ED-C 20.50

D1445306

PLAYS OF THE IRISH RENAISSANCE

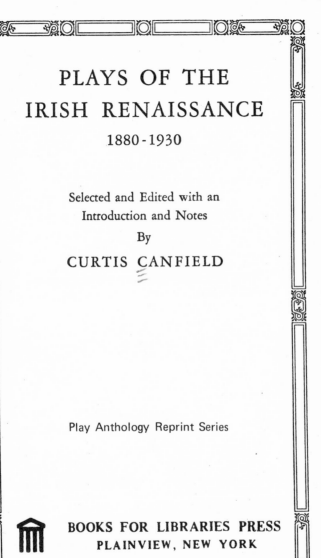

PLAYS OF THE
IRISH RENAISSANCE
1880-1930

Selected and Edited with an
Introduction and Notes

By

CURTIS CANFIELD

Play Anthology Reprint Series

BOOKS FOR LIBRARIES PRESS
PLAINVIEW, NEW YORK

First Published 1929

Reprinted 1974

Library of Congress Cataloging in Publication Data

Canfield, Fayette Curtis, 1903–   ed.
    Plays of the Irish renaissance, 1880–1930.

    (Play anthology reprint series)
    Reprint of the 1929 ed. published by Washburn,
New York.
    CONTENTS: Yeats, W. B. On Baile's strand.—Yeats,
W. B. The only jealousy of Emer.—Russell, G. W.
Deirdre.—Gregory, A. Hyacinth Halvey.—Hyde, D.   The
twisting of the rope. ₍etc.₎
    1. English drama—Irish authors. I. Title.
PR8865.C3 1974   822'.9'1208   73–4881
ISBn 0–8369–8248–7

To

K. N. C. and D. M.
THIS SMALL TOKEN OF MY GRATITUDE

PREFACE

THIS book traces and illustrates by means of thirteen typical plays the general historical development of Ireland's drama from the beginning to the present time. The drama is treated as a part of the current Irish literary movement, and the plays themselves furnish a starting point for a discussion of the major aspects of Irish character manifested in them. By virtue of its drama and its lyric poetry the movement has become known, in part, to most of the world. It is not unnatural that we find the Irish genius speaking most often in terms of lyric poetry and lyrical drama. By what means could a nation with so much pride in its singing speech, such love for a well-told story, such passion for the defense of a romantic and patriotic idealism more fittingly express itself? There is no other book treating the dramatic movement as a whole which attempts to define it with a list of outstanding plays and authors. This book, then, has a duality of purpose: to supply the present deficiency in American-published Irish plays, and to commemorate the fiftieth anniversary of the inception of the Literary Renaissance in Ireland in which the dramatic movement has an important and integral part. In the companion field of Irish poetry David Morton has selected and set down material in a book called *The Renaissance of Irish Poetry*. It is hoped that the two volumes together will suffice to give the general reader and the student an adequate approach to the movement as it reaches its first half-century milestone. The one underlying quality which binds both plays and poems together as a homogeneous national expression is the rhythmic rise and fall of the Anglo-Irish idiom.

My wish, at the beginning, was not especially to record the dramaturgic development of each individual writer by critical comparisons with other authors from any technical standpoint, but now I find that I have succumbed to the temptation in some places. I have simply taken plays which most appealed to me as best illustrating and defining the five groups into which I have arbitrarily divided the whole field. The choice of group titles is based on the general differentiation in the subject matter which seems to concern the Irish more deeply and more insistently than any others. The one important consideration governing my selection of the plays was that they be solely in the Irish tradition—reflecting the life, thought, and emotion of Ireland in the past or present by means which are recognized as characteristically national. Plays rising from English or other foreign traditions, have naturally been excluded. This division into groups has prevented me from fitting the plays together in chronological order; but the groups themselves broadly indicate a successive movement although the plays within them do not necessarily follow each other in point of time. The groups are as follows:

    I. Plays Based on Ancient Gaelic Legend and Mythology

    II. Plays of the Peasant Character: Comedy

    III. Plays of the Peasant Character: Tragedy

    IV. Plays of Patriotism

    V. Plays of the Modern Movement

It must be kept in mind that these groups are not, nor are they intended to be, rigid classifications. In many plays a blending of two or even three elements treated separately in the foregoing list is noticeable. For example, the plays based on legendary subjects often have a double motive involving both religion and patriotism, and *Maeve* is, in essence, a fantasy. Again, practically all the plays comprising the first three groups were written for the purpose of stimulating consciousness of the race and the nation by an appeal to the minds and hearts of the people. By virtue of this fact they may all be considered patriotic plays; and, at the same time, the legendary plays are valuable educationally. So the classification is no better than any other tabulation dealing with a literary or artistic movement except in so far as it clarifies and localizes our approach to the study of the whole movement.

It is unfortunate that the Irish drama is little known here in the United States, except for three or four writers whose plays have been published in collected editions, while many writers of almost equal merit remain unnoticed. Neither is the interesting fact very widespread that the Irish drama and Irish literature in general were revived through the conscious effort of a small group of enthusiasts after the literature of the Gael had lain forgotten for five centuries.

Since the movement is essentially a "Little Theater" movement and a literary one, it is evident that these plays herein included to define it, with the exception of the Plays of the Modern Movement in Group IV, will hardly prove successes of the Broadway type. In fact, I have purposely weeded out plays which were "theatrical" rather than literary. But I am sure that the intimate appeal of the plays themselves, coupled with some preparation for their reception by directors of progressive amateurs which may relate the play to the movement as a whole, will result in satisfaction for the most critical audience. The Anglo-Irish idiom, so captivating when spoken correctly, is a welcome challenge for the ambitious producer.

Dublin,   C.C.
July, 1929

CONTENTS

PLAYS OF THE IRISH RENAISSANCE

GROUP I

Plays Based on Ancient Gaelic Legend and Mythology

There had been no national drama in Ireland since some unknown scribe of the eleventh or twelfth century had copied out a semi-humorous dialogue between Ossian and St. Patrick from a still more ancient manuscript. Later, when the drama of Europe was being shaped by the newly discovered knowledge of the Renaissance, Ireland was so torn by wave after wave of invasions that it partook but little in this widespread development. Its drama did not develop at all, but, like much of its literature, leaked out through the lips of its *shanachies* or wandering minstrels and was all but lost. Again, the fact that the Church looked on the infant drama with some suspicion after the Protestants had taken over the management of the acting guilds may account for the long darkness which inclosed it until the end of the nineteenth century. When the drama finally emerged from the shadow of English tradition, its origins were as threads inextricably interwoven into the political history of the country from 1880 to 1890. The agitation attendant on the struggle for national freedom bears so pertinently on the sudden outburst of literary enthusiasm which followed a period of acute political disappointment, that we may be allowed to recall, in brief, the important events leading up to the collapse of the national hero, Charles Stewart Parnell, and the ultimate effect this collapse had on the young Ireland of the time. Holding the balance of power as head of the Irish Parliamentary Party at Westminster, Parnell obstructed and delayed all business in the House of Commons until England was forced to listen to his demands for Home Rule. And for the first time in history it seemed that the goal would be won. Concessions came one after another, Land Acts favorable to the Irish farmer were passed (1881 and 1885), and coercion methods were discontinued. As a result, the whole country rejoiced in the thought that after seven centuries of oppression Ireland would soon be free. But suddenly their hope turned to dismay. Lord Frederick Cavendish, coming from England in 1882 as Chief Secretary under the new and friendly terms of the Kilmainham Treaty, was assassinated in Phoenix Park along with a Castle official. England rose in wrath, renounced all its concessions, passed additional Coercion Acts, and imprisoned Parnell for complicity in the murders. He was released shortly afterwards, however, when it was proved that he had been unjustly convicted. With its hero free, Ireland once more took heart, but it was not for long. Shortly afterwards Parnell was implicated in a wretched divorce case and his career ruined. The idol had fallen and the people were in despair. The Irish Party split hopelessly into opposite factions, and the chance for freedom without bloodshed seemed lost forever when it had been so close at hand. But the Irish are resilient. Their failure to obtain emancipation in one direction spurred and goaded them to obtain it in another.

The spark of a less sanguinary rebellion in the field of national literature had been faintly glowing as early as 1880, when Standish O'Grady's bardic *History of Ireland* was published. This book was acknowledged by many writers as the driving force, the initial impetus which caused them to begin expressing themselves in terms of their country and their race. It brought them closer to the realization that Ireland had had a glorious past; it showed them that they had a real tradition on which to build a new literature.

Then it was as if Ireland had suddenly become possessed of a voice. The Irish National Literary Society was founded in 1891, and the Irish Literary Society, less interested in political propaganda than its predecessor, in 1893. These organizations, out of which eventually flowed the National Theatre, were set up, in the words of Lennox Robinson, as defensive movements "to counter the disillusionment of Parnell's fall." In 1893 Dr. Douglas Hyde and Eoin MacNeill established the Gaelic League, an organization designed to preserve, and to disseminate interest in, the native tongue. All were concrete manifestations of the awakening impulse to understand Ireland, and to cause her to be understood by the outside world. Where there had been no strength remaining for literary creativeness, there was now desire enough, and consequently time enough on hand to create a new literature and a new drama where there had been none before. This drama's form sprung from the determined efforts of William Butler Yeats and Lady Gregory to give direction and support to the sudden and contagious desire for a national drama born in despair.

In an attempt to ascertain, then, the motives underlying the movement, we discover first of all a deep bitterness against England supplementing and coloring the urge to create a distinctly Irish literature. The English theater as it was organized in Ireland was purely a commercial affair. Its unliterary themes and second-hand methods were extremely distasteful to the Nationalists. They wanted a theater and a drama not only reflecting the thoughts and lives of the Irish people, but serving at the same time to correct the absurd notion of Ireland and Irishmen spread far and wide by English and American dramatists in the form of that grotesque caricature, the Stage Paddy. They were actuated too by an intense fervor of patriotism. Irish culture of ancient time was either unknown or misunderstood outside Ireland. They became zealots in the idealistic cause of acquainting the world with their past attainments and their aspirations for the future. They began to realize that the printed word was as valuable for the accomplishment of their purpose as had been the sword. So the dramatic revival, at once the offspring of an intense love and a passionate dislike, came into being in Ireland with the performance of Yeats's *The Countess Cathleen* at the Ancient Concert Rooms on May 8, 1899.

The pioneers under the guidance of Mr. Yeats and Lady Gregory first turned their attention to the great mass of legendary material which was already at hand. As it happened they had to choose between two courses of procedure—that of dramatizing the heroic legends, on one side, or writing in the yet to be discovered Irish tradition of contemporaneous matters, on the other. The first choice was the more natural one because it was consistent with the fundamental ideal of the writers of the movement: the inauguration of a dramatic literature having roots in the past but still sustaining its national and racial identity in the present.

These legendary subjects, too, afforded an immediate escape from the poverty, violence, and factional strife surrounding the material existence of poets and people alike in the first years of the twentieth century. The dramatists by steeping themselves in the past were able to draw the world of the imagination closer about them. They have always cherished this world as a psychological substitute for the concrete reality. Although their feet were in the clay they found refuge in the vague and dreamy mists in which the stories of other happier times enveloped them. One finds in the great majority of the plays the continual recurrence of this conflict between reality and dream. It stands as so prominent a characteristic that one is inclined to say that it is an integral part, if not the foundation, of all Irish literature of the Renaissance. Here was Ireland stripped of the best of her manhood by war, famine, and emigration. It was without resources, even without a name, facing poverty and complete desolation. No wonder the Irish chose to see their future not by the light of this gloomy actuality but mellowed, softened, and if possible explained away by an idealistic philosophy carrying them off to the dream world of the spirit. The movement began by running counter to the Realism of Ibsen which swept England and the northern countries. It affiliated itself with that type of drama written in Italy by Gabriele d'Annunzio; in France by Edmond Rostand; and in Belgium by the chief seer of the Symbolist playwrights, Maurice Maeterlinck. But in the beginning it went even beyond Romanticism to the more soothing Nirvana of Mysticism, and, in the case of Yeats's later plays, to Occultism.

I do not know that it was a preconceived plan on the part of Yeats and his followers, but this dramatization of heroic legend with which they elected to start the movement offers the only recent analogy to the development of the Greek Classical Drama. Some one in that country, whom we know by the name of Homer collected the remnants of a bardic literature; and the Greek drama was simply a retelling of his stories about ancient kings and heroes, and their perpetuation by means of the theater. For the Irish this use of legendary material was historically auspicious because it paralleled the Greek method of writing plays with legendary and mythological backgrounds. All heroic characters regardless of country or language are struck from the same mold. Time and distance have no effect on their ultimate kinship. Each hero is the personification of an ideal—a popular conception

Plays Based on Ancient Gaelic Legend   19

of might and strength—actuated primarily by elemental emotions engendered by War and Love. Agamemnon, King of Mycenæ, has his Irish counterpart in Conchubar,[1] High King of Ulster, and Achilles has his in Cuchulain, King of Muirthemne.[2] The princess Antigone, who dies for the preservation of family honor, and Princess Deirdre,[3] who dies for true love, each exemplifies the nobility of the feminine heroic character in tragic circumstances. Although the methods used by the poets of the two countries in shaping their stories into dramatic form are distinctly different, as are the later developments of the two literatures, the classical ideal made fortunate impress on the best Irish dramatic poets at the beginning of the movement.

It might be well to mention at this time something about the happenings during the first few years after the formation of the Irish Literary Theatre in 1898. In its brief period of existence the organization was not successful. Within two years we see the movement splitting up and breaking away from its first course; and men like George Moore and Edward Martyn, who had been instrumental in starting the Irish Literary Theatre, withdrew from participation therein. Some idea of the swift changes the theater and its policies underwent may be found in the variety of names given to the succeeding developments of the original undertaking. First it was known as the Irish Literary Theatre, under whose auspices Edward Martyn's *The Heather Field* was performed on May 9, 1899. It was shortly after that Yeats, having determined on the policy of writing plays concerning Ireland's poetic past rather than the social and psychological plays of *The Heather Field* type, welcomed the schism which inevitably followed this divergence of opinion. In the meantime a company of Irish players (the actors in the Irish Literary Theatre were English) had been gathered together by the brothers, W. G. and F. J. Fay. They were separate from the Irish Literary Theatre and first called themselves the Irish National Theatre and later (1902) the Irish National Dramatic Company. Yeats found the directors and the members of this company in sympathy with his ideas of what direction the nascent drama should take and, ac-

[1] Pronounced Con-a-choor.
[2] Cuhoolin of Mŭr-hĕv-na.
[3] Deer'dree.

cordingly, affiliated himself with it. By 1903 he had become its president; its name had become the Irish National Theatre Society; and the brothers Fay had become discontented with the shift in power from the hands of the actor-manager to those of the dramatist. They remained in the Society, however, until 1908—W. G. as its leading actor, and F. J. as its valued director. The last change in title came in 1904. It was then known as the National Theatre Society, and from this branch, aided by Miss A. E. F. Horniman's philanthropy, the Abbey Theatre budded in 1904. Ernest Boyd has written the best succinct estimation of this early history in his excellent volume, *Ireland's Literary Renaissance.*[4]

Two of the three plays in the first group are from the pen of William Butler Yeats, who has been mentioned as the leading literary spirit of the Renaissance as far as the theater is concerned. He discovered Synge in a student hotel in Paris and persuaded him, as he did many other writers, to turn to the theater, the Irish theater, as a medium of expression. It was owing to his complete detachment from actuality that the first efforts of the Irish theater were, on the whole, romantic and mystical. These two plays are characteristic of the majority of his works, and although written ten years apart they offer an interesting unity in time and story sequence. Their subject matter is admittedly taken from Lady Gregory's remarkable collection of Gaelic lore under the title *Cuchulain of Muirthemne.*[5]

On Baile's Strand,[6] a dramatization of the Irish version of the Sohrab and Rustum legend, contains two cardinal principles which Yeats advanced as the fundamentals of the new art—beauty of structure and beauty of language. We may detect in the use of the first principle an additional influence of the classical ideal. Although one of the earliest plays of the movement,[7] it is at least one ample exception to the blanket

[4] New York: Alfred A. Knopf, 1922. Chapters XII–XIV. See also Lady Gregory's *Our Irish Theatre.* New York: G. P. Putman's Sons, 1914. After this was written a lengthy historical and critical account of the movement came into my hands. It is Andrew E. Malone's *The Irish Drama* (London: Constable & Co. Ltd., 1929).

[5] London: John Murray, 1902.

[6] Boy-lez.

[7] The first performance of the first version occurred at the opening of

criticism leveled at the Irish dramatists' lack of attention to technical requirements. Yeats, while cautioning the tyros to "learn construction from the masters," is careful to add, "but dialogue from ourselves." Surely the Irish have not erred in using construction as the skeleton and not, like the French and English dramatists of the late nineteenth century, as the flesh and blood of the plays as well. But, in this connection, it must be repeated that the drama was an untried field for the Irish; and their inexperience demanded a period of apprenticeship. Yeats was busy at the time soliciting many people, preferably amateurs, to donate their services to the movement by writing or acting Irish plays. Although in many cases he uncovered rich sources of theatrical material, there were many authors contributing to the Irish Literary Theatre and later to the National Theatre Society whose dramaturgic inexpertness overshadowed their enthusiasm. We must excuse these novices for the sin of overeagerness in serving the cause without proper grounding in the fundamentals of playwriting. But such incautious idealism was not foreign to people whose lives had been spent in fighting seemingly insurmountable odds.

In this play, Yeats avoids another unfortunate characteristic common to many Irish dramatists—the willingness to say more than enough. *On Baile's Strand* is shorn clean of all superfluity. A minimum number of primary characters employ few words which are unnecessary to the development of the plot. It is a pity that other dramatists of the movement disregard this economy of means. One is impressed by the fact that by embedding the tragic seed of the story in the center of the play between scenes of lighter import, Yeats has made such simple yet judicious use of form. It enables him neatly to explain the play's underlying moral—that life lies between a Fool and a Blindman, the one symbolizing Instinct, the other, Reason. *On Baile's Strand* is the first good example of the so-called circular or "sandwich" method applied to one-act playwriting. The unity and final completeness this employment of form arouses is one of the play's chief pleasures, because not its words alone but its craftsmanship contributes to the significance of its idea.

There is no need to spend a great deal of time calling at-

the Abbey Theatre, December 27, 1904. The revised version included in this collection was played in the same theater in 1906.

tention to the second artistic principle—beauty of language
—embodied in *On Baile's Strand*. Although the Anglo-Irish
idiom is conspicuously absent, such rich felicities of phrase
as "My teeth are growing long with the hunger," and the
extraordinary descriptive power of the diction give ample
evidence of the author's Celtic literary ancestry. The language with all its color and lyricism is the essence of an
idealized Irish speech. The interpolated songs and the rather
complicated ritual with sword and fire delight the peasant
audience, and at the same time, they provide a telling pan-
tomimic accompaniment to the text. In spite of the fact
that the characters are enveloped in an ancient atmosphere of
mist and shadow, there is nothing unreal about them. Indeed
their very genuine humanness is reminiscent of the flesh and
blood characters that Euripides set against a similar legendary
background. In this play we must not confuse the hazy
Maeterlinckian setting with the decidedly unmystical portrai-
ture of the central personages, although the influence of the
Belgian dramatist is noticeable in the stress Yeats places on
symbolic action. The dramatic irony with which he treats
the situation, the use of *anagnorisis* in Cuchulain's realization
that he has killed his son, the *peripeteia* following immediately
after Cuchulain's oath to Conchobar, and the bloody combat
behind the scenes are all further evidences of close application
to the rules of the masters.

Yeats, writing at Dublin in 1912, says that *On Baile's
Strand* is one of a cycle of plays dealing with Cuchulain and
his friends and enemies. I have included the next play in this
cycle, having as its principal motive the "power of witches
over Cuchulain's life." A contrast and comparison of his
treatment of the Cuchulain legend in *On Baile's Strand* and in
the next play of this group, *The Only Jealousy of Emer*
(1919), may help the reader toward a better understanding
of the plays themselves, and serve as the basis for discovering
the direction Yeats's dramatic development has taken. And it
will show, in a way, the difference ten years' experience with a
living theater has made in his conception of such a theater
as an ideal vehicle for his poetry.

Yeats is content to make *On Baile's Strand* comparatively
objective. Some slight changes and compressions for purposes
of dramatic emphasis occur in transcribing and adapting the

ancient legend as it is set down in *Cuchulain of Muirthemne*.[8] There is also some necessary elaboration to project the characters in sharper outline for the theater. Where the legend confines itself to a broad outline of external events, Yeats infuses the story with subtleties relating to emotional conflicts within the characters. He makes it his own by supplying ampler motives, cross-purposes, and inner significances lacking in the original. The most important addition he makes to the legend, however, is the creation of these conflicting motives which develop the action. For example, in the saga, the Son of Aoife [9] kills a warrior of the Red Branch, a chivalric order, because the latter insists on learning his identity as he approaches the enemies' stronghold. Cuchulain then attacks him to revenge the death of his comrade. There is no sudden entrance into the dun of the hostile kings; no challenge to equal the dramatic explanation for the visitor's presence there — "I have come alone in the midst of you to weigh my sword against Cuchulain's sword!" Then too, there are none of the devices Yeats employs to retard the approach of the inevitable climax: Cuchulain's unwillingness to fight the bold young warrior for whom a strange affection has arisen; his dismay at being forced to do so by the King who has just had his oath of obedience. And finally Yeats has superimposed the allegorical scenes on the original material.

In *The Only Jealousy of Emer* we find something more than the process of refining and sharpening character and situation. Yeats has shifted his point of attack from the dramatization of external events to the dramatization of an imaginative psychic interlude, stuffed with an extraneous mystical philosophy not present in the text of the epic narrative. It is a change from the theater of the many to the theater of the few. It is drama grown too complex, too special, too subjectively intricate for the æsthetic appetites of the urbanized peasants who comprised his first audiences. The play treats of the period between Cuchulain's battle with the waves, which marks the end of *On Baile's Strand*, and his slow recovery to consciousness in a hut near the shore. In Lady Gregory's version, the incidents connected with this particular episode take place before and not after the slay-

[8] Chapter XVIII *The Only Son of Aoife*, pp. 313–319.
[9] *Eefa* (Eva).

ing of the son of Aoife. According to her, Cuchulain had been whipped by magic rods in the hands of a woman of the Sidhe,[10] one Fand, who has fallen in love with him. She is the wife of Mananaan, King of the Country-under-the-Wave. On recovering from the love-beating, Cuchulain went into Fand's domain and after a battle there, "stopped a month in the country with her." Emer, Cuchulain's enraged wife, descends upon the lovers to avenge her husband's unfaithfulness. Her anger is allayed, however, when Fand, hearing that Emer's company still pleases Cuchulain, heroically decides to return to her husband, Mananaan. The Druids then give a drink of forgetfulness to Cuchulain, and also to Emer, who return to their native Emain Macha.[11] "And after that, Mananaan shook his cloak between Cuchulain and Fand, the way they should never meet again." [12]

It is evident that the tortuous subjectivity of the play is a far cry from the naïve simplicity of the tale from which it is derived. It is another good indication of the swerving course of the dramatic movement. The fact is that Yeats has ceased to use the legends as a dramatic medium whereby he might excite popular interest in the Irish Literary Revival. The theater itself has become too popular for him. The rising tide of realists and realistic methods has proved too threatening for his delicate bark. So, while continuing to remain on the directorate of the Abbey Theatre, he has practically withdrawn from active participation as a contributing playwright. He has, however, recently given to the Abbey his version of Sophocles' *Œdipus Rex*, and it was highly successful. He is also preparing a version of *Œdipus at Colonnus* for publication next year.

Yeats is the one remaining romantic poet of any dimensions writing for the theater today who has consistently resisted and survived the Ibsen tidal wave. Consequently *The Only Jealousy of Emer* was written for a drawing-room audience of not more than fifty people selected for their interest in and appreciation of poetry. True, the legend is still used as

[10] Pronounced *Shee*—from the word meaning the place where spirits dwell, hence—fairies, "other people."

[11] Pronounced *Avvin-Ma-ha,* Navan fort near Armagh, Conchubar's capital.

[12] Cuchulain of Muirthemne, Chapter XIV, p. 293.

a starting point, but only as the instrument for the poet's subjective self-expression. The Japanese Noh has replaced the classic play as his structural model; but the shift from the Greek form has not been inconsistent with the sensuous, Oriental coloring of his later work with its masks, its moon-phases, and its mystic music. Yeats realizes his anomolous position in the modern theater in a note to *Four Plays for Dancers*, which volume contains *The Only Jealousy of Emer* — "In writing these little plays, I knew I was creating something which could only fully succeed in a civilization very unlike ours." And it is thus he signs his epitaph as a predominant figure in the Dramatic Renaissance.

The rebuke offered his type of drama by the younger realists following the new standard of John M. Synge was enough to turn his eyes, never strong for gazing on the world outside, further within himself. In judging him, not as an individual author but as a part of the whole movement he is accredited with beginning, we must allow that he remains as a distinguished pioneer. It rose under his hand into something different from that which he had anticipated, got further away from him as time went on, and eventually, like water bursting through a dam, submerged him in its flood.

A book of plays purporting to represent the Irish drama, would hardly be complete without some dramatization of the Deirdre legend. Practically every Irish writer of importance, in verse, fiction or drama, has at one time or another treated this sad and lovely story. The three best dramatic versions belong to Yeats, Synge, and A. E. Each has his own point of attack, his own style and method, his individual conception of the sorrowful Queen. While Yeats and A. E. are bound by a common feeling of spirituality in handling the theme, Synge is alone in his thoroughly realistic treatment of it. I have included A. E.'s play because it preserves the unity of mood evoked by the preceding plays in this group, and because it contains those special qualities of delicate feeling and poetic imagination I want to associate with these early struggles to lay the foundation for a national drama. It has also a point in common with Classical Drama: the curse on the house of Conchubar, as on the house of Laius, crosses the lives of all the characters in the tragedy. And an additional reason is the fact that the author has distinguished himself in service to Ireland in so many fields—journalism, art, economics, poetry, history, and politics—that we are likely to forget his one dramatic contribution to Irish letters which is important enough to be included with the best of its genre.

I have a letter from A. E. which will serve as an interesting commentary on the movement as well as give us some idea of the ardor of the men connected with the enterprise in its young and somewhat feverish beginnings. He writes, "Deirdre was written at a time when I do not believe I had been in a theater twice in my life and I knew absolutely nothing about stage technique or the construction of a play. It was written hastily in response to the request of two young actors, William and Frank Fay, who asked me to complete a scene I had written which formed the first act. The first act was written in one night without any idea of being staged at all. The second and third acts were written with the knowledge that the play would be spoken on a stage. It was intended to be acted behind a gauze curtain to give a remote and legendary character to all that took place on the stage, and was so staged on its first performance. This first and only attempt at playwriting was made with the high confidence of absolute ignorance of the stage." There is no doubt that whether *Deirdre* was written in one week or one year it remains as a sincere and careful dramatization of this favorite subject.[13]

[13] My original plan was to include all three plays relating to the Deirdre saga but, owing to the limitations in the size of this edition, it had to be abandoned. Students interested in comparing the three plays should supplement the reading of them by an interesting article in the *Irish Review*, July, 1912, by Francis Bickley under the title "Deirdre."

ON BAILE'S STRAND

By William Butler Yeats

PERSONS IN THE PLAY

A FOOL
A BLIND MAN
CUCHULAIN, *King of Muirthemne*
CONCHUBAR, *High King of Uladh*
A YOUNG MAN, *Son of Cuchulain*
KINGS AND SINGING WOMEN

SCENE: *A great hall at Dundealgan, not "Cuchulain's great ancient house" but an assembly house nearer to the sea. A big door at the back, and through the door misty light as of sea mist. There are many chairs and one long bench. One of these chairs, which is towards the front of the stage, is bigger than the others. Somewhere at the back there is a table with flagons of ale upon it and drinking-horns. There is a small door at one side of the hall. A* FOOL *and* BLIND MAN, *both ragged, and their features made grotesque and extravagant by masks, come in through the door at the back. The* BLIND MAN *leans upon a staff.*

FOOL. What a clever man you are though you are blind! There's nobody with two eyes in his head that is as clever as you are. Who but you could have thought that the hen-wife sleeps every day a little at noon? I would never be able to steal anything if you didn't tell me where to look for it. And what a good cook you are! You take the fowl out of my hands after I have stolen it and plucked it, and you put it into the big pot at the fire there, and I can go out and run races with the witches at the edge of the waves and get an appetite, and when I've got it, there's the hen waiting inside for me, done to the turn.

BLIND MAN [*who is feeling about with his stick*]. Done to the turn.

FOOL [*putting his arm round* BLIND MAN's *neck*]. Come now, I'll have a leg and you'll have a leg, and we'll draw lots for the wishbone, I'll be praising you, I'll be praising you while we're eating it, for your good plans and for your good cooking. There's nobody in the world like you, Blind Man. Come, come. Wait a minute. I shouldn't have closed the door. There are some that look for me, and I wouldn't like them not to find me. Don't tell it to anybody, Blind Man. There are some that follow me. Boann herself out of the river and Fand out of the deep sea. Witches they are, and they come by in the wind, and they cry, "Give a kiss, Fool, give a kiss," that's what they cry. That's wide enough. All the witches can come in now. I wouldn't have them beat at the door and say: "Where is the Fool? Why has he put a lock on the door?" Maybe they'll hear the bubbling of the pot and come in and sit on the ground. But we won't give them any of the fowl. Let them go back to the sea, let them go back to the sea.

BLIND MAN [*feeling legs of big chair with his hands*]. Ah! [*Then, in a louder voice as he feels the back of it.*] Ah—ah—

FOOL. Why do you say "Ah-ah"?

BLIND MAN. I know the big chair. It is today the High King Conchubar is coming. They have brought out his chair. He is going to be Cuchulain's master in earnest from this day out. It is that he's coming for.

FOOL. He must be a great man to be Cuchulain's master.

BLIND MAN. So he is. He is a great man. He is over all the rest of the kings of Ireland.

FOOL. Cuchulain's master! I thought Cuchulain could do anything he liked.

BLIND MAN. So he did, so he did. But he ran too wild, and Conchubar is coming today to put an oath upon him that will stop his rambling and make him as biddable as a house-dog and keep him always at his hand. He will sit in this chair and put the oath upon him.

FOOL. How will he do that?

BLIND MAN. You have no wits to understand such things. [*The* BLIND MAN *has got into the chair.*] He will sit up in this chair and he'll say: "Take the oath, Cuchulain. I bid you take the oath. Do as I tell you. What are your wits compared with mine, and what are your riches compared with mine? And what sons have you to pay your debts and to put a stone over you when you die? Take the oath, I tell you. Take a strong oath."

FOOL [*crumpling himself up and whining*]. I will not. I'll take no oath. I want my dinner.

BLIND MAN. Hush, hush! It is not done yet.

FOOL. You said it was done to a turn.

BLIND MAN. Did I, now? Well, it might be done, and not done. The wings might be white, but the legs might be red. The flesh might stick hard to the bones and not come away in the teeth. But, believe me, Fool, it will be well done before you put your teeth in it.

FOOL. My teeth are growing long with the hunger.

BLIND MAN. I'll tell you a story—the kings have story-tellers while they are waiting for their dinner—I will tell you a story with a fight in it, a story with a champion in it, and a ship and a queen's son that has his mind set on killing somebody that you and I know.

FOOL. Who is that? Who is he coming to kill?

BLIND MAN. Wait, now, till you hear. When you were stealing the fowl, I was lying in a hole in the sand, and I heard three men coming with a shuffling sort of noise. They were wounded and groaning.

FOOL. Go on. Tell me about the fight.

BLIND MAN. There had been a fight, a great fight, a tremendous great fight. A young man had landed on the shore, the guardians of the shore had asked his name, and he had refused to tell it, and he had killed one, and others had run away.

FOOL. That's enough. Come on now to the fowl. I wish it was bigger. I wish it was as big as a goose.

BLIND MAN. Hush! I haven't told you all. I know who that young man is. I heard the men who were running away say he had red hair, that he had come from Aoife's country, that he was coming to kill Cuchulain.

FOOL. Nobody can do that.

[*To a tune.*]

Cuchulain has killed kings,
Kings and sons of kings,

Dragons out of the water,
And witches out of the air,
Banachas and Bonachas and people of the woods.

BLIND MAN. Hush! hush!
FOOL [*still singing*].

Witches that steal the milk,
Fomor that steal the children,
Hags that have heads like hares,
Hares that have claws like witches,
All riding a cock-horse.

[*Spoken.*]

Out of the very bottom of the bitter black north.
BLIND MAN. Hush, I say!
FOOL. Does Cuchulain know that he is coming to kill him?
BLIND MAN. How would he know that with his head in the clouds? He doesn't care for common fighting. Why would he put himself out, and nobody in it but that young man? Now if it were a white fawn that might turn into a queen before morning—
FOOL. Come to the fowl. I wish it was as big as a pig; a fowl with goose grease and pig's crackling.
BLIND MAN. No hurry, no hurry. I know whose son it is. I wouldn't tell anybody else, but I will tell you—a secret is better to you than your dinner. You like being told secrets.
FOOL. Tell me the secret.
BLIND MAN. That young man is Aoife's son. I am sure it is Aoife's son, it flows in upon me that it is Aoife's son. You have often heard me talking of Aoife, the great woman-fighter Cuchulain got the mastery over in the north?
FOOL. I know, I know. She is one of those cross queens that live in hungry Scotland.
BLIND MAN. I am sure it is her son. I was in Aoife's country for a long time.
FOOL. That was before you were blinded for putting a curse upon the wind.

BLIND MAN. There was a boy in her house that had her own red color on him and everybody said he was to be brought up to kill Cuchulain, that she hated Cuchulain. She used to put a helmet on a pillar-stone and call it Cuchulain and set him casting at it. There is a step outside—Cuchulain's step.

[CUCHULAIN *passes by in the mist outside the big door.*]

FOOL. Where is Cuchulain going?

BLIND MAN. He is going to meet Conchubar that has bidden him to take the oath.

FOOL. Ah, an oath, Blind Man. How can I remember so many things at once? Who is going to take an oath?

BLIND MAN. Cuchulain is going to take an oath to Conchubar who is High King.

FOOL. What a mix-up you make of everything, Blind Man! You were telling me one story, and now you are telling me another story. . . . How can I get the hang of it at the end if you mix everything at the beginning? Wait till I settle it out. There now, there's Cuchulain [*he points to one foot*], and there is the young man [*he points to the other foot*] that is coming to kill him, and Cuchulain doesn't know. But where's Conchubar? [*Takes bag from side.*] That's Conchubar with all his riches—Cuchulain, young man, Conchubar. —And where's Aoife? [*Throws up cap.*] There is Aoife, high up on the mountains in high hungry Scotland. Maybe it is not true after all. Maybe it was your own making up. It's many a time you cheated me before with your lies. Come to the cooking-pot, my stomach is pinched and rusty. Would you have it to be creaking like a gate?

BLIND MAN. I tell you it's true. And more than that is true. If you listen to what I say, you'll forget your stomach.

FOOL. I won't.

BLIND MAN. Listen. I know who the young man's father is, but I won't say. I would be afraid to say. Ah, Fool, you would forget everything if you could know who the young man's father is.

FOOL. Who is it? Tell me now quick, or I'll shake you. Come, out with it, or I'll shake you.

[*A murmur of voices in the distance.*]

BLIND MAN. Wait, wait. There's somebody coming. . . . It is Cuchulain is coming. He's coming back with the High

King. Go and ask Cuchulain. He'll tell you. It's little you'll care about the cooking-pot when you have asked Cuchulain that . . .

[BLIND MAN *goes out by side door.*]

FOOL. I'll ask him. Cuchulain will know. He was in Aoife's country. [*Goes up stage.*] I'll ask him. [*Turns and goes down stage.*] But, no, I won't ask him, I would be afraid. [*Going up again.*] Yes, I will ask him. What harm in asking? The Blind Man said I was to ask him. [*Going down.*] No, no. I'll not ask him. He might kill me. I have but killed hens and geese and pigs. He has killed kings. [*Goes up again almost to big door.*] Who says I'm afraid? I'm not afraid. I'm no coward. I'll ask him. No, no, Cuchulain, I'm not going to ask you.

> He has killed kings,
> Kings and sons of kings,
> Dragons out of the water,
> And witches out of the air,
> Banachas and Bonachas and people of the woods.

[FOOL *goes out by side door, the last words being heard outside.* CUCHULAIN *and* CONCHUBAR *enter through the big door at the back. While they are still outside,* CUCHULAIN'S *voice is heard raised in anger. He is a dark man, something over forty years of age.* CONCHUBAR *is much older and carries a long staff, elaborately carved or with an elaborate gold handle.*]

CUCHULAIN. Because I have killed men without your
    bidding;
And have rewarded others at my own pleasure,
Because of half a score of trifling things
You'd lay this oath upon me, and now—and now
You add another pebble to the heap,
And I must be your man, well-nigh your bondsman,
Because a youngster out of Aoife's country
Has found the shore ill-guarded.

CONCHUBAR.   He came to land
While you were somewhere out of sight and hearing,
Hunting or dancing with your wild companions.

CUCHULAIN. He can be driven out. I'll not be bound.

I'll dance or hunt, or quarrel or make love,
Wherever and whenever I've a mind to.
If time had not put water in your blood,
You never would have thought it.
     CONCHUBAR.   I would leave
A strong and settled country to my children.
     CUCHULAIN. And I must be obedient in all things;
Give up my will to yours; go where you please;
Come when you call; sit at the council-board
Among the unshapely bodies of old men;
I whose mere name has kept this country safe,
I that in early days have driven out
Maeve of Cruachan and the northern pirates,
The hundred kings of Sorcha, and the kings
Out of the Garden in the East of the World.
Must I, that held you on the throne when all
Had pulled you from it, swear obedience
As if I were some cattle-raising king?
Are my shins speckled with the heat of the fire,
Or have my hands no skill but to make figures
Upon the ashes with a stick? Am I
So slack and idle that I need a whip
Before I serve you?
     CONCHUBAR.   No, no whip, Cuchulain,
But every day my children come and say:
"This man is growing harder to endure.
How can we be at safety with this man
That nobody can buy or bid or bind?
We shall be at his mercy when you are gone;
He burns the earth as if he were a fire,
And time can never touch him."
     CUCHULAIN.   And so the tale
Grows finer yet; and I am to obey
Whatever child you set upon the throne,
As if it were yourself!
     CONCHUBAR.   Most certainly.
I am High King, my son shall be High King;
And you for all the wildness of your blood,
And though your father came out of the sun,
Are but a little king and weigh but light
In anything that touches government,

If put into the balance with my children.

    CUCHULAIN. It's well that we should speak our minds out
      plainly,
For when we die we shall be spoken of
In many countries. We in our young days
Have seen the heavens like a burning cloud
Brooding upon the world, and being more
Than men can be now that cloud's lifted up,
We should be the more truthful. Conchubar,
I do not like your children—they have no pith,
No marrow in their bones, and will lie soft
Where you and I lie hard.

    CONCHUBAR.   You rail at them
Because you have no children of your own.

    CUCHULAIN.   I think myself most lucky that I leave
No pallid ghost or mockery of a man
To drift and mutter in the corridors,
Where I have laughed and sung.

    CONCHUBAR.   That is not true,
For all your boasting of the truth between us;
For there is no man having house and lands,
That have been in the one family
And called by the one name for centuries,
But is made miserable if he know
They are to pass into a stranger's keeping,
As yours will pass.

    CUCHULAIN.   The most of men feel that,
But you and I leave names upon the harp.

    CONCHUBAR.   You play with arguments as lawyers do,
And put no heart in them. I know your thoughts,
For we have slept under the one cloak and drunk
From the one wine cup. I know you to the bone.
I have heard you cry, aye in your very sleep,
"I have no son," and with such bitterness
That I have gone upon my knees and prayed
That it might be amended.

    CUCHULAIN.   For you thought
That I should be as biddable as others
Had I their reason for it; but that's not true;
For I would need a weightier argument
Than one that marred me in the copying,

As I have that clean hawk out of the air
That, as men say, begot this body of mine
Upon a mortal woman.
    CONCHUBAR.   Now as ever
You mock at every reasonable hope,
And would have nothing, or impossible things.
What eye has ever looked upon the child
Would satisfy a mind like that?
    CUCHULAIN.   I would leave
My house and name to none that would not face
Even myself in battle.
    CONCHUBAR.   Being swift of foot,
And making light of every common chance,
You should have overtaken on the hills
Some daughter of the air, or on the shore
A daughter of the Country-under-Wave.
    CUCHULAIN. I am not blasphemous.
    CONCHUBAR.   Yet you despise
Our queens, and would not call a child your own,
If one of them had borne him.
    CUCHULAIN.   I have not said it.
    CONCHUBAR. Ah! I remember I have heard you boast,
When the ale was in your blood, that there was one
In Scotland, where you had learnt the trade of war,
That had a stone-pale cheek and red-brown hair;
And that although you had loved other women,
You'd sooner that fierce woman of the camp
Bore you a son than any queen among them.
    CUCHULAIN. You call her a "fierce woman of the camp,"
For having lived among the spinning-wheels,
You'd have no woman near that would not say,
"Ah! how wise!" "What will you have for supper?"
"What shall I wear that I may please you, sir?"
And keep that humming through the day and night
For ever. A fierce woman of the camp!
But I am getting angry about nothing.
You have never seen her. Ah! Conchubar, had you seen her
With that high, laughing, turbulent head of hers
Thrown backward, and the bowstring at her ear,
Or sitting at the fire with those grave eyes
Full of good counsel as it were with wine,

Or when love ran through all the lineaments
Of her wild body—although she had no child,
None other had all beauty, queen, or lover,
Or was so fitted to give birth to kings.
    CONCHUBAR. There's nothing I can say but drifts you
      farther
From the one weighty matter. That very woman—
For I know well that you are praising Aoife—
Now hates you and will leave no subtlety
Unknotted that might run into a noose
About your throat, no army in idleness
That might bring ruin on this land you serve.
    CUCHULAIN. No wonder in that, no wonder at all in that.
I never have known love but as a kiss
In the mid-battle, and a difficult truce
Of oil and water, candles and dark night,
Hillside and hollow, the hot-footed sun,
And the cold, sliding, slippery-footed moon—
A brief forgiveness between opposites
That have been hatreds for three times the age
Of this long-'stablished ground.
    CONCHUBAR.   Listen to me.
Aoife makes war on us, and every day
Our enemies grow greater and beat the walls
More bitterly, and you within the walls
Are every day more turbulent; and yet,
When I would speak about these things, your fancy
Runs as it were a swallow on the wind.
    [*Outside the door in the blue light of the sea mist are
many old and young* KINGS; *amongst them are three* WOMEN,
*two of whom carry a bowl of fire. The third, in what follows,
puts from time to time fragrant herbs into the fire so that it
flickers up into brighter flame.*]
Look at the door and what men gather there—
Old counselors that steer the land with me,
And younger kings, the dancers and harp-players
That follow in your tumults, and all these
Are held there by the one anxiety.
Will you be bound into obedience
And so make this land safe for them and theirs?
You are but half a king and I but half!

I need your might of hand and burning heart,
And you my wisdom.

CUCHULAIN [*going near to door*]. Nestlings of a high
    nest,
Hawks that have followed me into the air
And looked upon the sun, we'll out of this
And sail upon the wind once more. This king
Would have me take an oath to do his will,
And having listened to his tune from morning,
I will no more of it. Run to the stable
And set the horses to the chariot-pole,
And send a messenger to the harp-players.
We'll find a level place among the woods,
And dance awhile.

A YOUNG KING. Cuchulain, take the oath.
There is none here that would not have you take it.

CUCHULAIN. You'd have me take it? Are you of one mind?

THE KINGS. All, all, all, all!

A YOUNG KING. Do what the High King bids you.

CONCHUBAR. There is not one but dreads this turbulence
Now that they're settled men.

CUCHULAIN.   Are you so changed,
Or have I grown more dangerous of late?
But that's not it. I understand it all.
It's you that have changed. You've wives and children now,
And for that reason cannot follow one
That lives like a bird's flight from tree to tree.—
It's time the years put water in my blood
And drowned the wildness of it, for all's changed,
But that unchanged.—I'll take what oath you will:
The moon, the sun, the water, light or air,
I do not care how binding.

CONCHUBAR.   On this fire
That has been lighted from your hearth and mine;
The older men shall be my witnesses,
The younger, yours. The holders of the fire
Shall purify the thresholds of the house
With waving fire, and shut the outer door,
According to the custom; and sing rhyme
That has come down from the old law-makers
To blow the witches out. Considering

That the wild will of man could be oath-bound,
But that a woman's could not, they bid us sing
Against the will of woman at its wildest
In the shape-changers that runs upon the wind.

[CONCHUBAR *has gone on to his throne.*]

THE WOMEN. [*They sing in a very low voice after the first
few words so that the others all but drown their words.*]

> May this fire have driven out
> The shape-changers that can put
> Ruin on a great king's house
> Until all be ruinous.
> Names whereby a man has known
> The threshold and the hearthstone,
> Gather on the wind and drive
> The women, none can kiss and thrive,
> For they are but whirling wind,
> Out of memory and mind.
> They would make a prince decay
> With light images of clay,
> Planted in the running wave;
> Or, for many shapes they have,
> They would change them into hounds
> Until he had died of his wounds,
> Though the change were but a whim;
> Or they'd hurl a spell at him,
> That he follow with desire
> Bodies that can never tire,
> Or grow kind, for they anoint
> All their bodies, joint by joint,
> With a miracle-working juice
> That is made out of the grease
> Of the ungoverned unicorn.
> But the man is thrice forlorn,
> Emptied, ruined, wracked, and lost,
> That they follow, for at most
> They will give him kiss for kiss;
> While they murmur, "After this
> Hatred may be sweet to the taste."
> Those wild hands that have embraced
> All his body can but shove

At the burning wheel of love,
Till the side of hate comes up.
Therefore in this ancient cup
May the sword-blades drink their fill
Of the homebrew there, until
They will have for masters none
But the threshold and hearthstone.

CUCHULAIN [*speaking, while they are singing*]. I'll take
        and keep this oath, and from this day
I shall be what you please, my chicks, my nestlings.
Yet I had thought you were of those that praised
Whatever life could make the pulse run quickly,
Even though it were brief, and that you held
That a free gift was better than a forced.—
But that's all over.—I will keep·it, too,
I never gave a gift and took it again.
If the wild horse should break the chariot-pole,
It would be punished. Should that be in the oath?
    [*Two of the* WOMEN, *still singing, crouch in front of
    him holding the bowl over their heads. He spreads his hands
    over the flame.*]
I swear to be obedient in all things
To Conchubar, and to uphold his children.
    CONCHUBAR. We are one being, as these flames are one:
I give my wisdom, and I take your strength.
Now thrust the swords into the flame, and pray
That they may serve the threshold and the hearthstone
With faithful service.
    [THE KINGS *kneel in a semicircle before the two* WOMEN
    and CUCHULAIN, *who thrusts his sword into the flame. They
    all put the points of their swords into the flame. The third*
    WOMAN *is at the back near the big door.*]
    CUCHULAIN.   O pure, glittering ones
That should be more than wife or friend or mistress,
Give us the enduring will, the unquenchable hope,
The friendliness of the sword!—
    [*The song grows louder, and the last words ring out
    clearly. There is a loud knocking at the door, and a cry of
    "Open! open!"*]

CONCHUBAR. Some king that has been loitering on the
    way.
Open the door, for I would have all know
That the oath's finished and Cuchulain bound,
And that the swords are drinking up the flame.
    [*The door is opened by the third* WOMAN, *and a* YOUNG
MAN *with a drawn sword enters.*]
    YOUNG MAN. I am of Aoife's country.
    [*The* KINGS *rush towards him.* CUCHULAIN *throws himself
between.*]
    CUCHULAIN.   Put up your swords.
He is but one. Aoife is far away.
    · YOUNG MAN. I have come alone into the midst of you
To weigh this sword against Cuchulain's sword.
    CONCHUBAR. And are you noble? for if of common seed,
You cannot weigh your sword against his sword
But in mixed battle.
    YOUNG MAN.   I am under bonds
To tell my name to no man; but it's noble.
    CONCHUBAR. But I would know your name and not your
    bonds.
You cannot speak in the Assembly House,
If you are not noble.
    FIRST OLD KING. Answer the High King!
    YOUNG MAN. I will give no other proof than the hawk
    gives—
That it's no sparrow!
    [*He is silent for a moment, then speaks to all.*]
                        Yet look upon me, kings.
I, too, am of that ancient seed, and carry
The signs about this body and in these bones.
    CUCHULAIN. To have shown the hawk's gray feather is
    enough,
And you speak highly, too. Give me that helmet.
I'd thought they had grown weary sending champions.
That sword and belt will do. This fighting's welcome.
The High King there has promised me his wisdom;
But the hawk's sleepy till its well-beloved
Cries out amid the acorns, or it has seen
Its enemy like a speck upon the sun.

What's wisdom to the hawk, when that clear eye
Is burning nearer up in the high air?
   [*Looks hard at* YOUNG MAN; *then comes down steps and grasps* YOUNG MAN *by shoulder.*]
Hither into the light.
[*To* CONCHUBAR.]   The very tint
Of her that I was speaking of but now.
Not a pin's difference.
[*To* YOUNG MAN.]   You are from the North
Where there are many that have that tint of hair—
Red-brown, the light red-brown. Come nearer, boy,
For I would have another look at you.
There's more likeness—a pale, a stone-pale cheek.
What brought you, boy? Have you no fear of death?
   YOUNG MAN.   Whether I live or die is in the gods' hands.
   CUCHULAIN. That is all words, all words; a young man's
    talk.
I am their plow, their harrow, their very strength;
For he that's in the sun begot this body
Upon a mortal woman, and I have heard tell
It seemed as if he had outrun the moon;
That he must follow always through waste heaven,
He loved so happily. He'll be but slow
To break a tree that was so sweetly planted.
Let's see that arm. I'll see it if I choose.
That arm had a good father and a good mother,
But it is not like this.
   YOUNG MAN.   You are mocking me;
You think I am not worthy to be fought.
But I'll not wrangle but with this talkative knife.
   CUCHULAIN. Put up your sword; I am not mocking you.
I'd have you for my friend, but if it's not
Because you have a hot heart and a cold eye,
I cannot tell the reason.
[*To* CONCHUBAR.]   He has got her fierceness,
And nobody is as fierce as those pale women.
But I will keep him with me, Conchubar,
That he may set my memory upon her
When the day's fading.—You will stop with us,
And we will hunt the deer and the wild bulls;

And, when we have grown weary, light our fires
Between the wood and water, or on some mountain
Where the shape-changers of the morning come.
The High King there would make a mock of me
Because I did not take a wife among them.
Why do you hang your head? It's a good life:
The head grows prouder in the light of the dawn,
And friendship thickens in the murmuring dark
Where the spare hazels meet the wool-white foam.
But I can see there's no more need for words
And that you'll be my friend from this day out.

    CONCHUBAR.   He has come hither not in his own name
But in Queen Aoife's and has challenged us
In challenging the foremost man of us all.

    CUCHULAIN. Well, well, what matter?

    CONCHUBAR. You think it does not matter;
And that a fancy lighter than the air,
A whim of the moment has more matter in it.
For having none that shall reign after you,
You cannot think as I do, who would leave
A throne too high for insult.

    CUCHULAIN.   Let your children
Remortar their inheritance, as we have,
And put more muscle on.—I'll give you gifts,
But I'd have something too—that arm-ring, boy.
We'll have this quarrel out when you are older.

    YOUNG MAN. There is no man I'd sooner have my friend
Than you, whose name has gone about the world
As if it had been the wind; but Aoife'd say
I had turned coward.

    CUCHULAIN.   I will give you gifts
That Aoife'll know, and all her people know,
To have come from me. [*Showing cloak.*]
                       My father gave me this.
He came to try me, rising up at dawn
Out of the cold dark of the rich sea.
He challenged me to battle, but before
My sword had touched his sword, told me his name,
Gave me this cloak, and vanished. It was woven
By women of the Country-under-Wave
Out of the fleeces of the sea. O! tell her

I was afraid, or tell her what you will.
No; tell her that I heard a raven croak
On the north side of the house, and was afraid.

   CONCHUBAR. Some witch of the air has troubled Cuchu-
    lain's mind.

   CUCHULAIN. No witchcraft. His head is like a woman's
    head
I had fancy for.

   CONCHUBAR.   A witch of the air
Can make a leaf confound us with memories.
They run upon the wind and hurl the spells
That make us nothing, out of the invisible wind.
They have gone to school to learn the trick of it.

   CUCHULAIN. No, no—there's nothing out of common
    here;
The winds are innocent.—That arm-ring, boy.

   A KING. If I've your leave I'll take this challenge up.

   ANOTHER KING. No, give it me, High King, for this wild
    Aoife
Has carried off my slaves.

   ANOTHER KING.   No, give it me,
For she has harried me in house and herd.

   ANOTHER KING. I claim this fight.

   OTHER KINGS [together]. And I! And I! And I!

   CUCHULAIN. Back! back! Put up your swords! Put up your
    swords!
There's none alive that shall accept a challenge
I have refused. Laegaire, put up your sword!

   YOUNG MAN. No, let them come. If they've a mind for it,
I'll try it out with any two together.

   CUCHULAIN. That's spoken as I'd have spoken at your
    age.
But you are in my house. Whatever man
Would fight with you shall fight it out with me.
They're dumb, they're dumb. How many of you would meet
    [Draws sword.]
This mutterer, this old whistler, this sandpiper,
This edge that's grayer than the tide, this mouse
That's gnawing at the timbers of the world,
This, this— Boy, I would meet them all in arms
If I'd a son like you. He would avenge me

When I have withstood for the last time the men
Whose fathers, brothers, sons, and friends I have killed
Upholding Conchubar, when the four provinces
Have gathered with the ravens over them.
But I'd need no avenger. You and I
Would scatter them like water from a dish.

    YOUNG MAN. We'll stand by one another from this out.
Here is the ring.

    CUCHULAIN.   No, turn and turn about.
But my turn's first because I am the older.

    [*Spreading out cloak.*]
Nine queens out of the Country-under-Wave
Have woven it with the fleeces of the sea
And they were long embroidering at it.—Boy,
If I had fought my father, he'd have killed me,
As certainly as if I had a son
And fought with him, I should be deadly to him;
For the old fiery fountains are far off
And every day there is less heat o' the blood.

    CONCHUBAR [*in a loud voice*]. No more of this. I will
    not have this friendship.
Cuchulain is my man, and I forbid it.
He shall not go unfought, for I myself—

    CUCHULAIN. I will not have it.

    CONCHUBAR. You lay commands on me?

    CUCHULAIN [*seizing* CONCHUBAR]. You shall not stir,
    High King. I'll hold you there.

    CONCHUBAR. Witchcraft has maddened you.

    THE KINGS [*shouting*]. Yes, witchcraft! witchcraft!

    FIRST OLD KING. Some witch has worked upon your mind,
    Cuchulain.
The head of that young man seemed like a woman's
You'd had a fancy for. Then of a sudden
You laid your hands on the High King himself!

    CUCHULAIN. And laid my hands on the High King him-
    self?

    CONCHUBAR. Some witch is floating in the air above us.

    CUCHULAIN. Yes, witchcraft, witchcraft! Witches of the
    air!

[*To* YOUNG MAN.] Why did you? Who was it set you to
this work?

Out, out! I say, for now it's sword on sword!

YOUNG MAN. But . . . but I did not.

CUCHULAIN.   Out, I say, out, out!

[YOUNG MAN *goes out followed by* CUCHULAIN. *The* KINGS *follow them out with confused cries, and words one can hardly hear because of the noise. Some cry,* "Quicker, quicker!" "Why are you so long at the door?" "We'll be too late!" "Have they begun to fight?" "Can you see if they are fighting?" *and so on. Their voices drown each other. The three* WOMEN *are left alone.*]

FIRST WOMAN. I have seen, I have seen!

SECOND WOMAN. What do you cry aloud?

FIRST WOMAN. The ever-living have shown me what's to come.

THIRD WOMAN. How? Where?

FIRST WOMAN. In the ashes of the bowl.

SECOND WOMAN. While you were holding it between your hands?

THIRD WOMAN. Speak quickly!

FIRST WOMAN. I have seen Cuchulain's roof-tree
Leap into fire, and the walls split and blacken.

SECOND WOMAN. Cuchulain has gone out to die.

THIRD WOMAN.   O! O!

SECOND WOMAN. Who could have thought that one so great as he
Should meet his end at this unnoted sword!

FIRST WOMAN. Life drifts between a fool and a blind man
To the end, and nobody can know his end.

SECOND WOMAN. Come, look upon the quenching of this greatness.

[*The other two go to the door, but they stop for a moment upon the threshold and wail.*]

FIRST WOMAN. No crying out, for there'll be need of cries
And rending of the hair when it's all finished.

[*The* WOMEN *go out. There is the sound of clashing swords from time to time during what follows.*]

[*Enter the* FOOL *dragging the* BLIND MAN.]

FOOL. You have eaten it, you have eaten it! You have left me nothing but the bones.

[*He throws* BLIND MAN *down by big chair.*]

BLIND MAN. Oh, that I should have to endure such a

plague! Oh, I ache all over! Oh, I am pulled to pieces! This is the way you pay me all the good I have done you.

FOOL. You have eaten it! You have told me lies. I might have known you had eaten it when I saw your slow, sleepy walk. Lie there till the kings come. Oh, I will tell Conchubar and Cuchulain and all the kings about you!

BLIND MAN. What would have happened to you but for me, and you without your wits? If I did not take care of you, what would you do for food and warmth!

FOOL. You take care of me? You stay safe, and send me into every kind of danger. You sent me down the cliff for gulls' eggs while you warmed your blind eyes in the sun; and then you ate all that were good for food. You left me the eggs that were neither egg nor bird. [BLIND MAN *tries to rise;* FOOL *makes him lie down again.*] Keep quiet now, till I shut the door. There is some noise outside—a high vexing noise, so that I can't be listening to myself. [*Shuts the big door.*] Why can't they be quiet! why can't they be quiet! [BLIND MAN *tries to get away.*] Ah! you would get away, would you! [*Follows* BLIND MAN *and brings him back.*] Lie there! lie there! No, you won't get away! Lie there till the kings come. I'll tell them all about you. I will tell it all. How you sit warming yourself, when you have made me light a fire of sticks, while I sit blowing it with my mouth. Do you not always make me take the windy side of the bush when it blows, and the rainy side when it rains?

BLIND MAN. Oh, good Fool! listen to me. Think of the care I have taken of you. I have brought you to many a warm hearth, where there was a good welcome for you, but you would not stay there; you were always wandering about.

FOOL. The last time you brought me in it was not I who wandered away, but you that got put out because you took the crubeen out of the pot when nobody was looking. Keep quiet, now!

CUCHULAIN [*rushing in*]. Witchcraft! There is no witchcraft on the earth, or among the witches of the air, that these hands cannot break.

FOOL. Listen to me, Cuchulain. I left him turning the fowl at the fire. He ate it all, though I had stolen it. He left me nothing but the feathers.

CUCHULAIN. Fill me a horn of ale!

BLIND MAN. I gave him what he likes best. You do not know how vain this fool is. He likes nothing so well as a feather.

FOOL. He left me nothing but the bones and feathers. Nothing but the feathers, though I had stolen it.

CUCHULAIN. Give me that horn. Quarrels here, too! [*Drinks.*] What is there between you two that is worth a quarrel? Out with it!

BLIND MAN. Where would he be but for me? I must be always thinking—thinking to get food for the two of us, and when we've got it, if the moon is at the full or the tide on the turn, he'll leave the rabbit in the snare till it is full of maggots, or let the trout slip back through his hands into the stream.

[*The* FOOL *has begun singing while the* BLIND MAN *is speaking.*]

FOOL [*singing*].

> When you were an acorn on the tree-top,
>   Then was I an eagle cock;
> Now that you are a withered old block,
>   Still am I an eagle cock.

BLIND MAN. Listen to him, now. That's the sort of talk I have to put up with day out, day in.

[*The* FOOL *is putting the feathers into his hair.* CUCHULAIN *takes a handful of feathers out of a heap the* FOOL *has on the bench beside him, and out of the* FOOL's *hair, and begins to wipe the blood from his sword with them.*]

FOOL. He has taken my feathers to wipe his sword. It is blood that he is wiping from his sword.

CUCHULAIN [*goes up to door at back and throws away feathers*]. They are standing about his body. They will not awaken him, for all his witchcraft.

BLIND MAN. It is that young champion that he has killed. He that came out of Aoife's country.

CUCHULAIN. He thought to have saved himself with witchcraft.

FOOL. That blind man there said he would kill you. He

came from Aoife's country to kill you. That blind man said they had taught him every kind of weapon that he might do it. But I always knew that you would kill him.

CUCHULAIN [*to the* BLIND MAN]. You knew him, then?

BLIND MAN. I saw him, when I had my eyes, in Aoife's country.

CUCHULAIN. You were in Aoife's country?

BLIND MAN. I knew him and his mother there.

CUCHULAIN. He was about to speak of her when he died.

BLIND MAN. He was a queen's son.

CUCHULAIN. What queen? what queen? [*Seizes* BLIND MAN, *who is now sitting upon the bench.*] Was it Scathach? There were many queens. All the rulers there were queens.

BLIND MAN. No, not Scathach.

CUCHULAIN. It was Uathach, then? Speak! speak!

BLIND MAN. I cannot speak; you are clutching me too tightly. [CUCHULAIN *lets him go.*] I cannot remember who it was. I am not certain. It was some queen.

FOOL. He said a while ago that the young man was Aoife's son.

CUCHULAIN. She? No, no! She had no son when I was there.

FOOL. That blind man there said that she owned him for her son.

CUCHULAIN. I had rather he had been some other woman's son. What father had he? A soldier out of Alba? She was an amorous woman—a proud, pale, amorous woman.

BLIND MAN. None knew whose son he was.

CUCHULAIN. None knew! Did you know, old listener at doors?

BLIND MAN. No, no; I knew nothing.

FOOL. He said a while ago that he heard Aoife boast that she'd never but the one lover, and he the only man that had overcome her in battle. [*Pause.*]

BLIND MAN. Somebody is trembling, Fool! The bench is shaking. Why are you trembling? Is Cuchulain going to hurt us? It was not I who told you, Cuchulain.

FOOL. It is Cuchulain who is trembling. It is Cuchulain who is shaking the bench.

BLIND MAN. It is his own son he has slain.

CUCHULAIN. 'Twas they that did it, the pale windy people.

Where? where? where? My sword against the thunder!
But no, for they have always been my friends;
And though they love to blow a smoking coal
Till it's all flame, the wars they blow aflame
Are full of glory, and heart up-lifting pride,
And not like this. The wars they love awaken
Old fingers and the sleepy strings of harps.
Who did it then? Are you afraid? Speak out!
For I have put you under my protection.
And will reward you well. Dubthach the Chafer?
He'd an old grudge. No, for he is with Maeve.
Laegaire did it! Why do you not speak?
What is this house? [*Pause.*] Now I remember all.

    [*Comes before* CONCHUBAR'S *chair, and strikes out with his sword, as if* CONCHUBAR *was sitting upon it.*]
'Twas you who did it—you who sat up there
With your old rod of kingship, like a magpie
Nursing a stolen spoon. No, not a magpie,
A maggot that is eating up the earth!
Yes, but a magpie, for he's flown away.
Where did he fly to?

    BLIND MAN.   He is outside the door.

    CUCHULAIN. Outside the door?

    BLIND MAN. Between the door and the sea.

    CUCHULAIN. Conchubar, Conchubar! the sword into your heart!

    [*He rushes out. Pause.* FOOL *creeps up to the big door and looks after him.*]

    FOOL. He is going up to King Conchubar. They are all about the young man. No, no, he is standing still. There is a great wave going to break, and he is looking at it. Ah! now he is running down to the sea, but he is holding up his sword as if he were going into a fight. [*Pause.*] Well struck! well struck!

    BLIND MAN. What is he doing now?

    FOOL. Oh! he is fighting the waves!

    BLIND MAN. He sees King Conchubar's crown on every one of them.

    FOOL. There, he has struck at a big one! He has struck the crown off it; he has made the foam fly. There again, another big one!

BLIND MAN. Where are the kings? What are the kings doing?

FOOL. They are shouting and running down to the shore, and the people are running out of the houses. They are all running.

BLIND MAN. You say they are running out of the houses? There will be nobody left in the houses. Listen, Fool!

FOOL. There, he is down! He is up again. He is going out in the deep water. There is a big wave. It has gone over him. I cannot see him now. He has killed kings and giants, but the waves have mastered him, the waves have mastered him!

BLIND MAN. Come here, Fool!

FOOL. The waves have mastered him.

BLIND MAN. Come here!

FOOL. The waves have mastered him.

BLIND MAN. Come here, I say.

FOOL [*coming towards him, but looking backwards towards the door*]. What is it?

BLIND MAN. There will be nobody in the houses. Come this way; come quickly! The ovens will be full. We will put our hands into the ovens. [*They go out.*]

THE ONLY JEALOUSY OF EMER

By William Butler Yeats

PERSONS OF THE PLAY

THREE MUSICIANS (*their faces made up to resemble masks*)
THE GHOST OF CUCHULAIN (*wearing a mask*)
THE FIGURE OF CUCHULAIN (*wearing a mask*)
EMER ⎱ (*masked, or their faces made up to re-*
EITHNE INGUBA ⎰ *semble masks*)
WOMAN OF THE SIDHE (*wearing a mask*)

Enter Musicians, who are dressed and made up as in "At the Hawk's Well." [1] They have the same musical instruments, which can either be already upon the stage or be brought in by the FIRST MUSICIAN before he stands in the center with the cloth between his hands, or by a player when the cloth has been unfolded. The stage as before can be against the wall of any room, and the same black cloth can be used as in "At the Hawk's Well."

[*Song for the folding and unfolding of the cloth.*]

FIRST MUSICIAN. A woman's beauty is like a white
Frail bird, like a white sea-bird alone
At daybreak after stormy night
Between two furrows upon the plowed land:
A sudden storm and it was thrown
Between dark furrows upon the plowed land.
How many centuries spent
The sedentary soul
In toils of measurement
Beyond eagle or mole,
Beyond hearing or seeing,
Or Archimedes guess,
To raise into being
That loveliness?

[1] See *Four Plays for Dancers*, New York: The Macmillan Company, 1929.

A strange unserviceable thing,
A fragile, exquisite, pale shell,
That the vast troubled waters bring
To the loud sands before day has broken.
The storm arose and suddenly fell
Amid the dark before day had broken.
What death? what discipline?
What bonds no man could unbind
Being imagined within
The labyrinth of the mind,
What pursuing or fleeing,
What wounds, what bloody press
Dragged into being
This loveliness?

> [*When the cloth is folded again the Musicians take
> their places against the wall. The folding of the
> cloth shows on one side of the stage the curtained
> bed or litter on which lies a man in his grave-
> clothes. He wears an heroic mask. Another man
> with exactly similar clothes and mask crouches
> near the front.* EMER *is sitting beside the bed.*]

FIRST MUSICIAN [*speaking*]. I call before the eyes a roof
With cross-beams darkened by smoke;
A fisher's net hangs from a beam,
A long oar lies against the wall.
I call up a poor fisher's house;
A man lies dead or swooning,
That amorous man,
That amorous, violent man, renowned Cuchulain,
Queen Emer at his side.
At her own bidding all the rest have gone;
But now one comes on hesitating feet,
Young Eithne Inguba, Cuchulain's mistress.
She stands a moment in the open door,
Beyond the open door the bitter sea,
The shining, bitter sea, is crying out,
[*singing*] White shell, white wing!
I will not choose for my friend
A frail unserviceable thing
That drifts and dreams, and but knows
That waters are without end

And that wind blows.

EMER [*speaking*]. Come hither, come sit down beside the
    bed;
You need not be afraid, for I myself
Sent for you, Eithne Inguba.

EITHNE INGUBA.   No, madam,
I have too deeply wronged you to sit there.

EMER. Of all the people in the world we two,
And we alone, may watch together here,
Because we have loved him best.

EITHNE INGUBA.   And is he dead?

EMER. Although they have dressed him out in his grave-
    clothes
And stretched his limbs, Cuchulain is not dead;
The very heavens when that day's at hand,
So that his death may not lack ceremony,
Will throw out fires, and the earth grow red with blood.
There shall not be a scullion but foreknows it
Like the world's end.

EITHNE INGUBA. How did he come to this?

EMER. Towards noon in the assembly of the kings
He met with one who seemed a while most dear.
The kings stood around; some quarrel was blown up;
He drove him out and killed him on the shore
At Baile's tree, and he who was so killed
Was his own son begot of some wild woman
When he was young, or so I have heard it said;
And thereupon, knowing what man he had killed,
And being mad with sorrow, he ran out;
And after, to his middle in the foam
With shield before him and with sword in hand,
He fought the deathless sea. The kings looked on
And not a king dared stretch an arm, or even
Dared call his name, but all stood wondering
In that dumb stupor like cattle in a gale,
Until at last, as though he had fixed his eyes
On a new enemy, he waded out
Until the water had swept over him;
But the waves washed his senseless image up
And laid it at this door.

EITHNE INGUBA.   How pale he looks!

EMER. He is not dead.

EITHNE INGUBA.   You have not kissed his lips
Nor laid his head upon your breast.

EMER.   It may be
An image has been put into his place,
A sea-borne log bewitched into his likeness,
Or some stark horseman grown too old to ride
Among the troops of Mananan, Son of the Sea,
Now that his joints are stiff.

EITHNE INGUBA.   Cry out his name.
All that are taken from our sight, they say,
Loiter amid the scenery of their lives
For certain hours or days, and should he hear
He might, being angry, drive the changeling out.

EMER.   It is hard to make them hear amid their darkness,
And it is long since I could call him home;
I am but his wife, but if you cry aloud
With that sweet voice that is so dear to him
He cannot help but listen.

EITHNE INGUBA.   He loves me best,
Being his newest love, but in the end
Will love the woman best who loved him first
And loved him through the years when love seemed lost.

EMER. I have that hope, the hope that some day somewhere
We'll sit together at the hearth again.

EITHNE INGUBA. Women like me, the violent hour passed
    over,
Are flung into some corner like old nutshells.
Cuchulain, listen.

EMER.   No, not yet, for first
I'll cover up his face to hide the sea;
And throw new logs upon the hearth and stir
The half-burnt logs until they break in flame.
Old Mananan's unbridled horses come
Out of the sea, and on their backs his horsemen;
But all the enchantments of the dreaming foam
Dread the hearth-fire.

> [*She pulls the curtains of the bed so as to hide the
> sick man's face, that the actor may change his mask
> unseen. She goes to one side of platform and moves*

her hand as though putting logs on a fire and stir-
ring it into a blaze. While she makes these move-
ments the Musicians play, marking the movements
with drum and flute perhaps.

   Having finished she stands beside the imaginary
fire at a distance from CUCHULAIN *and* EITHNE
INGUBA.]
                     Call on Cuchulain now.
EITHNE INGUBA. Can you not hear my voice?
EMER.   Bend over him;
Call out dear secrets till you have touched his heart
If he lies there; and if he is not there
Till you have made him jealous.
EITHNE INGUBA.   Cuchulain, listen.
EMER. Those words sound timidly; to be afraid
Because his wife is but three paces off,
When there is so great a need, were but to prove
The man that chose you made but a poor choice:
We're but two women struggling with the sea.
EITHNE INGUBA. O my beloved, pardon me, that I
Have been ashamed and you in so great need.
I have never sent a message or called out,
Scarce had a longing for your company
But you have known and come; and if indeed
You are lying there, stretch out your arms and speak;
Open your mouth and speak, for to this hour
My company has made you talkative.
What ails your tongue, or what has closed your ears?
Our passion had not chilled when we were parted
On the pale shore under the breaking dawn.
He cannot speak: or else his ears are closed
And no sound reaches him.
EMER.   Then kiss that image;
The pressure of your mouth upon his mouth
May reach him where he is.
EITHNE INGUBA [*starting back*]. It is no man.
I felt some evil thing that dried my heart
When my lips touched it.
EMER.   No, his body stirs;
The pressure of your mouth has called him home;

He has thrown the changeling out.

EITHNE INGUBA [*going further off*]. Look at that arm;
That arm is withered to the very socket.

    EMER [*going up to the bed*]. What do you come for; and
        from where?

    FIGURE OF CUCHULAIN. I have come
From Mananan's court upon a bridleless horse.

    EMER.   What one among the Sidhe has dared to lie
Upon Cuchulain's bed and take his image?

    FIGURE OF CUCHULAIN. I am named Bricriu—not the man
    —that Bricriu,
Maker of discord among gods and men,
Called Bricriu of the Sidhe.

    EMER.   Come for what purpose?

    FIGURE OF CUCHULAIN [*sitting up parting curtain and
        showing its distorted face, as* EITHNE INGUBA *goes out*].
        I show my face and everything he loves
Must fly away.

    EMER.   You people of wind
Are full of lying speech and mockery:
I have not fled your face.

    FIGURE OF CUCHULAIN. You are not loved.

    EMER.   And therefore have no dread to meet your eyes
And to demand him of you.

    FIGURE OF CUCHULAIN. For that I have come.
You have but to pay the price and he is free.

    EMER. Do the Sidhe bargain?

    FIGURE OF CUCHULAIN. When they would free a captive
They take in ransom a less valued thing.
The fisher when some knowledgeable man
Restores to him his wife, or son, or daughter,
Knows he must lose a boat or net, or it may be
The cow that gives his children milk; and some
Have offered their own lives. I do not ask
Your life, or any valuable thing;
You spoke but now of the mere chance that some day
You'd be the apple of his eye again
When old and ailing, but renounce that chance
And he shall live again.

    EMER.   I do not question
But you have brought ill luck on all he loves;

And now, because I am thrown beyond your power
Unless your words are lies, you come to bargain.

FIGURE OF CUCHULAIN. You loved your mastery, when but
newly married,
And I love mine for all my withered arm;
You have but to put yourself into that power
And he shall live again.

EMER.   No, never, never.

FIGURE OF CUCHULAIN. You dare not be accursed, yet he
has dared.

EMER. I have but two joyous thoughts, two things I
prize,
A hope, a memory, and now you claim that hope.

FIGURE OF CUCHULAIN. He'll never sit beside you at the
hearth
Or make old bones, but die of wounds and toil
On some far shore or mountain, a strange woman
Beside his mattress.

EMER.   You ask for my one hope
That you may bring your curse on all about him.

FIGURE OF CUCHULAIN. You've watched his loves and you
have not been jealous
Knowing that he would tire, but do those tire
That love the Sidhe?

EMER.   What dancer of the Sidhe,
What creature of the reeling moon has pursued him?

FIGURE OF CUCHULAIN. I have but to touch your eyes and
give them sight;
But stand at my left side.

    [*He touches her eyes with his left hand, the right
    being withered.*]

EMER.   My husband there.

FIGURE OF CUCHULAIN. But out of reach—I have dis-
solved the dark
That hid him from your eyes, but not that other
That's hidden you from his.

EMER.   Husband, husband!

FIGURE OF CUCHULAIN. Be silent, he is but a phantom now
And he can neither touch, nor hear, nor see;
The longing and the cries have drawn him hither.
He heard no sound, heard no articulate sound;

They could but banish rest, and make him dream,
And in that dream, as do all dreaming shades
Before they are accustomed to their freedom,
He has taken his familiar form; and yet
He crouches there not knowing where he is
Or at whose side he is crouched.

> [*A* WOMAN OF THE SIDHE *has entered and stands a
> little inside the door.*]

EMER.   Who is this woman?
FIGURE OF CUCHULAIN. She has hurried from the Country-
    under-Wave
And dreamed herself into that shape that he
May glitter in her basket; for the Sidhe
Are dextrous fishers and they fish for men
With dreams upon the hook.

EMER.   And so that woman
Has hid herself in this disguise and made
Herself into a lie.

FIGURE OF CUCHULAIN. A dream is body;
The dead move ever towards a dreamless youth
And when they dream no more return no more;
And those more holy shades that never lived
But visit you in dreams.

EMER.   I know her sort.
They find our men asleep, weary with war,
Or weary with the chase, and kiss their lips
And drop their hair upon them; from that hour
Our men, who yet know nothing of it all,
Are lonely, and when at fall of night we press
Their hearts upon our hearts their hearts are cold.

> [*She draws a knife from her girdle.*]

FIGURE OF CUCHULAIN. And so you think to wound her
    with a knife.
She has an airy body. Look and listen;
I have not given you eyes and ears for nothing.

> [*The* WOMAN OF THE SIDHE *moves round the crouch-
> ing* GHOST OF CUCHULAIN *at front of stage in a
> dance that grows gradually quicker, as he slowly
> awakes. At moments she may drop her hair upon
> his head but she does not kiss him. She is accom-
> panied by string and flute and drum. Her mask and*

clothes must suggest gold or bronze or brass or silver, so that she seems more an idol than a human being. This suggestion may be repeated in her movements. Her hair, too, must keep the metallic suggestion.]

GHOST OF CUCHULAIN. Who is it stands before me there
Shedding such light from limb and hair
As when the moon, complete at last
With every laboring crescent past,
And lonely with extreme delight,
Flings out upon the fifteenth night?

WOMAN OF THE SIDHE. Because I long I am not complete.
What pulled your hands about your feet
And your head down upon your knees,
And hid your face?

GHOST OF CUCHULAIN. Old memories:
A dying boy, with handsome face
Upturned upon a beaten place;
A sacred yew-tree on a strand;
A woman that held in steady hand,
In all the happiness of her youth
Before her man had broken troth,
A burning wisp to light the door;
And many a round or crescent more;
Dead men and women. Memories
Have pulled my head upon my knees.

WOMAN OF THE SIDHE. Could you that have loved many
    a woman
That did not reach beyond the human,
Lacking a day to be complete,
Love one that though her heart can beat,
Lacks it but by an hour or so?

GHOST OF CUCHULAIN.   I know you now, for long ago
I met you on the mountain-side,
Beside a well that seemed long dry,
Beside old thorns where the hawk flew.
I held out arms and hands; but you,
That now seem friendly, fled away
Half woman and half bird of prey.

WOMAN OF THE SIDHE. Hold out your arms and hands
    again;

You were not so dumbfounded when
I was that bird of prey, and yet
I am all woman now.
    GHOST OF CUCHULAIN. I am not
The young and passionate man I was
And though that brilliant light surpass
All crescent forms, my memories
Weigh down my hands, abash my eyes.
    WOMAN OF THE SIDHE. Then kiss my mouth. Though
      memory
Be beauty's bitterest enemy
I have no dread, for at my kiss
Memory on the moment vanishes:
Nothing but beauty can remain.
    GHOST OF CUCHULAIN.   And shall I never know again
Intricacies of blind remorse?
    WOMAN OF THE SIDHE. Time shall seem to stay his course;
When your mouth and my mouth meet
All my round shall be complete
Imagining all its circles run;
And there shall be oblivion
Even to quench Cuchulain's drouth,
Even to still that heart.
    GHOST OF CUCHULAIN. Your mouth.
      [*They are about to kiss, he turns away.*]
O Emer, Emer.
    WOMAN OF THE SIDHE. So then it is she
Made you impure with memory.
    GHOST OF CUCHULAIN. Still in that dream I see you stand,
A burning wisp in your right hand,
To wait my coming to the house,
As when our parents married us.
    WOMAN OF THE SIDHE. Being among the dead you love her
That valued every slut above her
While you still lived.
    GHOST OF CUCHULAIN. O my lost Emer.
    WOMAN OF THE SIDHE. And there is not a loose-tongued
      schemer
But could draw you, if not dead,
From her table and her bed.
But what could make you fit to wive

With flesh and blood, being born to live
Where no one speaks of broken troth,
For all have washed out of their eyes
Wind-blown dirt of their memories
To improve their sight?
    GHOST OF CUCHULAIN. Your mouth, your mouth.
       [*Their lips approach, but* CUCHULAIN *turns away as*
       EMER *speaks.*]
    EMER. If but the dead will set him free
That I may speak with him at whiles
By the hearthstone, I am content—
Content that he shall turn on me
Eyes that the cold moon, or the vague sea,
Or what I know not's made indifferent.
    GHOST OF CUCHULAIN. What a wise silence has fallen in
      this dark!
I know you now in all your ignorance
Of all whereby a lover's quiet is rent.
What dread so great as that he should forget
The least chance sight or sound, or scratch or mark
On an old door, or frail bird heard and seen
In the incredible clear light love cast
All round about her some forlorn lost day?
That face, though fine enough, is a fool's face
And there's a folly in the deathless Sidhe
Beyond man's reach.
    WOMAN OF THE SIDHE. I told you to forget
After my fashion; you would have none of it;
So now you may forget in a man's fashion.
There's an unbridled horse at the sea's edge;
Mount; it will carry you in an eye's wink
To where the King of Country-under-Wave,
Old Mananan, nods above the board and moves
His chessmen in a dream. Demand your life
And come again on the unbridled horse.
    GHOST OF CUCHULAIN. Forgive me those rough words.
      How could you know
That man is held to those whom he has loved
By pain they gave, or pain that he has given,
Intricacies of pain.
    WOMAN OF THE SIDHE. I am ashamed

That being of the deathless shades I chose
A man so knotted to impurity.
            [*The* GHOST OF CUCHULAIN *goes out.*]
    WOMAN OF THE SIDHE [*to* FIGURE OF CUCHULAIN]. To
        you that have no living light, being dropped
From a last leprous crescent of the moon,
I owe it all.
    FIGURE OF CUCHULAIN. Because you have failed
I must forego your thanks, I that took pity
Upon your love and carried out your plan
To tangle all his life and make it nothing
That he might turn to you.
    WOMAN OF THE SIDHE.   Was it from pity
You taught the woman to prevail against me?
    FIGURE OF CUCHULAIN. You know my nature—by what
        name I am called.
    WOMAN OF THE SIDHE. Was it from pity that you hid
        the truth
That men are bound to women by the wrongs
They do or suffer?
    FIGURE OF CUCHULAIN. You know what being I am.
    WOMAN OF THE SIDHE. I have been mocked and disobeyed
        —your power
Was more to you than my good will, and now
I'll have you learn what my ill will can do;
I lay you under bonds upon the instant
To stand before your King and face the charge
And take the punishment.
    FIGURE OF CUCHULAIN. I'll stand there first,
And tell my story first, and Mananan
Knows that his own harsh sea made my heart cold.
    WOMAN OF THE SIDHE. My horse is there and shall out-
        run your horse.
            [*The* FIGURE OF CUCHULAIN *falls back, the* WOMAN
                OF THE SIDHE *goes out. Drum taps, music re-
                sembling horse hoofs.*]
    EITHNE INGUBA [*entering quickly*]. I heard the beat of
        hoofs, but saw no horse,
And then came other hoofs, and after that
I heard low angry cries and thereupon
I ceased to be afraid.

EMER.   Cuchulain wakes.
>   [*The figure turns round. It once more wears the
>   heroic mask.*]

CUCHULAIN. Your arms, your arms. O Eithne Inguba,
I have been in some strange place and am afraid.
>   [*The* FIRST MUSICIAN *comes to the front of stage, the
>   others from each side and unfold the cloth singing.*]

[*Song for the unfolding and folding of the cloth.*]

THE MUSICIANS

>   Why does your heart beat thus?
>   Plain to be understood
>   I have met in a man's house
>   A statue of solitude,
>   Moving there and walking;
>   Its strange heart beating fast
>   For all our talking.
>   O still that heart at last.
>
>   O bitter reward
>   Of many a tragic tomb!
>   And we though astonished are dumb
>   And give but a sigh and a word,
>   A passing word.
>
>   Although the door be shut
>   And all seem well enough,
>   Although wide world hold not
>   A man but will give you his love
>   The moment he has looked at you,
>   He that has loved the best
>   May turn from a statue
>   His too human breast.
>
>   O bitter reward
>   Of many a tragic tomb!
>   And we though astonished are dumb
>   Or give but a sigh and a word,
>   A passing word.

What makes your heart so beat?
Is there no man at your side?
When beauty is complete
Your own thought will have died
And danger not be diminished;
Dimmed at three-quarter light
When moon's round is finished
The stars are out of sight.

O bitter reward
Of many a tragic tomb!
And we though astonished are dumb
Or give but a sigh and a word,
A passing word.

[*When the cloth is folded again the stage is bare.*]

Note on *The Only Jealousy of Emer*

"While writing these plays, intended for some fifty people in a drawing-room or a studio, I have so rejoiced in my freedom from the stupidity of an ordinary audience that I have filled *The Only Jealousy of Emer* with convictions about the nature and history of a woman's beauty, which Robartes found in the *Speculum* of Gyraldus and in Arabia Deserta among the Judwalis. The soul through each cycle of its development is held to incarnate through twenty-eight typical incarnations, corresponding to the phases of the moon, the light part of the moon's disc symbolizing the subjective and the dark part the objective nature, the wholly dark moon (called Phase 1) and the wholly light (called Phase 15) symbolizing complete objectivity and complete subjectivity respectively. In a poem called 'The Phases of the Moon' in *The Wild Swans at Coole* I have described certain aspects of this symbolism, which needs, however, 100 pages or more for its exposition, for it purports to be a complete classification and analysis of every possible type of human intellect, Phase 1 and Phase 15 symbolizing, however, two incarnations not visible to human eyes nor having human characteristics. The invisible fifteenth incarnation is that of the greatest possible bodily beauty, and the fourteenth and sixteenth those of the greatest beauty visible to human eyes. Much that Robartes has found might be a commentary on Castiglione's saying that the physical beauty of woman is the spoil or monument of the victory of the soul, for physical beauty, only possible to subjective natures, is described as the result of emotional toil in past lives. Objective natures are declared to be always ugly, hence the disagreeable appearance of politicians, reformers, philanthropists, and men of science. A saint or sage before his final deliverance has one incarnation as a woman of supreme beauty.

In writing these little plays I knew that I was creating something which could only fully succeed in a civilization very unlike ours. I think they should be written for some country where all classes share in a half-mythological, half-philosophical folk-belief which the writer and his small audience lift into a new subtlety. All my life I have longed for such a country, and always found it quite impossible to write without having as much belief in its real existence as a child has in that of the wooden birds, beasts, and persons of his toy Noah's ark. I have now found all the mythology and philosophy I need."

WILLIAM BUTLER YEATS

DEIRDRE

A LEGEND IN THREE ACTS

By George William Russell (A. E.)

DRAMATIS PERSONÆ

CONCOBAR, *Ardrie of Ulla*
NAISI
AINLE } *Brothers of Naisi*
ARDAN
FERGUS, *Former Ardrie*
BUINNE } *Sons of Fergus*
ILANN
CATHVAH, *A Druid*
DEIRDRE, *Daughter of Felim*
LAVARCAM, *A Druidess*
Herdsman, Messenger

ACT I

SCENE: *The dun of* DEIRDRE'S *captivity.* LAVARCAM, *a Druidess, sits before the door in the open air.* DEIRDRE *comes out of the dun.*

DEIRDRE. Dear fostermother, how the spring is beginning! The music of the Father's harp is awakening the flowers. Now the winter's sleep is over, and the spring flows from the lips of the harp. Do you not feel the thrill in the wind— a joy answering the trembling strings? Dear fostermother, the spring and the music are in my heart!

LAVARCAM. The harp has but three notes; and, after sleep and laughter, the last sound is of weeping.

DEIRDRE. Why should there be any sorrow while I am with you? I am happy here. Last night in a dream I saw the blessed Sidhe upon the mountains, and they looked on me with eyes of love.

66

[*An old* HERDSMAN *enters, who bows before* LAVARCAM.]

HERDSMAN. Lady, the High King is coming through the woods.

LAVARCAM. Deirdre, go to the grianan for a little. You shall tell me your dream again, my child.

DEIRDRE. Why am I always hidden from the king's sight.

LAVARCAM. It is the king's will you should see no one except these aged servants.

DEIRDRE. Am I indeed fearful to look upon, fostermother? I do not think so, or you would not love me.

LAVARCAM. It is the king's will.

DEIRDRE. Yet why must it be so, fostermother? Why must I hide away? Why must I never leave the valley?

LAVARCAM. It is the king's will.

[*While she is speaking* CONCOBAR *enters. He stands still and looks on* DEIRDRE. DEIRDRE *gazes on the* KING *for a moment, and then covering her face with her hands, she hurries into the dun. The* HERDSMAN *goes out.* LAVARCAM *sees and bows before the* KING.]

CONCOBAR. Lady, is all well with you and your charge?

LAVARCAM. All is well.

CONCOBAR. Is there peace in Deirdre's heart?

LAVARCAM. She is happy, not knowing a greater happiness than to roam the woods or to dream of what the immortal ones can bring her.

CONCOBAR. Fate has not found her yet hidden in this valley.

LAVARCAM. Her happiness is to be here. But she asks why must she never leave the glen. Her heart quickens within her. Like a bird she listens to the spring, and soon the valley will be narrow as a cage.

CONCOBAR. I cannot open the cage. Less ominous the Red Swineherd at a feast than this beautiful child in Ulla. You know the word of the Druids at her birth.

LAVARCAM. Aye, through her would come the destruction of the Red Branch. But sad is my heart, thinking of her lonely youth.

CONCOBAR. The gods did not guide us how the ruin might be averted. The Druids would have slain her, but I set myself against the wise ones, thinking in my heart that the chivalry of the Red Branch would be already gone if this child were slain. If we are to perish it shall be nobly, and without any departure from the laws of our order. So I have hidden her away from men, hoping to stay the coming of fate.

LAVARCAM. King, your mercy will return to you, and if any of the Red Branch fall, you will not fall.

CONCOBAR. If her thoughts turned only to the Sidhe her heart would grow cold to the light love that warriors give. The birds of Angus cannot breathe or sing their maddening song in the chill air that enfolds the wise. For this, Druidess, I made thee her fosterer. Has she learned to know the beauty of the ever-living ones, after which the earth fades and no voice can call us back?

LAVARCAM. The immortals have appeared to her in vision and looked on her with eyes of love.

CONCOBAR. Her beauty is so great it would madden whole hosts, and turn them from remembrance of their duty. We must guard well the safety of the Red Branch. Druidess, you have seen with subtle eyes the shining life beyond this. But through the ancient traditions of Ulla, which the bards have kept and woven into song, I have seen the shining law enter men's minds, and subdue the lawless into love of justice. A great tradition is shaping an heroic race; and the gods who fought at Moytura are descending and dwelling in the heart of the Red Branch. Deeds will be done in our time as mighty as those wrought by the giants who battled at the dawn; and through the memory of our days and deeds the gods will build themselves an eternal empire in the mind of the Gael. Wise woman, guard well this beauty which fills my heart with terror. I go now, and will doubly warn the spearmen at the passes, but will come hither again and speak with thee of these things, and with Deirdre I would speak also.

LAVARCAM. King of Ulla, be at peace. It is not I who will break through the design of the gods. [CONCOBAR *goes through the woods, after looking for a time at the door of the dun.*] But Deirdre is also one of the immortals. What the gods desire will utter itself through her heart. I will seek counsel from the gods.

[DEIRDRE *comes slowly through the door.*]

DEIRDRE. Is he gone? I fear this stony king with his implacable eyes.

LAVARCAM. He is implacable only in his desire for justice.

DEIRDRE. No! No! There is a hunger in his eyes for I know not what.

LAVARCAM. He is the wisest king who ever sat on the chair of Macha.

DEIRDRE. He has placed a burden on my heart. Oh! fostermother, the harp of life is already trembling into sorrow!

LAVARCAM. Do not think of him. Tell me your dream, my child.

[DEIRDRE *comes from the door of the dun and sits on a deerskin at* LAVARCAM'S *feet.*]

DEIRDRE. Tell me, do happy dreams bring happiness, and do our dreams of the Sidhe ever grow real to us as you are real to me? Do their eyes draw nigh to ours, and can the heart we dream of ever be a refuge for our hearts.

LAVARCAM. Tell me your dream.

DEIRDRE. Nay; but answer first of all, dear fostermother —you who are wise, and who have talked with the Sidhe.

LAVARCAM. Would it make you happy to have your dream real, my darling?

DEIRDRE. Oh, it would make me happy!

[*She hides her face on* LAVARCAM'S *knees.*]

LAVARCAM. If I can make your dream real, I will, my beautiful fawn.

DEIRDRE. Dear fostermother, I think my dream is coming near to me. It is coming to me now.

LAVARCAM. Deirdre, tell me what hope has entered your heart?

DEIRDRE. In the night I saw in a dream the top of the mountain yonder, beyond the woods, and three hunters stood there in the dawn. The sun sent its breath upon their faces, but there was a light about them never kindled at the sun. They were surely hunters from some heavenly field, or the three gods whom Lu condemned to wander in mortal form, and they are come again to the world to seek some greater treasure.

LAVARCAM. Describe to me these immortal hunters. In Eiré we know no gods who take such shape appearing unto men.

DEIRDRE. I cannot now make clear to thee my remembrance of two of the hunters, but the tallest of the three—oh, he stood like a flame against the flameless sky, and the whole sapphire of the heavens seemed to live in his fearless eyes! His hair was darker than the raven's wing, his face dazzling in its fairness. He pointed with his great flame-bright spear to the valley. His companions seemed in doubt, and pointed east and west. Then in my dream I came nigh him and whispered in his ear, and pointed the way through the valley to our dun. I looked into his eyes, and he started like one who sees a vision; and I know, dear fostermother, he will come here, and he will love me Oh, I would die if he did not love me!

LAVARCAM. Make haste, my child, and tell me was there aught else memorable about this hero and his companions?

DEIRDRE. Yes, I remember each had the likeness of a torch shedding rays of gold embroidered on the breast.

LAVARCAM. Deirdre, Deirdre, these are no phantoms, but living heroes! O wise king, the eyes of the spirit thou wouldst open have seen farther than the eyes of the body thou wouldst blind! The Druid vision has only revealed to this child her destiny.

DEIRDRE. Why do you talk so strangely, fostermother?

LAVARCAM. Concobar, I will not fight against the will of the immortals. I am not thy servant, but theirs. Let the Red Branch fall! If the gods scatter it they have chosen to guide the people of Ulla in another path.

DEIRDRE. What has disturbed your mind, dear fostermother? What have I to do with the Red Branch? And why should the people of Ulla fall because of me?

LAVARCAM. O Deirdre, there were no warriors created could overcome the Red Branch. The gods have but smiled on this proud chivalry through thine eyes, and they are already melted. The waving of thy hand is more powerful to subdue than the silver rod of the king to sustain. Thy golden hair shall be the flame to burn up Ulla.

DEIRDRE. Oh, what do you mean by these fateful prophecies? You fill me with terror. Why should a dream so gentle and sweet portend sorrow?

LAVARCAM. Dear golden head, cast sorrow aside for a time.

The Father has not yet struck the last chords on the harp of life. The chords of joy have but begun for thee.

DEIRDRE. You confuse my mind, dear fostermother, with your speech of joy and sorrow. It is not your wont. Indeed, I think my dream portends joy.

LAVARCAM. It is love, Deirdre, which is coming to thee. Love, which thou hast never known.

DEIRDRE. But I love thee, dearest and kindest of guardians.

LAVARCAM. Oh, in this love heaven and earth will be forgotten, and your own self unremembered, or dim and far off as a home the spirit lives in no longer.

DEIRDRE. Tell me, will the hunter from the hills come to us? I think I could forget all for him.

LAVARCAM. He is not one of the Sidhe, but the proudest and bravest of the Red Branch, Naisi, son of Usna. Three lights of valor among the Ultonians are Naisi and his brothers.

DEIRDRE. Will he love me, fostermother, as you love me, and will he live with us here?

LAVARCAM. Nay, where he goes you must go, and he must fly afar to live with you. But I will leave you now for a little, child, I would divine the future.

[LAVARCAM *kisses* DEIRDRE *and goes within the dun.* DEIRDRE *walks to and fro before the door.* NAISI *enters. He sees* DEIRDRE, *who turns and looks at him, pressing her hands to her breast.* NAISI *bows before* DEIRDRE.]

NAISI. Goddess, or enchantress, thy face shone on me at dawn on the mountain. Thy lips called me hither, and I have come.

DEIRDRE. I called thee, dear Naisi.

NAISI. Oh, knowing my name, never before having spoken to me, thou must know my heart also.

DEIRDRE. Nay, I know not. Tell me what is in thy heart.

NAISI. O enchantress, thou art there. The image of thine eyes is there and thy smiling lips, and the beating of my heart is muffled in a cloud of thy golden tresses.

DEIRDRE. Say on, dear Naisi.

NAISI. I have told thee all. Thou only art in my heart.

DEIRDRE. But I have never ere this spoken to any man. Tell me more.

NAISI. If thou hast never before spoken to any man, then

indeed art thou one of the immortals, and my hope is vain. Hast thou only called me to thy world to extinguish my life hereafter in memories of thee?

DEIRDRE. What wouldst thou with me, dear Naisi?

NAISI. I would carry thee to my dun by the sea of Moyle, O beautiful woman, and set thee there on an ivory throne. The winter would not chill thee there, nor the summer burn thee, for I would enfold thee with my love, enchantress, if thou camest to my world. Many warriors are there of the clan Usna, and two brothers I have who are strong above any hosts, and they would all die with me for thy sake.

DEIRDRE [*taking the hands of* NAISI]. I will go with thee where thou goest. [*Leaning her head on* NAISI'S *shoulder.*] Oh, fostermother, too truly hast thou spoken! I know myself not. My spirit has gone from me to this other heart forever.

NAISI. Dost thou forego thy shining world for me?

LAVARCAM [*coming out of the dun*]. Naisi, this is the Deirdre of the prophecies.

NAISI. Deirdre! Deirdre! I remember in some old tale of my childhood that name. [*Fiercely.*] It was a lying prophecy. What has this girl to do with the downfall of Ulla?

LAVARCAM. Thou art the light of the Ultonians, Naisi, but thou art not the star of knowledge. The Druids spake truly. Through her, but not through her sin, will come the destruction of the Red Branch.

NAISI. I have counted death as nothing battling for the Red Branch; and I would not, even for Deirdre, war upon my comrades. But Deirdre I will not leave nor forget for a thousand prophecies made by the Druids in their dotage. If the Red Branch must fall, it will fall through treachery; but Deirdre I will love, and in my love is no dishonor, nor any broken pledge.

LAVARCAM. Remember, Naisi, the law of the king. It is death to thee to be here. Concobar is even now in the woods, and will come hither again.

DEIRDRE. Is it death to thee to love me, Naisi? Oh, fly quickly, and forget me. But first, before thou goest, bend down thy head—low—rest it on my bosom. Listen to the beating of my heart. That passionate tumult is for thee!

There, I have kissed thee. I have sweet memories for everlasting. Go now, my beloved, quickly. I fear—I fear for thee this stony king.

NAISI. I do not fear the king, nor will I fly hence. It is due to the chief of the Red Branch that I should stay and face him, having set my will against his.

LAVARCAM. You cannot remain now.

NAISI. It is due to the king.

LAVARCAM. You must go; both must go. Do not cloud your heart with dreams of a false honor. It is not your death only, but Deirdre's which will follow. Do you think the Red Branch would spare her, after your death, to extinguish another light of valor, and another who may wander here?

NAISI. I will go with Deirdre to Alba.

DEIRDRE. Through life or to death I will go with thee, Naisi.

[*Voices of* AINLE *and* ARDAN *are heard in the wood.*]

ARDAN. I think Naisi went this way.

AINLE. He has been wrapt in a dream since the dawn. See! This is his footstep in the clay!

ARDAN. I heard voices.

AINLE [*entering with* ARDAN]. Here is our dream-led brother.

NAISI. Ainle and Ardan, this is Deirdre, your sister. I have broken through the command of the king, and fly with her to Alba to avoid warfare with the Red Branch.

ARDAN. Our love to thee, beautiful sister.

AINLE. Dear maiden, thou art already in my heart with Naisi.

LAVARCAM. You cannot linger here. With Concobar the deed follows swiftly the counsel; tonight his spearmen will be on your track.

NAISI. Listen, Ainle and Ardan. Go you to Emain Macha. It may be the Red Branch will make peace between the king and myself. You are guiltless in this flight.

AINLE. Having seen Deirdre, my heart is with you, brother, and I also am guilty.

ARDAN. I think, being here, we, too, have broken the command of the king. We will go with thee to Alba, dear brother and sister.

LAVARCAM. Oh, tarry not, tarry not! Make haste while there is yet time. The thoughts of the king are circling around Deirdre as wolves around the fold. Try not the passes of the valley, but over the hills. The passes are all filled with the spearmen of the king.

NAISI. We will carry thee over the mountains, Deirdre, and tomorrow will see us nigh to the isles of Alba.

DEIRDRE. Farewell, dear fostermother. I have passed the faëry sea since dawn, and have found the Island of Joy. Oh, see! what bright birds are around us, with dazzling wings! Can you not hear their singing? Oh, bright birds, make music forever around my love and me!

LAVARCAM. They are the birds of Angus. Their singing brings love—and death.

DEIRDRE. Nay, death has come before love, dear foster-mother, and all I was has vanished like a dewdrop in the sun. Oh, beloved, let us go. We are leaving death behind us in the valley.

[DEIRDRE *and the brothers go through the wood.* LAVARCAM *watches, and when they are out of sight sits by the door of the dun with her head bowed to her knees. After a little* CONCOBAR *enters.*]

CONCOBAR. Where is Deirdre?

LAVARCAM [*not lifting her head*]. Deirdre has left death behind her, and has entered into the Kingdom of her Youth.

CONCOBAR. Do not speak to me in portents. Lift up your head, Druidess. Where is Deirdre?

LAVARCAM [*looking up*]. Deirdre is gone!

CONCOBAR. By the high gods, tell me whither, and who has dared to take her hence?

LAVARCAM. She has fled with Naisi, son of Usna, and is beyond your vengeance, king.

CONCOBAR. Woman, I swear by Balor, Tethra, and all the brood of demons, I will have such a vengeance a thousand years hereafter shall be frightened at the tale. If the Red Branch is to fall, it will sink at least in the seas of the blood of the clan Usna.

LAVARCAM. O king, the doom of the Red Branch had already gone forth when you suffered love for Deirdre to enter your heart.

[*Scene closes.*]

ACT II

SCENE: *In a dun by Loch Etive. Through the open door can be seen lakes and wooded islands in a silver twilight.* DEIRDRE *stands at the door looking over the lake.* NAISI *is within binding a spear-head to the shaft.*

DEIRDRE. How still is the twilight! It is the sunset, not of one, but of many days—so still, so still, so living! The enchantment of Dana is upon the lakes and islands and woods, and the Great Father looks down through the deepening heavens.

NAISI. Thou art half of their world, beautiful woman, and it seems fair to me, gazing on thine eyes. But when thou art not beside me the flashing of spears is more to be admired than a whole heavenful of stars.

DEIRDRE. O Naisi! still dost thou long, for the Red Branch and the peril of battles and death.

NAISI. Not for the Red Branch, nor the peril of battles, nor death, do I long. But—

DEIRDRE. But what, Naisi? What memory of Eri hast thou hoarded in thy heart?

NAISI [*bending over his spear*]. It is nothing, Deirdre.

DEIRDRE. It is a night of many days, Naisi. See, all the bright day had hidden is revealed! Look, there! A star! and another star! They could not see each other through the day, for the hot mists of the sun were about them. Three years of the sun have we passed in Alba, Naisi, and now, O star of my heart, truly do I see you, this night of many days.

NAISI. Though my breast lay clear as a crystal before thee, thou couldst see no change in my heart.

DEIRDRE. There is no change, beloved; but I see there one memory warring on thy peace.

NAISI. What is it then, wise woman?

DEIRDRE. O Naisi, I have looked within thy heart, and thou hast there imagined a king with scornful eyes thinking of thy flight.

NAISI. By the gods, but it is true! I would give this kingdom I have won in Alba to tell the proud monarch I fear him not.

DEIRDRE. O Naisi, that thought will draw thee back to Eri, and to I know not what peril and death beyond the seas.

NAISI. I will not war on the Red Branch. They were ever faithful comrades. Be at peace, Deirdre.

DEIRDRE. Oh, how vain it is to say to the heart, "Be at peace," when the heart will not rest! Sorrow is on me, beloved, and I know not wherefore. It has taken the strong and fast place of my heart, and sighs there hidden in my love for thee.

NAISI. Dear one, the songs of Ainle and the pleasant tales of Ardan will drive away thy sorrow.

DEIRDRE. Ainle and Ardan! Where are they? They linger long.

NAISI. They are watching a sail that set hitherward from the south.

DEIRDRE. A sail!

NAISI. A sail! What is there to startle thee in that? Have not a thousand galleys lain in Loch Etive since I built this dun by the sea.

DEIRDRE. I do not know, but my spirit died down in my heart as you spake. I think the wind that brings it blows from Eri, and it is it has brought sorrow to me.

NAISI. My beautiful one, it is but a fancy. It is some merchant comes hither to barter Tyrian cloths for the cunning work of our smiths. But glad would I be if he came from Eri, and I would feast him here for a night, and sit round a fire of turves and hear of the deeds of the Red Branch.

DEIRDRE. Your heart forever goes out to the Red Branch, Naisi. Were there any like unto thee, or Ainle, or Ardan?

NAISI. We were accounted most skillful, but no one was held to be braver than another. If there were one it was great Fergus who laid aside the silver rod which he held as Ardrie of Ulla, but he is in himself greater than any king.

DEIRDRE. And does one hero draw your heart back to Eri?

NAISI. A river of love, indeed, flows from my heart unto Fergus, for there is no one more noble. But there were many others, Conal, and the boy we called Cuculain, a dark, sad child, who was the darling of the Red Branch, and truly he seemed like one who would be a world-famous warrior. There were many held him to be a god in exile.

DEIRDRE. I think we, too, are in exile in this world. But tell me who else among the Red Branch do you think of with love?

NAISI. There was the Ardrie, Concobar, whom no man knows, indeed, for he is unfathomable. But he is a wise king, though moody and passionate at times, for he was cursed in his youth for a sin against one of the Sidhe.

DEIRDRE. Oh, do not speak of him! My heart falls at the thought of him as into a grave, and I know I will die when we meet.

NAISI. I know one who will die before that, my fawn.

DEIRDRE. Naisi! You remember when we fled that night; as I lay by thy side—thou wert yet strange to me—I heard voices speaking out of the air. The great ones were invisible, yet their voices sounded solemnly. "Our brother and our sister do not remember," one said; and another spake: "They will serve the purpose all the same," and there was more which I could not understand, but I knew we were to bring some great gift to the Gael. Yesternight, in a dream, I heard the voices again, and I cannot recall what they said; but as I woke from sleep my pillow was wet with tears falling softly, as out of another world, and I saw before me thy face, pale and still, Naisi, and the king, with his implacable eyes. Oh, pulse of my heart, I know the gift we shall give to the Gael will be a memory to pity and sigh over, and I shall be the priestess of tears. Naisi, promise me you will never go back to Ulla—swear to me, Naisi.

NAISI. I will, if—

[*Here* AINLE *and* ARDAN *enter.*]

AINLE. Oh, great tidings, brother!

DEIRDRE. I feel fate is stealing on us with the footsteps of those we love. Before they speak, promise me, Naisi.

AINLE. What is it, dear sister? Naisi will promise thee anything, and if he does not we will make him do it all the same.

DEIRDRE. Oh, let me speak! Both Death and the Heart's Desire are speeding to win the race. Promise me, Naisi, you will never return to Ulla.

ARDAN. Naisi, it were well to hear what tale may come from Emain Macha. One of the Red Branch displays our banner on a galley from the south. I have sent a boat to bring this warrior to our dun. It may be Concobar is dead.

DEIRDRE. Why should we return? Is not the Clan Usna greater here than ever in Eri.

AINLE. Dear sister, it is the land which gave us birth, which ever like a mother whispered to us, and its whisper is sweeter than the promise of beloved lips. Though we are kings here in Alba we are exiles, and the heart is afar from its home.

[*A distant shout is heard.*]

NAISI. I hear a call like the voice of a man of Eri.

DEIRDRE. It is only a herdsman calling home his cattle. [*She puts her arms round* NAISI'S *neck.*] Beloved, am I become so little to you that your heart is empty, and sighs for Eri?

NAISI. Deirdre, in my flight I have brought with me many whose desire is afar, while you are set as a star by my side. They have left their own land and many a maiden sighs for the clansmen who never return. There is also the shadow of fear on my name, because I fled and did not face the king. Shall I swear to keep my comrades in exile, and let the shame of fear rest on the chieftain of their clan?

DEIRDRE. Can they not go? Are we not enough for each other, for surely to me thou art hearth and home, and where thou art there the dream ends, and beyond it there is no other dream.

[*A voice is heard without, more clearly calling.*]

AINLE. It is a familiar voice that calls! And I thought I heard thy name, Naisi.

ARDAN. It is the honey-sweet speech of a man of Eri.

DEIRDRE. It is one of our own clansmen. Naisi, will you not speak? The hour is passing, and soon there will be naught but a destiny.

FERGUS [*without*]. Naisi! Naisi!

NAISI. A deep voice, like the roar of a storm god! It is Fergus who comes from Eri.

ARDAN. He comes as a friend. There is no treachery in the Red Branch.

AINLE. Let us meet him, and give him welcome!

[*The brothers go to the door of the dun.* DEIRDRE *leans against the wall with terror in her eyes.*]

DEIRDRE [*in a low broken voice*]. Naisi! [NAISI *returns to her side.* AINLE *and* ARDAN *go out.* DEIRDRE *rests one hand on* NAISI's *shoulder and with the other points upwards.*] Do you not see them? The bright birds which sang at our flight! Look, how they wheel about us as they sing! What a heart-rending music! And their plumage, Naisi! It is all dabbled with crimson; and they shake a ruddy dew from their wings upon us! Your brow is stained with the drops. Let me clear away the stains. They pour over your face and hands. Oh!

[*She hides her face on* NAISI's *breast.*]

NAISI. Poor, frightened one, there are no birds! See, how clear are my hands! Look again on my face.

DEIRDRE [*looking up for an instant*]. Oh! blind, staring eyes.

NAISI. Nay, they are filled with love, light of my heart. What has troubled your mind? Am I not beside you, and a thousand clansmen around our dun?

DEIRDRE. They go, and the music dies out. What was it Lavarcam said? "Their singing brings love and death."

NAISI. What matters death, for love will find us among the Ever Living Ones. We are immortals, and it does not become us to grieve.

DEIRDRE. Naisi, there is some treachery in the coming of Fergus.

NAISI. I say to you, Deirdre, that treachery is not to be spoken of with Fergus. He was my fosterer, who taught me all a chieftain should feel, and I shall not now accuse him on the foolish fancy of a woman. [*He turns from* DEIRDRE, *and as he nears the door* FERGUS *enters with hands laid affectionately on a shoulder of each of the brothers;* BUINNE *and* ILANN *follow.*] Welcome, Fergus! Glad is my heart at your coming, whether you bring good tidings or ill!

FERGUS. I would not have crossed the sea of Moyle to bring thee ill tidings, Naisi. [*He sees* DEIRDRE.] My coming has affrighted thy lady, who shakes like the white wave trembling before its fall. I swear to thee, Deirdre, that the sons of Usna are dear to me as children to a father.

DEIRDRE. The Birds of Angus showed all fiery and crimson as you came!

BUINNE. If we are not welcome in this dun let us return!

FERGUS. Be still, hasty boy.

ILANN. The lady Deirdre has received some omen or warning on our account. When the Sidhe declare their will, we should with due awe consider it.

ARDAN. Her mind has been troubled by a dream of some ill to Naisi.

NAISI. It was not by dreaming evils that the sons of Usna grew to be champions in Ulla. And I took thee to my heart, Deirdre, though the Druids trembled to murmur thy name.

FERGUS. If we listened to dreamers and foretellers the sword would never flash from its sheath. In truth, I have never found the Sidhe send omens to warriors; they rather bid them fly to herald our coming.

DEIRDRE. And what doom comes with thee now that such omens fled before thee? I fear thy coming, warrior. I fear the Lights of Valor will be soon extinguished.

FERGUS. Thou shalt smile again, pale princess, when thou hast heard my tale. It is not to the sons of Usna I would bring sorrow. Naisi, thou art free to return to Ulla.

NAISI. Does the king then forego his vengeance?

DEIRDRE. The king will never forego his vengeance. I have looked on his face—the face of one who never changes his purpose.

FERGUS. He sends forgiveness and greetings.

DEIRDRE. O Naisi, he sends honied words by the mouth of Fergus, but the pent-up death broods in his own heart.

BUINNE. We were tempest-beaten, indeed, on the sea of Moyle, but the storm of this girl's speech is more fearful to face.

FERGUS. Your tongue is too swift, Buinne. I say to you, Deirdre, that if all the kings of Eri brooded ill to Naisi, they dare not break through my protection.

NAISI. It is true, indeed, Fergus, though I have never asked any protection save my own sword. It is a chill welcome you give to Fergus and his sons, Deirdre. Ainle, tell them within to make ready the feasting hall.

[AINLE *goes into an inner room.*]

DEIRDRE. I pray thy pardon, warrior. Thy love for Naisi I do not doubt. But in this holy place there is peace, and the doom that Cathvah the Druid cried cannot fall. And oh, I feel, too, there is One here among us who pushes us silently from the place of life, and we are drifting away—away from the world, on a tide which goes down into the darkness!

ARDAN. The darkness is in your mind alone, poor sister. Great is our joy to hear the message of Fergus.

NAISI. It is not like the king to change his will. Fergus, what has wrought upon his mind?

FERGUS. He took counsel with the Druids and Lavarcam, and thereafter spake at Emain Macha, that for no woman in the world should the sons of Usna be apart from the Red Branch. And so we all spake joyfully; and I have come with the king's message of peace, for he knew that for none else wouldst thou return.

NAISI. Surely, I will go with thee, Fergus. I long for the shining eyes of friends and the fellowship of the Red Branch, and to see my own country by the sea of Moyle. I weary of this barbarous people in Alba.

DEIRDRE. O children of Usna, there is death in your going! Naisi, will you not stay the storm bird of sorrow? I forehear the falling of tears that cease not, and in generations unborn the sorrow of it all that will never be stilled!

NAISI. Deirdre! Deirdre! It is not right for you, beautiful woman, to come with tears between a thousand exiles and their own land! Many battles have I fought, knowing well there would be death and weeping after. If I feared to trust to the word of great kings and warriors, it is not with tears I would be remembered. What would the bards sing of Naisi —without trust! afraid of the outstretched hand!—frightened by a woman's fears! By the gods, before the clan Usna were so shamed I would shed my blood here with my own hand.

DEIRDRE. O stay, stay your anger! Have pity on me, Naisi! Your words, like lightnings, sear my heart. Never again will I seek to stay thee. But speak to me with love once more, Naisi. Do not bend your brows on me with anger; for, oh! but a little time remains for us to love!

FERGUS. Nay, Deirdre, there are many years. Thou shalt yet smile back on this hour in thy old years thinking of the love and laughter between.

AINLE [*entering*]. The feast is ready for our guests.

ARDAN. The bards shall sing of Eri tonight. Let the harpers sound their gayest music. Oh, to be back once more in royal Emain!

NAISI. Come, Deirdre, forget thy fears. Come, Fergus, I

long to hear from thy lips of the Red Branch and Ulla.

FERGUS. It is geasa with me not to refuse a feast offered by one of the Red Branch.

[FERGUS, BUINNE, ILANN, *and the sons of Usna go into the inner room.* DEIRDRE *remains silently standing for a time, as if stunned. The sound of laughter and music floats in. She goes to the door of the dun, looking out again over the lakes and islands.*]

DEIRDRE. Farewell, O home of happy memories. Though thou art bleak to Naisi, to me thou art bright. I shall never see thee more, save as shadows we wander here, weeping over what is gone. Farewell, O gentle people, who made music for me on the hills. The Father has struck the last chord on the Harp of Life, and the music I shall hear hereafter will be only sorrow. O Mother Dana, who breathed up love through the dim earth to my heart, be with me where I am going. Soon shall I lie close to thee for comfort, where many a broken heart has lain and many a weeping head.

[*Music of harps and laughter again floats in.*]

VOICES. Deirdre! Deirdre! Deirdre!

[DEIRDRE *leaves the door of the dun, and the scene closes as she flings herself on a couch, burying her face in her arms.*]

ACT III

SCENE: *The House of the Red Branch at Emain Macha. There is a door covered with curtains, through which the blue light of evening can be seen.* CONCOBAR *sits at a table on which is a chessboard, with figures arranged.* LAVARCAM *stands before the table.*

CONCOBAR. The air is dense with omens, but all is uncertain. Cathvah, for all his Druid art, is uncertain, and cannot foresee the future; and in my dreams, too, I again see Macha, who died at my feet, and she passes by me with a secret exultant smile. O Druidess, is the sin of my boyhood to be avenged by this woman, who comes back to Eri in a cloud of prophecy?

LAVARCAM. The great beauty has passed from Deirdre in

her wanderings from place to place and from island to island. Many a time has she slept on the bare earth ere Naisi won a kingdom for himself in Alba. Surely the prophecy has already been fulfilled, for blood has been shed for Deirdre, and the Red Branch divided on her account. To Naisi the Red Branch are as brothers. Thou hast naught to fear.

CONCOBAR. Well, I have put aside my fears and taken thy counsel, Druidess. For the sake of the Red Branch I have forgiven the sons of Usna. Now, I will call together the Red Branch, for it is my purpose to bring the five provinces under our sway, and there shall be but one kingdom in Eri between the seas. [*A distant shouting of many voices is heard.* LAVARCAM *starts, clasping her hands.*] Why dost thou start, Druidess? Was it not foretold from of old that the gods would rule over one people in Eri? I sometimes think the warrior soul of Lu shines through the boy Cuculain, who, after me, shall guide the Red Branch; aye, and with him are many of the old company who fought at Moytura, come back to renew the everlasting battle. Is not this the Isle of Destiny, and the hour at hand? [*The clamor is again renewed.*] What is this clamor as if men hailed a king? [*Calls.*] Is there one without there? [ILANN *enters.*] Ah! returned from Alba with the fugitives!

ILANN. King, we have fulfilled our charge. The sons of Usna are with us in Emain Macha. Whither is it your pleasure they should be led?

CONCOBAR. They shall be lodged here, in the House of the Red Branch. [ILANN *is about to withdraw.*] Yet, wait, what mean all these cries as of astonished men?

ILANN. The lady, Deirdre, has come with us, and her beauty is a wonder to the gazers in the streets, for she moves among them like one of the Sidhe, whiter than ivory, with long hair of gold, and her eyes, like the blue flame of twilight, make mystery in their hearts.

CONCOBAR [*starting up*]. This is no fading beauty who returns! You hear, Druidess!

ILANN. Ardrie of Ulla, whoever has fabled to thee that the beauty of Deirdre is past has lied. She is sorrowful, indeed, but her sadness only bows the heart to more adoration than her joy, and pity for her seems sweeter than the dream of love. Fading! Yes, her yesterday fades behind her every morning, and every changing mood seems only an unveiling to bring her nearer to the golden spirit within. But how could I describe Deirdre? In a little while she will be here, and you shall see her with your own eyes.

[ILANN *bows and goes out.*]

CONCOBAR. I will, indeed, see her with my own eyes. I will not, on the report of a boy, speak words that shall make the Red Branch to drip with blood. I will see with my own eyes. [*He goes to the door.*] But I swear to thee, Druidess, if thou hast plotted deceit a second time with Naisi, that all Eri may fall asunder, but I will be avenged.

[*He holds the curtain aside with one hand and looks out. As he gazes his face grows sterner, and he lifts his hand above his head in menace.* LAVARCAM *looks on with terror, and as he drops the curtain and looks back on her, she lets her face sink in her hands.*]

CONCOBAR [*scornfully*]. A Druid makes prophecies and a Druidess schemes to bring them to pass! Well have you all worked together! A fading beauty was to return, and the Lights of Valor to shine again in the Red Branch! And I, the Ardrie of Ulla and the head of the Red Branch, to pass by the broken law and the after deceit! I, whose sole thought was of the building up of a people, to be set aside! The high gods may judge me hereafter, but tonight shall see the broken law set straight, and vengeance on the traitors to Ulla!

LAVARCAM. It was all my doing! They are innocent! I loved Deirdre, O king! let your anger be on me alone.

CONCOBAR. Oh, tongue of falsehood! Who can believe you! The fate of Ulla was in your charge, and you let it go forth at the instant wish of a man and a girl's desire. The fate of Ulla was too distant, and you must bring it nigher— the torch to the pile! Breakers of the law and makers of lies, you shall all perish together!

[CONCOBAR *leaves the room.* LAVARCAM *remains, her being shaken with sobs. After a pause* NAISI *enters with* DEIRDRE. AINLE, ARDAN, ILANN, *and* BUINNE *follow. During the dialogue which ensues,* NAISI *is inattentive, and is curiously examining the chessboard.*]

DEIRDRE. We are entering a house of death! Who is it that weeps so? I, too, would weep, but the children of Usna are too proud to let tears be seen in the eyes of their women.

[*She sees* LAVARCAM, *who raises her head from the table.*]
O fostermother, for whom do you sorrow? Ah! it is for us.
You still love me, dear fostermother; but you, who are wise,
could you not have warned the Lights of Valor? Was it kind
to keep silence, and only meet us here with tears?

LAVARCAM. O Deirdre, my child! my darling! I have let
love and longing blind my eyes. I left the mountain home of
the gods for Emain Macha, and to plot for your return. I—
I deceived the king. I told him your loveliness was passed, and
the time of the prophecy gone by. I thought when you came
all would be well. I thought wildly, for love had made a
blindness in my heart, and now the king has discovered the deceit; and, oh! he has gone away in wrath, and soon his terrible hand will fall!

DEIRDRE. It was not love made you all blind, but the high
gods have deserted us, and the demons draw us into a trap.
They have lured us from Alba, and they hover here above us
in red clouds—cloud upon cloud—and await the sacrifice.

LAVARCAM. Oh, it is not yet too late! Where is Fergus? The
king dare not war on Fergus. Fergus is our only hope.

DEIRDRE. Fergus has bartered his honor for a feast. He remained with Baruch that he might boast he never refused the
wine cup. He feasts with Baruch, and the Lights of Valor who
put their trust in him—must die.

BUINNE. Fergus never bartered his honor. I do protest, girl,
against your speech. The name of Fergus alone would protect
you throughout all Eri; how much more here, where he is
champion in Ulla. Come, brother, we are none of us needed
here. [BUINNE *leaves the room.*]

DEIRDRE. Father and son alike desert us! O fostermother, is
this the end of all? Is there no way out? Is there no way out?

ILANN. I will not desert you, Deirdre, while I can still
thrust a spear. But you fear overmuch without a cause.

LAVARCAM. Bar up the door and close the windows. I will
send a swift messenger for Fergus. If you hold the dun until
Fergus comes all will yet be well. [LAVARCAM *hurries out.*]

DEIRDRE [*going to* NAISI]. Naisi, do you not hear? Let the
door be barred! Ainle and Ardan, are you still all blind? Oh!
must I close them with my own hand!

[DEIRDRE *goes to the window, and lays her hand on the
bars.* NAISI *follows her.*]

NAISI. Deirdre, in your girlhood you have not known of the ways of the Red Branch. This thing you fear is unheard of in Ulla. The king may be wrathful; but the word, once passed, is inviolable. If he whispered treachery to one of the Red Branch he would not be Ardrie tomorrow. Nay, leave the window unbarred, or they will say the sons of Usna have returned timid as birds! Come, we are enough protection for thee. See, here is the chessboard of Concobar, with which he is wont to divine, playing a lonely game with fate. The pieces are set. We will finish the game, and so pass the time until the feast is ready. [*He sits down.*] The golden pieces are yours and the silver mine.

AINLE [*looking at the board*]. You have given Deirdre the weaker side.

NAISI. Deirdre always plays with more cunning skill.

DEIRDRE. O fearless one, if he who set the game played with fate, the victory is already fixed, and no skill may avail.

NAISI. We will see if Concobar has favorable omens. It is geasa for him always to play with silver pieces. I will follow his game. It is your move. Dear one, will you not smile? Surely, against Concobar you will play well.

DEIRDRE. It is too late. See, everywhere my king is threatened!

ARDAN. Nay, your game is not lost. If you move your king back all will be well.

MESSENGER [*at the door*]. I bear a message from the Ardrie to the sons of Usna.

NAISI. Speak out thy message, man. Why does thy voice tremble? Who art thou? I do not know thee. Thou art not one of the Red Branch. Concobar is not wont to send messages to kings by such as thou.

MESSENGER. The Red Branch are far from Emain Macha— but it matters not. The king has commanded me to speak thus to the sons of Usna. You have broken the law of Ulla when you stole away the daughter of Felim. You have broken the law of the Red Branch when you sent lying messages through Lavarcam plotting to return. The king commands that the daughter of Felim be given up, and—

AINLE. Are we to listen to this?

ARDAN. My spear will fly of itself if he does not depart.

NAISI. Nay, brother, he is only a slave. [*To the* MES-

SENGER.] Return to Concobar, and tell him that tomorrow the Red Branch will choose another chief. There, why dost thou wait? Begone! [*To* DEIRDRE.] Oh, wise woman, truly did you see the rottenness in this king!

DEIRDRE. Why did you not take my counsel, Naisi? For now it is too late—too late.

NAISI. There is naught to fear. One of us could hold this dun against a thousand of Concobar's household slaves. When Fergus comes tomorrow there will be another king in Emain Macha.

ILANN. It is true, Deirdre. One of us is enough for Concobar's household slaves. I will keep watch at the door while you play at peace with Naisi.

[ILANN *lifts the curtain of the door and goes outside. The play at chess begins again.* AINLE *and* ARDAN *look on.*]

AINLE. Naisi, you play wildly. See, your queen will be taken.

[*A disturbance without and the clash of arms.*]

ILANN [*without*]. Keep back! Do you dare?

NAISI. Ah! the slaves come on, driven by the false Ardrie! When the game is finished we will sweep them back and slay them in the Royal House before Concobar's eyes. Play! You forget to move, Deirdre.

[*The clash of arms is renewed.*]

ILANN [*without*]. Oh! I am wounded. Ainle! Ardan! To the door!

[AINLE *and* ARDAN *rush out. The clash of arms renewed.*]

DEIRDRE. Naisi, I cannot. I cannot. The end of all has come. Oh, Naisi!

[*She flings her arms across the table, scattering the pieces over the board.*]

NAISI. If the end has come we should meet it with calm. It is not with sighing and tears the Clan Usna should depart. You have not played this game as it ought to be played.

DEIRDRE. Your pride is molded and set like a pillar of bronze. O warrior, I was no mate for you. I am only a woman, who has given her life into your hands, and you chide me for my love.

NAISI [*caressing her head with his hands*]. Poor timid dove, I had forgotten thy weakness. I did not mean to wound thee, my heart. Oh, many will shed hotter tears than these for thy sorrow! They will perish swiftly who made Naisi's queen to weep! [*He snatches up a spear and rushes out. There are cries, and then a silence.*]

LAVARCAM [*entering hurriedly*]. Bear Deirdre swiftly away through the night. [*She stops and looks around.*] Where are the sons of Usna? Oh! I stepped over many dead bodies at the door. Surely the Lights of Valor were not so soon overcome! Oh, my darling! come away with me from this terrible house.

DEIRDRE [*slowly*]. What did you say of the Lights of Valor? That—they—were dead?

[NAISI, AINLE, *and* ARDAN *reënter.* DEIRDRE *clings to* NAISI.]

NAISI. My gentle one, do not look so pale nor wound me with those terror-stricken eyes. Those base slaves are all fled. Truly, Concobar is a mighty king without the Red Branch!

LAVARCAM. Oh, do not linger here. Bear Deirdre away while there is time. You can escape through the city in the silence of the night. The king has called for his Druids: soon the magic of Cathvah will enfold you, and your strength will be all withered away.

NAISI. I will not leave Emain Macha until the head of this false king is apart from his shoulders. A spear can pass as swiftly through his Druid as through one of his slaves. Oh, Cathvah, the old mumbler of spells and of false prophecies, who caused Deirdre to be taken from her mother's breast! Truly, I owe a deep debt to Cathvah, and I will repay it.

LAVARCAM. If you love Deirdre, do not let pride and wrath stay your flight. You have but an instant to fly. You can return with Fergus and a host of warriors in the dawn. You do not know the power of Cathvah. Surely, if you do not depart, Deirdre will fall into the king's hands, and it were better she had died in her mother's womb.

DEIRDRE. Naisi, let us leave this house of death.

.[*The sound of footsteps without.*]

LAVARCAM. It is too late!

[AINLE *and* ARDAN *start to the door, but are stayed at the sound of* CATHVAH'S *voice.* DEIRDRE *clings to* NAISI.]

CATHVAH [*chanting without*].
>Let the Faed Fia fall;
>Mananaun Mac Lir.
>Take back the day

> Amid days unremembered.
> Over the warring mind
> Let thy Faed Fia fall,
> Mananaun Mac Lir!

NAISI. Why dost thou weep, Deirdre, and cling to me so?
The sea is calm. Tomorrow we will rest safely at Emain Macha
with the great Ardrie, who has forgiven all.

LAVARCAM. The darkness is upon his mind. Oh, poor
Deirdre!

CATHVAH [*without*].

> Let thy waves rise,
> Mananaun Mac Lir.
> Let the earth fail
> Beneath their feet,
> Let thy waves flow over them,
> Mananaun:
> Lord of ocean!

NAISI. Our galley is sinking—and no land in sight! I did
not think the end would come so soon. O pale love, take
courage. Is death so bitter to thee? We shall go down in each
other's arms; our hearts shall beat out their love together, and
the last of life we shall know will be our kisses on each other's
lips. [AINLE *and* ARDAN *stagger outside. There is a sound of
blows and a low cry.*] Ainle and Ardan have sunk in the
waters! We are alone. Still weeping! My bird, my bird, soon
we shall fly together to the bright kingdom in the West, to
Hy Brazil, amid the opal seas.

DEIRDRE. Naisi, Naisi, shake off the magic dream. It is here
in Emain Macha we are. There are no waters. The spell of the
Druid and his terrible chant have made a mist about your eyes.

NAISI. Her mind is wandering. She is distraught with terror
of the king. There, rest your head on my heart. Hush! hush!
The waters are flowing upward swiftly. Soon, when all is over,
you will laugh at your terror. The great Ardrie will sorrow
over our death.

DEIRDRE. I cannot speak. Lavarcam, can you not break the
enchantment?

LAVARCAM. My limbs are fixed here by the spell.

NAISI. There was music a while ago. The swans of Lir, with
their slow, sweet faëry singing. There never was a sadder tale
than theirs. They must roam for ages, driven on the sea of

Moyle, while we shall go hand in hand through the country of immortal youth. And there is Mananaun, the dark blue king, who looks at us with a smile of welcome. Ildathach is lit up with its shining mountains, and the golden phantoms are leaping there in the dawn! There is a path made for us! Come, Deirdre, the god has made for us an island on the sea. [Naisi *goes through the door, and falls back, smitten by a spear-thrust.*] The Druid Cathvah!—The king!—O Deirdre!

[*He dies.* Deirdre *bends over the body, taking the hands in hers.*]

Lavarcam. O gentle heart, thy wounds will be more bitter than his. Speak but a word. That silent sorrow will kill thee and me. My darling, it was fate, and I was not to blame. Come, it will comfort thee to weep beside my breast. Leave the dead for vengeance, for heavy is the vengeance that shall fall on this ruthless king.

Deirdre. I do not fear Concobar any more. My spirit is sinking away from the world. I could not stay after Naisi. After the Lights of Valor had vanished, how could I remain? The earth has grown dim and old, fostermother. The gods have gone far away, and the lights from the mountains and the Lions of the Flaming Heart are still. O fostermother, when they heap the cairn over him, let me be beside him in the narrow grave. I will still be with the noble one.

[Deirdre *lays her head on* Naisi's *body.* Concobar *enters, standing in the doorway.* Lavarcam *takes* Deirdre's *hand and drops it.*]

Lavarcam. Did you come to torture her with your presence? Was not the death of Naisi cruelty enough? But now she is past your power to wound.

Concobar. The death of Naisi was only the fulfilling of the law. Ulla could not hold together if its ancient laws were set aside.

Lavarcam. Do you think to bind men together when you have broken their hearts? O fool, who would conquer all Eri! I see the Red Branch scattered and Eri rent asunder, and thy memory a curse after many thousand years. The gods have overthrown thy dominion, proud king, with the last sigh from this dead child; and out of the pity for her they will build up an eternal kingdom in the spirit of man.

[*An uproar without and the clash of arms.*]

VOICES. Fergus! Fergus! Fergus!

LAVARCAM. The avenger has come! So perishes the Red Branch! [*She hurries out wildly.*]

CONCOBAR [*slowly, after a pause*]. I have two divided kingdoms, and one is in my own heart. Thus do I pay homage to thee, O queen, who will rule, being dead.

[*He bends over the body of* DEIRDRE *and kisses her hand.*]

FERGUS [*without*]. Where is the traitor Ardrie?

[CONCOBAR *starts up, lifting his spear.* FERGUS *appears at the doorway, and the scene closes.*]

GROUP II

PLAYS OF THE PEASANT CHARACTER: COMEDY

THE PASSING OF THE SHEE

(after looking at one of A. E.'s pictures)

Adieu, sweet Angus, Maeve, and Fand,
  Ye plumed yet skinny Shee,
That poets played with hand in hand
  To learn their ecstasy.

We'll stretch in Red Dan Sally's ditch,
  And drink in Tubber Fair,
Or poach with Red Dan Philly's bitch
  The badger and the hare.[1]

WE hear in these few lines of playful heresy the battle cry of the realists against the ideals of spirituality and remoteness which Yeats had advocated. They state, by implication, the duality informing the Irish dramatic movement and, incidentally, the Irish character. It is the paradoxical nature of the Celt to vacillate continually between the conflicting issues of reality and ideality, of fact and dream, the world of nature and the world of the imagination. He is at once the visionary and the man of action. It is this paradox again which gives us from John M. Synge *Riders to the Sea* in one breath, so to speak, and *The Playboy of the Western World* in the other—one a heart-rending tragic cry, the other a raw and devastating comic satire. We have seen in the preceding plays distinct examples of the "poetic" Celt. Let us look for a moment at some of the others, who express themselves through the medium of prose, contemporary characters, and settings re-

[1] The works of John M. Synge. Maunsel and Company, Dublin, 1910, Vol. II, p. 215.

flecting the home life of the Irish peasantry. It so happens that these three peasant plays are seeking to catch the humor, not the sadness in the peasant life and character.

The tradition of reality, founded on the few plays of John Millington Synge, represents the reverse of the same medal which on its face fascinated Yeats and his visionaries. In the light of the movement as a whole the realists are not in opposition to the poets who molded their themes with so much ecstasy; and, though they changed the complexion of subsequent Irish drama, the prose plays were natural corollaries to the poetic plays, each was a step forward in the fervid desire to express and interpret Ireland. Synge saw that both types were needed to guarantee a complete and healthy native dramatic tradition, since the poetic play tended to place dramatic subject matter too far away from the simple, everyday life of the people who came to witness it. The difference between these prose plays and those of the first group is in many respects a difference of degree and not of kind. Both alike contain the essentials of a poetic speech but the prose plays have more emphatically an Irish poetic speech drawn directly from the mouths of the peasantry. Synge realized, furthermore, the value of a drama sustaining itself thus by the speech of the people and he set about fulfilling this apparent necessity by observing the way they spoke and felt in remote, poorly populated areas in Ireland. The part which attracted him most and where *Riders to the Sea* is laid was the Aran Islands to the south of Connemara in Galway Bay. For realists like Synge the peasant idiom, with its Elizabethan flavor, he heard spoken there held as much inherent beauty as the eloquence of heroic kings did for Yeats. By Synge's treatment, the language was transmuted into a lyric pattern rivaling verse. He labored always for the right word, for subtlety of nuance, for a variety of shades of meaning, and for a simplicity of expression. And his influence on Irish dramatists following in his footsteps has been so great that it is only at the present time that the Irish are beginning to see how unfortunate for their drama has been this persistent imitation of him, because after Synge had written about the peasantry of Ireland there was much left to say about them but little to be as well remembered. Lately, in the hands of his host of imitators tragedy has tended to fade to melodrama, and comedy to slapstick farce.

In view of the extraordinary amount of notoriety, discussion, controversy, violent opposition, and ardent defense stirred up in Ireland and in the United States by *The Playboy of the Western World*, I must ask the indulgence of the reader in saying something about this play although it is not included in this edition since its American publishers considered *Riders to the Sea* to be ample representation of this author. With *The Playboy of the Western World*, "so superb and wild in reality," Synge and the Irish movement attained world-wide recognition. Organized opposition to the Abbey Theatre's presentation of it in the United States during their 1911–1912 tour by people who regarded it as an immoral excoriation of Irish life and character only served to stimulate the enthusiasm of those who appreciated its ultimate value as a work of art. First produced by the Abbey Theatre Company (National Theatre Society) on January 26, 1907, it has never, in the opinion of many, lost its position as the foremost Irish comedy and is regarded as the keystone play of the movement.

Among foibles of the peasant character Synge treats with such brilliance and pungent wit none is so amusing as the romantic awe with which the peasants regard the fugitive from justice. The villain in *The Playboy of the Western World* becomes a hero in the villagers' eyes in proportion to the daring of his deed. The suddenness of the transformation of Christy's character and its swift development when he realizes that his supposed crime need not be kept shamefully to himself but may be openly admitted, even bragged about to the world in general as an efficient method for securing glory; and the reversal of Pegeen's attitude toward her "only playboy," near the end of the play, showing her outward bitterness and inward woe, are a few characteristics of Synge's sly yet benign humor. As is the case in most of Lady Gregory's comedies, a real affection is aroused for the person in the play who inclines toward such a pleasing rascality. Pegeen's disillusionment on discovering that her hero has tumbled from his pedestal, and that he is not the man she took him for, again helps to underline the superiority of the imagination over reality as it presents itself to the peasant mind when a choice has to be made between the two. Her change of feeling shows that the love she manifests for the *idea* of heroism is more permanent and more comforting than the love for the hero himself. This behavior on her part may perhaps be taken as a psychological compensation for the lack of those gallant duelists and reckless horsemen who filled the popular imagination of western Ireland in the eighteenth century. The girls like Pegeen may be starving for swains like the Galway young bloods whose lives gave the truth to Michael's statement that "a daring fellow is the jewel of the world." As a comedy based on the national psychology it shows an uncanny insight into the minds of the people and as such reaches the highest ideal of Meredith's definition.

The humorous group completes and balances the preceding spiritual tragedies and the following realistic tragedies of the third group. They also had a more immediate value in the programs of the Abbey Theatre. Here they furnished pleasing relaxation from the grimness of the tragedies, and relieved the strain of concentration necessary for the proper assimilation of the poetic legends. Lady Gregory mentions the importance of this factor when she tells us that she reworked as comedy many ideas for plays (*Spreading the News* is one) which had first presented themselves to her as tragedy, because she felt the need of variety in the Abbey productions.

One thing above all others serves to make the Irish Drama as a whole intensely interesting. That is its naturalness. Its picturesque vividness depends largely on the apparent absence of conscious artifice in the writing of the plays. If they have been formulated according to the capricious laws of various schools of playwriting, they are all the more valuable because they do not show it. And we may say with certainty, now that thirty-five years have passed since the dramatic portion of the Irish Renaissance began, that plays written according to the Ibsen method have not survived as well as those written by playwrights who have evolved new dramaturgic methods in keeping with the original purpose of the movement. Lady Gregory's originality and freshness of style bespeak her affiliation with the latter group.

None of the following comedies is lacking in uniqueness. Their widely diversified subject matter outlines sufficiently the major characteristics of Irish Comedy. At the same time no one will deny that each author invests his plot with a decidedly Irish flavor without resorting to the banalities of popular comedy writing. Lady Gregory and Dr. Hyde, by setting a highly individual or "different" character against a background of familiar and usual peasant types, and by elaborating the ensuing conflict between them, bring out the idiosyncrasies of both contestants in clear comic relief. By the use of this simple but none the less effective method, they go a long step forward in an attempt to isolate and crystallize at least a part of the contradictory Celtic temperament. The function of true comedy is evident in these plays: to cause the absurdities and incongruities in the national character to be laughed out of existence by the very people who possess them. In *Hyacinth Halvey* we find as the principal motive the Irishman's reluctance to change his opinion of a man's character, especially when his estimate of the man is reënforced by a similar collective estimate, and this in spite of overwhelming proof that he is wrong! The action is pyramided in such a way that the accumulated absurdities involved in the plot reach a highly mirthful degree of concentration. It is not, however, from stupidity or stubbornness that in *Hyacinth Halvey* the natives shut their eyes against the acceptance of facts which might reveal Halvey's true nature. We have here again an echo of the theme in *The Playboy of the Western World*—the pathetic humor evinced by people who need some ideal, some hero no matter how weak or small on whom they may pin their faith and trust. And in this play the ideal once more transcends and extinguishes the real.

The Twisting of the Rope, in addition to its intrinsic merit, has an added historical value because it was the first play to be spoken in the Gaelic tongue on any stage.[2] Its author is the distinguished Irish scholar Dr. Douglas Hyde, whose *Literary History of Ireland* is one of the outstanding books of the movement. *The Twisting of the Rope* is a humorous incident rather than a fully-developed play but even its brevity and its tenuous plot do not detract from the significance of the idea underlying it. It recalls the absolute tyranny which wandering singers exercised over the whole countryside in the Middle Ages. At that time the singers were highly organized in a Druidic society known as the Bardic Association, and they wielded great power by virtue of their knowledge and use of witchcraft. The bards were protected, like Hanrahan,

[2] October 21, 1901.

by the potency of their curses, and they preyed on the credulity and superstitious fear of the ancient folk with increasing rapacity until St. Patrick removed from them their evil charms and powers though he allowed them to continue the comparatively harmless practice of composing and reciting verses. Hanrahan is evidently a lineal descendant of the most overbearing of these bardic strollers. The mirth of the situation springs from his humiliation at the hands of the wary peasants whose hospitality he has flouted. Their deception in this case is justified because Hanrahan has abused his power. The tension of the final scene is enhanced by our realization that the plotters are in immediate danger of the singer's blasting curse until he is safely outside the house where his wrath becomes impotent. Some critics have been able to discover in the peasants' attitude toward Hanrahan the symbol of the ancient Irish poetic spirit forced to wander up and down the roads suffering rebuke from an ignorant and unpoetic peasantry at every step, and under no condition being allowed entrance into either their huts or their hearts. From this point of view, the play is an ironic comedy and presumes first of all an alignment of our sympathies with Hanrahan, the personification of the unhappy poetic spirit. The incompatability of this interpretation is clear. The poet's fiery truculence hardly permits of any such sympathetic attitude toward him. At the end of the play we are perfectly willing to see the disturber outwitted and shown the door, while the dance goes on merrily without further interruption.

The Twisting of the Rope hints at the importance the Irish attach to the element of the supernatural, but *The Dandy Dolls*, by George Fitzmaurice, brings it out on the stage in full view of the audience. The belief in fairies is still widespread in rural Ireland, but perhaps we have been led to think of the "other world" inhabitants as the "gentlefolk"—like the tiny leprechauns you may be able to catch by the heel and force to divulge the hiding place of their bag of gold; or else as national benefactors like Kathleen Ni Houlihan. Less common are the fairies of the "Old Hag" type, who, with her deviling son, appears in this play. *The Dandy Dolls* is an excellent example of the Irish imagination taking the form of wild fantasy, such as is found in *The Playboy of the Western World* and in *Hyacinth Halvey*, though there constrained and diluted by the essential reality of the characters. Fitzmaurice is not bound in an way to the requirements of verisimilitude. Since his plays are peopled by fairies, he can make them behave in any way he wishes without having to make their actions seem probable or natural. This freedom of handling applies also to the ordinary persons in the play who are affected by the spirits and whose behavior, therefore, is unaccountable. He adds to the grotesque situation in *The Dandy Dolls* the same commentary that Padraic Colum makes in *The Fiddler's House,* on the difference of opinion among Irishmen in regard to profitable and useless employment. In this case, the making of the dolls becomes the symbol of artistic or moral endeavor frustrated by poverty, by the petty demands of a harsh and unsympathetic domesticity, and by the prevalent superstition that such images as dolls are the devil's work and should be left to him and his kind. The rich extravagance of the idiom places the author with the best of those whose delight it is to capture and transcribe peasant speech. The opening dialogue between Cauth and the Old Gray Man shows the loquacity of the peasant and confirms the well-known saying that an Irishman always uses ten words when one will suffice. But the color and vigor of the riotous speeches throughout the play compensate for the time the author takes for exposition.

The peasant comedies as a group are filled with the laughter and wit of the unspoiled Irish countryside. They are often coarse and blatant, the laughter in them loud and raucous. But Ireland is still largely a nation of peasants except in the two large cities, we can expect little from their drama in the way of subtleties and sophistication.

HYACINTH HALVEY

By Lady Augusta Gregory

PERSONS

HYACINTH HALVEY
JAMES QUIRKE, *a butcher*
FARDY FARRELL, *a telegraph boy*
SERGEANT CARDEN
MRS. DELANE, *Postmistress at Cloon*
MISS JOYCE, *the Priest's Housekeeper*

SCENE: *Outside the Post Office at the little town of Cloon.*
MRS. DELANE *at Post Office door.* MR. QUIRKE *sitting on
a chair at butcher's door. A dead sheep hanging beside it,
and a thrush in a cage above.* FARDY FARRELL *playing on a
mouth organ. Train whistle heard.*

MRS. DELANE. There is the four o'clock train, Mr. Quirke.

MR. QUIRKE. Is it now, Mrs. Delane, and I not long after
rising? It makes a man drowsy to be doing the half of his
work in the night time. Going about the country, looking for
little stags of sheep, striving to knock a few shillings together.
That contract for the soldiers gives me a great deal to attend to.

MRS. DELANE. I suppose so. It's hard enough on myself to
be down ready for the mail car in the morning, sorting letters
in the half dark. It's often I haven't time to look who are the
letters from—or the cards.

MR. QUIRKE. It would be a pity you not to know any little
news might be knocking about. If you did not have information of what is going on who should have it? Was it you,
ma'am, was telling me that the new Sub-Sanitary Inspector
would be arriving today?

MRS. DELANE. Today it is he is coming, and it's likely he
was in that train. There was a card about him to Sergeant
Carden this morning.

MR. QUIRKE. A young chap from Carrow they were saying he was.

MRS. DELANE. So he is, one Hyacinth Halvey; and indeed if all that is said of him is true, or if a quarter of it is true, he will be a credit to this town.

MR. QUIRKE. Is that so?

MRS. DELANE. Testimonials he has by the score. To Father Gregan they were sent. Registered they were coming and going. Would you believe me telling you that they weighed up to three pounds?

MR. QUIRKE. There must be great bulk in them indeed.

MRS. DELANE. It is no wonder he to get the job. He must have a great character so many persons to write for him as what there did.

FARDY. It would be a great thing to have a character like that.

MRS. DELANE. Indeed I am thinking it will be long before you will get the like of it, Fardy Farrell.

FARDY. If I had the like of that of a character it is not here carrying messages I would be. It's in Noonan's Hotel I would be, driving cars.

MR. QUIRKE. Here is the priest's housekeeper coming.

MRS. DELANE. So she is; and there is the Sergeant a little while after her.

[*Enter* MISS JOYCE.]

MRS. DELANE. Good evening to you, Miss Joyce. What way is his Reverence today? Did he get any ease from the cough?

MISS JOYCE. He did not indeed, Mrs. Delane. He has it sticking to him yet. Smothering he is in the night time. The most thing he comes short in is the voice.

MRS. DELANE. I am sorry, now, to hear that. He should mind himself well.

MISS JOYCE. It's easy to say let him mind himself. What do you say to him going to the meeting tonight? [*Sergeant comes in.*] It's for his Reverence's *Freeman* I am come, Mrs. Delane.

MRS. DELANE. Here it is ready. I was just throwing an eye on it to see was there any news. Good evening, Sergeant.

SERGEANT [*holding up a placard*]. I brought this notice, Mrs. Delane, the announcement of the meeting to be held tonight in the Courthouse. You might put it up here convenient to the window. I hope you are coming to it yourself?

MRS. DELANE. I will come, and welcome. I would do more than that for you, Sergeant.

SERGEANT. And you, Mr. Quirke.

MR. QUIRKE. I'll come, to be sure. I forget what's this the meeting is about.

SERGEANT. The Department of Agriculture is sending round a lecturer in furtherance of the moral development of the rural classes. [*Reads.*] "A lecture will be given this evening in Cloon Courthouse, illustrated by magic lantern slides—". Those will not be in it; I am informed they were all broken in the first journey, the railway company taking them to be eggs. The subject of the lecture is "The Building of Character."

MRS. DELANE. Very nice, indeed. I knew a girl lost her character, and she washed her feet in a blessed well after, and it dried up on the minute.

SERGEANT. The arrangements have all been left to me, the Archdeacon being away. He knows I have a good intellect for things of the sort. But the loss of those slides puts a man out. The thing people will not see it is not likely it is the thing they will believe. I saw what they call tableaux—standing pictures, you know—one time in Dundrum—

MRS. DELANE. Miss Joyce was saying Father Gregan is supporting you.

SERGEANT. I am accepting his assistance. No bigotry about me when there is a question of the welfare of any fellow creatures. Orange and green will stand together tonight. I myself and the station master on the one side; your parish priest in the chair.

MISS JOYCE. If his Reverence would mind me he would not quit the house tonight. He is no more fit to go speak at a meeting than [*pointing to the one hanging outside* QUIRKE'S *door*] that sheep.

SERGEANT. I am willing to take the responsibility. He will have no speaking to do at all, unless it might be to bid them give the lecturer a hearing. The loss of those slides now is a great annoyance to me—and no time for anything. The lecturer will be coming by the next train.

MISS JOYCE. Who is this coming up the street, Mrs. Delane?

MRS. DELANE. I wouldn't doubt it to be the new Sub-Sanitary Inspector. Was I telling you of the weight of the testimonials he got, Miss Joyce?

MISS JOYCE. Sure I heard the curate reading them to his Reverence. He must be a wonder for principles.

MRS. DELANE. Indeed it is what I was saying to myself, he must be a very saintly young man.

[*Enter* HYACINTH HALVEY. *He carries a small bag and a large brown paper parcel. He stops and nods bashfully.*]

HYACINTH. Good evening to you. I was bid to come to the Post Office—

SERGEANT. I suppose you are Hyacinth Halvey? I had a letter about you from the Resident Magistrate.

HYACINTH. I heard he was writing. It was my mother got a friend he deals with to ask him.

SERGEANT. He gives you a very high character.

HYACINTH. It is very kind of him indeed, and he not knowing me at all. But indeed all the neighbors were very friendly. Anything anyone could do to help me they did it.

MRS. DELANE. I'll engage it is the testimonials you have in your parcel? I know the wrapping paper, but they grew in bulk since I handled them.

HYACINTH. Indeed I was getting them to the last. There was not one refused me. It is what my mother was saying, a good character is no burden.

FARDY. I would believe that indeed.

SERGEANT. Let us have a look at the testimonials. [HYACINTH HALVEY *opens parcel, and a large number of envelopes fall out.*]

SERGEANT [*opening and reading one by one*]. "He possesses the fire of the Gael, the strength of the Norman, the vigor of the Dane, the stolidity of the Saxon"—

HYACINTH. It was the Chairman of the Poor Law Guardians wrote that.

SERGEANT. "A magnificent example to old and young"—

HYACINTH. That was the Secretary of the De Wet Hurling Club—

SERGEANT. "A shining example of the value conferred by an eminently careful and high class education"—

HYACINTH. That was the National Schoolmaster.

SERGEANT. "Devoted to the highest ideals of his Motherland to such an extent as is compatible with a hitherto non-parliamentary career"—

HYACINTH. That was the Member for Carrow.

SERGEANT. "A splendid exponent of the purity of the race"—

HYACINTH. The Editor of the *Carrow Champion*.

SERGEANT. "Admirably adapted for the efficient discharge of all possible duties that may in future be laid upon him"—

HYACINTH. The new Station Master.

SERGEANT. "A champion of every cause that can legitimately benefit his fellow creatures"— Why, look here, my man, you are the very one to come to our assistance tonight.

HYACINTH. I would be glad to do that. What way can I do it?

SERGEANT. You are a newcomer—your example would carry weight—you must stand up as a living proof of the beneficial effect of a high character, moral fiber, temperance—there is something about it here I am sure—[*Looks.*] I am sure I saw "unparalleled temperance" in some place—

HYACINTH. It was my mother's cousin wrote that—I am no drinker, but I haven't the pledge taken—

SERGEANT. You might take it for the purpose.

MR. QUIRKE [*eagerly*]. Here is an anti-treating button. I was made a present of it by one of my customers—I'll give it to you, [*sticks it in* HYACINTH's *coat*] and welcome.

SERGEANT. That is it. You can wear the button on the platform—or a bit of blue ribbon—hundreds will follow your example—I know the boys from the Workhouse will—

HYACINTH. I am in no way wishful to be an example—

SERGEANT. I will read extracts from the testimonials. "There he is," I will say, "an example of one in early life who by his own unaided efforts and his high character has obtained a profitable situation"—[*Slaps his side.*] I know what I'll do. I'll engage a few corner-boys from Noonan's bar, just as they are, greasy and sodden, to stand in a group—there will be the contrast— The sight will deter others from a similar fate— That's the way to do a tableau—I knew I could turn out a success.

HYACINTH. I wouldn't like to be a contrast—

SERGEANT [*puts testimonials in his pocket*]. I will go now

and engage those lads—sixpence each, and well worth it—
Nothing like an example for the rural classes.

[*Goes off,* HYACINTH *feebly trying to detain him.*]

MRS. DELANE. A very nice man indeed. A little high up in
himself, may be. I'm not one that blames the police. Sure they
have their own bread to earn like every other one. And indeed
it is often they will let a thing pass.

MR. QUIRKE [*gloomily*]. Sometimes they will, and more
times they will not.

MISS JOYCE. And where will you be finding a lodging, Mr.
Halvey?

HYACINTH. I was going to ask that myself, ma'am. I don't
know the town.

MISS JOYCE. I know of a good lodging, but it is only a very
good man would be taken into it.

MRS. DELANE. Sure there could be no objection there to
Mr. Halvey. There is no appearance on him but what is good,
and the Sergeant after taking him up the way he is doing.

MISS JOYCE. You will be near to the Sergeant in the lodging I speak of. The house is convenient to the barracks.

HYACINTH [*doubtfully*]. To the barracks?

MISS JOYCE. Alongside of it and the barrack yard behind.
And that's not all. It is opposite to the priest's house.

HYACINTH. Opposite, is it?

MISS JOYCE. A very respectable place, indeed, and a very
clean room you will get. I know it well. The curate can see
into it from his window.

HYACINTH. Can he now?

FARDY. There was a good many, I am thinking, went into
that lodging and left it after.

MISS JOYCE [*sharply*]. It is a lodging you will never be
let into or let stop in, Fardy. If they did go they were a good
riddance.

FARDY. John Hart, the plumber, left it—

MISS JOYCE. If he did it was because he dared not pass the
police coming in, as he used, with a rabbit he was after
snaring in his hand.

FARDY. The schoolmaster himself left it.

MISS JOYCE. He needn't have left it if he hadn't taken to
card-playing. What way could you say your prayers, and
shadows shuffling and dealing before you on the blind?

HYACINTH. I think maybe I'd best look around a bit before I'll settle in a lodging—

MISS JOYCE. Not at all. *You* won't be wanting to pull down the blind.

MRS. DELANE. It is not likely *you* will be snaring rabbits.

MISS JOYCE. Or bringing in a bottle and taking an odd glass the way James Kelly did.

MRS. DELANE. Or writing threatening notices, and the police taking a view of you from the rear.

MISS JOYCE. Or going to roadside dances, or running after good-for-nothing young girls—

HYACINTH. I give you my word I'm not so harmless as you think.

MRS. DELANE. Would you be putting a lie on these, Mr. Halvey? [*Touching testimonials.*] I know well the way *you* will be spending the evenings, writing letters to your relations—

MISS JOYCE. Learning O'Growney's exercises—

MRS. DELANE. Sticking post cards in an album for the convent bazaar.

MISS JOYCE. Reading the *Catholic Young Man*—

MRS. DELANE. Playing the melodies on a melodeon—

MISS JOYCE. Looking at the pictures in the *Lives of the Saints*. I'll hurry on and engage the room for you.

HYACINTH. Wait. Wait a minute—

MISS JOYCE. No trouble at all. I told you it was just opposite. [*Goes.*]

MR. QUIRKE. I suppose I must go upstairs and ready myself for the meeting. If it wasn't for the contract I have for the soldiers' barracks and the Sergeant's good word, I wouldn't go anear it. [*Goes into shop.*]

MRS. DELANE. I should be making myself ready too. I must be in good time to see you being made an example of, Mr. Halvey. It is I myself was the first to say it; you will be a credit to the town. [*Goes.*]

HYACINTH [*in a tone of agony*]. I wish I had never seen Cloon.

FARDY. What is on you?

HYACINTH. I wish I had never left Carrow. I wish I had been drowned the first day I thought of it, and I'd be better off.

FARDY. What is it ails you?

HYACINTH. I wouldn't for the best pound ever I had be in this place today.

FARDY. I don't know what you are talking about.

HYACINTH. To have left Carrow, if it was a poor place, where I had my comrades, and an odd spree, and a game of cards—and a coursing match coming on, and I promised a new gray-hound from the city of Cork. I'll die in this place, the way I am. I'll be too much closed in.

FARDY. Sure it mightn't be as bad as what you think.

HYACINTH. Will you tell me, I ask you, what way can I undo it?

FARDY. What is it you are wanting to undo?

HYACINTH. Will you tell me what way can I get rid of my character?

FARDY. To get rid of it, is it?

HYACINTH. That is what I said. Aren't you after hearing the great character they are after putting on me?

FARDY. That is a good thing to have.

HYACINTH. It is not. It's the worst in the world. If I hadn't it, I wouldn't be like a prize mangold at a show with every person praising me.

FARDY. If I had it, I wouldn't be like a head in a barrel, with every person making hits at me.

HYACINTH. If I hadn't it, I wouldn't be shoved into a room with all the clergy watching me and the police in the back yard.

FARDY. If I had it, I wouldn't be but a message carrier now, and a clapper scaring birds in the summertime.

HYACINTH. If I hadn't it, I wouldn't be wearing this button and brought up for an example at the meeting.

FARDY [*whistles*]. Maybe you're not, so, what those papers make you out to be?

HYACINTH. How would I be what they make me out to be? Was there ever any person of that sort since the world was a world, unless it might be St. Antony of Padua looking down from the chapel wall? If it is like that I was, isn't it in Mount Melleray I would be, or with the Friars at Esker? Why would I be living in the world at all, or doing the world's work?

FARDY [*taking up parcel*]. Who would think, now, there would be so much lies in a small place like Carrow?

HYACINTH. It was my mother's cousin did it. He said I was not reared for laboring—he gave me a new suit and bid me never to come back again. I daren't go back to face him —the neighbors knew my mother had a long family—bad luck to them the day they gave me these. [*Tears letters and scatters them.*] I'm done with testimonials. They won't be here to bear witness against me.

FARDY. The Sergeant thought them to be great. Sure he has the samples of them in his pocket. There's not one in the town but will know before morning that you are the next thing to an earthly saint.

HYACINTH [*stamping*]. I'll stop their mouths. I'll show them I can be a terror for badness. I'll do some injury. I'll commit some crime. The first thing I'll do I'll go and get drunk. If I never did it before I'll do it now. I'll get drunk —then I'll make an assault—I tell you I'd think as little of taking a life as of blowing out a candle.

FARDY. If you get drunk you are done for. Sure that will be held up after as an excuse for any breaking of the law.

HYACINTH. I will break the law. Drunk or sober I'll break it. I'll do something that will have no excuse. What would you say is the worst crime that any man can do?

FARDY. I don't know. I heard the Sergeant saying one time it was to obstruct the police in the discharge of their duty—

HYACINTH. That won't do. It's a patriot I would be then, worse than before, with my picture in the weeklies. It's a red crime I must commit that will make all respectable people quit minding me. What can I do? Search your mind now.

FARDY. It's what I heard the old people saying there could be no worse crime than to steal a sheep—

HYACINTH. I'll steal a sheep—or a cow—or a horse—if that will leave me the way I was before.

FARDY. It's maybe in jail it will leave you.

HYACINTH. I don't care—I'll confess—I'll tell why I did it —I give you my word I would as soon be picking oakum or breaking stones as to be perched in the daylight the same as that bird, and all the town chirruping to me or bidding me chirrup—

FARDY. There is reason in that, now.

HYACINTH. Help me, will you?

FARDY. Well, if it is to steal a sheep you want, you haven't far to go.

HYACINTH [*looking round wildly*]. Where is it? I see no sheep.

FARDY. Look around you.

HYACINTH. I see no living thing but that thrush—

FARDY. Did I say it was living? What is that hanging on Quirke's rack?

HYACINTH. It's [*fingers it*] a sheep, sure enough—

FARDY. Well, what ails you that you can't bring it away?

HYACINTH. It's a dead one—

FARD. What matter if it is?

HYACINTH. If it was living I could drive it before me—

FARDY. You could. Is it to your own lodging you would drive it? Sure everyone would take it to be a pet you brought from Carrow.

HYACINTH. I suppose they might.

FARDY. Miss Joyce sending in for news of it and it bleating behind the bed.

HYACINTH [*distracted*]. Stop! Stop!

MRS. DELANE [*from upper window*]. Fardy! Are you there, Fardy Farrell?

FARDY. I am, ma'am.

MRS. DELANE [*from window*]. Look and tell me is that the telegraph I hear ticking?

FARDY [*looking in at door*]. It is, ma'am.

MRS. DELANE. Then botheration to it, and I not dressed or undressed. Wouldn't you say, now, it's to annoy me it is calling me down. I'm coming! I'm coming! [*Disappears.*]

FARDY. Hurry on, now! hurry! She'll be coming out on you. If you are going to do it, do it, and if you are not, let it alone.

HYACINTH. I'll do it! I'll do it!

FARDY [*lifting the sheep on his back*]. I'll give you a hand with it.

HYACINTH [*goes a step or two and turns round*]. You told me no place where I could hide it.

FARDY. You needn't go far. There is the church beyond

at the side of the Square. Go round to the ditch behind the wall—there's nettles in it.

HYACINTH. That'll do.

FARDY. She's coming out—run! run!

HYACINTH [*runs a step or two*]. It's slipping!

FARDY. Hoist it up! I'll give it a hoist! [HALVEY *runs out.*]

MRS. DELANE [*calling out*]. What are you doing Fardy Farrell? Is it idling you are?

FARDY. Waiting I am, ma'am, for the message—

MRS. DELANE. Never mind the message yet. Who said it was ready? [*Going to door.*] Go ask for the loan of—no, but ask news of— Here, now go bring that bag of Mr. Halvey's to the lodging Miss Joyce has taken—

FARDY. I will, ma'am. [*Takes bag and goes out.*]

MRS. DELANE [*coming out with a telegram in her hand.*] Nobody here? [*Looks round and calls cautiously.*] Mr. Quirke! Mr. Quirke! James Quirke!

MR. QUIRKE [*looking out of his upper window with soap-suddy face.*] What is it, Mrs. Delane?

MRS. DELANE [*beckoning*]. Come down here till I tell you.

MR. QUIRKE. I cannot do that. I'm not fully shaved.

MRS. DELANE. You'd come if you knew the news I have.

MR. QUIRKE. Tell it to me now. I'm not so supple as I was.

MRS. DELANE. Whisper now, have you an enemy in any place?

MR. QUIRKE. It's likely I may have. A man in business—

MRS. DELANE. I was thinking you had one.

MR. QUIRKE. Why would you think that at this time more than any other time?

MRS. DELANE. If you could know what is in this envelope you would know that, James Quirke.

MR. QUIRKE. Is that so? And what, now, is there in it?

MRS. DELANE. Who do you think now is it addressed to?

MR. QUIRKE. How would I know that, and I not seeing it?

MRS. DELANE. That is true. Well, it is a message from Dublin Castle to the Sergeant of Police!

MR. QUIRKE. To Sergeant Carden, is it?

MRS. DELANE. It is. And it concerns yourself.

MR. QUIRKE. Myself, is it? What accusation can they be bringing against me? I'm a peaceable man.

MRS. DELANE. Wait till you hear.

Mr. Quirke. Maybe they think I was in that moonlighting case—

Mrs. Delane. That is not it—

Mr. Quirke. I was not in it—I was but in the neighboring field—cutting up a dead cow, that those never had a hand in—

Mrs. Delane. You're out of it—

Mr. Quirke. They had their faces blackened. There is no man can say I recognized them.

Mrs. Delane. That's not what they're saying—

Mr. Quirke. I'll swear I did not hear their voices or know them if I did hear them.

Mrs. Delane. I tell you it has nothing to do with that. It might be better for you if it had.

Mr. Quirke. What is it, so?

Mrs. Delane. It is an order to the Sergeant bidding him immediately to seize all suspicious meat in your house. There is an officer coming down. There are complaints from the Shannon Fort Barracks.

Mr. Quirke. I'll engage it was that pork.

Mrs. Delane. What ailed it for them to find fault?

Mr. Quirke. People are so hard to please nowadays, and I recommended them to salt it.

Mrs. Delane. They had a right to have minded your advice.

Mr. Quirke. There was nothing on that pig at all but that it went mad on poor O'Grady that owned it.

Mrs. Delane. So I heard, and went killing all before it.

Mr. Quirke. Sure it's only in the brain madness can be. I heard the doctor saying that.

Mrs. Delane. He should know.

Mr. Quirke. I give you my word I cut the head off it. I went to the loss of it, throwing it to the eels in the river. If they had salted the meat, as I advised them, what harm would it have done to any person on earth?

Mrs. Delane. I hope no harm will come on poor Mrs. Quirke and the family.

Mr. Quirke. Maybe it wasn't that but some other thing—

Mrs. Delane. Here is Fardy. I must send the message to the Sergeant. Well, Mr. Quirke, I'm glad I had the time to give you a warning.

MR. QUIRKE. I'm obliged to you, indeed. You were always very neighborly, Mrs. Delane. Don't be too quick now sending the message. There is just one article I would like to put away out of the house before the Sergeant will come. [*Enter* FARDY.]

MRS. DELANE. Here now, Fardy—that's not the way you're going to the barracks. Any one would think you were scaring birds yet. Put on your uniform. [FARDY *goes into office.*] You have this message to bring to the Sergeant of Police. Get your cap now, it's under the counter.

[FARDY *reappears, and she gives him telegram.*]

FARDY. I'll bring it to the station. It's there he was going.

MRS. DELANE. You will not, but to the barracks. It can wait for him there.

[FARDY *goes off.* MR. QUIRKE *has appeared at door.*]

MR. QUIRKE. It was indeed a very neighborly act, Mrs. Delane, and I'm obliged to you. There is just *one* article to put out of the way. The Sergeant may look about him then and welcome. It's well I cleared the premises on yesterday. A consignment to Birmingham I sent. The Lord be praised, isn't England a terrible country with all it consumes?

MRS. DELANE. Indeed you always treat the neighbors very decent, Mr. Quirke, not asking them to buy from you.

MR. QUIRKE. Just one article. [*Turns to rack.*] That sheep I brought in last night. It was for a charity indeed I bought it from the widow woman at Kiltartan Cross. Where would the poor make a profit out of their dead meat without me? Where now is it? Well, now, I could have swore that that sheep was hanging there on the rack when I went in—

MRS. DELANE. You must have put it in some other place.

MR. QUIRKE [*going in and searching and coming out*]. I did not; there is no other place for me to put it. Is it gone blind I am, or is it not in it, it is?

MRS. DELANE. It's not there now anyway.

MR. QUIRKE. Didn't you take notice of it there yourself this morning?

MRS. DELANE. I have it in my mind that I did; but it's not there now.

MR. QUIRKE. There was no one here could bring it away?

MRS. DELANE. Is it me myself you suspect of taking it, James Quirke?

MR. QUIRKE. Where is it at all? It is certain it was not of itself it walked away. It was dead, and very dead, the time I bought it.

MRS. DELANE. I have a pleasant neighbor indeed that accuses me that I took his sheep. I wonder, indeed, you to say a thing like that! I to steal your sheep or your rack or anything that belongs to you or to your trade! Thank you, James Quirke. I am much obliged to you indeed.

MR. QUIRKE. Ah, be quiet, woman; be quiet—

MRS. DELANE. And let me tell you, James Quirke, that I would sooner starve and see everyone belonging to me starve than to eat the size of a thimble of any joint that ever was on your rack or that ever will be on it, whatever the soldiers may eat that have no other thing to get, or the English that devour all sorts, or the poor ravenous people that's down by the sea! [*She turns to go into shop.*]

MR. QUIRKE [*stopping her*]. Don't be talking foolishness, woman. Who said you took my meat? Give heed to me now. There must some other message have come. The Sergeant must have got some other message.

MRS. DELANE [*sulkily*]. If there is any way for a message to come that is quicker than to come by the wires, tell me what it is and I'll be obliged to you.

MR. QUIRKE. The Sergeant was up here making an excuse he was sticking up that notice. What was he doing here, I ask you?

MRS. DELANE. How would I know what brought him?

MR. QUIRKE. It is what he did; he made as if to go away —he turned back again and I shaving—he brought away the sheep—he will have it for evidence against me—

MRS. DELANE [*interested*]. That might be so.

MR. QUIRKE. I would sooner it to have been any other beast nearly ever I had upon the rack.

MRS. DELANE. Is that so?

MR. QUIRKE. I bade the Widow Early to kill it a fortnight ago—but she would not, she was that covetous!

MRS. DELANE. What was on it?

MR. QUIRKE. How would I know what was on it? Whatever was on it, it was the will of God put it upon it—wasted it was, and shivering and refusing its share.

MRS. DELANE. The poor thing.

MR. QUIRKE. Gone all to nothing—wore away like a flock of thread. It did not weigh as much as a lamb of two months.

MRS. DELANE. It is likely the Inspector will bring it to Dublin?

MR. QUIRKE. The ribs of it streaky with the dint of patent medicines—

MRS. DELANE. I wonder is it to the Petty Sessions you'll be brought or is it to the Assizes?

MR. QUIRKE. I'll speak up to them. I'll make my defense. What can the Army expect at fippence a pound?

MRS. DELANE. It is likely there will be no bail allowed?

MR. QUIRKE. Would they be wanting me to give them good quality meat out of my own pocket? Is it to encourage them to fight the poor Indians and Africans they would have me? It's the Anti-Enlisting Societies should pay the fine for me.

MRS. DELANE. It's not a fine will be put on you, I'm afraid. It's five years in jail you will be apt to be getting. Well, I'll try and be a good neighbor to poor Mrs. Quirke.

[MR. QUIRKE, *who has been stamping up and down, sits down and weeps.* HALVEY *comes in and stands on one side.*]

MR. QUIRKE. Hadn't I heart-scalding enough before, striving to rear five weak children?

MRS. DELANE. I suppose they will be sent to the Industrial Schools?

MR. QUIRKE. My poor wife—

MRS. DELANE. I'm afraid the workhouse—

MR. QUIRKE. And she out in an ass-car at this minute helping me to follow my trade.

MRS. DELANE. I hope they will not arrest her along with you.

MR. QUIRKE. I'll give myself up to justice. I'll plead guilty! I'll be recommended to mercy!

MRS. DELANE. It might be best for you.

MR. QUIRKE. Who would think so great a misfortune could come upon a family through the bringing away of one sheep!

HYACINTH [*coming forward*]. Let you make yourself easy.

MR. QUIRKE. Easy! It's easy to say let you make yourself easy.

HYACINTH. I can tell you where it is.

MR. QUIRKE. Where what is?

HYACINTH. The sheep you are fretting after.

MR. QUIRKE. What do you know about it?

HYACINTH. I know everything about it.

MR. QUIRKE. I suppose the Sergeant told you?

HYACINTH. He told me nothing.

MR. QUIRKE. I suppose the whole town knows it, so?

HYACINTH. No one knows it, as yet.

MR. QUIRKE. And the Sergeant didn't see it?

HYACINTH. No one saw it or brought it away but myself.

MR. QUIRKE. Where did you put it at all?

HYACINTH. In the ditch behind the church wall. In among the nettles it is. Look at the way they have me stung. [*Holds out hands.*]

MR. QUIRKE. In the ditch! The best hiding place in the town.

HYACINTH. I never thought it would bring such great trouble upon you. You can't say anyway I did not tell you.

MR. QUIRKE. You yourself that brought it away and that hid it! I suppose it was coming in the train you got information about the message to the police.

HYACINTH. What now do you say to me?

MR. QUIRKE. Say! I say I am as glad to hear what you said as if it was the Lord telling me I'd be in heaven this minute.

HYACINTH. What are you going to do to me?

MR. QUIRKE. Do, is it? [*Grasps his hand.*] Any earthly thing you would wish me to do, I will do it.

HYACINTH. I suppose you will tell—

MR. QUIRKE. Tell! It's I that will tell when all is quiet. It is I will give you the good name through the town!

HYACINTH. I don't well understand.

MR. QUIRKE [*embracing him*]. The man that preserved me!

HYACINTH. That preserved you?

MR. QUIRKE. That kept me from ruin!

HYACINTH. From ruin?

MR. QUIRKE. That saved me from disgrace!

HYACINTH [*to* MRS. DELANE]. What is he saying at all?

MR. QUIRKE. From the Inspector!

HYACINTH. What is he talking about?

MR. QUIRKE. From the magistrates!

HYACINTH. He is making some mistake.

MR. QUIRKE. From the Winter Assizes!

HYACINTH. Is he out of his wits?

MR. QUIRKE. Five years in jail!

HYACINTH. Hasn't he the queer talk?

MR. QUIRKE. The loss of the contract!

HYACINTH. Are my own wits gone astray?

MR. QUIRKE. What way can I repay you?

HYACINTH [*shouting*]. I tell you I took the sheep—

MR. QUIRKE. You did, God reward you!

HYACINTH. I stole away with it—

MR. QUIRKE. The blessing of the poor on you!

HYACINTH. I put it out of sight—

MR. QUIRKE. The blessing of my five children—

HYACINTH. I may as well say nothing—

MRS. DELANE. Let you be quiet now, Quirke. Here's the Sergeant coming to search the shop—

[SERGEANT *comes in:* QUIRKE *leaves go of* HALVEY, *who arranges his hat, etc.*]

SERGEANT. The Department to blazes!

MRS. DELANE. What is it is putting you out?

SERGEANT. To go to the train to meet the lecturer, and there to get a message through the guard that he was unavoidably detained in the South, holding an inquest on the remains of a drake.

MRS. DELANE. The lecturer, is it?

SERGEANT. To be sure. What else would I be talking of? The lecturer has failed me, and where am I to go looking for a person that I would think fitting to take his place?

MRS. DELANE. And that's all? And you didn't get any message but the one?

SERGEANT. Is that all? I am surprised at you, Mrs. Delane. Isn't it enough to upset a man, within three quarters of an hour of the time of the meeting? Where, I would ask you, am I to find a man that has education enough and wit enough and character enough to put up speaking on the platform on the minute?

MR. QUIRKE [*jumps up*]. It is I myself will tell you that.

SERGEANT. You!

MR. QUIRKE [*slapping* HALVEY *on the back*]. Look at here, Sergeant. There is not one word was said in all those papers about this young man before you but it is true. And there could be no good thing said of him that would be too good for him.

SERGEANT. It might not be a bad idea.

MR. QUIRKE. Whatever the paper said about him, Sergeant, I can say more again. It has come to my knowledge—by chance—that since he came to this town that young man has saved a whole family from destruction.

SERGEANT. That is much to his credit—helping the rural classes—

MR. QUIRKE. A family and a long family, big and little, like sods of turf—and they depending on a—on one that might be on his way to dark trouble at this minute if it was not for his assistance. Believe me, he is the most sensible man, and the wittiest, and the kindest, and the best helper of the poor that ever stood before you in this Square. Is not that so, Mrs. Delane?

MRS. DELANE. It is true indeed. Where he gets his wisdom and his wit and his information from I don't know, unless it might be that he is gifted from above.

SERGEANT. Well, Mrs. Delane, I think we have settled that question. Mr. Halvey, you will be the speaker at the meeting. The lecturer sent these notes—you can lengthen them into a speech. You can call to the people of Cloon to stand out, to begin the building of their character. I saw a lecturer do it one time at Dundrum. "Come up here," he said, "Dare to be a Daniel," he said—

HYACINTH. I can't—I won't—

SERGEANT [*looking at papers and thrusting them into his hand*]. You will find it quite easy. I will conduct you to the platform—these papers before you and a glass of water— That's settled. [*Turns to go.*] Follow me on to the Courthouse in half an hour—I must go to the barracks first—I heard there was a telegram— [*Calls back as he goes.*] Don't be late, Mrs. Delane. Mind, Quirke, you promised to come.

MRS. DELANE. Well, it's time for me to make an end of settling myself—and indeed, Mr. Quirke, you'd best do the same.

MR. QUIRKE [*rubbing his cheek*]. I suppose so. I had best

keep on good terms with him for the present. [*Turns.*] Well, now, I had a great escape this day.

[*Both go in as* FARDY *reappears whistling.*]

HYACINTH [*sitting down*]. I don't know in the world what has come upon the world that the half of the people of it should be cracked!

FARDY. Weren't you found out yet?

HYACINTH. Found out, is it? I don't know what you mean by being found out.

FARDY. Didn't he miss the sheep?

HYACINTH. He did, and I told him it was I took it—and what happened I declare to goodness I don't know— Will you look at these? [*Holds out notes.*]

FARDY. Papers! Are they more testimonials?

HYACINTH. They are what is worse. [*Gives a hoarse laugh.*] Will you come and see me on the platform—these in my hand—and I speaking—giving out advice. [FARDY *whistles.*] Why didn't you tell me, the time you advised me to steal a sheep, that in this town it would qualify a man to go preaching, and the priest in the chair looking on.

FARDY. The time I took a few apples that had fallen off a stall, they did not ask me to hold a meeting. They welted me well.

HYACINTH [*looking round*]. I would take apples if I could see them. I wish I had broke my neck before I left Carrow and I'd be better off! I wish I had got six months the time I was caught setting snares—I wish I had robbed a church.

FARDY. Would a Protestant church do?

HYACINTH. I suppose it wouldn't be so great a sin.

FARDY. It's likely the Sergeant would think worse of it— Anyway, if you want to rob one, it's the Protestant church is the handiest.

HYACINTH [*getting up*]. Show me what way to do it?

FARDY [*pointing*]. I was going around it a few minutes ago, to see might there be e'er a dog scenting the sheep, and I noticed the window being out.

HYACINTH. Out, out and out?

FARDY. It was, where they are putting colored glass in it for the distiller—

HYACINTH. What good does that do me?

FARDY. Every good. You could go in by that window if

you had some person to give you a hoist. Whatever riches there is to get in it then, you'll get them.

HYACINTH. I don't want riches. I'll give you all I will find if you will come and hoist me.

FARDY. Here is Miss Joyce coming to bring you to your lodging. Sure I brought your bag to it, the time you were away with the sheep—

HYACINTH. Run! Run!

[*They go off. Enter* MISS JOYCE.]

MISS JOYCE. Are you here, Mrs. Delane? Where, can you tell me, is Mr. Halvey?

MRS. DELANE [*coming out dressed*]. It's likely he is gone on to the Courthouse. Did you hear he is to be in the chair and to make an address to the meeting?

MISS JOYCE. He is getting on fast. His Reverence says he will be a good help in the parish. Who would think, now, there would be such a godly young man in a little place like Carrow!

[*Enter* SERGEANT *in a hurry, with telegram.*]

SERGEANT. What time did this telegram arrive, Mrs. Delane?

MRS. DELANE. I couldn't be rightly sure, Sergeant. But sure it's marked on it, unless the clock I have is gone wrong.

SERGEANT. It is marked on it. And I have the time I got it marked on my own watch.

MRS. DELANE. Well, now, I wonder none of the police would have followed you with it from the barracks—and they with so little to do—

SERGEANT [*looking in at* QUIRKE'S *shop*]. Well, I am sorry to do what I have to do, but duty is duty. [*He ransacks shop.* MRS. DELANE *looks on.* MR. QUIRKE *puts his head out of window.*]

MR. QUIRKE. What is that going on inside? [*No answer.*] Is there anyone inside, I ask? [*No answer.*] It must be that dog of Tannian's—wait till I get at him.

MRS. DELANE. It is Sergeant Carden, Mr. Quirke. He would seem to be looking for something—

[MR. QUIRKE *appears in shop.* SERGEANT *comes out, makes another dive, taking up sacks, etc.*]

MR. QUIRKE. I'm greatly afraid I am just out of meat,

Sergeant—and I'm sorry now to disoblige you, and you not being in the habit of dealing with me—

SERGEANT. I should think not, indeed.

MR. QUIRKE. Looking for a tender little bit of lamb, I suppose you are, for Mrs. Carden and the youngsters?

SERGEANT. I am not.

MR. QUIRKE. If I had it now, I'd be proud to offer it to you, and make no charge. I'll be killing a good kid tomorrow. Mrs. Carden might fancy a bit of it—

SERGEANT. I have had orders to search your establishment for unwholesome meat, and I am come here to do it.

MR. QUIRKE [*sitting down with a smile*]. Is that so? Well, isn't it a wonder the schemers does be in the world.

SERGEANT. It is not the first time there have been complaints.

MR. QUIRKE. I suppose not. Well, it is on their own head it will fall at the last!

SERGEANT. I have found nothing so far.

MR. QUIRKE. I suppose not, indeed. What is there you could find, and it not in it?

SERGEANT. Have you not meat at all upon the premises?

MR. QUIRKE. I have, indeed, a nice barrel of bacon.

SERGEANT. What way did it die?

MR. QUIRKE. It would be hard for me to say that. American it is. How would I know what way they do be killing the pigs out there? Machinery, I suppose, they have—steam hammers—

SERGEANT. Is there nothing else here at all?

MR. QUIRKE. I give you my word, there is no meat living or dead in this place, but yourself and myself and that bird above in the cage.

SERGEANT. Well, I must tell the Inspector I could find nothing. But mind yourself for the future.

MR. QUIRKE. Thank you, Sergeant. I will do that. [*Enter* FARDY. *He stops short.*]

SERGEANT. It was you delayed that message to me, I suppose? You'd best mend your ways or I'll have something to say to you. [*Seizes and shakes him.*]

FARDY. That's the way everyone does be faulting me. [*Whimpers.*]

[*The* SERGEANT *gives him another shake. A half-crown falls out of his pocket.*]

MISS JOYCE [*picking it up*]. A half-a-crown! Where, now, did you get that much, Fardy?

FARDY. Where did I get it, is it!

MISS JOYCE. I'll engage it was no honest way you got it.

FARDY. I picked it up in the street—

MISS JOYCE. If you did, why didn't you bring it to the Sergeant or to his Reverence?

MRS. DELANE. And some poor person, may be, being at the loss of it.

MISS JOYCE. I'd best bring it to his Reverence. Come with me, Fardy, till he will question you about it.

FARDY. It was not altogether in the street I found it—

MISS JOYCE. There, now! I knew you got it in no good way! Tell me, now.

FARDY. It was playing pitch and toss I won it—

MISS JOYCE. And who would play for half-crowns with the like of you, Fardy Farrell? Who was it, now?

FARDY. It was—a stranger—

MISS JOYCE. Do you hear that? A stranger! Did you see e'er a stranger in this town, Mrs. Delane, or Sergeant Carden, or Mr. Quirke?

MR. QUIRKE. Not a one.

SERGEANT. There was no stranger here.

MRS. DELANE. There could not be one here without me knowing it.

FARDY. I tell you there was.

MISS JOYCE. Come on, then, and tell who was he to his Reverence.

SERGEANT [*taking other arm*]. Or to the bench.

FARDY. I did get it, I tell you, from a stranger.

SERGEANT. Where is he, so?

FARDY. He's in some place—not far away.

SERGEANT. Bring me to him.

FARDY. He'll be coming here.

SERGEANT. Tell me the truth and it will be better for you.

FARDY [*weeping*]. Let me go and I will.

SERGEANT [*letting go*]. Now—who did you get it from?

FARDY. From that young chap came today, Mr. Halvey.

ALL. Mr. Halvey!

MR. QUIRKE [*indignantly*]. What are you saying, you young ruffian you? Hyacinth Halvey to be playing pitch and toss with the like of you!

FARDY. I didn't say that.

MISS JOYCE. You did say it. You said it now.

MR. QUIRKE. Hyacinth Halvey! The best man that ever came into this town!

MISS JOYCE. Well, what lies he has!

MR. QUIRKE. It's my belief the half-crown is a bad one. May be it's to pass it off it was given to him. There were tinkers in the town at the time of the fair. Give it here to me. [*Bites it.*] No, indeed, it's sound enough. Here, Sergeant, it's best for you take it.

[*Gives it to* SERGEANT, *who examines it.*]

SERGEANT. Can it be? Can it be what I think it to be?

MR. QUIRKE. What is it? What do you take it to be?

SERGEANT. It is, it is. I know it. I know this half-crown—

MR. QUIRKE. That is a queer thing, now.

SERGEANT. I know it well. I have been handling it in the church for the last twelvemonth—

MR. QUIRKE. Is that so?

SERGEANT. It is the nest-egg half-crown we hand round in the collection plate every Sunday morning. I know it by the dint on the Queen's temples and the crooked scratch under her nose.

MR. QUIRKE [*examining it*]. So there is, too.

SERGEANT. This is a bad business. It has been stolen from the church.

ALL. O! O! O!

SERGEANT [*seizing* FARDY]. You have robbed the church!

FARDY [*terrified*]. I tell you I never did!

SERGEANT. I have the proof of it.

FARDY. Say what you like! I never put a foot in it!

SERGEANT. How did you get this, so?

MISS JOYCE. I suppose from the *stranger*?

MRS. DELANE. I suppose it was Hyacinth Halvey gave it to you, now?

FARDY. It was so.

SERGEANT. I suppose it was he robbed the church?

FARDY [*sobs*]. You will not believe me if I say it.

MR. QUIRKE. O! the young vagabond! Let me get at him!

MRS. DELANE. Here he is himself now!

[HYACINTH *comes in.* FARDY *releases himself and creeps behind him.*]

MRS. DELANE. It is time you to come, Mr. Halvey, and shut the mouth of this young schemer.

MISS JOYCE. I would like you to hear what he says of you, Mr. Halvey. Pitch and toss, he says.

MR. QUIRKE. Robbery, he says.

MRS. DELANE. Robbery of a church.

SERGEANT. He has had a bad name long enough. Let him go to a reformatory now.

FARDY [*clinging to* HYACINTH]. Save me, save me! I'm a poor boy trying to knock out a way of living; I'll be destroyed if I go to a reformatory. [*Kneels and clings to* HYACINTH's *knees.*]

HYACINTH. I'll save you easy enough.

FARDY. Don't let me be jailed!

HYACINTH. I am going to tell them.

FARDY. I'm a poor orphan—

HYACINTH. Will you let me speak?

FARDY. I'll get no more chance in the world—

HYACINTH. Sure I'm trying to free you—

FARDY. It will be tasked to me always.

HYACINTH. Be quiet, can't you.

FARDY. Don't you desert me!

HYACINTH. Will you be silent?

FARDY. Take it on yourself.

HYACINTH. I will if you'll let me.

FARDY. Tell them you did it.

HYACINTH. I am going to do that.

FARDY. Tell them it was you got in at the window.

HYACINTH. I will! I will!

FARDY. Say it was you robbed the box.

HYACINTH. I'll say it! I'll say it!

FARDY. It being open!

HYACINTH. Let me tell, let me tell.

FARDY. Of all that was in it.

HYACINTH. I'll tell them that.

FARDY. And gave it to me.

HYACINTH [*putting hand on his mouth and dragging him up*]. Will you stop and let me speak?

SERGEANT. We can't be wasting time. Give him here to me.

HYACINTH. I can't do that. He must be let alone.

SERGEANT [*seizing him*]. He'll be let alone in the lock-up.

HYACINTH. He must not be brought there.

SERGEANT. I'll let no man get him off.

HYACINTH. I will get him off.

SERGEANT. You will not!

HYACINTH. I will.

SERGEANT. Do you think to buy him off?

HYACINTH. I will buy him off with my own **confession**.

SERGEANT. And what will that be?

HYACINTH. It was I robbed the church.

SERGEANT. That is likely indeed!

HYACINTH. Let him go, and take me. I tell you I did it.

SERGEANT. It would take witnesses to prove that.

HYACINTH [*pointing to* FARDY]. He will be witness.

FARDY. O! Mr. Halvey, I would not wish to do that. Get me off and I will say nothing.

HYACINTH. Sure you must. You will be put on oath in the court.

FARDY. I will not! I will not! All the world knows I don't understand the nature of an oath!

MR. QUIRKE [*coming forward*]. Is it blind ye all are?

MRS. DELANE. What are you talking about?

MR. QUIRKE. Is it fools ye all are?

MISS JOYCE. Speak for yourself.

MR. QUIRKE. Is it idiots ye all are?

SERGEANT. Mind who you're talking to.

MR. QUIRKE [*seizing* HYACINTH's *hands*]. Can't you see? Can't you hear? Where are your wits? Was ever such a thing seen in this town?

MRS. DELANE. Say out what you have to say.

MR. QUIRKE. A walking saint he is!

MRS. DELANE. Maybe so.

MR. QUIRKE. The preserver of the poor! Talk of the holy martyrs! They are nothing at all to what he is! Will you look at him! To save that poor boy he is going! To take the blame on himself he is going! To say he himself did the robbery he is going! Before the magistrate he is going! To jail he is going! Taking the blame on his own head! Putting the sin on his own shoulders! Letting on to have done a robbery! Telling a lie—that it may be forgiven him—to his own injury! Doing all that I tell you to save the character of a miserable slack lad, that rose in poverty.

[*Murmur of admiration from all.*]

MR. QUIRKE. Now, what do you say?

SERGEANT [*pressing his hand*]. Mr. Halvey, you have given us all a lesson. To please you, I will make no information against the boy. [*Shakes him and helps him up.*] I will put back the half-crown in the poor-box next Sunday. [*To* FARDY.] What have you to say to your benefactor?

FARDY. I'm obliged to you, Mr. Halvey. You behaved very decent to me, very decent indeed. I'll never let a word be said against you if I live to be a hundred years.

SERGEANT [*wiping eyes with a blue handkerchief*]. I will tell it at the meeting. It will be a great encouragement to them to build up their character. I'll tell it to the priest and he taking the chair—

HYACINTH. O stop, will you—

MR. QUIRKE. The chair. It's in the chair he himself should be. It's in a chair we will put him now. It's to chair him through the streets we will. Sure he'll be an example and a blessing to the whole of the town. [*Seizes* HALVEY *and seats him in chair.*] Now, Sergeant, give a hand. Here, Fardy.

[*They all lift the chair with* HALVEY *in it, wildly protesting.*]

MR. QUIRKE. Come along now to the Courthouse. Three cheers for Hyacinth Halvey! Hip! hip! hoora!

[*Cheers heard in the distance as the curtain drops.*]

THE TWISTING OF THE ROPE

A COMEDY IN ONE ACT

By Douglas Hyde

DRAMATIS PERSONÆ

HANRAHAN, *a wandering poet*
SHEAMUS O'HERAN, *engaged to Oona*
MAURYA, *the woman of the house*
SHEELA, *a neighbor*
OONA, *Maurya's daughter*
Neighbors and a piper who have come to MAURYA's *house for a dance*

SCENE: *A farmer's house in Munster a hundred years ago. Men and women moving about and standing round the walls as if they had just finished a dance.* HANRAHAN, *in the foreground, talking to* OONA.
The piper is beginning a preparatory drone for another dance, but SHEAMUS *brings him a drink and he stops. A man has come and holds out his hand to* OONA, *as if to lead her out, but she pushes him away.*

OONA. Don't be bothering me now; don't you see I'm listening to what he is saying? [*To* HANRAHAN.] Go on with what you were saying just now.

HANRAHAN. What .did that fellow want of you?

OONA. He wanted the next dance with me, but I wouldn't give it to him.

HANRAHAN. And why would you give it to him? Do you think I'd let you dance with anyone but myself, and I here? I had no comfort or satisfaction this long time until I came here tonight, and till I saw yourself.

OONA. What comfort am I to you?

HANRAHAN. When a stick is half burned in the fire, does it not get comfort when water is poured on it?

OONA. But, sure, you are not half burned.

HANRAHAN. I am; and three-quarters of my heart is burned, and scorched and consumed, struggling with the world, and the world struggling with me.

OONA. You don't look that bad.

HANRAHAN. O, Oona ni Regaun, you have not knowledge of the life of a poor bard, without house or home or havings, but he going and ever going a drifting through the wide world, without a person with him but himself. There is not a morning in the week when I rise up that I do not say to myself that it would be better to be in the grave than to be wandering. There is nothing standing to me but the gift I got from God, my share of songs; when I begin upon them, my grief and my trouble go from me; I forget my persecution and my ill luck; and now since I saw you, Oona, I see there is something that is better even than the songs.

OONA. Poetry is a wonderful gift from God; and as long as you have that, you are richer than the people of stock and store, the people of cows and cattle.

HANRAHAN. Ah, Oona, it is a great blessing, but it is a great curse as well for a man, he to be a poet. Look at me: have I a friend in this world? Is there a man alive that has a wish for me? is there the love of anyone at all on me? I am going like a poor lonely barnacle goose throughout the world; like Oisin after the Fenians; every person hates me: you do not hate me, Oona?

OONA. Do not say a thing like that; it is impossible that anyone would hate you.

HANRAHAN. Come and we will sit in the corner of the room together; and I will tell you the little song I made for you; it is for you I made it.

[*They go to a corner and sit down together.* SHEELA *comes in at the door.*]

SHEELA. I came to you as quick as I could.

MAURYA. And a hundred welcomes to you.

SHEELA. What have you going on now?

MAURYA. Beginning we are; we had one jig, and now the piper is drinking a glass. They'll begin dancing again in a minute when the piper is ready.

SHEELA. There are a good many people gathering in to you tonight. We will have a fine dance.

MAURYA. Maybe so, Sheela; but there's a man of them there, and I'd sooner him out than in.

SHEELA. It's about the long red man you are talking, isn't it—the man that is in close talk with Oona in the corner? Where is he from, and who is he himself?

MAURYA. That's the greatest vagabond ever came into Ireland; Tumaus Hanrahan they call him; but it's Hanrahan the rogue he ought to have been christened by right. Aurah, wasn't there the misfortune on me, him to come in to us at all tonight?

SHEELA. What sort of a person is he? Isn't he a man that makes songs, out of Connacht? I heard talk of him before; and they say there is not another dancer in Ireland so good as him. I would like to see him dance.

MAURYA. Bad luck to the vagabond! It is well I know what sort he is; because there was a kind of friendship between himself and the first husband I had; and it is often I heard from poor Diarmuid—the Lord have mercy on him!—what sort of a person he was. He was a schoolmaster down in Connacht; but he used to have every trick worse than another; ever making songs he used to be, and drinking whiskey and setting quarrels afoot among the neighbors with his share of talk. They say there isn't a woman in the five provinces that he wouldn't deceive. He is worse than Donal no Greina long ago. But the end of the story is that the priest routed him out of the parish altogether; he got another place then, and followed on at the same tricks until he was routed out again, and another again with it. Now he has neither place nor house nor anything, but he to be going the country, making songs and getting a night's lodging from the people; nobody will refuse him, because they are afraid of him. He's a great poet, and maybe he'd make a rann on you that would stick to you forever, if you were to anger him.

SHEELA. God preserve us; but what brought him in tonight?

MAURYA. He was traveling the country and he heard there was to be a dance here, and he came in because he knew us; he was rather great with my first husband. It is wonderful how he is making out his way of life at all, and he with nothing but his share of songs. They say there is no place that he'll go to, that the women don't love him, and that the men don't hate him.

SHEELA [*catching* MAURYA *by the shoulder*]. Turn your head, Maurya; look at him now, himself and your daughter, and their heads, together; he's whispering in her ear; he's after making a poem for her and he's whispering it in her ear. Oh, the villain, he'll be putting his spells on her now.

MAURYA. Ohone, go deo! isn't it a misfortune that he came? He's talking every moment with Oona since he came in three hours ago. I did my best to separate them from one another, but it failed me. Poor Oona is given up to every sort of old songs and old made-up stories; and she thinks it sweet to be listening to him. The marriage is settled between herself and Sheamus O'Heran there, a quarter from today. Look at poor Sheamus at the door, and he watching them. There is grief and hanging of the head on him; it's easy to see that he'd like to choke the vagabond this minute. I am greatly afraid that the head will be turned on Oona with his share of blathering. As sure as I am alive there will come evil out of this night.

SHEELA. And couldn't you put him out?

MAURYA. I could. There's no person here to help him unless there would be a woman or two; but he is a great poet, and he has a curse that would split the trees, and that would burst the stones. They say the seed will rot in the ground and the milk go from the cows when a poet like him makes a curse, if a person routed him out of the house; but if he was once out, I'll go bail I wouldn't let him in again.

SHEELA. If himself were to go out willingly, there would be no virtue in his curse then.

MAURYA. There would not, but he will not go out willingly, and I cannot rout him out myself for fear of his curse.

SHEELA. Look at poor Sheamus. He is going over to her.

[SHEAMUS *gets up and goes over to her*.]

SHEAMUS. Will you dance this reel with me, Oona, as soon as the piper is ready?

HANRAHAN [*rising up*]. I am Tumaus Hanrahan, and I am speaking now to Oona ni Regaun; and as she is willing to be talking to me, I will allow no living person to come between us.

SHEAMUS [*without heeding* HANRAHAN]. Will you not dance with me, Oona?

HANRAHAN [*savagely*]. Didn't I tell you now that it was to me Oona ni Regaun was talking? Leave that on the spot, you clown, and do not raise a disturbance here.

SHEAMUS. Oona—

HANRAHAN [*shouting*]. Leave that! [SHEAMUS *goes away, and comes over to the two old women.*]

SHEAMUS. Maurya Regaun, I am asking leave of you to throw that ill-mannerly, drunken vagabond out of the house. Myself and my two brothers will put him out if you will allow us; and when he's outside I'll settle with him.

MAURYA. Sheamus, do not; I am afraid of him. That man has a curse they say that would split the trees.

SHEAMUS. I don't care if he had a curse that would overthrow the heavens; it is on me it will fall, and I defy him! If he were to kill me on the moment, I will not allow him to put his spells on Oona. Give me leave, Maurya.

SHEELA. Do not, Sheamus. I have a better advice than that.

SHEAMUS. What advice is that?

SHEELA. I have a way in my head to put him out. If you follow my advice, he will go out himself as quiet as a lamb; and when you get him out, slap the door on him, and never let him in again.

MAURYA. Luck from God on you, Sheela, and tell us what's in your head.

SHEELA. We will do it as nice and easy as you ever saw. We will put him to twist a hay rope till he is outside, and then we will shut the door on him.

SHEAMUS. It's easy to say, but not easy to do. He will say to you, "Make a hay rope yourself."

SHEELA. We will say then that no one ever saw a hay rope made, that there is no one at all in the house to make the beginning of it.

SHEAMUS. But will *he* believe that we never saw a hay rope?

SHEELA. He believe it, is it? He'd believe anything; he'd believe that himself is king over Ireland when he has a glass taken, as he has now.

SHEAMUS. But what excuse can we make for saying we want a hay rope?

MAURYA. Can't you think of something yourself, Sheamus?

SHEAMUS. Sure, I can say the wind is rising, and I must bind the thatch, or it will be off the house.

SHEELA. But he'll know the wind is not rising if he does but listen at the door. You must think of some other excuse, Sheamus.

SHEAMUS. Wait, I have a good idea now; say there is a coach upset at the bottom of the hill, and that they are asking for a hay rope to mend it with. He can't see as far as that from the door, and he won't know it's not true it is.

MAURYA. That's the story, Sheela. Now, Sheamus, go among the people and tell them the secret. Tell them what they have to say, that no one at all in this country ever saw a hay rope, and put a good skin on the lie yourself. [SHEAMUS *goes from person to person whispering to them, and some of them begin laughing. The piper has begun playing. Three or four couples rise up.*]

HANRAHAN [*after looking at them for a couple of minutes*]. Whisht! Let ye sit down! Do ye call that dragging, dancing? You are tramping the floor like so many cattle. You are as heavy as bullocks, as awkward as asses. May my throat be choked if I would not sooner be looking at as many lame ducks hopping on one leg through the house. Leave the floor to Oona ni Regaun and to me.

ONE OF THE MEN GOING TO DANCE. And for what would we leave the floor to you?

HANRAHAN. The swan of the brink of the waves, the royal phœnix, the pearl of the white breast, the Venus amongst the women, Oona ni Regaun, is standing up with me, and any place she rises up, the sun and the moon bow to her, and so shall ye yet. She is too handsome, too sky-like for any other woman to be near her. But wait a while! Before I'll show you how the Connacht boy can dance, I will give you the poem I made on the star of the province of Munster, on Oona ni Regaun. Get up, O sun among women, and we will sing the song together, verse about, and then we'll show them what right dancing is! [OONA *rises.*]

HANRAHAN.

    She is white Oona of the yellow hair,
    The Coolin that was destroying my heart inside me;
    She is my secret love and my lasting affection;
    I care not forever for any woman but her.

OONA.

    O bard of the black eye, it is you
    Who have found victory in the world and fame;
    I call on yourself and I praise your mouth;
    You have set my heart in my breast astray.

HANRAHAN.

    O fair Oona of the golden hair,
    My desire, my affection, my love and my store,
    Herself will go with her bard afar;
    She has hurt his heart in his breast greatly.

OONA.

    I would not think the night long nor the day,
    Listening to your fine discourse;
    More melodious is your mouth than the singing of the
        birds;
    From my heart in my breast you have found love.

HANRAHAN.

    I walked myself the entire world,
    England, Ireland, France, and Spain;
    I never saw at home or afar
    Any girl under the sun like fair Oona.

OONA.

    I have heard the melodious harp
    On the streets of Cork playing to us;
    More melodious by far I thought your voice,
    More melodious by far your mouth than that.

HANRAHAN.

    I was myself one time a poor barnacle goose;
    The night was not plain to me more than the day
    Till I got sight of her; she is the love of my heart
    That banished from me my grief and my misery.

OONA.

I was myself on the morning of yesterday
Walking beside the wood at the break of day;
There was a bird there was singing sweetly,
How I love love, and is it not beautiful?

[*A shout and a noise, and* SHEAMUS O'HERAN *rushes in.*]
SHEAMUS. Ububu! Ohone-y-o, go deo! The big coach is
overthrown at the foot of the hill! The bag in which the
letters of the country are is bursted; and there is neither tie,
nor cord, nor rope, nor anything to bind it up. They are
calling out now for a hay sugaun—whatever kind of thing
that is; the letters and the coach will be lost for want of a
hay sugaun to bind them.

HANRAHAN. Do not be bothering us; we have our poem
done, and we are going to dance. The coach does not come
this way at all.

SHEAMUS. The coach does come this way now; but sure
you're a stranger, and you don't know. Doesn't the coach
come over the hill now, neighbors?

ALL. It does, it does, surely.

HANRAHAN. I don't care whether it does come or whether
it doesn't. I would sooner twenty coaches to be overthrown
on the road than the pearl of the white breast to be stopped
from dancing to us. Tell the coachman to twist a rope for
himself.

SHEAMUS. Oh! murder! he can't. There's that much vigor,
and fire, and activity, and courage in the horses, that my
poor coachman must take them by the ears; it's on the pinch
of his life he's able to control them; he's afraid of his soul
they'll go from him of a rout. They are neighing like anything; you never saw the like of them for wild horses.

HANRAHAN. Are there no other people in the coach that
will make a rope, if the coachman has to be at the horses'
heads? Leave that, and let us dance.

SHEAMUS. There are three others in it; but as to one of
them, he is one-handed, and another man of them, he's shaking and trembling with the fright he got; it's not in him
now to stand up on his two feet with the fear that's on
him; and as for the third man, there isn't a person in this
country would speak to him about a rope at all, for his own

father was hanged with a rope last year for stealing sheep.

HANRAHAN. Then let one of yourselves twist a rope so, and leave the floor to us. [*To* OONA.] Now, O star of women, show me how Juno goes among the gods, or Helen for whom Troy was destroyed. By my word, since Deirdre died, for whom Naoise, son of Usnech, was put to death, her heir is not in Ireland today but yourself. Let us begin.

SHEAMUS. Do not begin until we have a rope; we are not able to twist a rope; there's nobody here can twist a rope.

HANRAHAN. There's nobody here is able to twist a rope?

ALL. Nobody at all.

SHEELA. And that's true; nobody in this place ever made a hay sugaun. I don't believe there's a person in this house who ever saw one itself but me. It's well I remember when I was a little girsha that I saw one of them on a goat that my grandfather brought with him out of Connacht. All the people used to be saying: "Aurah, what sort of a thing is that at all?" And he said that it was a sugaun that was in it; and that people used to make the like of that down in Connacht. He said that one man would go holding the hay, and another man twisting it. I'll hold the hay now; and you'll go twisting it.

SHEAMUS. I'll bring in a lock of hay. [*He goes out.*]

HANRAHAN.
I will make a dispraising of the province of Munster:
They do not leave the floor to us;
It isn't in them to twist even a sugaun;
The province of Munster without nicety, without prosperity.

Disgust forever on the province of Munster,
That they do not leave us the floor;
The province of Munster for the foul clumsy people.
They cannot even twist a sugaun!

SHEAMUS [*coming back*]. Here's the hay now.

HANRAHAN. Give it here to me; I'll show ye what the well-learned, hardy, honest, clever, sensible Connachtman will do, that has activity and full deftness in his hands, and sense in his head, and courage in his heart; but that the misfortune and the great trouble of the world directed him among the *lebidins* of the province of Munster, without honor, without nobility, without knowledge of the swan beyond the duck, or of the gold beyond the brass, or of the lily beyond the thistle, or of the star of young women, and the pearl of the white breast, beyond their own share of sluts and slatterns. Give me a kippeen. [*A man hands him a stick; he puts a wisp of hay round it, and begins twisting it; and* SHEELA *giving him out the hay.*]

HANRAHAN.

There is a pearl of a woman giving light to us;
She is my love; she is my desire;
She is fair Oona, the gentle queen-woman.
And the Munstermen do not understand half her
    courtesy.

These Munstermen are blinded by God;
They do not recognize the swan beyond the gray duck;
But she will come with me, my fine Helen,
Where her person and her beauty shall be praised for-
    ever.

Arrah, wisha, wisha, wisha! isn't this the fine village? isn't this the exceeding village? The village where there be that many rogues hanged that the people have no want of ropes with all the ropes that they steal from the hangman!

The sensible Connachtman makes
    A rope for himself;
But the Munsterman steals it
    From the hangman;
That I may see a fine rope,
    A rope of hemp yet,
A stretching on the throats
    Of every person here!

On account of one woman only the Greeks departed, and they never stopped, and they never greatly stayed, till they destroyed Troy; and on account of one woman only this village shall be damned; *go deo, ma neoir,* and to the womb of judgment, by God of the graces, eternally and everlastingly, because they did not understand that Oona ni Regaun is the second Helen, who was born in their midst, and that she overcame in beauty Deirdre and Venus, and all that came before or that will come after her!

> But she will come with me, my pearl of a woman,
> To the province of Connacht of the fine people;
> She will receive feasts, wine, and meat,
> High dances, sport, and music!

Oh, wisha, wisha! that the sun may never rise upon this village; and that the stars may never shine on it; and that— [*He is by this time outside the door. All the men make a rush at the door and shut it.* OONA *runs towards the door, but the women seize her.* SHEAMUS *goes over to her.*]

OONA. Oh! oh! oh! do not put him out; let him back; that is Tumaus Hanrahan—he is a poet—he is a bard—he is a wonderful man. Oh, let him back; do not do that to him!

SHEAMUS. Oh Oona *bán, acushla dílis,* let him be; he is gone now, and his share of spells with him! He will be gone out of your head tomorrow; and you will be gone out of his head. Don't you know that I like you better than a hundred thousand Deirdres, and that you are my one pearl of a woman in the world?

HANRAHAN [*outside, beating on the door*]. Open, open, open; let me in! Oh, my seven hundred thousand curses on you—the curse of the weak and the strong—the curse of the poets and of the bards upon you! The curse of the priests on you and the friars! The curse of the bishops upon you, and the Pope! The curse of the widows on you, and the children! Open! [*He beats on the door again and again.*]

SHEAMUS. I am thankful to ye, neighbors; and Oona will be thankful to ye tomorrow. Beat away, you vagabond! Do your dancing out there with yourself now! Isn't it a fine thing for a man to be listening to the storm outside, and himself quiet and easy beside the fire? Beat away, beat away! Where's Connacht now?

THE DANDY DOLLS

By George Fitzmaurice

CHARACTERS

ROGER CARMODY
CAUTH, *his wife*
HIS CHILD
GRAY MAN
HAG'S SON ⎱ *boys*
TIMMEEN ⎰
FATHER JAMES
KEERBY, *the priest's clerk*
HAG OF BARNA

SCENE: *Interior of* ROGER'S *kitchen.* CAUTH *is sitting at fire, knitting. Child on hob. Enter the* GRAY MAN *humming "The Old Leathern Breeches." Continues humming when he enters, and does some capers about floor to air, then shuts half-door.*

GRAY MAN. God bless you, lady! [*Pause.*] God bless, honest woman! [*Pause.*] Sour female, it's God bless I'm saying!

CAUTH. Oh, God bless! But if it's alms you're wanting, Gray Fellow, I'm thinking you're come to the wrong shop. For there isn't meal in the house, or flour in the house, nor spuds in the house itself; in a manner there is nothing in the house but the red raw starvation, as might be plain to you by the cut of that ashy creature sitting there on the hob with the map of the world painted on his burnt spangled shins.

GRAY MAN. God bless the child, I say! But it's no alms I come for, woman dear, or no reception in the line of lodging or of food. Indeed, it's himself I'm wanting, your darling husband, Mr. Roger Carmody; and is himself at home?

CAUTH. Himself is at home, but I'm thinking he's engaged.

GRAY MAN [*with long intonation*]. Engaged! What sort of talk is that in a cabin black with soot? Engaged! Sure a man could be engaged and could spare a little time.

CAUTH. He could if he wasn't my man, that has time and playtime and whips of time again, but still for want of time is in such a devil's own fix that he can't renayge himself to put a sop in the thatch, fix a hoop in that leaking oven, or settle a pot-hook on which to hang the pot. He don't earn as much as a shilling in a week, and all the same he's engaged, sir, and always engaged is he.

GRAY MAN. That's like a riddle you'd hear from a child— I went to the wood and I picked a thorn, riddle-me-riddle-me-ree.

CAUTH [*sourly*]. A sore subject I'd be riddling on, then, that booby man of mine; for may the devil fly away with the day he drew on him that practice of making dandy dolls. Isn't he well engaged, glory be God?

GRAY MAN [*sitting down opposite* CAUTH]. So it seems. [*With a sniff.*] And isn't it a funny fancy game for a spade-man stuck in gripes? Capers?

CAUTH. Capers! Notions! A hobby, moryah! to keep him on the hearth, and he addicted to going marauding after poultry in the dark.

GRAY MAN. A holy thought, faith, if it's gay itself.

CAUTH. A holy thought! A fitter thing for him to exert himself in a proper laboring man, earn his coin for himself, and 'tisn't thinking of robbing he would be, with the tasby flattened in him when the night would come.

GRAY MAN. 'Tis you that's right.

CAUTH. 'Tis me that's right. But where's the good, and a bosthoon he? What harm—glory be to God!—but them dolls the biggest torment to him in the world. For the Hag's Son is against them to the death, and so sure as Roger makes a doll, so sure will the Hag's Son, soon or late, come at it, give it a knuckle in the navel, split it in two fair halves, collar the windpipe, and off with him carrying the squeaky-squeak.

GRAY MAN. Roger raging?

• CAUTH. Roger raging. Fit to stick. Teetotally mad itself. But, worse than all, after a doll is diddled, nothing for him but his plundering chase again.

GRAY MAN. From sheer disappointment?

CAUTH. From sheer disappointment. That's his excuse, and he'd be saying he'd be the honest man entirely if he could keep his doll from the power of the Barna brat; that he has such a grah for a dandy doll there wouldn't be a stir out of him while she would be fornenst him—he peeping at her delighted, and she sweet—smiling upon the clevvy. But 'tis equal which, for he isn't able to save his dolls, and isn't he the biggest looney not to stop his booby game?

GRAY MAN. He is, partly.

CAUTH. Partly! Only partly!

GRAY MAN. Partly. For if he robs a share itself, I'll engage them dolls have improved him generally in the line of virtue and of grace.

CAUTH. You'll engage them dolls have improved him generally in virtue and in grace? Faith, you'll engage no such thing, and though he is forty years at dolls, what occurred to him no further back than Thursday week—what occurred to him but to have him lep up in the bed to me in the middle of the night, sir, sweat pouring down off him after he waking out of a luscious dream, and there he commenced bawling till you'd think his heart would break lamenting all the opportunities he lost of collaring this and that in the line of fancy poultry the time he was a child, when no one suspected him, and he making rack there wasn't a thing in the world for him to come at now but the priest's geese!

GRAY MAN. A sort of fit?

CAUTH. A sort of fit. A spasm. An unholy spasm that never left him surely until the break of day. Likewise the devil a bit the better is he in the line of health. For, mind you, big as the mind he has for poultry, they never with his stomach would agree. But he was fairly before he started them dandy dolls—the time he'd take a notion for a bird and out the door he'd go. He'd have his little stew. He might get a change after it—a bit dull in himself—yawning and the like. But no alarm, no distress, unless some furry variations that would come upon his tongue.

GRAY MAN. Crawsick?

CAUTH. Crawsick—a thing could happen a man after a little booze. But 'tis different since, for, if them dolls do keep him in a bit itself, 'tis treble as ravenous he does be when he goes marauding on the new. And often I see him lick three geese in one almighty feed, his jaws going like a horse, he crunching and munching, and from the neck to the pope's nose there wouldn't be as much in the carcass left after him as would blind the eye of a Tommy Blue. Nor would that satisfy him, for, after all being over, 'tis many a time the baisht would turn around from that table there and, shameless to the world, call for the six loppeens.

GRAY MAN. Game to the heel?

CAUTH. Game to the heel. Ah, but my hand to you! he'd pay for his game, and in a bully soon time too. He'd be having the haycups, and there would come from him every belch. He'd be a show in the bed—a rattle—God save the hearers!— a rattle, and it going on in his guts.

GRAY MAN. Is it going on all night?

CAUTH. Going on all night. All the first night. For maybe 'tis the night after he'd be getting them sort of chills, when he'd be as cold as a dead pig, that was kilt, washed, shaved, and hanging on the gallows for twenty-four hours. And he'd be thumming himself, and he'd be scratching himself, trying to rise a heat, and there wouldn't be a stitch in the house but he'd have rolled about himself; but if you put a ton weight itself down on top of him 'twouldn't take that chill from his bones, and his teeth never stopping going like that. [Chatters.]

GRAY MAN [chattering]. Never stopping going like that?

CAUTH. Never stopping going like that.

GRAY MAN [shaking his head]. Faith, that was bad.

CAUTH. That was bad and very bad itself. But, bad as it was, worse was to happen to him before there would come back to him again the heart or the spirit or the tasby of a man. And for nights—for several nights indeed—the devil a kick would be out of him at all and he stiff. I'd be listening for a sound—no sound; I'd be feeling for his heart— no heart. Well, glory be to God, Gray Man, 'tis often I'd swear all the oaths in Ireland it's a pure corpse I had in him, and, fainting and shivering, it's by a struggle I'd crawl over him and out of the bed in the heel. I'd light the candle and I'd look at him, and it wouldn't be wishing to you to look at him and the cut of him in that hour, and he lying on the flat of his back, his eyes open in that sleep, his mouth open, but no breath coming; and no sort of expression on him was ever seen on the face of a Christian, but something in the shape of a damn ugly smile.

GRAY MAN. Woeful suffering.

CAUTH. Woeful suffering. And woeful suffering is all the benefit he has from his trumpery dandy dolls, we starved; and there is that leaking oven, and there is that hole in the thatch, and there we are without a pothooks on which to hang the pot. Lord above; isn't it the pity of the world I am with him surely, a mangy vomiting snooker itself to have beside me in the bed these forty years and more!

GRAY MAN. I can feel for you, and I felt for you before we ever met. For it's far and distant newses wander of the failings and the follies of a man. Faith, there's ballads sung about him in our quarter, and 'tis the youngsters itself could give you a flourishing account of Roger and his dandy dolls. Indeed, 'tis a great pity you are entirely, but I'll engage now—God bless the tears!—you find great relief from giving that share of talk.

CAUTH [*harshly*]. How simple I'd find relief in a share of talk! But if it's scoffing you are, such jokes don't match your beard, old fairy, or whatever you are, and wherever you rose out of this haunted eve of May.

GRAY MAN. Faith, out of a briny spot, then, a place where periwinkles are plenty, and there is dilisk thrown in heaps.

CAUTH [*drawing back her chair in terror*]. God knows, maybe 'tis the way you are really something queer! You're as white as Father Christmas, but, all the same, now that I take stock of you, I see there is a horrid cut about you I never seen in any ancient person in all the townlands bounding round this melted boggy spot.

GRAY MAN. Why, then, I'm thought uncommon noble by the mermaids near my home, and 'tis they are the damsels keep a sharp lookout for beauty and a handsome form, they brittle—half in bits—from the luscious thoughts of love.

CAUTH [*deliberately*]. 'Tis the way you are surely something queer, and, maybe, 'tis for some devil's purpose you were nudging me to blab about my man. But, bad as he is, 'tisn't the traitor I'd be acting to him in the heel, and 'tis little would make me give you that fist right in your grizzled puss. [*He puts hands on her knees; she tries to draw away from him.*] In the name of all that's good what pinching have you there?

GRAY MAN. Be easy now, and civil, most virtuous matron fair. And, though I'm a jolly sort of fellow when out for the day, faith, 'tisn't you, poor wrinkled screed, that would entice me to embrace you in your chair!

CAUTH. Let go my knees, I'm telling you. Glory be! A man I never seen before or don't know what's his name!

GRAY MAN. Counihan, then—one of the Counihans of the Isle of Doom. Martin I am, the youngest, for there is my elder brother James, and my father, old Mohoon. We do great business in the trumpery way, we make baubles for the globe, in a manner we are bauble makers to the King and Queen of Spain.

CAUTH. That's a bully make.

GRAY MAN. The devil a make. [*Handing her paper.*] And here's will tell you something and maybe something more.

CAUTH [*reading*]. "By royal appointment to the King and Queen of Spain. The Messrs. Counihan beg to intimate to the mainland people that, as usual, they are purchasing home-made trumperies, and especially are prepared to give bully prices for purty well-built dandy dolls." Is it prizes for dandy dolls?

GRAY MAN. Prizes for dandy dolls.

CAUTH [*suspiciously*]. Then it's about the dolls you came. Well I knew, old shaver, 'twas about the dolls you came.

GRAY MAN. Smart enough you spotted it, faith, you pleasant polite dame. Still, if you know more than your prayers 'tisn't the Counihans you should blame. For 'twas the sore day to us we offered them prizes, all through your husband man; with the Hag's Son coming to the mainland cliff right fornenst our home, and flinging the windpipes of Roger's dolls right down into the sea. Calling for his prizes he does be, the little blackguard brat, screeching laughing, and he turning every somersault for himself on the slippery green above. Shamed he has us, a peepshow itself to the laughing people passing by to Mass; in a manner we're in three gazaybos that were feared, respected, and venerated men. He has old Mohoon totally off his stems, his white head up day and night with fury going through his beard like a whirlwind through a bush. And brother James is worse, his feet all gored and bruised to bits from dancing raging horn-pipes on stumps of rocks and stones. And now, isn't that a purty fix for you from Roger's dandy dolls?

CAUTH. A purty fix, old shaver, and the devil fix you too, for that's what brought you here to fix it with my man.

GRAY MAN. Is it me fix him—me the most innocent poor slob in the world? I wouldn't hurt a bee. I'm only as you might say the garsoon, the messenger from James and old Mohoon. But there is more in that. Isn't there "warning" in it?

CAUTH [*reading*]. There is "warning." [*Reading slowly.*] "Warning . . ."

GRAY MAN. "It having come to the knowledge of the Messrs. Counihan . . ."

CAUTH [*reading*]. "It having come to the knowledge of the Messrs. Counihan, that the generality of the mainland people are nothing short of being a pack of the biggest thieves, rogues, and robbers, diddling each other at fairs over horses with blind eyes, cows with paralyzed udders, and so on in the line of blemishes, the Messrs. Counihan hereby give strict notice that if any person dare attempt to pass off on them a faulty or defective doll, they will soon and sudden take measures to chastise the thieving plunderers; in a manner they will rise every blister on his dirty yellow hide." [*Smiling*]. On his dirty yellow hide?

GRAY MAN. On his dirty yellow hide. You like that?

CAUTH. I like that.

GRAY MAN. No harm in that, says you, but maybe a deal of good.

CAUTH [*gleefully*]. My very thought. And my apologies to you, Gray Man, if my talk was cross or queer. Glory above! isn't it forty years wishing I am to see him tanned like that, and 'tis myself will hold him by the ears while you let his breeches down, and, with every wallop and flamm you'll give, I'll screech my loud hurrah! Faith, I'll call him in to you now, Gray Man, with a heart and more than a half. [*Rises. Goes towards door.*]

GRAY MAN [*sticking out his tongue and taking out of pocket an enormous black bottle which he slips furtively inside his overcoat*]. You're fine; you're thorough game itself, and upon my soul I love you more than all the dames of Doon.

CAUTH. Well, surely you're a droll fellow, old merryman so gay. [*Calling from doorstep.*] Roger-a-Roger-aboo-oo!

GRAY MAN. Was that snarl from a dog?

CAUTH. That snarl was from himself, out in the linnhe, the chronic! and he up to his ears this minute in making a brand-new dandy doll. For it's worse than a surly mastiff he is the time he does be manufacturing; and if a warrant rubbed a hair to him he'd make a ferocious grin at you that wouldn't shame the old boy himself that's below in the pit of hell. [*Calling.*] Roger! Roger! Aboo-oo! Roger! Roger! Aboo-oo! [*Running to hearth.*] Here he comes hopping, and, Lord! the countenance of the devil with the temper flying out of his two eyes. [*She sits down. Enter* ROGER *rapidly.*]

ROGER. In the name of God, is it in the other world I was, with yourself and your dinner-calls? The devil's cure to you for a bog-lark, what a burst of music comes from you in the heel of the day, the people raising their heads and gaping at you from far and near! The Lord be thanked my doll was finished, for there's a rasp in your cracked old windpipe that would frighten a horse from his oats, and many a time that same old screamer was the means of my making a faulty doll.

CAUTH. Now it's me is doing the harm, is it? But a time your old grandmother was the obstacle, not alluding to the day you aimed a pratie at her and hit her on that woeful polypus she had upon her nose. And what about Peg, and the time you used pull her by the hair of the head all round the kitchen floor?—your sister Peg I'm alluding to, crippled Peg with the crooked eye.

ROGER. Lies and damn lies!

CAUTH. Neither lies nor damn lies, and well it becomes you to be throwing the blame on more, you craven thing, hiding under the bed for yourself the time the Hag's Son would be coming onward on his prowl, leaving the tussle to Timmeen Faley, that little friend of yours that's always to the fore!

ROGER. More lies, for it's well yourself knows I used fight and struggle till I could fight no more. Timmeen, moryah! Timmeen is willing surely, but Timmeen is devilish weak.

CAUTH. Oh, glory, after all he done for you, the graceful nice garsoon! What harm if it's ever a bull's-eye you brought him from a pattern or a fair? But you're dirty mean and craven, and thankless now to boot.

ROGER. Peg away, old hairpin; but you'll fail this turn, whatever, to put me in a wax. For the joy of the world is in me over my new dandy doll. As sound as black oak it is, thanks be to God! [*Flourishes doll.*] Look at it so charming in its bib so gay. It's the finest doll I ever made, Cauth of the ugly snout!

CAUTH. That was the way with every doll the time when it was new. The last perfection always; no blemish on that, moryah! different altogether from all that went and fell before.

ROGER. I'm telling you there never was the beat of this.

CAUTH. And I'm telling you tell it first to the gallant horse marines.

ROGER [*in a rage*]. Psh! it's a gom I am to be bothering my napper with a poisoned whelp that the devil can't put a stop to ballyragging and clawfshawning from New Year's Day till New Year's Day again.

CAUTH. He turns it when he's beat. But what are you after now? Heavenly Father, 'tisn't fixing that doll you are in the place we eat our meals?

ROGER. I am, then, and with good tenpenny nails I'm fixing it itself. A deal a firmer place than the clevvy, woman, a place I'll have a view of it let me turn what way I will. 'Tisn't I'm afraid of this doll getting a knuckle or fifty knuckles itself, but to make it safer still I'll plant my dandy here.

CAUTH. Our fine table all destroyed! The only respectable thing in the house itself! Well, glory be to God, from Hell to Bedlam was there ever the match of you for a looney fool? [*Smiles.*] But, whisper! this Gray Man wants a talk with you if I rightly understand.

ROGER [*turning around and looking at* GRAY MAN *intently*]. Isn't it you I seen before? Where was it at all, or was it about the time I was turning into a man?

GRAY MAN. It could be.

ROGER. Where was this it was? There comes before me huge cliffs and a darksome sea.

GRAY MAN. The identical spot, then, and by the same token 'twas gone a quarter of the Christmas moon.

ROGER. 'Tis now I recollect. [*Drawing back in terror.*] Glory be to God, then, who is it? Glory be to God, 'tisn't one of the three Gray Men you are, who dwell in that rock in the heart of the fearsome bay of Doon, and come out on the battlements terrifying the people when the sea is roaring in the wild and dreary nights?

GRAY MAN [*pleasantly.*] Faith, then, it's one of them I am.

ROGER. And what might you want with me, hoary man of the ocean?

GRAY MAN [*handing bottle to* ROGER]. To give you a bottle. And if the Hag's Son whips the squeak from your new dandy doll, that mortal minute you'll drink the full of this. And he'll make for the doll this night itself at the hour of ten o'clock, for we are men can read the stars and prophesy of things that are to be.

ROGER. The doll is safe, but whether or which wherefore should I drink?

GRAY MAN. Your woman knows the wherefore and you'll soon know the why. But draw the cork from it, man, smell to it, it is sound and it is sweet.

ROGER [*drawing cork and smelling*]. Ptse! it's a rotten scent is from it, glory be to God! It's poison it is, and, win or lose, I'll not drink it, Gray Man from the sea.

GRAY MAN. You'll drink it and no thanks. For, if you dare resist, we have engines yonder would spatter a waterspout around your ears while you'd be asking the loan of a sack, or maybe 'tis a 'potamus we'd send up to your hall door to you that would take you in one gobble and, before you knew what o'clock was it, would sweep you holus-bolus to the bottom of the deep. Well, that's my message given, and now I must be going, for my time is running short. [*To* CAUTH, *who purses up lips and stares sourly in direction of auditorium.*] It grieves me sore to part, love, but we'll meet again in the gay soon time; so don't weep, my winsome purty, my beauteous fairy queen!

[*Strokes beard. Pulls out a little mirror and looks at himself. Puts mirror back in pocket. Whistles very softly "The Old Leathern Breeches," capering to air. Goes out and hums the air as he disappears.*]

CAUTH. Doll-di-do, this is what comes of the dandy dolls. [*Rises, goes to* ROGER.] And hammer away now, you mortal coward, but the sweat in lumps is clammy on your brow, and your two cheeks is the color of the clay.

ROGER. What way is it for you, woman, to be tormenting me now? Sure, if I was talking brave about my doll itself, what was it but to keep the heart in bloom, while all the time there was a little doubt, and like 'twould be in the air, for weeks past something was foreshowing me the calamity of this woeful hour. For it's as queer in myself I felt as ever I did after a topping feed of goose, the brain dull, a ton weight in every limb, and I walking the ground, and I couldn't lep the height of a sod of turf; the strangest things coming into my head; it's a fit of crying I got itself seeing the youngsters playing in Barton's field—it brought back to me so piercing the time I was likewise gay and hearty, tasby in me and high glee. But now it's miserable I do be, and dreary always, and 'tis God himself knows what mournful thoughts were brewing in me all through the Ree-Hee days. [*Hammers, then throws hammer aside on table.*] 'Tis no more hammering I can do, or battling I can do neither. Cauth, the heart and soul is gone out of me entirely, and there isn't the strength of a rush in my four bones.

CAUTH [*smelling to bottle*]. Whist now, maybe 'tisn't poison is in it at all. There is a heavy fume from it surely; still it might only be something will put you to sleep. But, whatever it is, Father James and his clerk are outside on the road, and rub the towel to your face for fear 'tis a notion they'd take to come in. Jawing they are, and 'tis like a dispute between them, the priest striving to bring Keerby this way, and Keerby wanting not. [*Turns away from window.*]

CHILD [*from door*]. Keerby has got away from him, mother. Oh J, the priest is after him again! Oh J, he has him by the ear! Oh J, he's driving him before him and rising every kick on his behind! By J, though, but Keerby is making tapes to pull away from him! Jaymini, they're leppin! Oh J, here they are full tally! Keerby and the priest himself, by J! [*Runs to fire.*]

CAUTH. Then where are my 'lastics—Lord, where are my 'lastic boots? [*Hides in corner.*]

ROGER. And the dickens where's that skillet—the dickens where's that towel?

[*Throws cloth over doll and stoops behind table. Enter* FATHER JAMES, *dragging* KEERBY *after him. They have a gun and a dog.*]

FATHER JAMES. Well, isn't it the show of the world I am with you, you stump of insubordination? Is there a priest in Ireland would put up with you itself, as bold as a pig, rising your voice cantankerous, and darring for to thwart me in my wishes and the way I want to go?

KEERBY. Sure 'tisn't striving to thwart you I am, your reverence. Isn't it for your own good I'm advising you, whatever'll become of your poultry not to have hand, act, or part in this man's dandy dolls? The world knows that in ways you're a man of the old times; but, faith, things is different, and if the Bishop hears of your capers maybe 'tis to pack you off he would to the wildest parish in the County Kerry, with sea on one side of you, and every day a fish Friday from Michaelmas to June!

FATHER JAMES. Tut for the Bishop. Tut for the Bishop, I'm saying, for amn't I a solid parish priest? and he dar say black your eye to me while I keep within the rules and regulations of Holy Church.

KEERBY. Why, then, that's the question, and if he wouldn't settle you himself, he might do worse. And maybe it's reported to Rome you'd be and excommunicated *per omnia sæcula sæculorum.*

FATHER JAMES. As there never was a law made against what I'm going to do in any Council of the Church, even in the Council of Trent itself, so that if I am reported to Rome, Mr. Bartholomew Keerby, by the time the Cardinals have settled the point I'm telling you there won't be many gray hairs left in your head, Mr. Bartholomew Keerby, or many gray hairs left in my head, Mr. Bartholomew Keerby, if there'll be a gray rib left in them at all itself.

KEERBY. So be it, your reverence, but I wished you'd let me absent myself whatever, as I don't want to have cut, shuffle, or deal with this man or his dandy dolls. There is a bad name on this house; in a manner the childer go a mile of around to avoid it. A blue light does be seen there all night, and 'tis said a small little man with a jim-crow hat appears on the top of the chimley regular every Christmas Eve. Sure, why not, and devilment of curse in them dandy dolls, and it well known that when Roger was a garsoon two black ravens would perch upon his shoulder every morning would rise over him and he marching off to school.

FATHER JAMES. So it's yourself is troubling you, you speechifying to me of Church law, and your thoughts all the time full of pagan pishogues! But isn't it as bold as the devil you are itself, and to dar spout them fables fornenst a man of my cloth! [*Loudly.*] But no more of it, I'm telling you. [*Gives him a push.*] Get along there—do your part in this business, and give me no more of your gab. Where's the people of this house, I'm saying, where's the people of this house?

[CAUTH *comes forward.* ROGER *rises.*]

CAUTH. Oh, welcome, your reverence; welcome kindly, Father James.

FATHER JAMES. Don't be welcoming me, sour woman; don't be welcoming me with that face on you like a high-fiddle, for 'tisn't welcomes I want from the thieves of the world, and it known to me at last the dog-fox which breaks into my back yard in the dead hour of the night. Roger Carmody, where are my geese?

ROGER. Your geese is ate. As your reverence knows the culprit, you might as well know that.

FATHER JAMES. Oh, you gulleter! oh, you panderer to the cravings of your dirty guts! Worse you are than the heretics itself, that think a good suit of clothes the best recommendation to a front seat in Glory; worse you are than the heretics, I'm saying, for you are foul outside as well as inside, and you have lost Paradise by stealing my geese.

·ROGER. Jesus, forgive me! Jesus, forgive me!

FATHER JAMES. Hypocrite, don't be blaspheming the holy name, and the feathers in your tick and the feathers in your bolster, the pluck from my old geese and the pluck from my old ganders! Ah, isn't it little would make me say them words would paralyze you on the mortal spot; and too long you have been running surely, corrupting the people, their mouths watering, and they passing by your half-door with the hot fumes coming out to them of the roast goose and the boiled goose, of the gravy and the giblet soup.

ROGER. God knows, then, Father James, 'tis the piercing sorrowful man I am I ever put a tooth in a goose.

FATHER JAMES. Sorrow me eye! Will that restore to me my poultry, or keep your hands off the new clutch of goslings I got from the Curtaynes? Will it keep you itself from stealing my fine young gray goose with the cuck on her that lays an egg for my breakfast all the mornings of the week? Sorrow me eye! Keep your sorrow for your guts, man, and fetch me that dandy doll I hear talks of. Fetch me the dandy doll 'tis said there is to be a battle about tonight, for if there is power in dolls to put you from stealing my geese, believe you me, I'll make a doll of it; in a manner I'm going to baptize it a good Catholic by the grace of God! Amn't I saying, fetch me the dandy doll?

CAUTH. Faith, she's right fornenst your reverence, if he'll only shift. [*To* ROGER.] Will you shift, I'm telling you, or is it shy or ashamed you are to let his reverence see the doll, or is it daft and dazzled you are entirely? Will you shift again? The dickens to you, and shift! [*Shoves* ROGER *aside and takes cloth off doll.*] There she is, your reverence, as large as life.

FATHER JAMES. My soul, she's fairly sweet! Well, missis, what name shall I put on her, if you please?

CAUTH [*moving away*]. Faith, you'll not put any name on her from me, your reverence; and let what will happen, I wouldn't acknowledge that bauble for daughter of mine, or have her called after one of my breed, if you were baptizing her from this till Michaelmas itself.

ROGER. Here's the holy water, your reverence, and don't mind that dreary whelp. Call the doll after my Aunt Jug.

FATHER JAMES. So be it, then, and Jug shall be her name. [*Baptizes doll.*] There, now, she's sanctified and sacramental sound, a match for all the hags and hags' sons from Barna to Kanturk. In holy armor, therefore, she's ready for the fray. And we'll be here to see it, Keerby; we'll come back to see the battle—faith, we'll come to see the sport. But, now, we want a corncrake to make a new mayfly. Away with us, we'll make her back to dinner! And, whist! she's screeching! Gayk-Gayk! Gayk-Gayk! she's in Curtin's rushy glen.

[*Exeunt* FATHER JAMES *and* KEERBY.]

CAUTH. We didn't think of telling the priest about the Gray Man, but I suppose it don't signify as he has baptized the doll. I'll bolt the door, for maybe the Hag's Son could be kept out altogether now, after the priest putting a blessing on the house. [*Comes and sits at fire opposite Roger.*] Take a doze for yourself to freshen you, and I'll take a doze for myself likewise, till 'tis near the battling hour. Well, 'twill be a great blessing if the Hag's Son fails, for they say if he is once cowarded he's done, and you'll be able to go to work tomorrow for yourself with the help of God—nine shillings a week, I hear, and great scoff at Horan's; then there is that sop to be put in the thatch, and a hoop for that leaking oven, and you must settle the pothooks, Roger, on which to hang the pot.

[CAUTH *and* ROGER *doze. They snore.* CHILD *sings "Oh, then, buttercups and daisies, and daisies and buttercups," to the air of "I'd mourn the hopes that leave me," and curtain falls.*]

SCENE II: *As curtain rises* CAUTH *and* ROGER *are still sleeping. It is within a minute of ten o'clock.*

CHILD [*playing marbles on floor*]. Into my first of nothing, into my second of nothing, into my last of thaw—game! [*Chalks a circle on floor and plays another game.*] Pinked! That's a button won. No! By J, I'm fat! [*Singing.*] "Oh, then, buttercups and daisies," etc. [*Looks at clock.* CAUTH *and* ROGER *wake up.*] Tick-tack! Tick-tack!

CAUTH. Stop, you ashy creature, hasn't the Hag's Son ears would hear a sound like that full fifty miles and more? So stop your tick-tack, for it might be will of God he'd forget the hour and maybe fall asleep.

. [*Clock strikes.*]

CHILD. Dong! Dong! Dong!

VOICE [*outside*]. Open! Open! Open, open, quick!

CAUTH. Stop outside now, you spawn of a mountainy hag! Stop outside now, be off and take your hook!

VOICE [*outside*]. It's me. It's Timmeen Faley. Open in the name of God! The Hag's Son is coming in one swoop down from the Barna hills.

[CAUTH *opens door.* TIMMEEN *comes in.* HAG'S SON *comes down from room.*]

CAUTH [*to* HAG'S SON]. The Hag's Son! You villain, is it in a slit in the window you came, or down a hole in the thatch?

HAG'S SON. Find out if you're fit, and give me none of your vulgar speech. Or is it the way you mistake me for your sweet bolster man? You green and withered female, I might give you a handsome pinch. [*Pinches her arm. She screams. He faces* TIMMEEN.] Good little boy, Timmeen, good little boy. I'd put a finger in your eye, Timmeen Faley.

TIMMEEN. Your talk is bold, Jackeen, the brat from Barna, but your pride might get a fall and your tail be under you when the who shall's finished for the dandy doll.

HAG'S SON. Is it himself will diddle me half-dozing in his chair; or is it herself will diddle me and she quavering after that pinch; or is it you, you little dribbler, will diddle me with only the breath left in you after that spell of the black north wind? Oh, Lord! look at the cut of him, with his little snuffle, his two dead blue eyes flat inside in his head, his little mouth half-open and the couple of ugly teeth showing themselves stuck in his lips; and it's you think yourself a match for me, you mangy puny thing—[*loudly*] a match for me, my chest a plate, my hands as hard as steel, every joint as supple as whalebone, and [*wheeling and turning about*] I've the fingers and toes of a midwife, as my gay old mother says.

TIMMEEN. 'Tis laughing I am, and you not knowing I have twenty points in my favor, and the priest after baptizing the dandy doll.

HAG'S SON [*laughing shrilly*]. A spit for his baptizing, for my old mother, the Hag, took the virtue out of it, and she, the minute he shook the holy water, giving me a puff of her breath in between the two eyes that blew me in a balloon right over the highest peak of the Barna hills. Likewise it's coming herself she is to help her darling son. Ha-ha! is it now you have the points in your favor? Ha-ha! it's now you're getting in dread.

TIMMEEN [*brandishing fist in* HAG'S SON's *face*]. Up to your pus, Jackeen, if I am, up to your pus! I'm as good as yourself, by damned, and I'm ready for the fray!

HAG'S SON. On for the battle, then, for Fontenoy and glory! On for the battle, then, and this is the way to smadher the grace of priest or parson!

TIMMEEN. And this is the way to break the melt in Jackeen, the brat from Barna.

[*They rush at doll. They drag it off table. They wheel about trying to take it from each other. Reënter* PRIEST *and* KEERBY.]

FATHER JAMES. The battle is raging. [*Handing gun to* KEERBY.] Here, hold that gun, till I make the sign of the cross, read from the book, and drive that Hag's Son up the chimley in one mortal flame of fire. [*Reads from book.*] You won't go up the chimley, you won't? Let us see what will come of a clout of a fist.

[*Makes at* HAG'S SON *and misses him.*]

CAUTH. That's the style, your reverence, murder him, ruin him; but keep me from the power of the Hag and I'll spoil him with the broom, I will.

KEERBY [*standing near dresser*]. And I'll make a shy at him with the stock of the gun when he comes around to where I am.

[*The fight continues, all going around in a ring.* CAUTH *and the* PRIEST *make efforts to hit the* HAG'S SON, *who dodges them. Sound of a lively jig being played on a fife outside.*]

CAUTH [*in terror*]. The Hag, the Hag herself! The Hag, the Hag of Barna!

[*Enter* HAG *playing a flute. She is a fantastically dressed old woman.*]

THE HAG [*taking flute from mouth*]. Ha-ha! is it flamming my little boy they are? [*Hits* CAUTH *with flute.*] Take that, old snotty nose! go wash your rotten rags and grease your creaking bones!

CAUTH. I'm kilt!

THE HAG [*hitting* PRIEST]. Ha-ha, shiny green coat, I have slaughtered a flay on the nape of your neck! [*Hits him again.*] Take that on the small of your back and scratch yourself!

FATHER JAMES [*itching himself*]. Botheration! In the name of the Father!

THE HAG [*to her son*]. Fight away, my gamey boy; fight away, my hearty. Your mother is up to your ear—[*singing*] and we'll rise a grand song and we'll rise a grand tune, going back to our home in Barna.

FATHER JAMES [*snatching broom from* CAUTH]. Give me that broom; no haunted hag shall daunt me; fight, slash, and batter—the power of man shall conquer the power—the power of the witch! [*They go round in a ring as before, fighting.*]

ROGER [*rising suddenly from seat near fire*]. They are treenahayla and striking wild. Priest, Cauth, and Keerby, it's walloping Timmeen ye are, and thinking you're striking the Hag and the Hag's Son. Divilment, divilment, you're blinked by divilment! Be careful in the name of God! will ye be careful in the name of God! [HAG'S SON *captures doll.*] He has it! Lord, he has it! Sure he had to have it, and where's the good in talking, and all to no use, for it's foredoomed I was, it's foredoomed I was. [HAG'S SON *pulls out windpipe and blows through it.*] But isn't it fierce all the same, and wherefore should this wrong thing be? But to hell with everything, I don't care, and by damned I'll have a goose! [*Enter* GRAY MAN *unperceived. He goes to other side of table opposite* ROGER.] Or a duck, a fat duck—I must have a duck! [*Moving jaws as if in eating.*] No, by Jabers, it's a turkey I must have, a good plump turkey! Oh, Lord, the turkey and the gravy fine! [*Sees* GRAY MAN.] Ah, the Gray Man, the Gray Man!

[GRAY MAN, *with grim smile, points to bottle.* ROGER *takes hold of it slowly. He puts it to his mouth, shaking like an aspen. He drinks. An explosion. Semi-darkness on stage. Noise as of a struggle. Dim figures of* GRAY MAN, ROGER, HAG, *and* HAG'S SON *seen going out,* ROGER *being dragged along. Total darkness.* HAG *and* HAG'S SON *heard singing* "My Bonnie Irish Boy." *Song dies away in distance. Stage clears.*]

FATHER JAMES. Is anyone kilt?

KEERBY. 'Tis a wonder we aren't and all devils here.

FATHER JAMES. Give me that gun, you awkward man.

KEERBY. Faith, the gun is innocent, whatever that bottle did he had in his mouth, for, after the report, didn't the bottom of it open like it would on a hinge, and what did I see inside but a batch of the finest horses, black as jet, with red eyes on them, prancing and pawing, fit to be off. The next minute what happened but out they galloped to me in a bully army, and captains, generals, soldiers, with their cannons, swords, and carabines, all in full bloom for war. Faith, this is no house for an honest man. [*Exit.*]

CAUTH [*rising as if in pain, from prostrate condition*]. Bad scran to him! it's scratched and ruinated I am on account of him, and there isn't a screed on me but is destroyed and tore. [*Looking about her vacantly.*] But the meila murdhre is over, and there isn't a trace of himself on the floor. The doll gone too; and mustn't it have been the rotten doll itself, when your reverence couldn't save it by the power of your calling, and the grace drawn down from the holy heavens above?

FATHER JAMES. 'Tis mysterious surely, and fantastic strange. Well, there's no more to be done, and I might as well be following Keerby.

[*Reënter* KEERBY.]

KEERBY. Your geese is safe, your reverence, for it's the wonderful thing entirely I now have seen. And the Bay of Doon that's ten miles distant looked as near to me as the cabbage haggart outside, and the three Gray Men were standing on the rock holding up an almighty torch that lit up all the black land lying to the east; and following the light didn't I see Roger being carried away by the Hag and the Son of the Hag. Riding on two Spanish asses they were, holding him between them by a whisker each, and his whiskers were the length of six feet you'd think, and his nose was the length of six feet you'd think, and his eyes were the size of turnips bulging outside his head. Galloping like the wind they were, through the pass of the Barna mountains, sweeping him along with them, forever and ever, to their woeful den in the heart of the Barna hills.

GROUP III

Plays of the Peasant Character: Tragedy

THE heritage of Ireland throughout its history has been the heritage of sorrow. Even the land, with its lonely roads, gray mists, and sudden fitful winds, attests an overhanging melancholy which must inevitably affect the peasant character. The country itself seems unable to dispel the memory of bitter wars, famine, and successive national disasters that have drained the blood but not the spirit of the people. It seems impossible that a nation could have survived the unbelievable hardships confronting it from the first Danish invasions to the civil war. The first two tragedies which follow are embedded in this sorrowful land and cry aloud its sorrowful name. They give us a composite picture of man's unending struggle against the land and the sea which at once offer life and death to him.

Because sadness and loneliness are paramount emotions enshrouding the Celtic spirit, we find that the sincerest utterance the Irish have is in the voice which sings of these emotions. And among the many who have written of Irish woe, John M. Synge in his *Riders to the Sea* cleaves deepest and comes nearest to the unhappy heart of the nation. And not of the Irish nation only. The spirit moving in old Maurya in her cottage on the grim dark island of Inishmaan where she lived is a fragment of the nobility springing from the hearts of all mothers who have given their loved ones to sudden and inescapable doom. That spirit transcends the lowly Aran cottage and reveals itself in universal terms in high as well as humble places where it becomes the common possession of all who are great and good in the face of suffering.

The artistic completeness of *Riders to the Sea* is manifest in every line. Those who quibble at its lack of length and contend that this defect militates against it in comparison with the classical drama confess the error of measuring the greatness of the tragic spirit by the number of lines used to contain it. There may be other arguments to show that it is inferior to the Greek tragedies but certainly its brevity is not one. What Synge was most intent on emphasizing was the fact that to these people living under primitive circumstances in a barren portion of our world, there came the philosophic peace of absolute frustration and, in the case of the mother, the ultimate survival of the spirit after receiving its utmost scourge of pain and heartbreak. And we are purged by pity and terror with watching them, knowing that their destiny matters nothing except to the handful of friends who share their sorrow. The poignant isolation of the tragedy and the terrible hardness of the setting contrasted with the yearning helplessness of the men and women set against it are added reminders of the conscious effort Synge made to intensify the pathos of the play by underlining its insignificance.

It is hard to say whether Irish landscape or Irish peasant life holds the more prominent place in *Riders to the Sea,* so closely has Synge joined them together. The rhythm of the keening of the swaying women who come to mourn Maurya's last son echoes the moaning and the beating of the relentless sea. Their speeches are most often concerned with the trivial material necessity, suffused with commonplace references to familiar and humble things which fill their everyday lives. These little things they talk about, like "the pig with the black feet," afford them some small comfort at the same time that they point the peasants' inability to cope with the abstract issues of the heavy, nameless fate which threatens them. Notice Maurya's inarticulate suspense and uneasiness at the beginning of the play and contrast it with the peacefulness of a later scene which shows her calmly making the ritual with holy water; and the hush of her voice saying near the end, "They're all gone now, and there isn't anything more the sea can do to me." It is thus she strikes the keynote of the play. To have heard these lovely, moving lines spoken by the players of the old Abbey Company, many of whom knew and loved the writer of them, with all the beauty and rhythm breathed into the play by that sorrowful and gentle man, was one of the richest experiences the theater of yesterday had to offer.

Just as the sea was the real protagonist in Synge's tragedy,

so the land is in Colum's. It may be necessary to explain
why I have placed what he calls an "Agrarian Comedy" in
this category. In a note to his *Three Plays*, he tells us that *The
Land* "was written to celebrate the redemption of the soil in
Ireland—an event made possible by the Land Act of 1903.
This event, as it represented the passing of Irish acres from
an alien landlordism, was considered to be of national importance." Another issue he dealt with was the alarming
wholesale emigration of the best Irish manhood and woman-
hood to the hospitable and profitable freedom of America.
Now, to the Irish people, these are not humorous subjects,
nor are they treated as such in the play. The implications and
overtones involved in the Cosgar-Douras relationship are serious, or at the least, tragi-comic. There is no light laughter
at the end, no feeling of self-satisfied mirth on the part of the
listener which greets him at the end of many Irish comedies.
There is rather a sad smile as we realize that Ellen and Matt
are justified in wanting to break away from the home and
the soil which offers them so little against the future compared to the romantic America of their dreams. We find
also, in the play, traces of what Colum calls the "human
comedy," a term which has always had a sardonic connota-
tion, in the characters of the indecisive Matt and of the stern
father whose pride and stubbornness close his mouth against
any word which might betray his sorrow at the thought of
his last son leaving him. We detect it also in the extreme independence of Ellen and in her selfish determination to as-
sert her individuality, and in the mimic Cornelius and the
stupid drudge who will become his wife. But in final analysis the play represents a tragic whole, although the parts
which make it up are, paradoxically enough, not tragic but
humorous. We are affected in much the same way as we are
by Ibsen's *The Wild Duck*. At the end of both plays we do
not know whether to be moved to sadness or to mirth, so
cunningly are these allied emotions aroused in us. Essentially, however, the play is serious. Murtagh Cosgar, hard,
with the hardness of a gnarled tree, and grown to the soil
which sustains him, is a not unfamiliar figure today in certain
parts of New England. His closest American dramatic counterpart is Ephraim Cabot in Eugene O'Neill's *Desire under
the Elms*. Ephraim, too, remains unmoved when his strong-

est sons leave him, for the same reason that Murtagh does—because the land has destroyed all feeling of affection for everything except itself.

The conflict between old and new Ireland is here also. It is always a favorite subject with Irish dramatists, Lennox Robinson having handled the theme in his skillful manner in *Harvest*. Another conflict to which Colum calls our attention is that between the family and the individual, a conflict here based on a custom prevailing to this day in Ireland, the power the head of the family has to regulate the marriages of his children. It is the custom for the girl to bring to her husband at the time of marriage as great a "fortune" as she can accumulate. The parent naturally selects the girl with the most money, although the son may have a different criterion. The situation becomes complex if the son has idealistic views regarding the comparative value of money and beauty. Variations on this theme serve as the starting point, the exciting force, in many plays of the Irish peasantry because they reveal with little effort the penuriousness and cupidity of a certain type of Irish farmer. *The Land* is too local and too timely to be set against *Riders to the Sea,* and it partakes but little of the latter's tragic stature. It has, nevertheless, a fitting place in this representation as a serious play dealing forcefully and intelligently with a grave social problem.

Birthright, written by an Irish schoolmaster who has contributed work of an excellent artistic standard to the drama of Ireland and America, is one of the best examples of modern domestic tragedy containing that which is usually reserved for and indiscriminately used as a *tour de force* in melodrama. It is the physical conflict between two principal characters at the catastrophic final curtain. The climax of this final scene, toward which the cunningly arranged plot leads, affords a striking contrast to the passive anticlimaxes in *Riders to the Sea* and *The Land*. The plot itself hinges on another curious custom. This custom decrees that the oldest son in a family will inherit, as his birthright, his father's property. However, in the play, the father considers the younger son, Shane, far more deserving of the land than his sporting elder brother. Another complication arises as the story reveals the mother's favoritism for her first-born and the father's for the son who must leave the farm. The play treats again the question of the individual circumstance refusing to be bound by and rebelling against universally accepted tradition.

Murray is a sympathetic realist. His characters are clearly and amply defined. The pitiful figure of Mrs. Morrissey stands out as one paralleling her namesake, Maurya, in *Riders to the Sea* because, in final analysis, she is the one who has to bear the burden of sorrow for her two sons. As may be self-evident from these two plays, this figure of the suffering Mother is a favorite with Irish authors and audiences.

There is another interesting fact about the Irish people which is touched upon in *Birthright*. They are enthusiastic lovers of sport and are prone to a national hero-worship for their brilliant athletes. Bat Morrissey's attitude toward the throngs who bear Hugh home in triumph is not the attitude of the younger generation. But then, like Murtagh Cosgar, he is the representative of that type of peasant who believes that nothing of worth can come from an activity which gives its participants pleasure. The accidental death of the mare, unpremeditated of course by the otherwise harmless crowd, only increases his bitterness against the elder son and moves him to the final decision to keep Shane on the land, which, with certain other coincidences, brings about the catastrophe. Peasant prejudice, narrowness of mind, and the capacity for violent emotional outbursts lie at the roots of the tragedy, and, on top of all these there is that ever-recurrent characteristic of the Irish mind—the inability or unwillingness to arbitrate and compromise.

RIDERS TO THE SEA [1]

A PLAY IN ONE ACT

by John Millington Synge

PERSONS

MAURYA, *an old woman*
BARTLEY, *her son*
CATHLEEN, *her daughter*
NORA, *a younger daughter*
MEN AND WOMEN

SCENE: *An Island off the west of Ireland. Cottage kitchen, with nets, oilskins, spinning wheel, some new boards standing by the wall, etc.* CATHLEEN, *a girl of about twenty, finishes kneading cake, and puts it down in the pot-oven by the fire; then wipes her hands, and begins to spin at the wheel.* NORA, *a young girl, puts her head in at the door.*

NORA [*in a low voice*]. Where is she?

CATHLEEN. She's lying down, God help her, and may be sleeping, if she's able.

[NORA *comes in softly, and takes a bundle from under her shawl.*]

CATHLEEN [*spinning the wheel rapidly*]. What is it you have?

NORA. The young priest is after bringing them. It's a shirt and a plain stocking were got off a drowned man in Donegal.

[CATHLEEN *stops her wheel with a sudden movement, and leans out to listen.*]

NORA. We're to find out if it's Michael's they are, some time herself will be down looking by the sea.

CATHLEEN. How would they be Michael's, Nora? How would he go the length of that way to the far north?

[1] *First performed at the Molesworth Hall, Dublin, February 25th, 1904.*

Nora. The young priest says he's known the like of it. "If it's Michael's they are," says he, "you can tell herself he's got a clean burial by the grace of God, and if they're not his, let no one say a word about them, for she'll be getting her death," says he, "with crying and lamenting."

[*The door which* Nora *half closed is blown open by a gust of wind.*]

Cathleen [*looking out anxiously*]. Did you ask him would he stop Bartley going this day with the horses to the Galway fair?

Nora. "I won't stop him," says he, "but let you not be afraid. Herself does be saying prayers half through the night, and the Almighty God won't leave her destitute," says he, "with no son living."

Cathleen. Is the sea bad by the white rocks, Nora?

Nora. Middling bad, God help us. There's a great roaring in the west, and it's worse it'll be getting when the tide's turned to the wind. [*She goes over to the table with the bundle.*] Shall I open it now?

Cathleen. Maybe she'd wake up on us, and come in before we'd done. [*Coming to the table.*] It's a long time we'll be, and the two of us crying.

Nora [*goes to the inner door and listens*]. She's moving about on the bed. She'll be coming in a minute.

Cathleen. Give me the ladder, and I'll put them up in the turf-loft, the way she won't know of them at all, and maybe when the tide turns she'll be going down to see would he be floating from the east.

[*They put the ladder against the gable of the chimney;* Cathleen *goes up a few steps and hides the bundle in the turf-loft.* Maurya *comes from the inner room.*]

Maurya [*looking up at* Cathleen *and speaking querulously*]. Isn't it turf enough you have for this day and evening?

Cathleen. There's a cake baking at the fire for a short space [*Throwing down the turf.*] and Bartley will want it when the tide turns if he goes to Connemara.

[Nora *picks up the turf and puts it round the pot-oven.*]

Maurya [*sitting down on a stool at the fire.*] He won't go this day with the wind rising from the south and west. He won't go this day, for the young priest will stop him surely.

Nora. He'll not stop him, mother, and I heard Eamon Simon and Stephen Pheety and Colum Shawn saying he would go.

Maurya. Where is he itself?

Nora. He went down to see would there be another boat sailing in the week, and I'm thinking it won't be long till he's here now, for the tide's turning at the green head, and the hooker's tacking from the east.

Cathleen. I hear some one passing the big stones.

Nora [*looking out*]. He's coming now, and he in a hurry.

Bartley [*comes in and looks round the room. Speaking sadly and quietly*]. Where is the bit of new rope, Cathleen, was bought in Connemara?

Cathleen [*coming down*]. Give it to him, Nora; it's on a nail by the white boards. I hung it up this morning, for the pig with the black feet was eating it.

Nora [*giving him a rope*]. Is that it, Bartley?

Maurya. You'd do right to leave that rope, Bartley, hanging by the boards. [Bartley *takes the rope*.] It will be wanting in this place, I'm telling you, if Michael is washed up tomorrow morning, or the next morning, or any morning in the week, for it's a deep grave we'll make him by the grace of God.

Bartley [*beginning to work with the rope*]. I've no halter the way I can ride down on the mare, and I must go now quickly. This is the one boat going for two weeks or beyond it, and the fair will be a good fair for horses I heard them saying below.

Maurya. It's a hard thing they'll be saying below if the body is washed up and there's no man in it to make the coffin, and I after giving a big price for the finest white boards you'd find in Connemara. [*She looks round at the boards.*]

Bartley. How would it be washed up, and we after looking each day for nine days, and a strong wind blowing a while back from the west and south?

Maurya. If it wasn't found itself, that wind is raising the sea, and there was a star up against the moon, and it rising in the night. If it was a hundred horses, or a thousand horses you had itself, what is the price of a thousand horses against a son where there is one son only?

BARTLEY [*working at the halter, to* CATHLEEN]. Let you go down each day, and see the sheep aren't jumping in on the rye, and if the jobber comes you can sell the pig with the black feet if there is a good price going.

MAURYA. How would the like of her get a good price for a pig?

BARTLEY [*to* CATHLEEN]. If the west wind holds with the last bit of the moon let you and Nora get up weed enough for another cock for the kelp. It's hard set we'll be from this day with no one in it but one man to work.

MAURYA. It's hard set we'll be surely the day you're drownd'd with the rest. What way will I live and the girls with me, and I an old woman looking for the grave?

[BARTLEY *lays down the halter, takes off his old coat, and puts on a newer one of the same flannel.*]

BARTLEY [*to* NORA]. Is she coming to the pier?

NORA [*looking out*]. She's passing the green head and letting fall her sails.

BARTLEY [*getting his purse and tobacco*]. I'll have half an hour to go down, and you'll see me coming again in two days, or in three days, or maybe in four days if the wind is bad.

MAURYA [*turning round to the fire, and putting her shawl over her head*]. Isn't it a hard and cruel man won't hear a word from an old woman, and she holding him from the sea?

CATHLEEN. It's the life of a young man to be going on the sea, and who would listen to an old woman with one thing and she saying it over?

BARTLEY [*taking the halter*]. I must go now quickly. I'll ride down on the red mare, and the gray pony'll run behind me. . . . The blessing of God on you. [*He goes out.*]

MAURYA [*crying out as he is in the door*]. He's gone now, God spare us, and we'll not see him again. He's gone now, and when the black night is falling I'll have no son left me in the world.

CATHLEEN. Why wouldn't you give him your blessing and he looking round in the door? Isn't it sorrow enough is on everyone in this house without your sending him out with an unlucky word behind him, and a hard word in his ear?

[MAURYA *takes up the tongs and begins raking the fire aimlessly without looking round.*]

NORA [*turning towards her*]. You're taking away the turf from the cake.

CATHLEEN [*crying out*]. The Son of God forgive us, Nora, we're after forgetting his bit of bread. [*She comes over to the fire.*]

NORA. And it's destroyed he'll be going till dark night, and he after eating nothing since the sun went up.

CATHLEEN [*turning the cake out of the oven*]. It's destroyed he'll be, surely. There's no sense left on any person in a house where an old woman will be talking forever.

[MAURYA *sways herself on her stool.*]

CATHLEEN [*cutting off some of the bread and rolling it in a cloth; to* MAURYA]. Let you go down now to the spring well and give him this and he passing. You'll see him then and the dark word will be broken, and you can say "God speed you," the way he'll be easy in his mind.

MAURYA [*taking the bread*]. Will I be in it as soon as himself?

CATHLEEN. If you go now quickly.

MAURYA [*standing up unsteadily*]. It's hard set I am to walk.

CATHLEEN [*looking at her anxiously*]. Give her the stick, Nora, or maybe she'll slip on the big stones.

NORA. What stick?

CATHLEEN. The stick Michael brought from Connemara.

MAURYA [*taking a stick* NORA *gives her*]. In the big world the old people do be leaving things after them for their sons and children, but in this place it is the young men do be leaving things behind for them that do be old. [*She goes out slowly.*]

[NORA *goes over to the ladder.*]

CATHLEEN. Wait, Nora, maybe she'd turn back quickly. She's that sorry, God help her, you wouldn't know the thing she'd do.

NORA. Is she gone round by the bush?

CATHLEEN [*looking out*]. She's gone now. Throw it down quickly, for the Lord knows when she'll be out of it again.

NORA [*getting the bundle from the loft*]. The young priest said he'd be passing tomorrow, and we might go down and speak to him below if it's Michael's they are surely.

CATHLEEN [*taking the bundle*]. Did he say what way they were found?

NORA [*coming down*]. "There were two men," says he, "and they rowing round with poteen before the cocks crowed, and the oar of one of them caught the body, and they passing the black cliffs of the north."

CATHLEEN [*trying to open the bundle*]. Give me a knife, Nora, the string's perished with the salt water, and there's a black knot on it you wouldn't loosen in a week.

NORA [*giving her a knife*]. I've heard tell it was a long way to Donegal.

CATHLEEN [*cutting the string*]. It is surely. There was a man in here a while ago—the man sold us that knife—and he said if you set off walking from the rocks beyond, it would be seven days you'd be in Donegal.

NORA. And what time would a man take, and he floating?

[CATHLEEN *opens the bundle and takes out a bit of a stocking. They look at them eagerly.*]

CATHLEEN [*in a low voice*]. The Lord spare us, Nora! isn't it a queer hard thing to say if it's his they are surely?

NORA. I'll get his shirt off the hook the way we can put the one flannel on the other. [*She looks through some clothes hanging in the corner.*] It's not with them, Cathleen, and where will it be?

CATHLEEN. I'm thinking Bartley put it on him in the morning, for his own shirt was heavy with the salt in it. [*Pointing to the corner.*] There's a bit of a sleeve was of the same stuff. Give me that and it will do.

[NORA *brings it to her and they compare the flannel.*]

CATHLEEN. It's the same stuff, Nora; but if it is itself aren't there great rolls of it in the shops of Galway, and isn't it many another man may have a shirt of it as well as Michael himself?

NORA [*who has taken up the stocking and counted the stitches, crying out*]. It's Michael, Cathleen, it's Michael; God spare his soul, and what will herself say when she hears this story, and Bartley on the sea?

CATHLEEN [*taking the stocking*]. It's a plain stocking.

NORA. It's the second one of the third pair I knitted, and I put up three score stitches, and I dropped four of them.

CATHLEEN [*counts the stitches*]. It's that number is in it. [*Crying out.*] Ah, Nora, isn't it a bitter thing to think of him floating that way to the far north, and no one to keen him but the black hags that do be flying on the sea?

NORA [*swinging herself round, and throwing out her arms on the clothes*]. And isn't it a pitiful thing when there is nothing left of a man who was a great rower and fisher, but a bit of an old shirt and a plain stocking?

CATHLEEN [*after an instant*]. Tell me is herself coming, Nora? I hear a little sound on the path.

NORA [*looking out*]. She is, Cathleen. She's coming up to the door.

CATHLEEN. Put these things away before she'll come in. Maybe it's easier she'll be after giving her blessing to Bartley, and we won't let on we've heard anything the time he's on the sea.

NORA [*helping* CATHLEEN *to close the bundle*]. We'll put them here in the corner. [*They put them into a hole in the chimney corner.* CATHLEEN *goes back to the spinning wheel.*]

NORA. Will she see it was crying I was?

CATHLEEN. Keep your back to the door the way the light'll not be on you.

[NORA *sits down at the chimney corner, with her back to the door.* MAURYA *comes in very slowly, without looking at the girls, and goes over to her stool at the other side of the fire. The cloth with the bread is still in her hand. The girls look at each other, and* NORA *points to the bundle of bread.*]

CATHLEEN [*after spinning for a moment*]. You didn't give him his bit of bread?

[MAURYA *begins to keen softly, without turning round.*]

CATHLEEN. Did you see him riding down? [MAURYA *goes on keening.*]

CATHLEEN [*a little impatiently*]. God forgive you; isn't it a better thing to raise your voice and tell what you seen, than to be making lamentation for a thing that's done? Did you see Bartley, I'm saying to you.

MAURYA [*with a weak voice*]. My heart's broken from this day.

CATHLEEN [*as before*]. Did you see Bartley?

MAURYA. I seen the fearfulest thing.

CATHLEEN [*leaves her wheel and looks out*]. God forgive

you; he's riding the mare now over the green head, and the gray pony behind him.

MAURYA [*starts, so that her shawl falls back from her head and shows her white tossed hair. With a frightened voice*]. The gray pony behind him.

CATHLEEN [*coming to the fire*]. What is it ails you, at all?

MAURYA [*speaking very slowly*]. I've seen the fearfulest thing any person has seen, since the day Bride Dara seen the dead man with the child in his arms.

CATHLEEN AND NORA. Uah.

[*They crouch down in front of the old woman at the fire.*]

NORA. Tell us what it is you seen.

MAURYA. I went down to the spring well, and I stood there saying a prayer to myself. Then Bartley came along, and he riding on the red mare with the gray pony behind him. [*She puts up her hands, as if to hide something from her eyes.*] The Son of God spare us, Nora!

CATHLEEN. What is it you seen?

MAURYA. I seen Michael himself.

CATHLEEN [*speaking softly*]. You did not, mother. It wasn't Michael you seen, for his body is after being found in the far north, and he's got a clean burial by the grace of God.

MAURYA [*a little defiantly*]. I'm after seeing him this day, and he riding and galloping. Bartley came first on the red mare; and I tried to say "God speed you," but something choked the words in my throat. He went by quickly; and "the blessing of God on you," says he, and I could say nothing. I looked up then, and I crying, at the gray pony, and there was Michael upon it—with fine clothes on him, and new shoes on his feet.

CATHLEEN [*begins to keen*]. It's destroyed we are from this day. It's destroyed, surely.

NORA. Didn't the young priest say the Almighty God wouldn't leave her destitute with no son living?

MAURYA [*in a low voice, but clearly*]. It's little the like of him knows of the sea. . . . Bartley will be lost now, and let you call in Eamon and make me a good coffin out of the white boards, for I won't live after them. I've had a husband, and a husband's father, and six sons in this house—six fine men, though it was a hard birth I had with every one of them and they coming to the world—and some of them were found and some of them were not found, but they're gone now the lot of them. . . . There were Stephen, and Shawn, were lost in the great wind, and found after in the Bay of Gregory of the Golden Mouth, and carried up the two of them on the one plank, and in by that door. [*She pauses for a moment, the girls start as if they heard something through the door that is half open behind them.*]

NORA [*in a whisper*]. Did you hear that, Cathleen? Did you hear a noise in the northeast?

CATHLEEN [*in a whisper*]. There's some one after crying out by the seashore.

MAURYA [*continues without hearing anything*]. There was Sheamus and his father, and his own father again, were lost in a dark night, and not a stick or sign was seen of them when the sun went up. There was Patch after was drowned out of a curagh that turned over. I was sitting here with Bartley, and he a baby, lying on my two knees, and I seen two women, and three women, and four women coming in, and they crossing themselves, and not saying a word. I looked out then, and there were men coming after them, and they holding a thing in the half of a red sail, and water dripping out of it— it was a dry day, Nora—and leaving a track to the door. [*She pauses again with her hand stretched out towards the door. It opens softly and old women begin to come in, crossing themselves on the threshold, and kneeling down in front of the stage with red petticoats over their heads.*]

MAURYA [*half in a dream, to* CATHLEEN]. Is it Patch, or Michael, or what is it at all?

CATHLEEN. Michael is after being found in the far north, and when he is found there how could he be here in this place?

MAURYA. There does be a power of young men floating round in the sea, and what way would they know if it was Michael they had, or another man like him, for when a man is nine days in the sea, and the wind blowing, it's hard set his own mother would be to say what man was it.

CATHLEEN. It's Michael, God spare him, for they're after sending us a bit of his clothes from the far north. [*She reaches out and hands* MAURYA *the clothes that belonged to* MICHAEL.

MAURYA *stands up slowly, and takes them in her hands.*
NORA *looks out.*]

NORA. They're carrying a thing among them and there's
water dripping out of it and leaving a track by the big stones.

CATHLEEN [*in a whisper to the women who have come
in*]. Is it Bartley it is?

ONE OF THE WOMEN. It is surely, God rest his soul.

[*Two younger women come in and pull out the table. Then
men carry in the body of* BARTLEY, *laid on a plank, with a
bit of a sail over it, and lay it on the table.*]

CATHLEEN [*to the women, as they are doing so*]. What
way was he drowned?

ONE OF THE WOMEN. The gray pony knocked him into
the sea, and he was washed out where there is a great surf
on the white rocks.

[MAURYA *has gone over and knelt down at the head of
the table. The women are keening softly and swaying themselves with a slow movement.* CATHLEEN *and* NORA *kneel
at the other end of the table. The men kneel near the door.*]

MAURYA [*raising her head and speaking as if she did not
see the people around her*]. They're all gone now, and there
isn't anything more the sea can do to me. . . . I'll have no
call now to be up crying and praying when the wind breaks
from the south, and you can hear the surf is in the east,
and the surf is in the west, making a great stir with the two
noises, and they hitting one on the other. I'll have no call
now to be going down and getting Holy Water in the dark
nights after Samhain, and I won't care what way the sea
is when the other women will be keening. [*To* NORA.] Give
me the Holy Water, Nora, there's a small sup still on the
dresser.

[NORA *gives it to her.*]

MAURYA [*drops* MICHAEL'S *clothes across* BARTLEY'S *feet,
and sprinkles the Holy Water over him*]. It isn't that I
haven't prayed for you, Bartley, to the Almighty God. It
isn't that I haven't said prayers in the dark night till you
wouldn't know what I'd be saying; but it's a great rest I'll
have now, and it's time surely. It's a great rest I'll have now,
and great sleeping in the long nights after Samhain, if it's
only a bit of wet flour we do have to eat, and maybe a fish

that would be stinking. [*She kneels down again, crossing herself, and saying prayers under her breath.*]

CATHLEEN [*to an old man*]. Maybe yourself and Eamon would make a coffin when the sun rises. We have fine white boards herself bought, God help her, thinking Michael would be found, and I have a new cake you can eat while you'll be working.

THE OLD MAN [*looking at the boards*]. Are there nails with them?

CATHLEEN. There are not, Colum; we didn't think of the nails.

ANOTHER MAN. It's a great wonder she wouldn't think of the nails, and all the coffins she's seen made already.

CATHLEEN. It's getting old she is, and broken.

[MAURYA *stands up again very slowly and spreads out the pieces of* MICHAEL's *clothes beside the body, sprinkling them with the last of the Holy Water.*]

NORA [*in a whisper to* CATHLEEN]. She's quiet now and easy; but the day Michael was drowned you could hear her crying out from this to the spring well. It's fonder she was of Michael, and would anyone have thought that?

CATHLEEN [*slowly and clearly*]. An old woman will be soon tired with anything she will do, and isn't it nine days herself is after crying and keening, and making great sorrow in the house?

MAURYA [*puts the empty cup mouth downwards on the table, and lays her hands together on* BARTLEY's *feet*]. They're all together this time, and the end is come. May the Almighty God have mercy on Bartley's soul, and on Michael's soul, and on the souls of Sheamus and Patch, and Stephen and Shawn [*bending her head*]; and may He have mercy on my soul, Nora, and on the soul of everyone is left living in the world. [*She pauses, and the keen rises a little more loudly from the women, then sinks away.*]

MAURYA [*continuing*]. Michael has a clean burial in the far north, by the grace of the Almighty God. Bartley will have a fine coffin out of the white boards, and a deep grave surely. What more can we want than that? No man at all can be living forever, and we must be satisfied. [*She kneels down again and the curtain falls slowly.*]

THE LAND

AN AGRARIAN COMEDY IN THREE ACTS

by Padraic Colum

CHARACTERS

MURTAGH COSGAR, *a farmer*
MATT, *his son*
SALLY, *his daughter*
MARTIN DOURAS, *a farmer*
CORNELIUS, *his son*
ELLEN, *his daughter*
A group of men
A group of boys and girls

The scene is laid in the Irish Midlands, present time.

ACT I

SCENE: *The interior of* MURTAGH COSGAR'S. *It is a large flagged kitchen with the entrance on the right. The dresser is below the entrance. There is a large fireplace in the back, and a room door to the left of the fireplace; the harness-rack is between room door and fireplace. The yard door is on the left. The table is down from the room door. There are benches around fireplace.*

It is the afternoon of a May day. SALLY COSGAR *is kneeling near the entrance chopping up cabbage leaves with a kitchen knife. She is a girl of twenty-five, dark, heavily built, with the expression of a half-awakened creature. She is coarsely dressed, and has a sacking apron. She is quick at work, and rapid and impetuous in speech. She is talking to herself.*

SALLY. Oh, you may go on grunting, yourself and your litter, it won't put me a bit past my own time. You oul'

171

black baste of a sow, sure I'm slaving to you all the spring. We'll be getting rid of yourself and your litter soon enough, and may the devil get you when we lose you.

[CORNELIUS *comes to the door. He is a tall young man with a slight stoop. His manners are solemn, and his expression somewhat vacant.*]

CORNELIUS. Good morrow, Sally. May you have the good of the day. [*He comes in.*]

SALLY [*impetuously*]. Ah, God reward you, Cornelius Douras, for coming in. I'm that busy keeping food to a sow and a litter of pigs that I couldn't get beyond the gate to see anyone.

CORNELIUS [*solemnly*]. You're a good girl, Sally. You're not like some I know. There are girls in this parish who never put hands to a thing till evening, when the boys do be coming in. Then they begin to stir themselves the way they'll be thought busy and good about a house.

SALLY [*pleased and beginning to chop again with renewed energy*]. Oh, it's true indeed for you, Cornelius. There are girls that be decking themselves, and sporting are themselves all day.

CORNELIUS. I may say that I come over to your father's, Murtagh Cosgar's house, this morning, thinking to meet the men.

SALLY. What men, Cornelius Douras?

CORNELIUS. Them that are going to meet the landlord's people with an offer for the land. We're not buying ourselves, unfortunately, but this is a great day—the day of the redemption, my father calls it—and I'd like to have some hand in the work if it was only to say a few words to the men.

SALLY. It's a wonder, Martin, your father isn't on the one errand with you.

CORNELIUS. We came out together, but the priest stopped father and us on the road. Father Bartley wanted his advice, I suppose. Ah, it's a pity the men won't have some one like my father with them! He was in jail for the Cause. Besides, he's a well-discoursed man, and a reading man, and, moreover, a man with a classical knowledge of English, Latin, and the Hibernian vernacular.

[MARTIN DOURAS *comes in. He is a man of about sixty,*

with a refined, scholarly look. His manner is subdued and nervous. He has a stoop, and is clean-shaven.]

CORNELIUS. I was just telling Sally here what a great day it is, father.

MARTIN DOURAS. Ay, it's a great day, no matter what our own troubles may be. I should be going home again. [*He takes a newspaper out of his pocket, and leaves it on the table.*]

CORNELIUS. Wait for the men, father.

MARTIN DOURAS. Maybe they'll be here soon. Is Murtagh in, Sally?

[CORNELIUS *takes the paper up, and begins to read it.*]

SALLY. He's down at the bottoms, Martin.

MARTIN DOURAS. He's going to Arvach Fair, maybe.

SALLY. He is in troth.

MARTIN DOURAS. I'll be asking him for a lift. He'll be going to the Fair when he come back from the lawyer's, I suppose?

SALLY. Ay, he'll be going tonight. [*She gathers the chopped cabbage into her apron, and goes to the door.*]

SALLY [*at the door*]. Cornelius.

[CORNELIUS *puts down the paper, and goes to the door.* SALLY *goes out.*]

MARTIN DOURAS. Cornelius!

[CORNELIUS *goes to* MARTIN.]

SALLY [*outside*]. Cornelius, give me a hand with this.

[CORNELIUS *turns again.*]

MARTIN DOURAS. Cornelius, I want to speak to you.

[CORNELIUS *goes to him.*]

MARTIN DOURAS. There is something on my mind, Cornelius.

CORNELIUS. What is it, father?

MARTIN DOURAS. It's about our Ellen. Father Bartley gave me news for her. "I've heard of a school that'll suit Ellen," says he. "It's in the County Leitrim."

CORNELIUS. If it was in Dublin itself, Ellen is qualified to take it on. And won't it be grand to have one of our family teaching in a school?

MARTIN DOURAS [*with a sigh*]. I wouldn't stand in her way, Cornelius; I wouldn't stand in her way. But won't it be a poor thing for an old man like me to have no one to discourse with in the long evenings? For when I'm talking with you, Cornelius, I feel like a boy who lends back all the marbles he's won, and plays again, just for the sake of the game.

CORNELIUS. We were in dread of Ellen going to America at one time, and then she went in for the school. Now Matt Cosgar may keep her from the school. Maybe we won't have to go further than this house to see Ellen.

MARTIN DOURAS. I'm hoping it'll be like that; but I'm in dread that Murtagh Cosgar will never agree to it. He's a hard man to deal with. Still Murtagh and myself will be on the long road tonight, and we might talk of it. I'm afeard of Ellen going.

CORNELIUS [*at the door*]. It's herself that's coming here, father.

MARTIN DOURAS. Maybe she has heard the news and is coming to tell us.

[ELLEN *comes in. She has a shawl over her head which she lays aside. She is about twenty-five, slightly built, nervous, emotional.*]

ELLEN. Is it only ourselves that's here?

MARTIN DOURAS. Only ourselves. Did you get any news to bring you over, Ellen?

ELLEN. No news. It was the shine of the day that brought me out; and I was thinking, too, of the girls that are going to America in the morning, and that made me restless.

[MARTIN *and* CORNELIUS *look significantly at each other.*]

MARTIN DOURAS. And did you see Matt, Ellen?

ELLEN. He was in the field and I coming up; but I did not wait for him, as I don't want people to see us together. [*Restlessly.*] I don't know how I can come into this house, for it's always like Murtagh Cosgar. There's nothing of Matt in it at all. If Matt would come away. There are little laborers' houses by the side of the road. Many's the farmer's son became a laborer for the sake of a woman he cared for!

CORNELIUS. And are you not thinking about the school at all, Ellen?

ELLEN. I'll hear about it some time, I suppose.

MARTIN DOURAS. You're right to take it that way, Ellen. School doesn't mean scholarship now. Many's the time I'm telling Cornelius that a man farming the land, with a few books on his shelf and a few books in his head, has more of the scholar's life about him than the young fellows who do be teaching in schools and teaching in colleges.

CORNELIUS. That's all very well, father. School and scholarship isn't the one. But think of the word "Constantinople"! I could leave off herding and digging every time I think on that word!

MARTIN DOURAS. Ah, it's a great word. A word like that would make you think for days. And there are many words like that.

ELLEN. It's not so much the long words that we've to learn and teach now. When will you be home, father? Will Cornelius be with you?

MARTIN DOURAS. Ellen, I have news for you. There is a school in Leitrim that Father Bartley can let you have.

ELLEN. In Leitrim! Did you tell Matt about it?

MARTIN DOURAS. I did not.

[SALLY *is heard calling* "Cornelius." CORNELIUS *goes to the door.*]

CORNELIUS. Here's Matt now. The benefit of the day to you, Matt.

[*He stands aside to let* MATT *enter.* MATT COSGAR *is a young peasant of about twenty-eight. He is handsome and well-built. He is dressed in a trousers, shirt, and coat, and has a felt hat on.* CORNELIUS *goes out.*]

MATT [*going to* ELLEN]. You're welcome, Ellen. Good morrow, Martin. It's a great day for the purchase, Martin.

MARTIN DOURAS. A great day, indeed, thank God.

MATT. Ah, it's a great thing to feel the ownership of the land, Martin.

MARTIN DOURAS. I don't doubt but it is.

MATT. Look at the young apple-trees, Ellen. Walking up this morning, I felt as glad of them as a young man would be glad of the sweetheart he saw coming towards him.

ELLEN. Ay, there's great gladness and shine in the day.

MATT. It seems to trouble you.

ELLEN. It does trouble me.

MATT. Why?

ELLEN. Everything seems to be saying, "There's something here, there's something going."

MATT. Ay, a day like this often makes you feel that way. It's a great day for the purchase though. How many years ought we to offer, Ellen?

[MARTIN *goes out.*]

ELLEN. Twenty years, I suppose—[*suddenly*] Matt!

MATT. What is it, Ellen?

ELLEN. I have got an offer of a school in the County Leitrim.

MATT. I wish they'd wait, Ellen. I wish they'd wait till I had something to offer you.

ELLEN. I'm a long time waiting here, Matt.

MATT. Sure we're both young.

ELLEN. This is summer now. There will be autumn in a month or two. The year will have gone by without bringing me anything.

MATT. He'll be letting me have my own way soon, my father will.

ELLEN. Murtagh Cosgar never let a child of his have their own way.

MATT. When the land's bought out, he'll be easier to deal with.

ELLEN. When he owns the land, he'll never let a son of his marry a girl without land or fortune.

MATT. Ellen, Ellen, I'd lose house and land for you. Sure you know that, Ellen. My brothers and sisters took their freedom. They went from this house and away to the ends of the world. Maybe I don't differ from them so much. But I've put my work into the land, and I'm beginning to know the land. I won't lose it, Ellen. Neither will I lose you.

ELLEN. O Matt, what's the land after all? Do you ever think of America? The streets, the shops, the throngs?

MATT. The land is better than that when you come to know it, Ellen.

ELLEN. May be it is.

MATT. I've set my heart on a new house. Ay and he'll build one for us when he knows my mind.

ELLEN. Do you think he'd build a new house for us, Matt? I could settle down if we were by ourselves. Maybe it's true that there are things stirring and we could begin a new life, even here.

MATT. We can, Ellen, we can. Hush! father's without.

[MARTIN DOURAS *and* MURTAGH COSGAR *are heard exchanging greetings. Then* MURTAGH *comes in,* MARTIN *behind him.* MURTAGH COSGAR *is about sixty. He is a hard, strong man, seldom-spoken, but with a flow of words and some satirical power. He is still powerful, mentally and physically. He is clean-shaven, and wears a sleeved waistcoat, heavy boots, felt hat. He goes towards* ELLEN.]

MURTAGH. Good morrow to you. [*Turning to* MATT.] When I get speaking to that Sally again, she'll remember what I say. Giving cabbage to the pigs, and all the bad potatoes in the house. And I had to get up in the clouds of the night to turn the cows out of the young meadow. No thought, no care about me. Let you take the harness outside and put a thong where there's a strain in it.

[MURTAGH *goes to the fire.* MATT *goes to the harness-rack.* MARTIN DOURAS *and* ELLEN *are at the door.*]

MARTIN DOURAS. Ellen, I'll have news for you when I see you again. I've made up my mind to that.

ELLEN. Are you going to the fair, father?

MARTIN DOURAS. Ay, with Murtagh.

ELLEN. God be with you, father. [*She goes out.*]

MARTIN DOURAS. What purchase are you thinking of offering, Murtagh?

MURTAGH COSGAR. Twenty years.

MARTIN DOURAS. It's fair enough. Oh, it's a great day for the country, no matter what our own troubles may be.

[MATT *has taken down the harness. He takes some of it up and goes out to yard.*]

MURTAGH COSGAR [*with some contempt*]. It's a pity you haven't a share in the day after all.

MARTIN DOURAS. Ay, it's a pity indeed.

[MURTAGH *goes to the door.*]

MURTAGH COSGAR [*with suppressed enthusiasm*]. From this day out we're planted in the soil.

MARTIN DOURAS. Ay, we're planted in the soil.

MURTAGH COSGAR. God, it's a great day.

[CORNELIUS *comes back.*]

CORNELIUS. This is a memorial occasion, Murtagh Cosgar, and I wish you the felicitations of it. I met the delegates and I coming in, and I put myself at the head of them. It's the day of the redemption, Murtagh Cosgar.

[MURTAGH, *without speaking, goes up to the room left.*]

CORNELIUS. He's gone up to get the papers. Father, we must give the men understanding for this business. They must demand the mineral rights. Here they are. Men of Ballykillduff, I greet your entrance.

[*Six men enter discussing.*]

FIRST MAN. We'll leave it to Murtagh Cosgar. Murtagh Cosgar isn't a grazier or a shopkeeper.

SECOND MAN. It's the graziers and shopkeepers that are putting a business head on this.

THIRD MAN. If we're all on the one offer, we can settle it at the lawyer's.

FOURTH MAN. Sure it's settled for twenty years on the first-term rents.

FIFTH MAN. There are some here that would let it go as high as twenty-three.

SIXTH MAN. What does Murtagh Cosgar say?

SOME OF THE MEN. We'll take the word from him.

MARTIN DOURAS. He mentioned twenty years.

SECOND MAN. Not as a limit, surely?

OTHER MEN. We're not for any higher offer.

SECOND MAN. Well, men, this is all I have to say. If you can get it for twenty, take it, and my blessing with it. But I want to be dealing with the Government, and not with landlords and agents. To have a straight bargain between myself and the Government, I'd put it up to twenty-three, ay, up to twenty-five years' purchase.

THIRD MAN. More power to you, Councilor. There's some sense in that.

SIXTH MAN. I'm with the Councilor.

FIRST MAN. It's all very well for graziers and shopkeepers to talk, but what about the small farmer?

FOURTH MAN. The small farmer. That's the man that goes under.

FIFTH MAN [*knocking at the table*]. Murtagh Cosgar! Murtagh Cosgar!

CORNELIUS. I tell you, men, that Murtagh Cosgar is in agreement with myself. Twenty years, I say, first term, no more. Let my father speak.

MARTIN DOURAS. There's a great deal to be said on both sides, men.

FIRST MAN. Here's Murtagh now.

MURTAGH COSGAR. Twenty years first term, that's what I agreed to.

SECOND MAN. And if they don't rise to that, Murtagh?

MURTAGH COSGAR. Let them wait. We can wait. I won't be going with you, men. I had a few words with the agent about the turbary this morning, and maybe you're better without me.

FIRST MAN. All right, Murtagh. We can wait.

FOURTH MAN. We know our own power now.

FIFTH MAN. Come on, men.

MURTAGH COSGAR. If they don't rise to it, bide a while. We can make a new offer.

SECOND MAN. We want to be settled by the fall.

THIRD MAN. The Councilor is right. We must be settled by the fall.

SIXTH MAN. A man who's a farmer only has little sense for a business like this.

SECOND MAN. We'll make the offer, Murtagh Cosgar, and bide a while. But we must be settled this side of the fall. We'll offer twenty years first term.

MURTAGH COSGAR. Do, and God speed you.

CORNELIUS [*to the men going out*]. I told you Murtagh Cosgar and myself are on the one offer. And Murtagh is right again when he says that you can bide your time. But make sure of the mineral rights, men; make sure of the mineral rights.

[*The men go out;* CORNELIUS *follows them.*]

MURTAGH COSGAR [*with irony*]. Musha, but that's a well-discoursed lad. It must be great to hear the two of you at it.

MARTIN DOURAS. God be good to Cornelius. There's little of the world's harm in the boy.

MURTAGH COSGAR. He and my Sally would make a great match of it. She's a bright one, too.

MARTIN DOURAS. Murtagh Cosgar, have you no feeling for your own flesh and blood?

MURTAGH COSGAR. Too much feeling, maybe. [*He stands*

at the door in silence. With sudden enthusiasm.] Ah, but that's the sight to fill one's heart. Lands plowed and spread. And all our own; all our own.

MARTIN DOURAS. All our own, ay. But we made a hard fight for them.

MURTAGH COSGAR. Ay.

MARTIN DOURAS. Them that come after us will never see them as we're seeing them now.

MURTAGH COSGAR [*turning round*]. Them that come after us. Isn't that a great thought, Martin Douras? and isn't it a great thing that we're able to pass this land on to them, and it redeemed forever? Ay, and their manhood spared the shame that our manhood knew. Standing in the rain with our hats off to let a landlord—ay, or a landlord's dog-boy—pass the way!

MARTIN DOURAS [*mournfully*]. May it be our own generation that will be in it. Ay, but the young are going fast; the young are going fast.

MURTAGH COSGAR [*sternly*]. Some of them are no loss.

MARTIN DOURAS. Ten of your own children went, Murtagh Cosgar.

MURTAGH COSGAR. I never think of them. When they went from my control, they went from me altogether. There's the more for Matt.

MARTIN DOURAS [*moistening his mouth, and beginning very nervously*]. Ay, Matt. Matt's a good lad.

MURTAGH COSGAR. There's little fear of him leaving now.

MARTIN DOURAS [*nervously*]. Maybe, maybe. But, mind you, Murtagh Cosgar, there are things—little things, mind you. Least ways, what we call little things. And, after all, who are we to judge whether a thing—

MURTAGH COSGAR. Is there anything on your mind, Martin Douras?

MARTIN DOURAS [*hurriedly*]. No; oh, no. I was thinking —I was thinking, maybe you'd give me a lift towards Arvach, if you'd be going that way this night.

MURTAGH COSGAR. Ay, why not?

MARTIN DOURAS. And we could talk about the land, and about Matt, too. Wouldn't it be a heartbreak if any of our children went—because of a thing we might—

MURTAGH COSGAR [*fiercely*]. What have you to say about Matt?

MARTIN DOURAS [*stammering*]. Nothing except in a— in what you might call a general way. There's many a young man left house and land for the sake of some woman, Murtagh Cosgar.

MURTAGH COSGAR. There's many a fool did it.

MARTIN DOURAS [*going to door*]. Ay, maybe; maybe. I'll be going now, Murtagh.

MURTAGH COSGAR. Stop! [*Clutching him.*] You know about Matt. What woman is he thinking of?

MARTIN DOURAS [*frightened*]. We'll talk about it again, Murtagh. I said I'd be back.

MURTAGH COSGAR. We'll talk about it now. Who is she? What name has she?

MARTIN DOURAS [*breaking from him and speaking with sudden dignity*]. It's a good name, Murtagh Cosgar; it's my own name.

MURTAGH COSGAR. Your daughter! Ellen! You're—

MARTIN DOURAS. Ay, a good name, and a good girl.

MURTAGH COSGAR. And do you think a son of mine would marry a daughter of yours?

MARTIN DOURAS. What great difference is between us, after all?

MURTAGH COSGAR [*fiercely*]. The daughter of a man who'd be sitting over his fire reading his paper, and the clouds above his potatoes, and the cows trampling his oats. [MARTIN *is beaten down.*] Do you know me at all, Martin Douras? I came out of a little house by the roadway and built my house on a hill. I had many children. Coming home in the long evenings, or kneeling still when the prayers would be over, I'd have my dreams. A son in Aughnalee, a son in Ballybrian, a son in Dunmore, a son of mine with a shop, a son of mine saying Mass in Killnalee. And I have a living name—a name in flesh and blood.

MARTIN DOURAS. God help you, Murtagh Cosgar.

MURTAGH COSGAR. But I've a son still. It's not your daughter he'll be marrying. [*He strides to the door and calls* MATT.]

MARTIN DOURAS [*going to him*]. Murtagh Cosgar—for God's sake—we're both old men, Murtagh Cosgar.

MURTAGH COSGAR. You've read many stories, Martin Douras, and you know many endings. You'll see an ending now, and it will be a strong ending, and a sudden ending.

[MATT *comes in.*]

MURTAGH COSGAR. You're wanted here.

MATT. I heard you call. [*He sits on table.*] So they're sticking to the twenty years.

MARTIN DOURAS [*eagerly*]. Twenty years, Matt, and they'll get it for twenty. Oh, it's a great day for you both! Father and son, you come into a single inheritance. What the father wins the son wields.

MURTAGH COSGAR. What the father wins, the son wastes.

MATT. What's the talk of father and son?

MARTIN DOURAS. They're the one flesh and blood. There's no more strife between them than between the right hand and the left hand.

MURTAGH COSGAR [*to* MATT]. We were talking about you. We were fixing a match for you.

MATT [*startled, looking at* MARTIN DOURAS]. Fixing a match for me? [*He rises.*]

MURTAGH COSGAR. Ay, Matt. Don't you think it's time to be making a match for you?

MATT [*sullenly, going to the door*]. Maybe it is. When you have chosen the woman, call. I'll be without.

MURTAGH COSGAR [*going to him*]. We haven't chosen yet. But it won't be Martin Douras' daughter, anyhow.

MATT. Stop. You drove all your living children away, except Sally and myself. You think Sally and myself are the one sort.

MURTAGH COSGAR [*tauntingly*]. Martin's daughter, Corney's sister. That's the girl for you!

MATT. We're not the one sort, I tell you. Martin Douras, isn't he a foolish old man that would drive all his children from him? What would his twenty years' purchase be to him then?

MURTAGH COSGAR. It wasn't for my children I worked. No, no; thank God; it wasn't for my children I worked. Go, if you will. I can be alone.

MARTIN DOURAS. O Murtagh, Murtagh, sure you know you can't be alone. We're two old men, Murtagh.

MURTAGH COSGAR. He daren't go.

MATT. Because I'm the last of them he thinks he can dare me like that.

MURTAGH COSGAR. There was more of my blood in the others.

MATT. Do you say that?

MARTIN DOURAS. Don't say it again. For God's sake, don't say it again, Murtagh.

MURTAGH COSGAR. I do say it again. Them who dared to go had more of my blood in them!

MATT. Ah, you have put me to it now, and I'm glad, glad. A little house, a bit of land. Do you think they could keep me here?

MURTAGH COSGAR [to MARTIN DOURAS]. It's his own way he wants. I never had my own way. [To MATT.] You're my last son. You're too young to know the hardship there was in rearing you.

MATT [exultantly]. Your last son; that won't keep me here. I'm the last of my name, but that won't keep me here. I leave you your lands, your twenty years' purchase. Murtagh Cosgar, Murtagh Cosgar! isn't that a great name, Martin Douras—a name that's well planted, a name for generations? Isn't he a lucky man that has a name for generations? [He goes out.]

MURTAGH COSGAR. He can't go. How could he go and he the last of the name. Close the door, I say.

MARTIN DOURAS. He'll go to Ellen, surely. We'll lose both of them. Murtagh Cosgar, God comfort you and me.

MURTAGH COSGAR. Ellen; who's Ellen? Ay, that daughter of yours. Close the door, I say.

[He sits down at fireplace. MARTIN DOURAS closes door and goes to him.]

ACT II

SCENE: Interior of MARTIN DOURAS's. The entrance is at back left. There is a dresser against wall back; a table down from dresser; room doors right and left. The fireplace is below the room door right; there are stools and chairs about it. There is a little bookcase left of the dresser, and a mirror beside it. There are patriotic and re-

ligious pictures on the wall. There are cups and saucers on table, and a teapot beside fire. It is afternoon still. ELLEN DOURAS is near the fire reading. CORNELIUS comes in slowly.

CORNELIUS. I left the men down the road a bit. We ought to take great pride out of this day, Ellen. Father did more than any of them to bring it about.

ELLEN. He suffered more than any of them. And it's little we'll get out of the day.

CORNELIUS. It's a great thing to have prophesied it, even. We'll be here to see a great change.

ELLEN. There will be no change to make things better!

CORNELIUS. Will you be taking that school, Ellen?

ELLEN. I'll wait a while.

[SALLY *coming in; she is hurried.*]

SALLY [*breathlessly*]. Oh, God save you, Cornelius. Tell me, is my father gone? I dread going back and he there! It was all over that baste of a sow that has kept me slaving all through the spring till I don't know whether greens or potatoes is the fittest for her!

CORNELIUS. He didn't go, Sally. I went down a bit of the road myself with the men.

SALLY. Oh, God help me! And I'll have to be going back to boil meal for her now. How are you, Ellen? [*She goes to* ELLEN.]

ELLEN. Sit down for a while, Sally; it's a long time since I was speaking to you.

[SALLY *sits down beside* ELLEN.]

CORNELIUS. I'll leave this paper where they won't be looking for pipe-lights. There are things in that paper I'd like to be saving. [*He takes a newspaper out of his pocket and goes to room right.*]

ELLEN [*to* SALLY, *who has been watching* CORNELIUS]. Tell me, Sally, are they always that busy in your house? Is your father as harsh as they say?

SALLY. Father 'ud keep us all working. He's a powerful great man.

ELLEN. Matt will be bringing a wife into the house soon, from all I hear. How would your father treat her?

SALLY. Oh, he'd have his way, and she'd have her way, I suppose.

ELLEN. And do you think your father will let him marry?

SALLY. Sure he must if the boy likes.

ELLEN. What would he say if Matt married a girl without a fortune?

SALLY. In my mother's country there are lots of girls with fortunes that Matt could have.

ELLEN. Supposing he wanted a girl that had no fortune?

SALLY. Oh, I suppose father would give in in the end. It wouldn't be clay against flint when Matt and father would be to it.

ELLEN. You're a good girl, Sally. If I was Matt's wife, do you think you'd be fond of me?

SALLY. I'd like you as well as another, Ellen.

[CORNELIUS *comes down from room.*]

CORNELIUS. I suppose they'll be here soon.

ELLEN. I have tea ready for them.

SALLY. Who's coming at all?

CORNELIUS. Some of the boys and girls that are for America. They are going to Gilroy's tonight, and are leaving from that in the morning. They are coming in to see Ellen on their way down.

SALLY. There are a good many going this flight. The land never troubles them in America, and they can wear fine clothes, and be as free as the larks over the bogs. It's a wonder you never thought of going, Ellen.

ELLEN. Father wouldn't like me to be far from him, and so I went in for the school instead.

SALLY. And now you've got a fine boy like Matt. It was lucky for you to be staying here.

ELLEN. Hush, Sally.

SALLY. Oh, I knew all about it before you talked to me at all. Matt always goes to the place where he thinks you'd be.

ELLEN [*rising*]. I'll be in the room when the girls come, Cornelius. [*She goes into room left.*]

SALLY [*going to* CORNELIUS]. God help us, but she's the silent creature. Isn't it a wonder she's not filled with talk of him after seeing him today? But Ellen's right. We shouldn't be talking about men, nor thinking about them either; and that's the way to keep them on our hands on the long run. I'll be going myself. [*She goes towards door.*]

CORNELIUS [*going to her*]. Don't be minding Ellen at all, Sally.

SALLY. Well, as high as she is, and as mighty as she is, she came into his own house to see Matt. God between us and harm, Cornelius, maybe they'll be saying I came into your house to see you.

CORNELIUS. Who'll know you came at all? And what isn't seen won't be spoken of.

SALLY. Would you like me to stay, Cornelius?

CORNELIUS. Ay, I would.

SALLY. Divil mind the sow.

[*They sit down together.*]

SALLY [*after a pause*]. Would you like me to knit you a pair of socks, Cornelius?

CORNELIUS. Oh, I would, Sally; I'd love to wear them.

SALLY. I'll knit them. We'll be getting rid of the sow tonight, maybe, and I'll have time after that.

CORNELIUS. And you come along the road when I'm herding. I don't want to be going near your father's house.

SALLY. Oh Cornelius, it won't be lucky for us when father hears about Ellen and Matt.

CORNELIUS. That's true. No man sees his house afire but looks to his rick.

SALLY. Come down a bit of the road with me, Cornelius. The sow will be grunting and grunting, reminding father that I'm away. Och, a minute ago I was as contented as if there was no land or pigs, or harsh words to trouble one. [*She goes to the door.*] The boys and girls for America are coming here.

CORNELIUS. Give me your hands to hold, Sally. [*She gives him her hands.*] We are as young as any of them after all.

[*They hold each other's hands, then stand apart.*]

SALLY. It's a fine time for them to be going when the leaves are opening on the trees.

[*Three boys and three girls enter. They are dressed for going away.*]

SALLY. God save you, girls. Good-by, Cornelius. I'll have to run like a redshank.

[SALLY *goes out.*]

CORNELIUS. I'll call Ellen down to you. [*He goes to the room door and calls.*] I'm going herding myself. Herding is pleasant when you have thoughts with you. [*He takes up the rod and goes out. The girls begin whispering, then chattering.*]

FIRST GIRL. Sure I know. Every night I'm dreaming of the sea and the great towns. Streets and streets of houses and every street as crowded as the road outside the chapel when the people do be coming from Mass.

FIRST BOY. I could watch the crowd in the street; I would think it better than any sight I ever knew.

SECOND GIRL. And the shops and the great houses.

SECOND BOY. There's no stir here. There's no fine clothes, nor fine manners, nor fine things to be seen.

THIRD BOY. There's no money. One could never get a shilling together here. In America there's money to have and to spend and to send home.

THIRD GIRL. Every girl gets married in America.

[ELLEN *comes down.*]

ELLEN. I'm glad you came. I have tea ready for you. I can't go to Gilroy's tonight.

[*Some come to the table and some remain near the door.*]

A GIRL [*at table, to* ELLEN]. They say that a peat fire like that will seem very strange to us after America. Bridget wondered at it when she came back. "Do civilized people really cook at the like of them?" said she.

A BOY. It's the little houses with only three rooms in them that will seem strange. I'm beginning to wonder myself at their thatch and their mud walls.

ANOTHER GIRL. Houses in bogs and fields. It was a heartbreak trying to keep them as we'd like to keep them.

A GIRL [*at door*]. Ah, but I'll never forget Gortan and the little road to Aughnalee.

ANOTHER GIRL. I think I'll be lonesome for a long time. I'll be thinking on my brothers and sisters. I nursed and minded all the little ones.

FIRST BOY. A girl like you, Ellen, is foolish to be staying here.

SECOND BOY. She'll be coming in the fall. We'll be glad to see you, Ellen.

ELLEN. I have no friends in America.

FIRST GIRL. I have no friends there, either. But I'll get on. You could get on better than any of us, Ellen.

SECOND GIRL. She's waiting for her school. It will be a little place by the side of a bog.

THIRD GIRL [*going to* ELLEN]. There would be little change in that. And isn't it a life altogether different from this life that we have been longing for? To be doing other work, and to be meeting strange people. And instead of bare roads and market-towns, to be seeing streets, and crowds, and theaters.

ELLEN [*passionately*]. Oh, what do you know about streets and theaters? You have only heard of them. They are finer than anything you could say. They are finer than anything you could think of, after a story, when you'd be young.

A GIRL. You'll be going after all, Ellen.

ELLEN. I won't be going.

FIRST GIRL. Well, maybe you'll be down at Gilroy's. We must go now.

[*The girls go to the door.* ELLEN *goes with them.*]

ONE OF THE BOYS. Phil said that an egg was all he could touch while he was on the sea.

SECOND BOY. God help us, if that was all Phil could take.

THIRD BOY. Light your pipes now, and we'll go.

[ELLEN *has parted with the girls. The boys light their pipes at fire. They go to door, and shake hands with* ELLEN. *The boys go out.*]

ELLEN. Theaters! What do they know of theaters? And it's their like will be enjoying them.

[SALLY *comes back. She is more hurried than before.*]

SALLY. Ellen! Ellen! I have wonders to tell. Where is Cornelius, at all? He's never here when you have wonders to tell.

ELLEN. What have you to tell?

SALLY. Oh, I don't know how I'll get it all out! Matt and father had an *odious* falling out, and it was about you. And Matt's going to America; and he's to bring you with him. And Cornelius was saying that if father found out about yourself and Matt—

ELLEN. Sally, Sally, take breath and tell it.

SALLY. Matt is going to America, like the others, and he's taking you with him.

ELLEN. Sally, Sally, is it the truth you're telling?

SALLY. It is the truth. Honest as day, it is the truth.

ELLEN. And I thought I'd be content with a new house. Now we can go away together. I can see what I longed to see. I have a chance of knowing what is in me. [*She takes* SALLY's *hands.*] It's great news you've brought me. No one ever brought me such news before. Take this little cross. You won't have a chance of getting fond of me after all. [*She wears a cross at her throat; she breaks the string, and gives it to* SALLY.]

SALLY. I don't know why I was so fervent to tell you. There's the stool before me that myself and Cornelius were sitting on, and he saying— [*She goes to the door.*] Here's Matt! Now we'll hear all about it.

ELLEN. So soon; so soon. [*She goes to the mirror. After a pause, turning to* SALLY.] Go down the road a bit, when he comes in. Sally, you have a simple mind; you might be saying a prayer that it will be for the best.

SALLY [*going to the door muttering*]. Go down the road a bit! 'Deed and I will not till I know the whole ins and outs of it. Sure I'm as much concerned in it as herself! "No man sees his house afire but watches his rick," he was saying. Ah, there's few of them could think of as fine a thing as that.

[MATT *comes in.*]

MATT. Well, Sally, were you home lately?

SALLY. I was—leastways as far as the door. Father and oul' Martin were discoorsing.

MATT. I've given them something to discoorse about. Maybe you'll be treated better from this day, Sally.

SALLY. O Matt, I'm sorry. [*She goes out.*]

MATT [*going to* ELLEN]. It happened at last, Ellen; the height of the quarrel came.

ELLEN. It was bound to come. I knew it would come, Matt.

MATT. He was a foolish man to put shame on me after all I did for the land.

ELLEN. You have too much thought for the land.

MATT. I had in troth. The others went when there was less to be done. They could not stand him. Even the girls stole away.

ELLEN. There was the high spirit in the whole of you.

MATT. I showed it to him. "Stop," said I; "no more, or I fling lands and house and everything aside."

ELLEN. You said that.

MATT. Ay. "Your other children went for less," said I; "do you think there's no blood in me at all?"

ELLEN. What happened then?

MATT. "I'm your last son," I said; "keep your land and your twenty years' purchase. I'm with the others; and it's poor your land will leave you, and you without a son to bring down your name. A bit of land, a house," said I; "do you think these will keep me here?"

ELLEN. I knew they could not keep you here, Matt. You have broken from them at last; and now the world is before us. Think of all that is before us—the sea, and the ships, the strange life, and the great cities.

MATT. Ay—there before us—if we like.

ELLEN. Surely we like.

MATT. I was always shy of crowds. I'm simple, after all, Ellen, and have no thought beyond the land.

ELLEN. You said that house and land could not keep you. You told him you were going as your brothers went.

MATT. And I felt I was going. I frightened him. He'll be glad to see me back. It will be long before he treats me that way again.

ELLEN [*suddenly*]. Matt!

MATT. What is it, Ellen?

ELLEN. I don't know—I was upset—thinking of the quarrel. [*Putting her hands on his shoulders.*] My poor Matt. It was about me you quarreled.

Matt. Ay, he spoke against you. I couldn't put up with that.

ELLEN. He does not know your high spirit. He does not know your strength.

MATT. Ellen, it's no shame for a man to have harsh words said to him when it's about a woman like you.

ELLEN. Let nothing come between us now. I saw you in

the winter making drains and ditches, and it wet. It's a poor story, the life of a man on the land.

MATT. I had too much thought for the land.

ELLEN. You had. Have thought for me now. There is no one in fair or market but would notice me. I was never a favorite. I lived to myself. I did not give my love about. You have never offered me anything. In the song a man offers towns to his sweetheart. You can offer me the sights of great towns, and the fine manners, and the fine life.

MATT. Ellen! [*He draws a little away.*] It's not me that could offer the like of that. I never had anything to my hand but a spade.

ELLEN. Your brothers—think of them.

MATT. They all left some one behind them. I am the last of my name.

ELLEN. Why should that keep you back?

MATT. His name is something to a man. Could you hear of your own name melting away without unease? And you are a woman. A man feels it more.

ELLEN. I do not understand men. Will you go back to your father's house after he shaming you out of it?

MATT. He'll be glad to see me back. He'll never cast it up to me that I went.

ELLEN. Matt, your father said words against me. Will you go to him and take his hand after that?

MATT. It was little he said against you. It was against your father he spoke.

ELLEN [*sinking down on a chair, and putting hands before her face*]. My God! after all my waiting, you talk like that.

MATT [*going to her*]. Ellen, Ellen, tell me what I can do for you? There's land and houses to be had here. Father will let me have my own way after this.

ELLEN [*rising, with anger*]. What does it matter to me whether he lets you have your own way or not? Do you think I could go into a farmer's house?

MATT. Ellen!

ELLEN. It's a bad hand I'd make of a farmer's house. I'm not the sort to be in one. I'm not like Sally.

MATT [*getting angry*]. Don't be talking that way, Ellen Douras.

ELLEN [*with great vehemence*]. I must be talking like this. If you take me, you will have to go from your father's house. I always knew it. You ought to know it now, Matt Cosgar.

MATT. You didn't know it always. And you have let some one come between us when you talk like that.

ELLEN. I'm not one to be listening to what people say about you. Nor do I be talking in the markets about you.

MATT. I suppose not. You wouldn't have people think you gave any thought to me; I'm not good enough for you. The people you know are better.

ELLEN. You are foolish to be talking like that. You are foolish, I say.

MATT. I know I am foolish. Fit only to be working in drains and ditches in the winter. That's what you think.

ELLEN. Maybe it is.

MATT. Ellen Douras! Ellen Douras! A farmer's roof will be high enough for you some day.

ELLEN. May I never see the day. Go back, go back. Make it up with your father. Your father will be glad of a laborer.

MATT. Maybe you won't be glad if I go back; thinking on what you've said.

ELLEN. I said too much. We don't know each other at all. Go back. You have made your choice. [*She goes up to room left.*]

MATT. Very well, then. God above, am I to be treated everywhere like a heifer strayed into a patch of oats? Neither man nor woman will make me put up with this any longer. [*Going to door.*] When Ellen Douras wants me, she knows the place to send to. [*He stands at door. There is no sound from room. Going back he speaks loudly.*] I'll be waiting two days or three days to hear from Ellen Douras.

[*There is no sound.* MATT *goes out. The room door is thrown open, and* ELLEN *comes down.*]

ELLEN [*furiously*]. Two days or three days he'll wait for me. As if I'd go into Murtagh Cosgar's house. As if I'd go into any farmer's house. As if I'd get married at all, and the world before me. Two days or three days you'll wait. Maybe it's lonesome, weary years you'll be waiting, Matt Cosgar.

CURTAIN

ACT III

SCENE: *Interior of* MURTAGH COSGAR'S. *It is towards sunset.* MURTAGH COSGAR *is standing before the door looking out.* MARTIN DOURAS *is sitting at the fire in an armchair.*

MARTIN DOURAS. It's getting late, Murtagh Cosgar.

MURTAGH COSGAR. Ay, it's getting late.

MARTIN DOURAS. It's time for me to be going home. I should be seeing Ellen. [*He rises.*]

MURTAGH COSGAR. Stay where you are. [*Turning round.*] We're two old men, as you say. We should keep each other's company for a bit.

MARTIN DOURAS. I should be going home to see Ellen.

MURTAGH COSGAR. If she's going, you can't stay her. Let you keep here.

MARTIN DOURAS. She'll be wondering what happened to me.

MURTAGH COSGAR. Divil a bit it will trouble her. You're going to the fair anyway?

MARTIN DOURAS. I have no heart to be going into a fair.

MURTAGH COSGAR. It's myself used to have the great heart. Driving in on my own side-car, and looking down on the crowd of them. It's twenty years since I took a sup of drink. Oh, we'll have drinking tomorrow that will soften the oul' skin of you. You'll be singing songs about the Trojans to charm every baste in the fair.

MARTIN DOURAS. We're both old men, Murtagh Cosgar.

MURTAGH COSGAR. And is there any reason in your scholarship why oul' men should be dry men? Answer me that!

MARTIN DOURAS. I won't answer you at all, Murtagh Cosgar. There's no use in talking to you.

MURTAGH COSGAR. Put it down on a piece of paper that oul' men should have light hearts when their care is gone from them. They should be like—

MARTIN DOURAS. There's nothing in the world like men with their rearing gone from them, and they old.

[SALLY *comes to the door. She enters stealthily.*]

MURTAGH COSGAR. Ha, here's one of the clutch home. Well, did you see that brother of yours?

SALLY. I did. He'll be home soon, father.

MURTAGH COSGAR. What's that you say? Were you talking to him? Did he say he'd be home?

SALLY. I heard him say it, father.

MARTIN DOURAS. God bless you for the news, Sally.

MURTAGH COSGAR. How could he go and he the last of them? Sure it would be against nature. Where did you see him, Sally?

SALLY. At Martin Douras's, father.

MURTAGH COSGAR. It's that Ellen Douras that's putting him up to all this. Don't you be said by her, Sally.

SALLY. No, father.

MURTAGH COSGAR. You're a good girl, and if you haven't wit, you have sense. He'll be home soon, did you say?

SALLY. He was coming home. He went round the long way, I'm thinking. Ellen Douras was vexed with him, father. She isn't going either, Matt says, but I'm thinking that you might as well try to keep a corn-crake in the meadow for a whole winter, as to try to keep Ellen Douras in Aughnalee.

MURTAGH COSGAR. Make the place tidy for him to come into. He'll have no harsh words from me. [*He goes up to the room.*]

SALLY. Father's surely getting ould.

MARTIN DOURAS [*sitting down*]. He's gone up to rest himself, God help him. Sally, *a stor*, I'm that fluttered, I dread going into my own house.

SALLY. I'll get ready now, and let you have a good supper before you go to the fair.

MARTIN DOURAS. Sit down near me, and let me hear everything, Sally. Was it Matt that told you, or were you talking to Ellen herself?

SALLY. Oh, indeed, I had a talk with Ellen, but she won't give much of her mind away. It was Matt that was telling me. "Indeed she's not going," said he, "and a smart young fellow like myself thinking of her. Ellen is too full of notions." Here's Matt himself. Father won't have a word to say to him. He's getting mild as he's getting ould, and maybe it's a fortune he'll be leaving to myself.

[MATT *comes to the door. He enters.*]

MATT. Where is he? He's not gone to the fair so early?

SALLY. He's in the room.

MATT. Were you talking to him at all? Were you telling him you saw myself?

SALLY. I was telling him that you were coming back.

MATT. How did he take it?

SALLY. Very quiet. God help us all; I think father's losing his spirit.

MATT [*going to* MARTIN]. Well, you see I've come back, Martin.

MARTIN DOURAS. Ay, you're a good lad. I always said you were a good lad.

MATT. How did father take it, Martin?

MARTIN DOURAS. Quietly, quietly. You saw Ellen?

MATT. Ay, I saw Ellen. [*Gloomily.*] She shouldn't talk the way she talks, Martin. What she said keeps coming into my mind, and I'm troubled. God knows I've trouble enough on my head.

MARTIN DOURAS [*eagerly*]. What did she say, Matt Cosgar?

MATT. It wasn't what she said. She has that school in her mind, I know.

MARTIN DOURAS. And is there anything to keep her here, Matt Cosgar?

MATT. I don't know that she thinks much of me now. We had a few words, but there's nothing in the world I put above Ellen Douras.

MARTIN DOURAS. I should be going to her.

MATT. Wait a bit, and I'll be going with you. Wait a bit. Let us talk it over. She wouldn't go from you, and you old.

MARTIN DOURAS. God forgive my age, if it would keep her here. Would I have my Ellen drawing turf, or minding a cow, or feeding pigs?

MATT. I'm fond of her, Martin. She couldn't go, and I so fond of her. What am I doing here? I should be making it up with her. What good will anything be if Ellen Douras goes? [*He turns to the door, then stops.*] I came to settle with him. I mustn't be running about like a frightened child.

[*The room door opens, and* MURTAGH COSGAR *is seen.* SALLY *has hung a pot over the fire, and is cleaning the dishes at the dresser.*]

MURTAGH COSGAR [*at the room door*]. Sally, it's time to be putting on the meal. If you have any cabbage left, put it through the meal. [*To* MATT.] You put the thong in the harness?

MATT. I did. [*Pause.*] Well, I've come back to you.

MURTAGH COSGAR. You're welcome. We were making ready for the fair.

MATT. I'll be going out again before nightfall.

MURTAGH COSGAR. I'll not be wanting you here, or at the fair.

MATT [*sullenly*]. There's no good talking to me like that.

MURTAGH COSGAR. You said, "I've come back," and I said, "you're welcome." You said, "I'm going out again," and I said, "I'll not be wanting you."

MATT. Father, have you no feeling for me at all?

MURTAGH COSGAR. Sure the wild raven on the tree has thought for her young.

MATT. Ay, but do you feel for me, and I standing here, trying to talk to you?

MURTAGH COSGAR. You're my son, and so I feel sorry for you; and you beginning to know your own foolishness. [*He turns to* SALLY.] I'm not taking the pigs. Put a fresh bedding under them tonight.

SALLY. I will, father.

MURTAGH COSGAR. Be up early, and let the cows along the road, or they'll be breaking into the young meadow.

SALLY. I'll do that, too.

MURTAGH COSGAR. Be sure to keep enough fresh milk for the young calf.

SALLY. I'll be sure to do it, father. [*She goes out.* MARTIN *takes out his paper, and begins to read it again.*]

MATT [*turning on* MURTAGH]. Before I go out again there's something I want settled.

MURTAGH COSGAR. What is it you want?

MATT. Would you have me go, or would you have me stay?

MURTAGH COSGAR. Don't be talking of going or staying, and you the last of them.

MATT. But I will be talking of it. You must treat me differently if you want me to stay. You must treat me differently to the way you treat Sally.

MURTAGH COSGAR. You were always treated differently, Matt. In no house that ever I remember was there a boy treated as well as you are treated here.

MATT. The houses that you remember are different from the houses that are now. Will you have me go, or will you have me stay?

MURTAGH COSGAR. You're very threatening. I'd have you stay. For the sake of the name, I'd have you stay.

MATT. Let us take hands on it, then.

MURTAGH COSGAR Wait, we'll see what you want first.

MATT. You have no feeling. I'd go out of this house, only I want to give you a chance.

MURTAGH COSGAR. Stop. We can have kindness in this. We needn't be beating each other down, like men at a fair.

MATT. We're not men at a fair. May God keep the kindness in our hearts.

[MARTIN *rises.*]

MURTAGH COSGAR. Don't be going, Martin Douras.

MATT. Don't be going yet. I'll be with you, when you're going.

[MARTIN *sits down.*]

MURTAGH COSGAR [*to* MATT]. You'll be getting married, I suppose, if you stay?

MATT. Maybe I will.

MURTAGH COSGAR [*bitterly*]. In the houses that are now, the young marry where they have a mind to. It's their own business, they say.

MATT. Maybe it is their own business. I'm going to marry Ellen Douras, if she'll have me.

MURTAGH COSGAR. Ellen is a good girl, and clever, I'm told. But I would not have you deal before you go into the fair.

MATT. I'm going to marry Ellen Douras.

MURTAGH COSGAR. Her father is here, and we can settle it now. What fortune will you be giving Ellen, Martin? That hundred pounds that was saved while you were in Maryborough jail?

[MARTIN *shakes his head.*]

MATT [*stubbornly*]. I'm going to marry Ellen Douras, with or without a fortune.

MURTAGH COSGAR [*passionately*]. Boy, your father built

this house. He got these lands together. He has a right to see that you and your generations are in the way of keeping them together.

MATT. I'll marry Ellen Douras, with or without a fortune.

MURTAGH COSGAR. Marry her, then. Marry Ellen Douras.

MATT. Now, Martin, we mustn't let an hour pass without going to her. [*He takes* MARTIN's *arm, and they go to the door.*]

MURTAGH COSGAR. Marry Ellen Douras, I bid you. Break what I have built, scatter what I have put together. That is what all the young will be doing.

[ELLEN DOURAS *comes to the door as* MATT *and* MARTIN *reach it.*]

MATT. Ellen!

[*She shrinks back.*]

ELLEN. It's my father I came to speak to.

MURTAGH COSGAR [*going to the door, and drawing the bolt from the half-door.*] When you come to my house, Ellen Douras, you are welcome within.

[ELLEN *comes in.*]

ELLEN. It's right that I should speak to you all. Matt Cosgar, I am going from here.

MATT. Ellen, Ellen, don't be saying that. Don't be thinking of the few words between us. It's all over now. Father agrees to us marrying. Speak, father, and let her hear yourself say it.

ELLEN. I can't go into a farmer's house.

MATT. You said that out of passion. Don't keep your mind on it any longer.

ELLEN. It's true, it's true. I can't go into a farmer's house. This place is strange to me.

MATT. How can you talk like that? I'm always thinking of you.

·ELLEN. I've stayed here long enough. I want my own way; I want to know the world.

MATT. If you go, how will I be living, day after day? The heart will be gone out of me.

MURTAGH COSGAR. You'll be owning the land, Matt Cosgar.

MATT [*passionately*]. I've worked on the land all my days. Don't talk to me about it now.

[ELLEN *goes to* MARTIN. MURTAGH *goes up to the door, and then turns and speaks.*]

MURTAGH COSGAR. Listen to me, Matt Cosgar; and you listen too, Ellen Douras. It's a new house you want maybe. This house was built for me and my generations; but I'll build a new house for you both. It's hard for a man to part with his land before the hour of his death; and it's hard for a man to break his lands; but I'll break them, and give a share of land to you.

ELLEN. You were never friendly to me; but you have the high spirit, and you deserve a better daughter than I would make. The land and house you offer would be a drag on me. [*She goes to the door.*]

MATT. Ellen, what he offers is nothing, after all; but I care for you. Sure you won't go from me like that?

ELLEN. Oh, can't you let me go? I care for you as much as I care for anyone. But it's my freedom I want.

MATT. Then you're going surely?

ELLEN. I am. Good-by.

[*She goes out,* MARTIN *follows her.* MATT *stands dazed.* MURTAGH *closes the door, then goes and takes* MATT's *arm, and brings him down.*]

MURTAGH COSGAR. Be a man. We offered her everything, and she went. There's no knowing what the like of her wants. The men will be in soon, and we'll drink to the new ownership.

MATT. Oh, what's the good in talking about that now? If Ellen was here, we might be talking about it.

MURTAGH COSGAR. Tomorrow you and me might go together. Ay, the bog behind the meadow is well drained by this, and we might put the plow over it. There will be a fine, deep soil in it, I'm thinking. Don't look that way, Matt, my son.

MATT. When I meet Ellen Douras again, it's not a farmer's house I'll be offering her, nor life in a country place.

MURTAGH COSGAR. No one could care for you as I care for you. I know the blood between us, and I know the thoughts I had as I saw each of you grow up.

[MATT *moves to the door.*]

MURTAGH COSGAR. Where are you going?

MATT. To see the boys that are going away.

MURTAGH COSGAR. Wait till the fall and I'll give you
money to go and come back. Farrell Kavanagh often goes
to America. You could go with him.

MATT. I'll go by myself, unless Ellen Douras comes now.
The creamery owes me money for the carting, and I'll get it.

MURTAGH COSGAR. Then go. Good-by to you, Matt Cosgar.

MATT. Good-by to you. [*He goes out.* MURTAGH *stands,
then moves about vaguely.*]

MURTAGH COSGAR. The floor swept, the hearth tidied.
It's a queer end to it all. Twenty years I bid them offer.
Twenty years, twenty years!

[MARTIN *comes back.*]

MURTAGH COSGAR. The men will be coming back.

MARTIN DOURAS. I suppose they will.

MURTAGH COSGAR. You're a queer fellow, Martin Douras.
You went to jail for some meeting.

MARTIN DOURAS. Ay.

MURTAGH COSGAR. Them was the stirring times. I can't
help but think of you in jail, and by yourself. What brings
you back now?

MARTIN DOURAS. Ellen told me to go back. I should say
something to Matt, I think.

MURTAGH COSGAR. He went out as you came in.

MARTIN DOURAS. I'll go in when the house is quiet. I'll
have a few prayers to be saying this night.

MURTAGH COSGAR. I'm going to the fair.

MARTIN DOURAS. I won't be going to the fair.

MURTAGH COSGAR. Why won't you be going to the fair?
Didn't you ask me for a lift? You'll be going with me.

MARTIN DOURAS. I won't be going, and don't be overbearing me now, Murtagh Cosgar.

MURTAGH COSGAR. You will be going to the fair, if it
was only to be showing that seemly face of yours. [*Going
to the door, he calls* "Sally!" *He turns to* MARTIN DOURAS.]
I've a daughter still, Martin Douras.

MARTIN DOURAS. You have, and I have a son.

MURTAGH COSGAR. What would you say to a match between them, Martin Douras?

MARTIN DOURAS. I have nothing to say again it.

MURTAGH COSGAR. Then a match it will be.

[SALLY *comes in from yard.*]

SALLY. If you fed that baste on honey, she'd turn on you. Cabbage I gave her and got into trouble for it, and now she's gone and trampled the bad potatoes till they're hardly worth the boiling. I'll put the bush in the gap when I'm going out again, father.

MURTAGH COSGAR. Ay. Is that Cornelius Douras that's coming up the path?

SALLY. Oh, faith it is. I'll get him to give me a hand with the trough.

[CORNELIUS *comes in.*]

CORNELIUS. Well, Murtagh Cosgar, a great and memorial day is ended. May you live long to enjoy the fruits of it. Twenty years on the first term, and the land is ours and our children's. I met the men.

MURTAGH COSGAR. Ours and our children's, ay. We've been making a match between yourself and Sally.

CORNELIUS. Between me and Sally.

SALLY. Between Cornelius and myself?

MURTAGH COSGAR. Ay, shake hands on it now.

CORNELIUS. And tell me one thing, Murtagh Cosgar. Is it true that Matt's going to America, and that Ellen will wait for him for a year at the school? I met them together, and they told me that.

MURTAGH COSGAR. What they say is true, I'm sure. The land is yours and your children's.

SALLY [*wiping her hands in her apron*]. O Cornelius.

CORNELIUS. Aren't they foolish to be going away like that, father, and we at the mouth of the good times? The men will be coming in soon, and you might say a few words. [MARTIN *shakes his head.*] Indeed you might, father; they'll expect it of you. [MARTIN *shakes his head.* MURTAGH *and* SALLY *try to restrain him.*] "Men of Ballykillduff," you might say, "stay on the land, and you'll be saved body and soul; you'll be saved in the man and in the nation. The nation, men of Ballykillduff, do you ever think of it at all? Do you ever think of the Irish nation that is waiting all this time to be born?" [*He becomes more excited; he is seen to be struggling with words.*]

BIRTHRIGHT [1]

by T. C. Murray

CHARACTERS

BAT MORRISSEY, *a farmer*
MAURA, *his wife*
HUGH, *his son*
SHANE, *a younger son*
DAN HEGARTY, *a neighbor*

SCENE: *Sunday evening. The interior of a farmhouse kitchen in the County Cork.* BAT MORRISSEY *is seated at the fire smoking. He is a hard-faced man of about sixty-five.* MAURA *is sorting a pile of new socks and removing them from the table to the deep window-sill. She is younger than her husband. Her face looks somewhat careworn. There are hints of a refined temperament in her quiet dress and apron, and in the appearance of the kitchen.* DAN HEGARTY *appears in the doorway. He leans comfortably on the half-door, and looks in, saluting them.*

ACT I

DAN. God bless all here!

MAURA. And you too [*turning round*]. Wisha, is that you, Dan Hegarty? Walk in. [*Unbolting the half-door.*] Sure it isn't coming from the play you are so soon?

DAN. 'Tis indeed, then, Mrs. Morrissey—though to tell you the honest truth I could hardly boast I saw the match at all.

MAURA. Well, now.

DAN. 'Twas only by a kind of chance like I come to see the finish of it. I missed all the rest o' the play.

BAT. An' that was no loss to you! Them matches are the

---

[1] (Revised version, 1928.)

curse o' the country with their drinking, an' their squabbling, an' their rowing—an' the Lord knows what! So they are.

DAN. Oh I don't know altogether about that now. Sure—

BAT. Well, I knows it. They're good for the publicans an' no one else, and signs on, they're the heads o' them always. . . . But 'tis the good sense you had yourself, Dan Hegarty, to be keeping far away from them till the play was nearly over—not like some belonging to this house who ought to know better.

DAN. Faith, I don't know altogether about the good sense, Bat. Sure 'twasn't that what kept me away at all.

BAT. An' what else then, I'd like to know? What else?

DAN. Well, then, 'twas this way with us.

MAURA [*giving him a chair*]. Sit down, Dan.

DAN. Thank you, ma'am. [*Sits down.*] The mason and the carpenter, they'll be coming over tomorrow to begin the new house, and 'twas only this morning the girl took it into her head to tell us the bag of flour was nearly out, an' that there was hardly the makings o' bread for our own supper tonight, not to mind the men's breakfast tomorrow morning. So, begor, Sunday and all as it was I had to tackle the horse an' go east to Macroon for a bag of flour—and I tell you 'twasn't too thankful to myself at all I was over it.

MAURA. Well, indeed, it was hard enough on you, and all the young people in the parish going to the match.

DAN. 'Tis many the big curse came out o' me, I tell you —God forgive me!—an' I jogging away to the town, an' meeting all the world against me going to the great match. 'Tis half ashamed like I felt passing the crowds.

BAT. *Ashamed*, is it? Well! well! [*Laughing derisively.*] An' I'd like to know now what was there to be ashamed of?

DAN. Sure I could hardly tell that—but, somehow, it was on my mind what 'ud the people be thinking—

BAT [*with contemptuous pity*]. Oh, wisha, Dan Hegarty, 'tis the quare world surely, an' 'tis the quare people that are in it!

DAN. Faith, that's the truth, Bat, an' the quarest people often are them that do be thinking they have the most sense. . . . But didn't ye hear at all the great work the parish done —an' the best team in Ireland again them?

BAT [*dryly*]. We didn't then—an' 'tis little we care aither. If they were playing in that field outside I wouldn't cross to the other side o' the road to see them.

DAN. You wouldn't indeed, an' your own son the captain of the team—an' he coming home to you this evening with another gold meddle?

BAT. Another gold meddle! I wouldn't give that much [*snapping his fingers*] for all the meddles there is in the City of Cork. Meddles! . . . I tell you, Dan Hegarty, 'twould be better for the peace o' this house if yer brave captain would stay at home an' mind his own business! So it would.

DAN. Yerra, don't be talking like that, man. Take the world a small bit aisy. Sure it isn't working on a Sunday you'd have him?

BAT. There's plenty work for a farmer, Sunday as well as Monday.

DAN. Maybe so, but 'tis the small farm we'll all be wanting when we're dead.

BAT. That's no talk at all.

DAN. Sure, man, we might as well break up the team altogether without Hugh in it. . . . Why, didn't Father Daly himself say the other day—'twas after he winning the meddle for the great verses he made for the *feis*—"there isn't," says he, "the beating of Hugh Morrissey in Ireland for anything." [*To* MAURA.] 'Twas east at the cross, Mrs. Morrissey, he said it. I heard him myself.

BAT [*crossly*]. Ah, don't annoy us with Father Daly an' his talk. 'Tis little him or his aquals cares about the likes of us. Destroying the parish he is, since he came into it, taking people away from their work an' putting notions into their heads. Father Daly!

DAN. Yeh, man, don't be talking like that a day like this! There isn't a mother's soul in this parish but yourself that wouldn't be out of his mind with delight this minute, and everyone to be praising his own flesh and blood! [*To* MAURA.] I'm sorry in my soul you didn't see the match, Mrs. Morrissey. I nearly killed the little mare and killed myself hurrying back from the town to see if I could see even the end of it. An' 'twas a grand sight surely.

MAURA. Wisha, God help us, Dan, I'm a bit too old now to be going to places like that.

DAN. Wisha indeed, and indeed you're not, ma'am. A person would think the way you talk you were drawing the pension. But sure whatever excuse there was for you there was none at all for himself here.

BAT. We'd look well, begor, Maura an' myself, going to yer tournament! [*Laughs derisively.*]

DAN. An' why not, Bat? Why not? The sight o' your son today would be giving you a kind of feeling, maybe, that your best cows and your heaviest pigs could never give you.

BAT [*shaking his head*]. God help you, Dan Hegarty! An' you a young man just beginning to rear a little family!

DAN. If I am then, Bat Morrissey, I only wish to God one o' them would grow up something like your Hugh! So I would. [*To* MAURA.] All the people, and the strangers even, were cheering like mad for him. Half a dozen times you'd be seeing the ball and it flying into the goal posts, an' your heart would be in your mouth thinking the other side had the goal, when you'd see him sending it back again with a puck into the middle of the field. 'Twas like a miracle the way he used to save it every time!

MAURA. Well! well!

DAN. I galloped away when it was over as I wanted to clear away before the crowds, but I gave one look back, an' they were shouldering him, an' cheering mad, an' shouting for him as if it was a member of Parliament he was.

BAT. An' for what now?

DAN [*with a gasp*]. For what?

BAT. Yes—for what, Dan Hegarty?

DAN. Didn't I tell you?

BAT. Is it because he hit a bit of a leather balleen with a twisted stick? Tch! tch! tch! [*Standing up and going towards room.*] 'Tis thinking I am that half the world is becoming a pack o' fools. [*Goes into room.*]

MAURA [*confidentially*]. I'd know could you tell me was he hurt at all, Dan?

DAN. I don't know then—I don't think so. . . . I'm almost sure he wasn't, now that I think of it.

MAURA. Thanks be to the Almighty God an' His Blessed Mother for that!

DAN. Bat isn't himself somehow this evening, Mrs. Morrissey?

MAURA. Shane's going away next Thursday morning that's upsetting him.

DAN. Ah, sure of course, I never thought of that. Wasn't it very sudden now, Mrs. Morrissey, that Shane got the notion to be going to America?

MAURA. 'Twas indeed, God help us. I couldn't speak with the fright when he told me first.

DAN. An' everyone thought he liked the farming greatly?

MAURA. And so he did—I don't know a boy in this townland that liked it better. But he was saying that Hugh would be getting married in a few years, an' then that 'twould be the poor lookout for him here. An' no matter what I said, or what his father said, or what anyone else said, it made no difference with him. "Rocking the cradle for Hugh, ye'd want me to be," says he.

DAN. Well, I suppose he's old enough to know his own business. . . . There's one thing anyway, there's no fear of him in the States.

MAURA. He's very steady, thank God.

DAN. Begor, 'tis too steady he is, if anything. To tell you the honest truth, I'd rather now a fellow with a bit o' spirit in him, so long as he'd have the good sense at the same time— just like Hugh.

MAURA. Sure their nature is God's blessed work and not their own, Dan Hegarty. And 'tis blaming Him you'll be if you talk that way.

DAN [*half skeptically.*] Well, now then, I suppose you're right there. [*Reënter* BAT.] I was saying to herself, Bat, that Shane will be the great loss to ye?

BAT. 'Tis little you know it, or any other man aither.

DAN. But 'twon't be long, never fear, till the fat checks be coming to you to make up for it!

BAT. *Tá go breagh!* 'Tis going out the money will be an' not coming in, I'm thinking. We can't work this place without extra help—an' good help, too—once Shane is gone from us. An' 'tis robbing to pay laborers now. Eggs they must be getting for breakfast, and tea after dinner. They'd break a man!

DAN. Yeh, man. You'll get used to that in time, like all the rest of us. [*To* MAURA.] But sure what made me call was about Shane's trunk. Herself tells me at home that 'tis the very dickens to get me out of a neighbor's chimney corner once I get in there an' begin the bit o' talk. An' faith, I'm thinking, 'tis the truth she's telling.

MAURA. Sure, not at all. 'Tis early yet. Why wouldn't you be a bit neighborly? And what message have you about the trunk, Dan?

DAN. When I was getting the flour at Ahern's they asked me to bring it. 'Twas Mrs. Ahern herself was there. She said you were hardly outside the town the fair day when the trunks came. Outside in the car it is. I've left the horse down a bit in the boreen. Mrs. Ahern herself put the label on it with the right directions for fear of any mistake. She said you told her.

MAURA. And so I did. I'm very thankful to you, Dan. 'Twas too much trouble entirely, but I was in a fright as it wasn't coming. Thursday, as you know, he'll be going, and I'd want to begin the packing soon, God help us.

DAN. Well, 'tis time for me to be turning home. I'm thinking 'tis in the great state they'll be for the flour. I'll be over Wednesday night to see Shane before he starts on the big journey next day. I hope he'll have the good weather for the voyage. Good-by for the present, Mrs. Morrissey.

MAURA. Good-by, and good luck, Dan.

DAN [*half jauntily*]. Come along, Bat. Come along.

[*He goes out, followed by* BAT. MAURA *makes the preliminary preparations for supper, pouring water into the kettle, setting it on the hangers over the fire, drawing the turf-embers round the pot-oven by the fire, etc.* BAT *returns, bearing on his shoulders an oak-colored tin trunk with brass lock. He lets it down on the floor.*]

BAT. 'Tis a fine trunk, isn't it?

MAURA [*after a pause*]. 'Tis a fine trunk, indeed, but 'tis the fineness of the coffin that's on it.

BAT. 'Tis a very dacent trunk, an' good value for six shillings.

MAURA [*after a pause*]. There was a shiver come over me, and a queer lonesome feeling, when I saw it on your shoulders. 'Twas the same as when you brought in the coffin for little Owen.

BAT [*lighting his pipe*]. 'Twill do all right.

MAURA. 'Twill, I suppose, God help us. [*She kneels down and opens the trunk.*]

MAURA. Isn't it the strong smell there is from it? I don't like it at all. 'Twill stick to the socks and the shirts for a long time.

[*There is a pause, during which is heard the strong puff-puff of a smoker whose pipe is in danger of going out.*]

MAURA. Maybe if I burned a small grain of the coffee in it 'twould make it wholesome?

BAT. Yerra, nonsense, woman! [*Puff-puff.*] Is it Shane to mind the smell o' the paint? Thank God, he's not that kind. [*Puff-puff.*] Sure I've seen him turn the strongest heap o' manure in the country, and he to mind it no more than if 'twas the fresh cut hay he was tossing on top o' the hayfork. [*Puff-puff.*]

MAURA. That's true, of course, but all the same, somehow—

BAT. Have sense, woman, have sense! . . . If 'twas the other boy, now, 'twould be different. There would be some reason then for talking. [*Laying down his pipe.*] Do you remember when we were carting out the manure to the western field last March, an' how white he got—like any poor creature of a woman—when myself an' Shane opened the heap; an' there was yourself running to get a drop o' whiskey for him. Well, begor [*laughing ironically*], 'tis something to have a real gentleman in the family.

MAURA. Sure he can't help his nature no more than ourselves.

BAT. 'Tis the quare nature he have—with his sporting, an' his fiddling, an' his *ráiméis* about the Irish—an' the Lord knows what! 'Tis the grand lookout for the future of this place, so it is. He'll be the man to mind it. . . . A fine lookout indeed.

MAURA. I'm sure he'll be able to mind it as well as the next. Isn't he as hardworking as anyone in this side of the parish—except Shane, of course; but sure everyone knows that he's an exception entirely.

BAT [*broodingly*]. A fine lookout, sure enough.

MAURA. Sure, God help us, everyone have their own faults.

BAT. He have enough o' them for twenty—so he have.

MAURA. Is it poor Hugh? Sure his faults are only the small faults. You're very hard on him, Bat—I don't know why—very, very hard on him entirely.

BAT [*angrily*]. What's that you're after saying? "Hard on him!" Hard, is it? That's the quare saying from your mouth. I'd like to know who is hard. When I bought this place thirty year ago with the bit o' money I made in the States what kind was it? Tell that an' spake the truth! Tell it now!

MAURA. A cold place it was surely—a cold, poor place, with more o' the rock, an' the brier, an' the sour weed than the sweet grass.

BAT. Well, an' who blasted every rock that was in it?

MAURA. Sure, 'twas no one but yourself, Bat.

BAT. An' who rooted out the briers, and often tore 'em out with his own two living hands?

MAURA [*conciliatory*]. 'Twas yourself I know. Alone you did it.

BAT [*with rising anger*]. An' maybe you'd tell me now again who drained the western field that was little better than a bog—an' who built the strong fences an' planted the thorn on them—an' who made the land kind where the grass was that dry an' coarse you'd think 'twas the strings o' the lash on that whip beyond? Tell me that, will you? Tell me that now?

MAURA. Sure, I know, Bat, 'twas yourself—and the good God that gave you the great strength.

BAT. *I'm hard*, am I? I've been out in the darkness before the dawn, an' remained stuck in the trench an' the furrow all day, till the black darkness came on me again, and the moon come up, and the faintness on me that I couldn't walk into this house for staggering no better than a cripple or a man that would be drunk. An' for what, I ask you? For what, Maura? For my brave Hugh, for an idler and a scamp and a-a-a worthless blackguard! I'm hard, Maura, am I?

MAURA. Wisht, sure I didn't mean it. I didn't mean it at all. I didn't, indeed, Bat.

BAT. I'm hard, am I? 'Tis your son is hard, and you know it. The sweat o' my body an' my life is in every inch o' the land, and 'tis little he cares, with his hurling an' his fiddling an' his versifying an' his confounded nonsense! . . . I tell you again—an' mind my words for it—'tis the black look-out for this place when *he* gets it, an' only for your talk, an' your crying, 'tis that blackguard's name an' not his brother's would be on that trunk there this night!

MAURA. Wouldn't it be the queer thing entirely, Bat, to send the eldest son away, and he with your own father's name on him?

BAT. Would it, then? Would it? Tell me, had I ever to go away myself? What was good enough for me ought to be good enough for my brave Hugh—but of course *I'm* only a poor ignorant plowman, and he's the scholar. The scholar! God bless us!

MAURA. Don't talk foolish, Bat. Sure no one thinks that way of you, and least of all the boy himself. . . . [*Half musingly.*] 'Tis the strange thing surely, his own father to be the only one in the parish that's not proud of him; and everyone talking of him, and the priest himself praising him, and his picture in the paper for the great rhymes he made for the *feis*.

BAT. That's more o' your foolish talk, an' 'tis you have helped to make him the kind he is. Your blood is in him. I see it in every twist and turn of his and every wild foolish thing coming from his mouth. . . . Good God, woman, will his grand rhymes an' his bits o' meddles an' his picture and the people's talk pay the rent for us? [*Folding his hands and looking at her with half-contemptuous pity.*] Well, surely, 'tis the foolish thing for a farmer to marry any but wan with the true farmer's blood in her. I should have guessed long ago what 'ud come of it when I married wan that had other blood in her veins. [*He goes towards the door and turns round.*] But Shane isn't gone yet—and maybe he'd never go! . . . Meddles!

[*He goes out.* MAURA *sits on the stool at the fireplace and looks vacantly into the fire.* SHANE *appears at the door and enters. He looks about twenty-three. He is rather low-sized, but the general physique indicates rough strength. There is a slight suggestion of hardness about the lines of the mouth.*]

SHANE. Will the supper soon be ready, mother? I feel a bit hungry.

MAURA [*starting*]. Oh, is that you, Shane? I never heard you coming in. 'Twill be on the table in five or ten minutes. [*Bustling towards dresser and putting cups on the table.*] I didn't expect you'd be back so soon.

SHANE. Oh, there's lots o' time.

MAURA. You got a lift, I suppose?

SHANE. No, then, I didn't. I came home across the fields.

MAURA. 'Tis wonderful the haste you must have made so! Dan Hegarty was here only a short while ago, and he had his horse, and he was saying he drove away the very minute the play was over.

SHANE. 'Twas how I left the field before the match was half over.

MAURA [*disappointed*]. Well! Well!

[BAT *reappears in the doorway. They are both unconscious of his presence till he speaks.*]

SHANE. It come into my head somehow that Hugh might be after forgetting to close up the gap this morning—he isn't over careful when them matches do be on—and I was thinking that the cows might be in the little patch o' winter cabbage, and as I was troubled about it I come away.

MAURA. Wisha, what a pity now! and Dan Hegarty was saying 'twas a grand sight altogether.

BAT. Was it now? Was it? If 'twas as grand again 'tis the hungry dinner 'twould make for us tomorrow, an' the day after, an' the day after that again.

MAURA. 'Twould so, I suppose.

BAT. You needn't be supposing it at all. You're the quare woman, Maura. 'Tisn't satisfied you are with wan of your sons making a fool of himself. . . . Have you candles in the house, and the lantern ready for the night?

MAURA. I'll see, Bat. I'll see this minute. . . . But why so?

BAT. We must be staying up, Shane and myself, with the sow tonight.

MAURA. Oh, I forgot. Sure of course. [*She opens the cupboard.*] There's plenty of candles. And as ye'll be in and out from the stall during the night 'twould be as well if Shane brought in a good *cireán* of turf to keep the fire up. Ye'll be wanting a sup o' hot milk or a cup o' tea at the latter end of the night.

SHANE. So we would. I'll bring in a good *bacal* of it after supper.

[MAURA *lifts cover of pot-oven to see the cake and removes the steaming kettle to the side of the hearth.* SHANE *and* BAT *sit on either side of the hearth opposite each other.*]

SHANE. Do you know I was thinking, an' I coming through the fields that 'twould be no harm for us to be turning in the cows o' nights from this out?

BAT. Sure we never housed them so soon after the Michaelmas?

SHANE. I know, but it looks as if there would be a great frost tonight.

MAURA. I was thinking so, too, from the look in the sky [*pointing west*]. Them red furrows in the west over the big hill is ever a token of the gray frost.

SHANE. 'Twould be a lot safer to turn them in.

BAT. Wait till I have a look out myself.

[*He goes towards the door for a moment.*]

BAT. 'Tis very chilly. There'll be a hard frost sure enough, and Shane is right.

[*He returns to the fireplace. There is a noise in the distance.*]

MAURA. What's that?

SHANE [*hurrying to door*]. 'Tis the people returning from the play. There's great crowds. I never seen such a sight o' people before. I hear them shouting. They're cheering for Hugh. Listen.

[*Shouting afar off.*]

MAURA [*shading her eyes*]. Glory be to God! was the like ever seen? 'Tis the end of the world you'd think it was. Where on earth did they all come from? For God's sake, come here and look at them, Bat. They're like a black flood covering the world.

BAT [*removing his pipe*]. That I may be blind if I will!

SHANE. They've a band too. The mare is up east on the little hill. If they give a blast of music 'twill frighten her. I'll run an' see after her. [*Going.*]

MAURA. Wisha, wait till you have a bit to eat? You didn't take a mouthful since one o'clock. She'll be all right, you'll find.

SHANE. I can't. Winnie is always a bit shy, an' 'tis a little thing would take a start out of her. [*Goes away hurriedly.*]

BAT [*with conviction*]. 'Tis more an' more I'm seeing the terrible loss that boy will be to us. . . . Isn't it a pity now the Great Man above didn't take it into His head to send him to us before the other?

MAURA. He knows Himself what's best, glory and honor to His Name. 'Tis queer for us—and the great blindness that's on us all—to be talking that way.

BAT. Yeh, have sense, have sense, woman.

MAURA. It can't be right at all. 'Tis many a man and woman in the big world that's hungry in their hearts for a little crying child this night, and you complaining that have two fine sons. I tell you, it can't be right at all, Bat.

BAT. Yeh, what nonsense!—that's no talk at all. . . . Where's Hugh? Isn't it time for him to be here now? Maybe 'tis missing the Rosary he'll be again tonight, like last Sunday?

MAURA. I'm sure he'll be here shortly. And sure if he wasn't in for the Rosary same he didn't forget to say it by himself. I was taking a pillow into his room, and 'twas on his two knees I saw him with the beads in his hands.

BAT. You're the great wan entirely for excusing him, no matter what divilment he does be at. 'Tis the quare prop he'll be for this house an' I'm greatly afeard 'tis the foolish thing I'm doing.

MAURA. Ah, sure, don't say that at all.

[*He goes towards the door slowly, and turns round speaking with measured deliberation.*]

BAT. 'Tis the foolish thing, Maura, when a man have the choice o' two poles to put under the roof of his house, to take that wan that is wake an' crooked an' rotten, just because it is a year or two older. . . . An' that's what I'm doing, Maura Morrissey. [*He goes out slowly.*]

[*After an interval* HUGH *is heard approaching. He enters with eager step.* MAURA *hastens to meet him. He is an open, lithe-limbed youth of twenty-five. He is in knickers, and his unbuttoned coat hangs loosely about him showing the crimson jersey beneath. In his hand is a hurley.*]

HUGH [*enthusiastically*]. Mother, glorious news! We've won the final after a splendid tussle. Isn't it great, and some of the best men in Ireland against us?

MAURA. Is there any hurt on you at all? Don't be telling me anything till I know that first.

HUGH [*laughing*]. Oh, make your mind easy. I escaped without a scratch.

MAURA. But is it the truth you're telling me?

HUGH. Oh, God knows, mother, it is.

MAURA [*doubtingly*]. Sure I can't trust you at all since the time your wrist was sprained, and all the lies you told to keep it from me.

HUGH [*playfully*]. Look here, you foolish little woman, will this set your mind at rest?

[*He dances a short sprightly step, whistling an accompaniment at the same time.*]

HUGH. Could a man do that and anything to be wrong with him?

MAURA [*laughing*]. Well, indeed, 'tis hardly. Thanks be to God that brought you home safe! But sure you must be weak with the hunger. I'll have the tea in half a minute. [*She bustles towards fireplace.*]

HUGH. Oh, look here, mother, 'tis hardly worth while. I'm in a desperate hurry.

MAURA [*surprised*]. What's that you're saying?

HUGH [*conciliatory*]. 'Tis how we're giving a little bit of a supper to the other team over at Pat Lacy's. There was a couple o' pounds left after paying the expenses of the tournament. 'Tis to be at six o'clock, and I just hurried over for a few minutes to tell you not to be staying up for me tonight. It may be half-past ten—or a little bit later—before I'll be home.

MAURA [*sitting down despondently*]. Oh, wisha! wisha! wisha!

HUGH. Yeh, what's the matter at all? What is it, mother?

MAURA [*rising with sudden energy*]. Hugh, boy, you'll stay at home this night, won't you?—won't you?

HUGH. And good heavens, why? Why, mother?

MAURA [*hesitatingly*]. Sure, just to please me, a poor old woman, Hugh, who—who haven't altogether too many pleasures in her life maybe. Won't you, Hugh?

HUGH. How can I, mother? How can I? 'Tis hard on me to be refusing, but sure *I* must be there whoever else will be there.

MAURA. And you won't do that small thing for me! O Hugh! Hugh! Hugh! [*She turns away reproachfully.*]

HUGH. For God's sake don't talk like that, mother. . . . I'd do anything in the world for your sake, and you know it.

MAURA. You'll not go then? I knew you wouldn't refuse me.

HUGH. Mother, look here. I'll not leave this roof tonight if
you'll be anyway against it when I tell you how it is with me.

MAURA. Thank God, Hugh, thank God! You don't know
the relief it is to my mind. You could be writing a message
to say to them you can't come. I'll run out to get some messenger to take it east for you. [*She puts on her shawl hastily,
and hurries towards the door.*] The bottle of ink is over there
near the brass candlestick. [*Going.*]

HUGH. Wait, mother, wait a minute. Sure I haven't told
you at all about it yet.

MAURA. It don't matter at all, when you're not going.
Maybe I'll find some one against the time you'll be writing the
letter. [*Going.*]

HUGH. But look here, mother.

MAURA [*anxiously*]. Well?

HUGH. How do you know but 'tis changing your mind
you'll be when I tell you the way 'tis with me about the business?

MAURA [*troubled*]. What is it, then?

HUGH. Here's a note I got from Father Daly. He got a
sick call before the match was over, and scribbled it on a leaf
of his notebook before he left the field. Curly Twomey that
brought it to me.

MAURA. Read it for me yourself. 'Tis cruel hard to make
out his writing always, God bless him.

HUGH. Very well. This is what he says:

"DEAR HUGH—I've met the Canon and spoken to him.
He has no objection whatever to the club entertaining themselves so long as I hold myself responsible. Unfortunately,
I've got a sick call at the other end of the parish and cannot
be present. In my absence it will remain entirely with you
to see that everything is seemly, and that there is no excess."
Listen to this, mother.

"Delighted with our men today. They were simply magnificent, and their captain's playing superb.

　　　　　　　　　　"Yours very faithfully,
　　　　　　　　　　　　　"CHARLES DALY."

HUGH. Well, mother?

MAURA [*after a pause*]. You can't refuse the priest.

HUGH [*in playful triumph*]. Didn't I say you would change your mind?

MAURA [*sadly*]. You did, indeed.

HUGH. But in any case, why on earth should you be uneasy about me? Surely I am able to take decent care of myself. Father Daly thinks so anyway . . . [*half bitterly*]. Is it because I had the misfortune to get drunk once in my life —and that three years ago—that you have so little trust in me?

MAURA. Oh, no, no, no, Hugh! 'Tis not that, indeed and indeed. 'Tis upset and troubled I was because of himself. It was, indeed.

HUGH. And why so, mother?

MAURA [*conciliatory*]. 'Twas how he was in a kind of temper all the evening since Dan Hegarty called with Shane's trunk. Dan would be talking about the goal and the great work entirely you done today, and you know that's the last thing that's good for him to hear. And 'tis greatly afraid I am that he'll be wild entirely with yourself and with us all when he finds you're not in the house for the Rosary tonight.

HUGH [*annoyed*]. That's most unfortunate! But what can I do? He seems to be getting more and more unreasonable every day. When a man does his big best for six days of the week 'tis hardly fair to grudge him Sunday! . . . Well, I'm bound to go all the same, no matter how he'll take it—but, indeed, I've no heart for pleasure now.

MAURA. Ah, well, sure, never mind—'tis only a little thing after all.

HUGH. I wouldn't care much for myself—I'd just as lief stay at home—but to be thinking of you sitting there quiet all night on that stool, and he opposite you, an' the hard word, an' the bitter word, coming in turn from his lips, and myself to be the cause of it all!

MAURA. Yeh, sure he don't mean the half of what he says. I don't mind him at all—sure, 'tis time for me now to be used to his ways. Don't be thinking of that at all or letting it trouble your mind. 'Tis half sorry I am for telling you at all.

HUGH. Oh, nonsense; why shouldn't you, mother? Why shouldn't you, indeed? And where is he now?

MAURA. He's out with Shane. They're looking after the mare, and they're thinking, too, of turning in the cows tonight.

HUGH. So soon?—but there's a frosty chill in the air. . . . [*More cheerfully.*] Look, mother. There's Father Daly's letter. If he says anything show it to him.

MAURA. 'Tis afraid I am 'twould only be making him worse. He can't bear to hear the name of Father Daly. "Destroying the parish," he says he is.

HUGH. There's not another priest in all this diocese like him! 'Tis the changed place the parish is since he came into it. And that's the thanks he's getting!

MAURA. 'Tis foolish for anyone to be expecting thanks in this world. 'Tis above he'll be getting a return for all the good he's after doing, so it is.

HUGH. That's about the truth of it, I'm thinking. [*Suddenly.*] 'Tis running a bit late, so I'll just run upstairs for a dash of cold water. I want to freshen myself up a bit for the night. . . . 'Tis too bad, but I suppose we can only let things take their course. He may say nothing after all.

MAURA. Maybe so, maybe so, indeed.

[*He hastily mounts the stairs to his room.* MAURA *prepares a cup of tea, which she is pouring out as he returns. He runs to a glass, tidying his hair.*]

MAURA. You weren't long. Here, take this and a cut of the hot cake. 'Tis easy to get a chill after the hot sweat o' the play, and 'twill warm you a bit.

HUGH. Thanks. Don't mind the cake. I won't eat anything. [*He gulps down the tea.*] That was a fine strong cup o' tea. It sent a warm wave like rushing all over me. I'll be going now; and I'm thinking, maybe, 'twould be no harm for all if you showed him the letter—the sight of the priest's name written by his own hand might soften him a bit, you know?

MAURA. Maybe so, then, with the help of God.

HUGH [*affectionately*]. And, mother, let the door on the latch, and I'll get to bed without disturbing anyone. I won't make a sound. I wouldn't have you wait up for all the world. [*Appealingly.*] Sure you won't now?

MAURA. No, I won't indeed, Hugh. I won't indeed. Make

your mind easy. . . . [*Playfully.*] Be off with yourself now, sir, I wouldn't have you a minute late after what the priest wrote.

HUGH [*pleasantly*]. You're right, mother. You're *always* right. Good-by. [*Going.*]

MAURA. Good-by, and God direct you!

[HUGH *goes out.* MAURA *stands a few moments at the door gazing after him. She returns and rearranges the supper table, removing cup and saucer to the dresser. After an interval a hurried step is heard.* SHANE *enters hastily, and with a show of strong excitement.*]

MAURA. What's the matter, Shane?

SHANE. Bad news enough then. The mare that's hurt on us.

MAURA. Virgin Mother! is it the truth you're saying?

SHANE. I'm not much given to joking. 'Tis for the gun I've come to put her out of pain. Her hind leg that's broken.

[*He stands on the chair and takes down the gun from the wall. He loads it in both barrels.*]

MAURA. *A Thighearna!* Isn't it terrible—terrible altogether? . . . And there's the plowing and everything else to be done by us, and no horse with us now—and the little foal not yet weaned.

SHANE [*bitterly*]. 'Twas the misfortunate match for us! Their cursed band that frightened her. Bad luck to the whole pack an' dice of them! That's what we've got by their tournament. [*He rushes out.*]

MAURA. 'Tis the terrible misfortune, surely. 'Tis the great loss entirely. . . . And Bat, sure 'twill kill him, and he always so proud of the brown mare. . . . The poor thing, and she always so good and willing, and the great worker for seven long years.

· [*A shot is heard.* MAURA *starts and cover her eyes. She remains thus till* SHANE *and* BAT *return.* SHANE *replaces the gun.* BAT *sits down in gloomy silence.*]

SHANE. All over, mother. One shot put an end to her.

MAURA. I heard it, God help us.

SHANE. She was the fine mare. She'll be the sore loss to ye.

MAURA. The sore loss, indeed.

SHANE. There wasn't another like her in the townland

for the work. 'Tis often I done nearly an acre o' plowing in the day with her, an' next morning she was as willing as ever again to take to the furrow; and it didn't matter whether 'twas uphill or downhill, or on the level *ban* she was. She was a great little woman—so she was.

MAURA. The poor thing!

SHANE. Do you know there was a kind of quare feeling come over me, an' I turning the gun at her?—a kind of shiver it was, an' a mist before my eyes.

MAURA. The poor dumb creature and she so kind.

SHANE. 'Tis strange I'll be feeling going across in the big ship, an' thinking of the lonely look in her big eyes with the death coming down on them like a dark dream. . . . Ah, well, ye'll have good reason to be remembering the great match whatever I'll do! 'Twas the dear match for ye! Thirty pounds she would be fetching as surely as she'd fetch a farthing. . . . And I suppose now you won't be entitled to any compensation, father?

BAT [*lifting his head*]. Where's Hugh?

MAURA. He's gone out.

BAT. Call him.

MAURA. There's no use. He's gone this half-hour or so. He won't be back for a bit.

BAT. An' why?

MAURA. The priest that sent for him on some business or other.

SHANE. 'Tis how Hugh's team are giving some kind of a spree to the other hurlers over at the village. I'm told there's to be great doings altogether, and there's to be a dance after.

MAURA [*with feverish eagerness*]. He won't be long at all. He said so going away. 'Tis only a supper they're having. 'Twas the priest himself asked him to look after things, and only for that he wouldn't be there at all. That's God's truth, Bat, so it is!

SHANE. They were saying it was to be a regular spree. But sure, whatever it is, 'twould be quare for the captain to be away from the diversions. 'Twould never do.

BAT. The black trouble is on this house this night, and feasting and drinking he is that should be here.

MAURA. Sure, God help us, he doesn't know it. How could he at all? And if he did, 'tis worse than Shane, or you or me, he'd feel, for he ever an' always loved the poor creature like a human thing.

BAT. A fine mare gone from us and he carousing . . . worth thirty pounds, Shane says. Worth every penny of forty pounds, I says. [*He stands up with an air of strong determination.*] Well, 'tis the long lane that have no turning, and my brave Hugh have come to the turning at last.

MAURA [*in alarm*]. What is it you're going to do at all, at all? Look, Bat, there's the priest's letter—written by his own blessed hand this day. [*Offering the letter.*] Only for it he'd be here in this kitchen this minute. God knows he would. [BAT *takes the letter. He goes towards the fireplace and with slow deliberation puts it into the fire unread. He watches it burn.*] Mother of God! What are you after doing? The letter that was written by the holy priest! There'll be no luck in this house forever again!

[BAT *goes calmly to the shelf over the fireplace, takes down pen and ink, and hands the pen to* SHANE.]

SHANE [*wonderingly*]. What's this for at all?

BAT. Wait. [*He goes to the trunk, takes out his penknife and carefully cuts off the label bearing* SHANE's *name. Handing label to* SHANE.] Read that for me.

SHANE [*reading*]. "John Morrissey, Passenger Queenstown to Boston, *via* Campania."

BAT. Good. Cross out the name that's on it, and write over it Hugh Morrissey. Make it plain and big. [SHANE *hesitates, looking questioningly.*]

BAT. What are you stopping for? Don't you understand plain talk?

SHANE. But, father—

BAT. Write it, I tell you, at wanst.

MAURA. But surely, surely, Bat— [*He pushes her roughly aside.*]

BAT. Shut your mouth, woman! 'Tis none o' your business! [*To* SHANE.] Write it—and write it at wanst, I say, or 'twill be worse for you!

[SHANE *writes slowly and carefully, and hands back the label to his father.*]

BAT [*looking at label in the stupid manner of a half-illiterate and handing it back to* SHANE]. Read it for me.

SHANE [*reading*]. "Hugh Morrissey, Passenger Queenstown to Boston, *via* Campania." [*He returns it to his father, who goes towards the trunk, and with a grim smile reattaches it to the handle.*]

BAT. Now, my fine captain, you may drink and feast to the devil!

[MAURA *sits in silent grief. There is a look of uncertain emotion on* SHANE'S *face as the curtain descends.*]

ACT II

SCENE: *The same. Midnight. There is a candle on the dresser throwing a dull light. In the middle of the room is a table laid for one.* MAURA, *worn and troubled, is kneeling at a chair, a Rosary bead in her hand. There is heard the sound of approaching footsteps, and the latch is lifted. She goes to unbolt the door in trembling haste.*

MAURA. Who's there? Is that yourself, Hugh?

HUGH. Open, mother.

[*She draws the bolt.* HUGH *comes in. She bolts the door again.*]

MAURA. What kept you at all, at all? I was getting very troubled about you.

HUGH. 'Twas how I couldn't manage to get away. I did my very best, honestly. God knows I did, mother.

MAURA. Sure, of course. I know, I know. But I was half uneasy like with the night passing and no sign of you at all.

HUGH [*dismally*]. Such a night of it as I'm after going through! 'Tis little notion Father Daly had the kind of task he was setting me! Good Heavens, such a night, mother!

MAURA. 'Twasn't too easy to manage them all, I suppose?

HUGH. Easy? Easy is it? [*Solemnly.*] I give you my word for it I'll be very, very slow to undertake the same responsibility again!

MAURA. Well, now.

HUGH. Some of the other team, when they had a small share of drink taken, were as cross as two sticks. 'Twas no joke at all to keep them in pleasant humor. 'Tisn't hard for men when they're after losing a great game to be losing their tempers after it.

MAURA. That's true, indeed. . . . But isn't it very pale entirely you're looking, Hugh? 'Tis whiter than the candle you are.

HUGH. I'm fagged out after the day. To tell you the honest truth, I never felt so tired in all my life. 'Twas awful to get the fellows away! I thought I could never get the last of them home. They'd stick on till daylight if I'd let them. One by one I had to force them into the wagonette—nearly twenty of them in all. [*Cheerfully.*] But, then, sure everything came right in the end.

MAURA. Thank God for that!

HUGH. 'Tis very late, I suppose?

MAURA. The clock is after striking twelve, but I'm thinking it must be a bit fast. I was afraid o' my life I'd be late for Mass this morning, but I was in a good while before the priest came on the altar.

HUGH [*reproachfully*]. And you stayed up for me after all your promises? Ah, mother, mother, mother!

MAURA [*extenuatingly*]. Well, now, I did and I didn't. 'Twas how I couldn't sleep. There was a kind of whirl and an aching in my head, and I thought 'twould ease it a bit if I came down here and busied myself a little till you came. There was plenty for me to be doing, I tell you.

HUGH. There you are!—always and ever thinking of everyone's comfort but your own. I'm sore afraid, you foolish little woman, you'll never learn sense. But there's no use talking to you.

MAURA. Wisha, don't be foolish. I've a nice little bit of supper for you here. 'Twill do you good, an' you want it.

HUGH. I couldn't touch a morsel, I'm so dead tired. Honestly, mother.

MAURA. I'll make the tea very hot, and I have a fine drop of goat's milk. 'Twill warm you a bit, and then you can run off to bed. 'Twon't take five minutes altogether.

HUGH. But sure I had tea before leaving Lacy's. Mrs. Lacy herself made me take a cup after all the others going away.

MAURA. What matter? There's a small bit o' meat since the dinner—'tis the ham, and 'tis very sweet. I thought you'd like it, you're always so fond of the ham.

HUGH [*yielding pleasantly*]. Very well so, let us have it.

MAURA. 'Twill be ready in half a minute. [*Puts tea to*

draw.] 'Tis terrible pale entirely you are after the day. You'd frighten a person. Look, while the tea'll be drawing I'll be taking off your boots for you. Put them up there on that little stool. [*Kneels down to remove his boots.*]

HUGH [*protestingly*]. Oh, nonsense, mother; nonsense! I'll take them off myself. I'm all right. I'm only a little tired, that's all.

MAURA. Ah, wisha, can't you let me—to please me this night?

HUGH [*half reluctantly*]. Well, so, if 'twill please you.

[*She begins to unfasten the lace when a man's heavy footsteps are heard on the stones outside approaching the door.*]

MAURA [*in a half-whisper*]. My God, Hugh, your father!

HUGH. And what matter, sure?

MAURA. Whisht! whisht! for God's sake, talk easy.

[*A hand lifts the latch and tries to push in the bolted door. They keep still.*]

BAT [*outside*]. Maura. [*There is no answer.*]

BAT [*more peremptorily*]. Maura! Maura!

[*There is still no answer. The footsteps are heard moving slowly away from the door.*]

MAURA. He thinks 'tis in the bed I am. He's going round to the back to rap at the bedroom window. Look, for God's sake! keep out of his way tonight. Run upstairs to your room till he's gone. Do, do, Hugh?

HUGH. Yeh, for what, mother? Have a bit of sense. What's the great harm I'm after doing at all?

MAURA. No harm, no harm, indeed. But he's in the black rage tonight. Ah, do, do! Won't you, Hugh?

HUGH [*half vexed*]. Mother, do you think 'tis a frightened child, I am?

MAURA. No, no, indeed I don't, Hugh; but there's a great fear in my heart—

HUGH. Yeh, nonsense. There's nothing at all to be troubled about. Nothing whatever. He'll say nothing, and if he does—sure let him.

MAURA. Well, so, won't you promise me not to mind at all whatever he'll be saying? 'Tis queer in himself he is, and greatly upset—for the mare that's after dying on us.

HUGH. What's that you say? Is it Winnie?

MAURA. She's dead. She broke her leg, and Shane had to

shoot her. [*Beseechingly.*] For the blessed Lord's sake, Hugh, don't heed anything at all your father'll say this night! 'Tis nearly out of his mind he is with the loss o' the mare.

[*A loud tapping is heard on the window of the bedroom off the kitchen.* MAURA *stands in the shadow of the doorway between kitchen and bedroom and feigns to answer from her bed.*]

BAT. Maura. Maura.

MAURA [*in half-drowsy tones*]. Who's there?

BAT [*roughly*]. Maura!

MAURA. Oh, is that yourself, Bat?

BAT. Get up and open the door. You put the bolt on it an' you going to bed. I want a candle, and I can't get in. The wan we have is nearly burned out.

MAURA. Just one minute, Bat—one minute. I'll have it opened against the time you'll be round. [*She reënters kitchen.*]

MAURA [*half distractedly*]. Promise me, Hugh, for God's sake, you won't take him up whatever he says. Won't you? Won't you? If you don't, God Himself only knows what might come of it. Look, on my two knees I'm begging you.

HUGH. For heaven's sake don't do that mother. I'll do anything you want—anything at all in the wide world. I'll not open my lips this night if you wish it. Now.

MAURA. God bless you, Hugh. God bless you for that, boy.

[BAT's *heavy step is heard again.* MAURA *throws a shawl around her and takes the candle off the dresser. As the latch is lifted she draws the bolt, and with feverish haste hands out the candle over the half-door to* BAT, *who is standing on the doorstep outside. The kitchen is very dimly lit by the glow of the fire.*]

BAT. Isn't it a great wandher you wouldn't think of laving the door on the latch, an' we wanting to be in and out? You must be always doing the quare thing an' the sthupid thing, Maura.

MAURA. I didn't notice myself bolting it, somehow, and I going to bed.

BAT. Well, notice it the next time, or 'tis out of your bed you'll have to be marching again—an' serve you right!

MAURA [*half-closing the door*]. Oh, I'll think of it this time, never mind.

BAT. Well, do so. [*He goes away slowly with the lighted candle in his hand.*]

MAURA [*fervently*]. Oh, thanks be to the Almighty God for that, Hugh! [*She lights a candle. Her hands are trembling.*]

HUGH [*with tender concern*]. You're trembling all over, mother.

MAURA. 'Twas foolish o' me to be so frightened, but—but I couldn't help it. Something in my heart that stirred when the latch rattled.

HUGH. Ah, sure, if I thought 'twould be like that at all with you I'd have gone up to the room the time you asked me, an' gladly too. I would, indeed.

MAURA. Sure it don't matter at all now that he's gone.

HUGH. It looked a cowardly thing, somehow, to be running away and a man after doing no wrong at all; but 'tis a lot more cowardly it looks now to be after remaining, and you to be the way you are this minute.

MAURA. Don't say that at all.

HUGH [*eagerly*]. Look here now. I'll go off straight to my room this minute for fear anything else might be bringing him back a second time. What do you say? Isn't it best?

MAURA. Well, maybe, 'twould be just as good. And I can take up the tea to you after.

HUGH. All right so.

[*He takes a candle and is lighting it at the fire when the latch is lifted again. The door is opened in.* MAURA *hastens towards it.* BAT *appears in the doorway.* HUGH *is in the shelter of the deep fireplace.*]

BAT [*to* MAURA]. Didn't you go back to bed since? Faith, 'tis hot in your blood you are! The night outside is getting very chilly, an' 'twould be no harm for me, I'm thinking, to be putting on my big coat against the frost. [*He advances into the room and sees* HUGH.]

BAT. So the spree is over at last?

MAURA. Wisha, say nothing to him tonight, Bat. He's not well at all. Look at the color he is, the Lord save us!

BAT [*in derision*]. Yes, look at him!—look at the cut of him!

MAURA [*appealingly*]. Wisha, Bat.

BAT [*with jeering mimicry*]. "Wisha, Bat." . . . Ah, Maura, Maura, 'tis you have the good right to be speaking for him—him that has the great love for you, keeping you up in the bitter night till near cockcrow. But sure he wouldn't be a rale gentleman an' he to come home earlier.

MAURA. No, no, Bat, you're wronging him. He didn't keep me up at all—he didn't, indeed. 'Twas the way I couldn't sleep with a queer pain in my head, and I thought 'twould do me good to come down to the fire for a little while.

BAT [*thunderingly*]. Hush your mouth, you!

BAT [*to* HUGH]. Have you any tongue in your head to-night, man? Maybe 'tis ashamed of yourself you are at last—you—you half-drunken scoundrel!

MAURA [*to* HUGH]. Don't mind him at all.

HUGH [*with quiet dignity*]. Those are hard words, father, but they're not true words.

MAURA [*to* HUGH]. Don't mind him this night at all, Hugh. Sure, thank God, no one could ever say that of you, and your father, he don't mean it at all.

BAT [*half savagely*]. Didn't I tell you hush your mouth before? Go in there straight to your bed, an' don't be interfering with what's no concern of yours! Do you hear me?

MAURA [*appealingly*]. Wisha, Bat—

BAT. Go at wanst, I tell you! Go now!

[*She goes towards her room, but lingers in the doorway.*]

BAT. Now, sir, I'm going to talk to you, an' 'tis the plain talk I'll give you. You're never in your life to spend another week under this roof.

[HUGH *starts and looks incredulous.*]

BAT. You think I don't mane it. Look here. By God, I swear it!

·HUGH [*distressfully*]. You wouldn't, father—you wouldn't, surely?

BAT. I've sworn it, sir. You'll lave this house instead of your brother on Thursday morning.

HUGH. You're not in earnest—you wouldn't be so hard—you wouldn't, surely? What wrong have I done?

BAT. Ah, 'tis well you're finding your tongue now, you

idle scoundrel! Go you must, an' go you will! Maybe 'tis perjuring myself you'd like me to be?

HUGH. 'Tis not, for you're not bound by such an oath. 'Tis unjust, and you know it.

BAT [*jeeringly*]. Is it so?

HUGH. Ever since I was a little child 'twas told to me that this place would be mine—you told me so yourself.

BAT. I don't care what I told you! This farm is my own and no one else's. I have put the whole work o' my life into it, and I'll do whatever I like with it. And out of this you'll march bag and baggage on Thursday morning! There! [*Taking trunk and flinging it towards him.*] You're a great scholar. You'll be able to read that label, I suppose.

MAURA [*rushing towards* BAT]. In the name of the good God, Bat—for the honor of Mary, His Mother—

[*He pushes her aside roughly, and goes out uttering half-smothered ejaculations. There is a long pause,* HUGH *sinks into a seat, his head buried in his hands. After a while* MAURA *goes to him timidly.*]

HUGH. Mother, don't come near me.

MAURA. Oh, Hugh!

HUGH. I'm sick of everything.

MAURA. *Dia linn as mhuire Mháthair!*

HUGH. The weight o' the world is on my heart . . . and that look on your face . . . 'tis the weight that's crushing it all down.

MAURA. Wisha, don't mind me at all, my poor boy. . . . Won't you be going to bed? 'Tis cold and white and shivering you are.

HUGH. 'Tis nothing—nothing at all. Let me by myself for a bit and I'll be better. 'Tis you want the rest, poor woman, and not I—'tis, indeed, mother.

MAURA [*with feigned cheerfulness*]. Sure not at all! I was always wonderful for staying up a night. [*Insinuatingly.*] Maybe you'll take a cup o' the tea after all? And I'll take a sup with you for the company. Do, Hugh.

HUGH. I couldn't, mother, I couldn't. Don't ask me.

MAURA. I won't then. I won't, Hugh.

HUGH [*going to her affectionately*]. Let me alone here by the fire for a little bit, mother, and I'll be all right very soon. You won't refuse me my last Sunday night here—you that never refused me anything in my life.

MAURA. Very well, Hugh, boy. I'll go if 'twill please you. *A Mhuire Mháthair!* What a black night! [*She leaves the room weeping silently.* HUGH *sits on the stool at the fire looking desolately into the dying embers.*]

HUGH. All over now. . . . A black night surely. . . . Poor Winnie dead, too, after all her years. Shot. The poor thing! The poor thing! . . . Thursday morning he said. Short shrift enough! 'Tis the hard landlord that gives only three days' notice. Well, 'tis many a better man has traveled the same road before. [*He looks at the trunk. He examines the label.*]

HUGH. Shane that wrote it! Shane! How could he do it? The miserable cur!—'tis only like him. A grabber—a mean, low grabber! Oh, such a piece of treachery! I could—yes, by God! I could choke the mean soul out of him this minute . . . yet for her sake, with her face full of sorrow, I'll say nothing. Poor mother! God help her! God help her!

[*There is a pause. He is halfway up the stairs, the candle in his hand, when the door opens and* SHANE *comes in. There is a look of eager questioning on his face.*]

SHANE. For God's sake, Hugh, what's up at all? My father went in for a candle, and ever since he come back he hasn't spoken a word or minded anything at all, but walking up and down the stall in a black silence.

HUGH. It doesn't matter—let me alone.

SHANE. Where's the harm in asking?

HUGH. Let me alone, I ask you, this night!

SHANE. And why so?

HUGH. Why so? Well, because—because the less talk between you and me just now the better maybe for both of us.

SHANE. Well, there's no doubt of it, but you're getting mighty civil, Hugh.

HUGH. Maybe 'tis too civil I am to a grabber.

SHANE. To what?

HUGH. I ask you again to get out of my sight!

SHANE [*threateningly*]. What's that you said first?

HUGH [*with a great effort of self-repression*]. In God's name, will you go or not?

SHANE. Who's a grabber?

HUGH. You are—and the meanest grabber that ever walked the earth.

SHANE. You drunken brute, if you say that again—

HUGH [*hotly*]. You're a liar, and I will say it again, and I'll say it till I'm hoarse, for there was never a dirtier grabber in all Ireland than yourself—grabbing a brother's land.

SHANE. That's a lie for you! What right had you to this place—you that never did an honest day's work in your life?

HUGH. What right had I?

SHANE. Yes, yes, what right? Is it because you were born a year or two before me? 'Tis the man's work an' not the reckoning of his years that makes the right! So it is!

HUGH. You may talk and argue till the Day of Judgment, but a grabber—a mean treacherous grabber you are and nothing else!

SHANE. Say that word again and by the Lord God— [*Pauses choked with passion.*]

HUGH [*confronting him*]. Well, what then? What then, Shaneen?—Shaneen the grabber?

SHANE [*making to strike him*]. Blast you!

[*They struggle with each other for a moment in a tempest of blind rage.* MAURA *rushes in.*]

MAURA. My God, what is it? What is up with ye at all? [*She rushes between them.*] Oh, shame, shame, shame, this holy night! Shame for you, Hugh—what has come over you at all? And black shame for you, Shane, and you knowing the great wrong done him—and the heavy load that is on his heart this night!

SHANE. He brought it on himself with his drunken lies. Don't be blaming me.

MAURA. For shame, Shane, don't be saying things like that.

SHANE. The whiskey was cheap tonight.

MAURA. If it was, there was none of it wet his lips, and you know it well, Shane. 'Tis the soft word, and the word of pity, and not the bitter thought should be on your lips this night.

SHANE. I'll say what I like. 'Twas he began it.

MAURA. 'Tis little heed you should be putting on his words an' his heart breaking.

SHANE. Oh, of course, of course. 'Tis the old story—taking his side always. There should be no favorites in this house, nor in any other house, neither.

MAURA. And sure, glory be to God, there isn't, boy?

SHANE. That's not true!—there is favorites here, an' for many a long day, too.

MAURA. Oh, Shane, boy, don't be talking like that. 'Tisn't true at all, and you know it well. Hush!

SHANE. I won't hush! You're always again me, whoever is in the wrong. 'Tisn't today nor yesterday I've seen it. I tell you 'tis the bad thing for any woman to be making distinctions between her own flesh and blood.

MAURA. Oh, Shane, sure you don't mean that at all? 'Tis the awful queer crooked fancy that's come into your mind. But 'tisn't true at all—indeed and indeed it isn't.

SHANE. That's a lie—and an infernal lie!

HUGH [*starting up.*] That's no way for you to speak to your mother! 'Tis only to a woman the like of you would say it.

SHANE. I don't want no words at all from you while the smell o' the drink is on them.

MAURA [*forcing* HUGH *into his seat*]. Whisht, whisht, for God's sake! Let us have no more words this blessed night. Say your prayers and go to bed, the two of ye, in the name of God. 'Tis very late. Won't you, Shane? Won't you, boy?

SHANE. I'll go when I'm after saying what I want to say, an' what's on my mind for many a day.

MAURA. Wisha, hush, hush, boy! 'Tis after one o'clock, and we're all dead tired.

SHANE. You says there is no favorite here.

MAURA. Wisha, Shane, *a chuid!*

SHANE. But I can swear it to you there is. I've seen it again and again since I was able to understand anything.

MAURA. Ah, wisha, Shane, boy, don't be thinking such a queer thought at all. There's no mortal reason for it—whatever put the foolish notion into your head.

SHANE. 'Tis no foolish notion, an' you know it too! When we were small boys an' we sitting there at that table, who always used to be given the white loaf, an' who used to get the strong cake? An' who was it always got the fine cloth from the shops in Macroom, an' which of us had to be wearing the gray homespun that was like what the poorhouse boys do be wearing, an' they walking out the country roads with their schoolmaster? An' who—

MAURA. Glory be to God, what's come over you? Sure ye were only the same to me as two lambs that would be on the one hill, only one o' ye being a bit stronger like than the other.

SHANE. 'Twas damn bad luck to be the strong lamb—so it was!

MAURA. Hugh hadn't the big strength that you had and he growing up, because that he grew so quick, and he had to be coaxed like to bring him on.

SHANE. Well, so, was it because he hadn't the strength that you used to be taking him to the town to see the fair an' the circus, an' leaving me at home thinking bitter things in my heart? An' was it because he hadn't the strength you got the priest to put him on the altar serving the Mass an' never thought o' me?

MAURA. Wisha, God help us, Shane, sure that was only because he was so quick at the learning.

SHANE. Oh, of course—of course! That was only one o' the distinctions you made between us when I was a boy, and if God made me rough, He didn't make me rough enough not to feel them and remember them to this hour. An' when we grew up 'tisn't one nor a dozen distinctions that was made between us, but a hundred and more. How could I have the soft feeling for you, or for him, or for anyone else? An' if I have the black hatred in my heart instead this night, is it your fault or my own?

MAURA. Shane, Shane, don't be saying such awful things. If I ever, ever made a difference 'twas unknownst to me. 'Twas indeed. Before God, I never meant them! I didn't, I— I didn't indeed. . . . [*Breaks off sobbingly.*]

HUGH [*passionately*]. You're a big cowardly brute to torture like that the woman that bore you. By God! I'll not listen to any more of it. If you dare to say another thing to her I'll—look—I'll choke the words in your throat, you— you mean hound, you—you—you miserable cur.

SHANE. Try it! do! I'll say what I like an' give you no thanks, great a hero as you are.

HUGH. Do it at your peril!

SHANE. You think I'm afraid of you?

MAURA. Ah, hush, let ye; hush, hush! [*To* HUGH.] Sure, Shane don't mean at all what he's saying.

SHANE. I do mean it—an' every single word of it.

MAURA. What harm? What harm?

HUGH [*scornfully*]. What could anyone expect from the likes of him after his treacherous work of this night?

MAURA. Ah, look, look now, the two of ye, have the grace of God about ye and go to bed?

HUGH. Is it me to lie on the same pillow with a man like him this night?

SHANE. No, I'm not a fine gentleman, and I drunk on other people's money—

HUGH. No, you're not, but do you know what you are? Do you? Do you? [*Approaching him threateningly.*]

MAURA. Stop! Stop!

HUGH [*passionately*]. You're a coward and you're a grabber! That's what you are, and nothing else.

[*At the word "grabber," Shane rushes wildly at HUGH. They get into handgrips and begin to struggle in blind and furious passion.*]

MAURA [*frantically, rushing out*]. Bat! Bat! for God's sake, run! They're killing each other!

[*The two men reel and stagger blindly. SHANE is seen to stumble and fall. Struggling onto his feet, he leaps at his brother. The impact brings them both to the ground. There is a horrid thud. HUGH lies perfectly still. Gathering himself up, SHANE looks on the prostrate figure. He is dazed and horrified. Pity and terror in his voice, he calls*

"Hugh! Hugh!"

There is only a dreadful stillness. He staggers out into the night crying "O God! O God!"

MAURA *rushes in and, bending distractedly over the boy's body, cries "Hugh! Hugh!" Bat is seen coming through the doorway, his face tense with alarm, as the curtain falls.*]

GROUP IV

PLAYS OF PATRIOTISM

THE SINGER is an attempt to explain the motives of idealism and self-sacrifice which at least one man felt during the Irish rebellion against the oppression of foreign overlords. Its author, Padraic Pearse, was a leader in the last organized movement against England culminating in the bloody Easter revolt in 1916. Pearse was executed in Kilmainham jail by the English government on May 3 of that year for his part in the Dublin uprising. Coming as it does from one who gave his life for Irish freedom, fulfilling his Singer's destiny as he himself had foretold, with love and pity without bitterness, the play has an added significance as an authentic spiritual biography.

The passion of patriotism, somewhat dimmed and foreign to us now after the mockery of the Great War, burns so brightly in these pages that it becomes a futile task to try and ascertain any philosophic worth which might be contained in them. *The Singer* pretends to be nothing more than the sudden outcry of a man facing imminent martyrdom, attempting to express, without attenuation, the emotional causes underlying his behavior. As a sincere projection of these emotions, the artistic integrity of the play is unquestioned. The patriotic drama of Ireland is as little for the cynic as it is for the academician. *The Singer* comes so close to the childlike heart of the Irish peasant that it has no protection from the smile of the sophisticate or the sneer of the cynic. Either of these would quench the bright flame of emotion the play gives off and crumble its beauty to ashes with a breath. The spirit in which it is written disarms criticism. So let us enter into that spirit as its Irish actors would enter into its playing, with a simplicity and a childlike sincerity. Then we may say all we need to say about

The Singer, as we finish it—this is deep, this is real, this is the Ireland that is like a child.

Maeve draws again for us the picture of Ireland, with Maeve as "the sweet symbol of her country in subjection," torn by the necessity of choosing either the actual world or the world of ancient dream. The symbolism is clear and consistent throughout. Ireland and England are separated by extreme racial differences. And these must ever continue between Celt and Anglo-Saxon because of their totally disparate temperaments. Faced with the prospect of forsaking the ideal beauty of her dream and the wonder of a poetic past, for a new, strange life with one who is at a far remove from the beliefs and traditions so meaningful to her, Maeve accepts the life in death which the Fairy Queen offers her. In a brilliant introduction to *The Heather Field and Maeve,*[1] George Moore says, "The idea of both plays is that silvery beauty which survives in the human heart, which we see shimmering to the horizon, leading our longings beyond the world, and we hear it in our hearts like silver harp strings, sounding seemingly of themselves, for no hand is by. The morning light, the hoar frost, the moonlight wandering among the mountains are the natural symbols of this divine beauty. Therefore Maeve is made of moonlight and hoar frost and light of morning. We do not discover her among our acquaintances, but everyone discovers her when he wills to do so in his own heart. Maeve is a character evolved out of a place; she is made out of the light of the keen bright Irish spring and the loneliness of the Clare mountains that surround her home, of the round tower, the masterwork of Goban, on which she gazes with intense eyes; of the legends of the ancient Irish gods, of the beauty of the Irish romanesque ornament, those exquisite traceries which are a reflection of the Byzantine, but more refined. Maeve is the spirit and sense of an ill-fated race, and she portrays its destiny and bears the still unextinguished light of its heroic period. Maeve is all ecstasy, tremulous white ecstasy, cold as ice and glittering like ice in the moonlight. She looks beyond the world for her love; she is haunted by the herolepsy of the plume and the spear of the warrior, and sees

[1] London: Duckworth & Co. (1899).

her lover the chiefest among the chieftains of Queen Maeve. Maeve's love is a cerebral erithism which shrinks from all contact or even thought of the contact of flesh. But this severance of her temperament from the strange fruition of all our holy and most tender aspirations does not alienate our sympathy from her. Although shorn of all common humanity our sympathy is with her, . . . and we cry, 'Believe in your warrior of long ago, and let go by you the young Englishman who seeks to rob you of your dream'; and to triumph thus over common instincts and infect the reader with sympathies and longings which lie beyond the world is surely to succeed where hitherto no modern English dramatist has even dreamed that drama was to be found."

THE SINGER

By *Padraic Pearse*

CHARACTERS

MACDARA, *the Singer*
COLM, *his Brother*
MAIRE NI FHIANNACHTA, *Mother of MacDara*
SIGHLE
MAOILSHEACHLAINN, *a Schoolmaster*
CUIMIN EANNA
DIARMAID *of the Bridge*

SCENE: *The wide, clean kitchen of a country house. To the left a door, which when open, shows a wild country with a background of lonely hills; to the right a fireplace, beside which another door leads to a room. A candle burns on the table.*

    MAIRE NI FHIANNACHTA, *a sad, gray-haired woman, is spinning wool near the fire.* SIGHLE, *a young girl, crouches in the inglenook, carding. She is barefooted.*

MAIRE. Mend the fire, Sighle, jewel.
SIGHLE. Are you cold?
MAIRE. The feet of me are cold.
    [SIGHLE *rises and mends the fire, putting on more turf; then she sits down again and resumes her carding.*]
    SIGHLE. You had a right to go to bed.
MAIRE. I couldn't have slept, child. I had a feeling that something was drawing near to us. That something or somebody was coming here. All day yesterday I heard footsteps abroad on the street.
SIGHLE. 'Twas the dry leaves. The quicken trees in the gap were losing their leaves in the high wind.

236

MAIRE. Maybe so. Did you think that Colm looked anxious in himself last night when he was going out?

SIGHLE. I may as well quench that candle. The dawn has whitened. [*She rises and quenches the candle; then resumes her place.*]

MAIRE. Did you think, daughter, that Colm looked anxious and sorrowful in himself when he was going out?

SIGHLE. I did.

MAIRE. Was he saying anything to you?

SIGHLE. He was. [*They work silently for a few minutes; then* SIGHLE *stops and speaks.*] Maire ni Fhiannachta, I think I ought to tell you what your son said to me. I have been going over and over it in my mind all the long hours of the night. It is not right for the two of us to be sitting at this fire with a secret like that coming between us. Will I tell you what Colm said to me?

MAIRE. You may tell me if you like, Sighle girl.

SIGHLE. He said to me that he was very fond of me.

MAIRE [*who has stopped spinning*]. Yes, daughter?

SIGHLE. And . . . and he asked me if he came safe out of the trouble, would I marry him.

MAIRE. What did you say to him?

SIGHLE. I told him that I could not give him any answer.

MAIRE. Did he ask you why you could not give him an answer?

SIGHLE. He did; and I didn't know what to tell him.

MAIRE. Can you tell me?

SIGHLE. Do you remember the day I first came to your house, Maire?

MAIRE. I do well.

SIGHLE. Do you remember how lonely I was?

MAIRE. I do, you creature. Didn't I cry myself when the priest brought you in to me? And you caught hold of my skirt and wouldn't let it go, but cried till I thought your heart would break. "They've put my mammie in the ground," you kept saying. "She was asleep, and they put her in the ground."

SIGHLE. And you went down on your knees beside me and put your two arms around me, and put your cheek against my cheek and said nothing but "God comfort you; God comfort you." And when I stopped crying a little, you brought me over to the fire. Your two sons were at the fire, Maire. Colm was in the ingle where I am now; MacDara was sitting where you are. MacDara stooped down and lifted me on to his knee—I was only a weeshy child. He stroked my hair. Then he began singing a little song to me, a little song that had sad words in it, but that had joy in the heart of it, and in the beat of it; and the words and the music grew very caressing and soothing like . . . like my mother's hand when it was on my cheek, or my mother's kiss on my mouth when I'd be half asleep—

MAIRE. Yes, daughter?

SIGHLE. And it soothed me, and soothed me; and I began to think that I was at home again, and I fell asleep in MacDara's arms—oh, the strong, strong arms of him, with his soft voice soothing me—when I woke up long after that I was still in his arms with my head on his shoulder. I opened my eyes and looked up at him. He smiled at me and said, "That was a good, long sleep." I . . . put up my face to him to be kissed, and he bent down his head and kissed me. He was so gentle, so gentle. [MAIRE *cries silently.*] I had no right to tell you all this. God forgive me for bringing those tears to you, Maire ni Fhiannachta.

MAIRE. Whist, girl. You had a right to tell me. Go on, jewel . . . my boy, my poor boy!

SIGHLE. I was only a weeshy child—

MAIRE. Eight years you were, no more, the day the priest brought you into the house.

SIGHLE. How old was MacDara?

MAIRE. He was turned fifteen. Fifteen he was on St. MacDara's day, the year your mother died.

SIGHLE. This house was as dear to me nearly as my mother's house from that day. You were good to me, Maire ni Fhiannachta, and your two boys were good to me, but—

MAIRE. Yes, daughter?

SIGHLE. MacDara was like sun and moon to me, like dew and rain to me, like strength and sweetness to me. I don't know did he know I was so fond of him. I think he did, because—

MAIRE. He did know, child.

SIGHLE. How do you know that he knew? Did he tell you? Did *you* know?

MAIRE. I am his mother. Don't I know every fiber of his body? Don't I know every thought of his mind? He never told me; but well I knew.

SIGHLE. He put me into his songs. That is what made me think he knew. My name was in many a song that he made. Often when I was at the *fosaidheacht* he would come up into the green *mám* to me, with a little song that he had made. It was happy for us in the green *mám* that time.

MAIRE. It was happy for us all when MacDara was here.

SIGHLE. The heart in the breast of me nearly broke when they banished him from us.

MAIRE. I knew it well.

SIGHLE. I used to lie awake in the night with his songs going through my brain, and the music of his voice. I used to call his name up in the green *mám*. At Mass his face used to come between me and the white Host.

MAIRE. We have both been lonely for him. The house has been lonely for him.

SIGHLE. Colm never knew I was so fond of MacDara. When MacDara went away Colm was kinder to me than ever—but, indeed, he was always kind.

MAIRE. Colm is a kind boy.

SIGHLE. It was not till yesterday he told me he was fond of me; I never thought it, I liked him well, but I never thought there would be word of marriage between us. I don't think he would have spoken if it was not for the trouble coming. He says it will be soon now.

MAIRE. It will be very soon.

SIGHLE. I shiver when I think of them all going out to fight. They will go out laughing: I see them with their cheeks flushed and their red lips apart. And then they will lie very still on the hillside—so still and white, with no red in their cheeks, but maybe a red wound in their white breasts, or on their white foreheads. Colm's hair will be dabbled with blood.

MAIRE. Whist, daughter. That is no talk for one that was reared in this house. I am his mother, and I do not grudge him.

SIGHLE. Forgive me, you have known more sorrow than I, and I think only of my own sorrow. [*She rises and kisses* MAIRE.] I am proud other times to think of so many young men, young men with straight, strong limbs, and smooth, white flesh, going out into great peril because a voice has called to them to right the wrong of the people. Oh, I would like to see the man that has set their hearts on fire with the breath of his voice! They say that he is very young. They say that he is one of ourselves—a mountainy man that speaks our speech, and has known hunger and sorrow.

MAIRE. The strength and the sweetness he has come, maybe, out of his sorrow.

SIGHLE. I heard Diarmaid of the Bridge say that he was at the fair of Uachtar Ard yesterday. There were hundreds in the streets striving to see him.

MAIRE. I wonder would he be coming here into Cois-Fhairrge, or is it into the Joyce country he would go? I don't know but it's his coming I felt all day yesterday, and all night. I thought, maybe, it might be—

SIGHLE. Who did you think it might be?

MAIRE. I thought it might be my son was coming to me.

SIGHLE. Is it MacDara?

MAIRE. Yes, MacDara.

SIGHLE. Do you think would he come back to be with the boys in the trouble?

MAIRE. He would.

SIGHLE. Would he be left back now?

MAIRE. Who would let or stay him and he homing like a homing bird? Death only; God between us and harm!

SIGHLE. Amen.

MAIRE. There is Colm in to us.

SIGHLE [*looking out of the window*]. Aye, he's on the street.

MAIRE. Poor Colm!

[*The door opens and* COLM *comes in. He is a lad of twenty.*]

COLM. Did you not go to bed, mother?

MAIRE. I did not, Colm. I was too uneasy to sleep. Sighle kept me company all night.

COLM. It's a pity of the two of you to be up like this.

MAIRE. We would be more lonesome in bed than here chatting. Had you many boys at the drill tonight?

COLM. We had, then. There were ten and three score.

MAIRE. When will the trouble be, Colm?

Colm. It will be tomorrow, or after tomorrow; or maybe sooner. There's a man expected from Galway with the word.

Maire. Is it the mountains you'll take to, or to march to Uachtar Ard or to Galway?

Colm. It's to march we'll do, I'm thinking. Diarmaid of the Bridge and Cuimin Eanna and the master will be into us shortly. We have some plans to make and the master wants to write some orders.

Maire. Is it you will be their captain?

Colm. It is, unless a better man comes in my place.

Maire. What better man would come?

Colm. There is talk of the Singer coming. He was at the fair of Uachtar Ard yesterday.

Maire. Let you put on the kettle, Sighle, and ready the room. The master will be asking a cup of tea. Will you lie down for an hour, Colm?

Colm. I will not. They will be in on us now.

Maire. Let you make haste, Sighle. Ready the room. Here, give me the kettle.

[Sighle, *who has brought a kettle full of water, gives it* to Maire, *who hangs it over the fire;* Sighle *goes into the room.*]

Colm [*after a pause*]. Was Sighle talking to you, mother?

Maire. She was, son.

Colm. What did she say?

Maire. She told me what you said to her last night. You must be patient, Colm. Don't press her to give you an answer too soon. She has strange thoughts in her heart, and strange memories.

Colm. What memories has she?

Maire. Many a woman has memories.

Colm. Sighle has no memories but of this house and of her mother. What is she but a child?

Maire. And what are you but a child? Can't you have patience? Children have memories, but the memories sometimes die. Sighle's memories have not died yet.

Colm. This is queer talk. What does she remember?

Maire. Whist, there's some one on the street.

Colm [*looking out of the window*]. It's Cuimin and the master.

MAIRE. Be patient, son. Don't vex your head. What are you both but children yet?

[*The door opens and* CUIMIN EANNA *and* MAOILSHEACH-LAINN *come in.* CUIMIN *is middle aged;* MAOILSHEACHLAINN *past middle age, turning gray, and a little stooped.*]

CUIMIN and MAOILSHEACHLAINN [*entering*]. God save all here.

MAIRE. God save you men. Will you sit? The kettle is on the boil. Give the master the big chair, Colm.

MAOILSHEACHLAINN [*sitting down near the fire on the chair which* COLM *places for him*]. You're early stirring, Maire.

MAIRE. I didn't lie down at all, master.

MAOILSHEACHLAINN. Is it to sit up all night you did?

MAIRE. It is, then. Sighle kept me company.

MAOILSHEACHLAINN. 'Tis a pity of the women of the world. Too good they are for us, and too full of care. I'm afraid that there was many a woman on this mountain that sat up last night. Aye, and many a woman in Ireland. 'Tis women that keep all the great vigils.

MAIRE. [*wetting the tea*]. Why wouldn't we sit up to have a cup of tea ready for you? Won't you go west into the room?

MAOILSHEACHLAINN. We'd as lief drink it here beside the fire.

MAIRE. Sighle is readying the room. You'll want the table to write on, maybe.

MAOILSHEACHLAINN. We'll go west so.

MAIRE. Wait till Sighle has the table laid. The tea will be drawn in a minute.

COLM [*to* MAOILSHEACHLAINN]. Was there any word of the messenger at the forge, master?

MAOILSHEACHLAINN. There was not.

CUIMIN. When we were coming up the boreen I saw a man breasting Cnoc an Teachta that I thought might be him.

MAOILSHEACHLAINN. I don't think it was him. He was walking slowly, and sure the messenger that brings that great story will come on the wings of the wind.

COLM. Perhaps it was one of the boys you saw going home from the drill.

CUIMIN. No, it was a stranger. He looked like a moun-tainy man that would be coming from a distance. He might be some one that was at the fair of Uachtar Ard yesterday, and that stayed the evening after selling.

MAOILSHEACHLAINN. Aye, there did a lot stay, I'm told, talking about the word that's expected.

CUIMIN. The Singer was there, I believe. Diarmaid of the Bridge said that he spoke to them all at the fair, and that there did a lot stay in the town after the fair thinking he'd speak to them again. They say he has the talk of an angel.

MAOILSHEACHLAINN. What sort is he to look at?

CUIMIN. A poor man of the mountains. Young they say he is, and pale like a man that lived in cities, but with the dress and the speech of a mountainy man; shy in himself and very silent, till he stands up to talk to the people. And then he has the voice of a silver trumpet, and words so beautiful that they make the people cry. And there is terrible anger in him, for all that he is shrinking and gentle. Diarmaid said that in the Joyce country they think it is some great hero that has come back again to lead the people against the Gall, or maybe an angel, or the Son of Mary Himself that has come down on the earth.

MAOILSHEACHLAINN [*looking towards the door*]. There's a footstep abroad.

MAIRE [*who has been sitting very straight in her chair listening intently*]. That is my son's step.

COLM. Sure, amn't I here, mother?

MAIRE. That is MacDara's step.

[*All start and look first towards* MAIRE, *then towards the door, the latch of which has been touched.*]

MAOILSHEACHLAINN. I wish it was MacDara, Maire. 'Tis maybe Diarmaid or the mountainy man we saw on the road.

MAIRE. It is not Diarmaid. It is MacDara.

[*The door opens slowly and* MACDARA, *a young man of perhaps twenty-five, dressed like a man of the mountains, stands on the threshold.*]

MACDARA. God save all here.

ALL. And you, likewise.

MAIRE [*who has risen and is stretching out her hands*]. I felt you coming to me, little son!

MacDara [*springing to her and folding her in his arms*].
Little mother! little mother!

[*While they still embrace* Sighle *reënters from the room
and stands still on the threshold looking at* MacDara.]

Maire [*raising her head*]. Along all the quiet roads and
across all the rough mountains, and through all the crowded
towns, I felt you drawing near to me.

MacDara. Oh, the long years, the long years!

Maire. I am crying for pride at the sight of you. Neighbors, neighbors, this is MacDara, the first child that I bore
to my husband.

MacDara [*kissing* Colm]. My little brother! [*To* Cuimin.] Cuimin Eanna! [*To* Maoilsheachlainn.] Master!
[*They shake hands.*]

Maoilsheachlainn. Welcome home.

Cuimin. Welcome home.

MacDara [*looking round*]. Where is . . . [*He sees*
Sighle *in the doorway.*] Sighle! [*He approaches her and takes
her hand.*] Little, little Sighle! . . . I . . . Mother, sometimes when I was in the middle of great crowds, I have seen
this fireplace, and you standing with your hands stretched out
to me as you stood a minute ago, and Sighle in the doorway of the room; and my heart has cried out to you.

Maire. I used to hear the crying of your heart. Often
and often here by the fireside or abroad on the street I would
stand and say, "MacDara is crying out to me now. The
heart in him is yearning." And this while back I felt you
draw near, draw near, step by step. Last night I felt you very
near to me. Do you remember me saying, Sighle, that I felt
some one coming, and that I thought maybe it might be
MacDara?

Sighle. You did.

Maire. I knew that something glorious was coming to the
mountain with today's dawn. Red dawns and white dawns
I have seen on the hills, but none like this dawn. Come in,
jewel, and sit down awhile in the room. Sighle has the table
laid. The tea is drawn. Bring in the griddlecakes, Sighle.
Come in, master. Come in, Cuimin.

Maoilsheachlainn. No, Maire, we'll sit here awhile.
You and the children will like to be by yourselves. Go in,

west, children. Cuimin and I have plans to make. We're
expecting Diarmaid of the Bridge in.

MAIRE. We don't grudge you a share in our joy, master.
Nor you, Cuimin.

CUIMIN. No, go on in, Maire. We'll go west after you.
We want to talk here.

MAIRE. Well, come in when you have your talk out. There's
enough tea on the pot for everybody. In with you, children.

[MACDARA, COLM, SIGHLE *and* MAIRE *go into the room,*
SIGHLE *carrying the griddlecakes and* MAIRE *the tea.*]

MAOILSHEACHLAINN. This is great news, MacDara to be
back.

CUIMIN. Do you think will he be with us?

MAOILSHEACHLAINN. Is it a boy with that gesture of
the head, that proud, laughing gesture, to be a coward
or a stag? You don't know the heart of this boy, Cuimin;
the love that's in it, and the strength. You don't know the
mind he has, so gracious, so full of wisdom. I taught him
when he was only a little ladeen. 'Tis a pity that he had ever
to go away from us. And yet, I think, his exile has made
him a better man. His soul must be full of great remem-
brances.

CUIMIN. I never knew rightly why he was banished.

MAOILSHEACHLAINN. Songs he was making that were setting the people's hearts on fire.

CUIMIN. Aye, I often heard his songs.

MAOILSHEACHLAINN. They were full of terrible love for
the people and of great anger against the Gall. Some said
there was irreligion in them and blasphemy against God.
But I never saw it, and I don't believe it. There are some
would have us believe that God is on the side of the Gall.
Well, word came down from Galway or from Dublin that
he would be put in prison, and maybe excommunicated if he
did not go away. He was only a gossoon of eighteen, or
maybe twenty. The priest counseled him to go, and not to
bring sorrow on his mother's house. He went away one
evening without taking farewell or leave of anyone.

CUIMIN. Where has he been since, I don't know?

MAOILSHEACHLAINN. In great cities, I'd say, and in lonely
places. He has the face of a scholar, or of a priest, or of a

clerk, on him. He must have read a lot, and thought a lot, and made a lot of songs.

CUIMIN. I don't know is he as strong a boy as Colm.

MAOILSHEACHLAINN. He's not as robust in himself as Colm is, but there was great strength in the grip of his hand. I'd say that he'd wield a *camán* or a pike with any boy on the mountain.

CUIMIN. He'll be a great backing to us if he is with us. The people love him on account of the songs he used to make. There's not a man that won't do his bidding.

MAOILSHEACHLAINN. That's so. And his counsel will be useful to us. He'll make better plans than you or I, Cuimin.

CUIMIN. I wonder what's keeping Diarmaid.

MAOILSHEACHLAINN. Some news that was at the forge or at the priest's house, maybe. He went east the road to see if there was sign of a word from Galway.

CUIMIN. I'll be uneasy till he comes. [*He gets up and walks to the window and looks out;* MAOILSHEACHLAINN *remains deep in thought by the fire.* CUIMIN *returns from the window and continues.*] Is it to march we'll do, or to fight here in the hills?

MAOILSHEACHLAINN. Out Maam Gap we'll go and meet the boys from the Joyce country. We'll leave some to guard the Gap and some at Leenane. We'll march the road between the lakes, through Maam and Cornamona and Clonbur to Cong. Then we'll have friends on our left at Ballinrobe and on our right at Taum. What is there to stop us but the few men the Gall have in Clifden?

CUIMIN. And if they march against us, we can destroy them from the mountains.

MAOILSHEACHLAINN. We can. It's into a trap they'll walk.

[MACDARA *appears in the doorway of the room with a cup of tea and some griddlecakes in his hand.*]

MACDARA. I've brought you out a cup of tea, master. I thought it long you were sitting here.

MAOILSHEACHLAINN [*taking it*]. God bless you, MacDara.

MACDARA. Go west, Cuimin. There's a place at the table for you now.

CUIMIN [*rising and going in*]. I may as well. Give me a call, boy, when Diarmaid comes.

MAOILSHEACHLAINN. This is a great day, MacDara.

MACDARA. It is a great day and a glad day, and yet it is a sorrowful day.

MAOILSHEACHLAINN. How can the day of your home-coming be sorrowful?

MACDARA. Has not every great joy a great sorrow at its core? Does not the joy of home-coming inclose the pain of departing? I have a strange feeling, master, I have only finished a long journey, and I feel as if I were about to take another long journey. I meant this to be a home-coming, but it seems only like a meeting on the way. . . . When my mother stood up to meet me with her arms stretched out to me, I thought of Mary meeting her Son on the Dolorous Way.

MAOILSHEACHLAINN. That was a queer thought. What was it that drew you home?

MACDARA. Some secret thing that I have no name for. Some feeling that I must see my mother, and Colm, and Sighle, again. A feeling that I must face some great adventure with their kisses on my lips. I seemed to see myself brought to die before a great crowd that stood cold and silent; and there were some that cursed me in their hearts for having brought death into their houses. Sad dead faces seemed to reproach me. Oh, the wise, sad faces of the dead —and the keening of women rang in my ears. But I felt that the kisses of those three, warm on my mouth, would be as wine in my blood, strengthening me to bear what men said, and to die with only love and pity in my heart, and no bitterness.

MAOILSHEACHLAINN. It was strange that you should see yourself like that.

MACDARA. It was foolish. One has strange, lonesome thoughts when one is in the middle of crowds. But I am glad of that thought, for it drove me home. I felt so lonely away from here. . . . My mother's hair is grayer than it was.

MAOILSHEACHLAINN. Aye, she has been ageing. She has had great sorrows: your father dead and you banished. Colm is grown a fine, strapping boy.

MACDARA. He is. There is some shyness between Colm and me. We have not spoken yet as we used to.

MAOILSHEACHLAINN. When boys are brought up together and then parted for a long time there is often shyness between them when they meet again. . . . Do you find Sighle changed?

MACDARA. No; and, yet—yes. Master, she is very beautiful. I did not know a woman could be so beautiful. I thought that all beauty was in the heart, that beauty was a secret thing that could be seen only with the eyes of reverie, or in a dream of some unborn splendor. I had schooled myself to think physical beauty an unholy thing. I tried to keep my heart virginal; and sometimes in the street of a city when I have stopped to look at the white limbs of some beautiful child, and have felt the pain that the sight of great beauty brings, I have wished that I could blind my eyes so that I might shut out the sight of everything that tempted me. At times I have rebelled against that, and have cried aloud that God would not have filled the world with beauty, even to the making drunk of the sight, if beauty were not of heaven. But, then, again, I have said, "This is the subtlest form of temptation; this is to give to one's own desire the sanction of God's will." And I have hardened my heart and kept myself cold and chaste as the top of a high mountain. But now I think I was wrong, for beauty like Sighle's must be holy.

MAOILSHEACHLAINN. Surely a good and comely girl is holy. You question yourself too much, MacDara. You brood too much. Do you remember when you were a gossoon, how you cried over the wild duck whose wing you broke by accident with a stone, and made a song about the crane whose nest you found ravished, and about the red robin you found perished on the doorstep? And how the priest laughed because you told him in confession that you had stolen drowned lilies from the river?

MACDARA [*laughing*]. Aye, it was at a station in Diarmaid of the Bridge's, and when the priest laughed my face got red, and everyone looked at us, and I got up and ran out of the house.

MAOILSHEACHLAINN [*laughing*]. I remember it well. We thought it was that you told him you were in love with his housekeeper.

MACDARA. It's little but I was, too. She used to give me

apples out of the priest's apple-garden. Little brown russet apples, the sweetest I ever tasted. I used to think that the apples of the Hesperides that the Children of Tuireann went to quest must have been like them.

MAOILSHEACHLAINN. It's a wonder but you made a poem about them.

MACDARA. I did. I made a poem in Deibhidhe of twenty quatrains.

MAOILSHEACHLAINN. Did you make many songs while you were away?

MACDARA. When I went away first my heart was as if dead and dumb and I could not make any songs. After a little while, when I was going through the sweet, green country, and I used to come to little towns where I'd see children playing, my heart seemed to open again like hard ground that would be watered with rain. The first song that I made was about the children that I saw playing in the street of Kilconnell. The next song that I made was about an old dark man that I met on the causeway of Aughrim. I made a glad, proud song when I saw the broad Shannon flow under the bridge of Athlone. I made many a song after that before I reached Dublin.

MAOILSHEACHLAINN. How did it fare with you in Dublin?

MACDARA. I went to a bookseller and gave him the book of my songs to print. He said that he dared not print them; that the Gall would put him in prison and break up his printing-press. I was hungry and I wandered through the streets. Then a man who saw me read an Irish poster on the wall spoke to me and asked me where I came from. I told him my story. In a few days he came to me and said that he had found work for me to teach Irish and Latin and Greek in a school. I went to the school and taught in it for a year. I wrote a few poems and they were printed in a paper. One day the Brother who was over the school came to me and asked me was it I that had written those poems. I said it was. He told me then that I could not teach in the school any longer. So I went away.

MAOILSHEACHLAINN. What happened to you after that?

MACDARA. I wandered in the streets until I saw a notice that a teacher was wanted to teach a boy. I went to the house and a lady engaged me to teach her little son for ten shillings a week. Two years I spent at that. The boy was a winsome child, and he grew into my heart. I thought it a wonderful thing to have the molding of a mind, of a life, in my hands. Do you ever think that, you who are a schoolmaster?

MAOILSHEACHLAINN. It's not much time I get for thinking.

MACDARA. I have done nothing all my life but think: think and make poems.

MAOILSHEACHLAINN. If the thoughts and the poems are good, that is a good life's work.

MACDARA. Aye, they say that to be busy with the things of the spirit is better than to be busy with the things of the body. But I am not sure, master. Can the Vision Beautiful alone content a man? I think true man is divine in this, that, like God, he must needs create, he must needs do.

MAOILSHEACHLAINN. Is not a poet a maker?

MACDARA. No, he is only a voice that cries out, a sigh that trembles into rest. The true teacher must suffer and do. He must break bread to the people: he must go into Gethsemane and toil up the steep of Golgotha. . . . Sometimes I think that to be a woman and to serve and suffer as women do is to be the highest thing. Perhaps that is why I felt it proud and wondrous to be a teacher, for a teacher does that. I gave to the little lad I taught the very flesh and blood and breath that were my life. I fed him on the milk of my kindness; I breathed into him my spirit.

MAOILSHEACHLAINN. Did he repay you for that great service?

MACDARA. Can any child repay its mother? Master, your trade is the most sorrowful of all trades. You are like a poor mother who spends herself in nursing children who go away and never come back to her.

MAOILSHEACHLAINN. Was your little pupil untrue to you?

MACDARA. Nay; he was so true to me that his mother grew jealous of me. A good mother and a good teacher are always jealous of each other. That is why a teacher's trade is the most sorrowful of all trades. If he is a bad teacher his pupil *wanders* away from him. If he is a good teacher his pupil's folk grow jealous of him. My little pupil's mother bade him choose between her and me.

MAOILSHEACHLAINN. Which did he choose?

MACDARA. He chose his mother. How could I blame him?

MAOILSHEACHLAINN. What did you do?

MACDARA. I shouldered my bundle and took to the roads.

MAOILSHEACHLAINN. How did it fare with you?

MACDARA. It fares ill with one who is so poor that he has no longer even his dreams. I was the poorest *shuiler* on the roads of Ireland, for I had no single illusion left to me. I could neither pray when I came to a holy well nor drink in a public-house when I had got a little money. One seemed to me as foolish as the other.

MAOILSHEACHLAINN. Did you make no songs in those days?

MACDARA. I made one so bitter that when I recited it at a wake they thought I was some wandering, wicked spirit, and they put me out of the house.

MAOILSHEACHLAINN. Did you not pray at all?

MACDARA. Once, as I knelt by the cross of Kilgobbin, it became clear to me, with an awful clearness, that there was no God. Why pray after that? I burst into a fit of laughter at the folly of men in thinking that there is a God. I felt inclined to run through the villages and cry aloud, "People, it is all a mistake; there is no God."

MAOILSHEACHLAINN. MacDara, this grieves me.

MACDARA. Then I said, "Why take away their illusion? If they find out that there is no God, their hearts will be as lonely as mine." So I walked the roads with my secret.

MAOILSHEACHLAINN. MacDara, I am sorry for this. You must pray, you must pray. You will find God again. He has only hidden His face from you.

MACDARA. No, He has revealed His Face to me. His Face is terrible and sweet, Maoilsheachlainn. I know It well now.

MAOILSHEACHLAINN. Then you found Him again?

MACDARA. His Name is suffering. His Name is loneliness. His Name is abjection.

MAOILSHEACHLAINN. I do not rightly understand you, and yet I think you are saying something that is true.

MACDARA. I have lived with the homeless and with the

breadless. Oh, Maoilsheachlainn, the poor, the poor! I have seen such sad childings, such bare marriage feasts, such candleless wakes! In the pleasant country places I have seen them, but oftener in the dark, unquiet streets of the city. My heart has been heavy with the sorrow of mothers, my eyes have been wet with the tears of children. The people, Maoilsheachlainn, the dumb, suffering people: reviled and outcast, yet pure and splendid and faithful. In them I saw, or seemed to see again, the Face of God. Ah, it is a tear-stained face, blood-stained, defiled with ordure, but it is the Holy Face!

[*There is a page of* MS. *missing here, which evidently covered the exit to the room of* MacDara *and the entrance of* Diarmaid.]

MAOILSHEACHLAINN. What news have you with you?

DIARMAID. The Gall have marched from Clifden.

MAOILSHEACHLAINN. Is it into the hills?

DIARMAID. By Letterfrack they have come, and the Pass of Kylemore, and through Glen Inagh.

COLM. And no word from Galway yet?

DIARMAID. No word, nor sign of a word.

COLM. They told us to wait for the word. We've waited too long.

MAOILSHEACHLAINN. The messenger may have been caught. Perhaps the Gall are marching from Galway too.

COLM. We'd best strike ourselves, so.

CUIMIN. Is it to strike before the word is given?

COLM. Is it to die like rats you'd have us because the word is not given?

CUIMIN. Our plans are not finished; our orders are not here.

COLM. Our plans will never be finished. Our orders may never be here.

CUIMIN. We've no one to lead us.

COLM. Didn't you elect me your captain?

CUIMIN. We did: but not to bid us rise out when the whole country is quiet. We were to get the word from the men that are over the people. They'll speak when the time comes.

COLM. They should have spoken before the Gall marched.

CUIMIN. What call have you to say what they should or what they should not have done? Am I speaking lie or truth, men? Are we to rise out before the word comes? I say we must wait for the word. What do you say, Diarmaid, you that was our messenger to Galway.

DIARMAID. I like the way Colm has spoken, and we may live to say that he spoke wisely as well as bravely; but I'm slow to give my voice to send out the boys of this mountain—our poor little handful—to stand with their poor pikes against the big guns of the Gall. If we had news that they were rising in the other countrysides; but we've got no news.

CUIMIN. What do you say, master? You're wiser than any of us.

MAOILSHEACHLAINN. I say to Colm that a greater one than he or I may give us the word before the day is old. Let you have patience, Colm—

COLM. My mother told me to have patience this morning, when MacDara's step was on the street. Patience, and I after waiting seven years before I spoke, and then to speak too late!

MAOILSHEACHLAINN. What are you saying at all?

COLM. I am saying this, master, that I'm going out the road to meet the Gall, if only five men of the mountain follow me.

[SIGHLE *has appeared in the doorway and stands terror-stricken.*]

CUIMIN. You will not, Colm.

COLM. I will.

DIARMAID. This is throwing away men's lives.

COLM. Men's lives get very precious to them when they have bought out their land.

MAOILSHEACHLAINN. Listen to me, Colm—

[COLM *goes out angrily, and the others follow him, trying to restrain him.* SIGHLE *comes to the fire, where she kneels.*]

SIGHLE [*as in a reverie*]. "They will go out laughing," I said, but Colm has gone out with anger in his heart. And he was so kind. . . . Love is a terrible thing. There is no pain so great as the pain of love. . . . I wish MacDara and

I were children in the green *mám* and that we did not know
that we loved each other. . . . Colm will lie dead on the
road to Glen Inagh, and MacDara will go out to die. . . .
There is nothing in the world but love and death.

[MacDara *comes out of the room.*]

MacDara [*in a low voice*]. She has dropped asleep,
Sighle.

Sighle. She watched long, MacDara. We all watched
long.

MacDara. Every long watch ends. Every traveler comes
home.

Sighle. Sometimes when people watch it is death that
comes.

MacDara. Could there be a royaler coming, Sighle? . . .
Once I wanted life. You and I to be together in one place
always: that is what I wanted. But now I see that we shall
be together for a little time only; that I have to do a hard,
sweet thing, and that I must do it alone. And because I
love you I would not have it different. . . . I wanted to
have your kiss on my lips, Sighle, as well as my mother's
and Colm's. But I will deny myself that. [Sighle *is crying.*]
Don't cry, child. Stay near my mother while she lives—
it may be for a little while of years. You poor women suffer
so much pain, so much sorrow and yet you do not die until
long after your strong, young sons and lovers have died.

[Maire's *voice is heard from the room, crying:* Mac-
Dara!]

MacDara. She is calling me.

[*He goes into the room;* Sighle *cries on her knees by the
fire. After a little while voices are heard outside, the latch
is lifted, and* Maoilsheachlainn *comes in.*]

Sighle. Is he gone, master?

Maoilsheachlainn. Gone out the road with ten or
fifteen of the young lads. Is MacDara within still?

Sighle. He was here in the kitchen awhile. His mother
called him and he went back to her.

[Maoilsheachlainn *goes over and sits down near the
fire.*]

Maoilsheachlainn. I think, maybe, that Colm did what
was right. We are too old to be at the head of work like
this. Was MacDara talking to you about the trouble?

SIGHLE. He said that he would have to do a hard, sweet thing, and that he would have to do it alone.

MAOILSHEACHLAINN. I'm sorry but I called him before Colm went out.

[*A murmur is heard as of a crowd of men talking as they come up the hill.*]

SIGHLE. What is that noise like voices?

MAOILSHEACHLAINN. It is the boys coming up the hillside. There was a great crowd gathering below at the cross.

[*The voices swell loud outside the door.* CUIMIN EANNA, DIARMAID, *and some others come in.*]

DIARMAID. The men say we did wrong to let Colm go out with that little handful. They say we should all have marched.

CUIMIN. And I say Colm was wrong to go before he got his orders. Are we all to go out and get shot down because one man is hotheaded? Where is the plan that was to come from Galway?

MAOILSHEACHLAINN. Men, I'm blaming myself for not saying the thing I'm going to say before we let Colm go. We talk about getting word from Galway. What would you say, neighbors, if the man that will give the word is under the roof of this house.

CUIMIN. Who is it you mean?

MAOILSHEACHLAINN [*going to the door of the room and throwing it open*]. Let you rise out, MacDara, and reveal yourself to the men that are waiting for your word.

ONE OF THE NEWCOMERS. Has MacDara come home?

[MACDARA *comes out of the room:* MAIRE NI FHIANNACHTA *stands behind him in the doorway.*]

DIARMAID [*starting up from where he has been sitting*]. That is the man that stood among the people in the fair of Uachtar Ard! [*He goes up to* MACDARA *and kisses his hand.*] I could not get near you yesterday, MacDara, with the crowds that were round you. What was on me that didn't know you? Sure, I had a right to know that sad, proud head. Maire ni Fhiannachta, men and women yet unborn will bless the pains of your first childing.

[MAIRE NI FHIANNACHTA *comes forward slowly and takes her son's hand and kisses it.*]

MAIRE [*in a low voice*]. Soft hand that played at my breast, strong hand that will fall heavy on the Gall, brave hand that will break the yoke! Men of this mountain, my son MacDara is the Singer that has quickened the dead years and all the quiet dust! Let the horsemen that sleep in Aileach rise up and follow him into the war! Weave your winding-sheets, women, for there will be many a noble corpse to be waked before the new moon!

[*Each comes forward and kisses his hand.*]

MAOILSHEACHLAINN. Let you speak, MacDara, and tell us is it time.

MACDARA. Where is Colm?

DIARMAID. Gone out the road to fight the Gall, himself and fifteen.

MACDARA. Has not Colm spoken by his deed already?

CUIMIN. You are our leader.

MACDARA. Your leader is the man that spoke first. Give me a pike and I will follow Colm. Why did you let him go out with fifteen men only? You are fourscore on the mountain.

DIARMAID. We thought it a foolish thing for fourscore to go into battle against four thousand, or, maybe, forty thousand.

MACDARA. And so it is a foolish thing. Do you want us to be wise?

CUIMIN. This is strange talk.

MACDARA. I will talk to you more strangely yet. It is for your own souls' sakes I would have had the fourscore go, and not for Colm's sake, or for the battle's sake, for the battle is won whether you go or not.

[*A cry is heard outside. One rushes in terror-stricken.*]

THE NEWCOMER. Young Colm has fallen at the Glen foot.

MACDARA. The fifteen were too many. Old men, you did not do your work well enough. You should have kept all back but one. One man can free a people as one Man redeemed the world. I will take no pike, I will go into the battle with bare hands. I will stand up before the Gall as Christ hung naked before men on the tree!

[*He moves through them, pulling off his clothes as he*

goes. As he reaches the threshold a great shout goes up from the people. He passes out and the shout dies slowly away. The other men follow him slowly. MAIRE NI FHIANNACHTA *sits down at the fire, where* SIGHLE *still crouches.*]

MAEVE

By Edward Martyn

(1899)

DRAMATIS PERSONÆ

THE O'HEYNES, Colman O'Heynes, *Prince of Burren*
MAEVE O'HEYNES, ⎫ *his daughters*
FINOLA O'HEYNES, ⎭
HUGH FITZ WALTER, *a young Englishman*
PEG INERNY, *a vagrant*

In the dream of Maeve appear Queen Maeve, a Boy Page, Chorus of Boy Pages, ancient Irish harpers, chieftains, warriors, people, etc.

The action takes place during the present time about and at O'Heynes Castle among the Burren Mountains of County Clare in Ireland.

ACT I

SCENE: *A ruined abbey in a green valley among mountains covered with layers of gray rock. At back a little removed is a cairn overgrown with grass. Gray limestones belonging to the ruin are strewn about the ground. At the left in the surrounding pasture of pale green, great leafless ash-trees stand among boulders spotted with white and orange lichen. It is a sunny evening in the month of March.*
MAEVE O'HEYNES—*a girl of about three and twenty with a fair complexion, gold hair, and a certain boyish beauty in the lines and movement of her slim figure, rests thoughtful and attentive on one of the fallen stones. She wears a red frieze dress with a black jacket and folding linen collar, and has on her head a sailor's cap of black wool.*

Finola O'Heynes—*a dark, rather submissive-looking girl somewhat younger, dressed simply in an ordinary gown, sits near on another stone.*

Finola [*reading from an old book*].
"Every hill which is at this Oenach
Hath under it heroes and queens,
And poets and distributors,
And fair fierce women."

Maeve [*rises and gazes before her as if in a dream*]. And fair fierce women!

Finola [*closing the book, goes to her*]. Maeve—what are you thinking of so earnestly?

Maeve [*recalled to herself*]. Visions—visions. That is all.

Finola. Has this old West Connacht poem brought you visions?

Maeve. Ah, the bard Dorban, who wrote it, was a poet! [*She sighs and covers her face with her hands.*]

Finola [*turning away*]. I am sorry I thought of reading it to you.

Maeve. Why, sister?

Finola. Because it seems to have called you back to your old self.

Maeve [*smiling sadly*]. My old self. As if I could ever have left my old self.

Finola. Oh, yes, you were peaceful and contented a little while ago.

Maeve. It seems so long ago, Finola.

Finola. Something strange has come over you now.

Maeve [*with restlessness*]. No, it is nothing. It is only the look of the evening.

Finola. But this is such a peaceful evening with that saffron sunlight over the ruins. Why should it make you anything else but peaceful?

Maeve. Oh, Finola, when I see the ruins like that, I know the visions are near me.

Finola. Then, after all, it was not because I read that poem?

Maeve. Yes—that, and the evening.

Finola [*looking at her anxiously*]. Why should the visions make you so sad, Maeve?

MAEVE [*wistfully*]. Such beautiful dead people! They used to walk in the oldest of these ruins before it was a ruin; they watched Goban, the great architect, building that round tower [*pointing to the right*], building his master-work. I see them now and I see others who lived long before them [*turns and looks to the back*], and are buried in that green cairn. Oh, I am dying because I am exiled from such beauty.

FINOLA [*with great gentleness*]. Darling, you must not think of these things. You know tomorrow—

MAEVE [*with a sudden chillness*]. Tomorrow—why do you speak of tomorrow while it is still today, and I can still think of my love?

FINOLA. Tomorrow when you are married, Maeve, it will be your husband who will be entitled to that love.

MAEVE [*significantly*]. He has not yet returned.

FINOLA. Hugh will certainly return before night.

MAEVE. But he has not yet returned, Finola.

FINOLA. Do you really think he will not return?

MAEVE [*with a baffled look*]. Oh, I don't know: but somehow I cannot believe that I am to be married tomorrow. [*Looks around.*] To leave all this for an English home—

FINOLA [*with increased anxiety*]. Maeve—

MAEVE. The very stones, as I wander among them, seem to forbid it. [*Exit among the ruins at back.*]

FINOLA [*walking about in agitation*]. Oh, why does not Hugh return? [*Then suddenly stopping.*] Here is father again. Poor father.

[THE O'HEYNES *enters from the left, leaning heavily on a stick. He is an old man, with thin, white disheveled hair almost falling to his shoulders, wears a tall hat and clothes of a somewhat bygone fashion; while about his whole appearance there is just a suggestion of the peasant.*]

THE O'HEYNES [*restlessly*]. Finola, I wonder will Hugh come after all?

FINOLA. Of course he will, father. Why have you been asking me this question all day?

THE O'HEYNES. Because he has been promising to come for ever so long, and he has not come.

FINOLA. Well—you know the reason.

THE O'HEYNES [*peevishly*]. Yes—yes—legal business—always the same excuse.

FINOLA. You surely must understand that he had to consult the lawyers about many matters before his marriage with Maeve.

THE O'HEYNES. When he left here for England he said it would only be for a little time, and here he has been away more than two months.

FINOLA. The delay was very unfortunate, but necessary, I suppose. You see every sort of legal business is so tedious.

THE O'HEYNES. I don't know—I don't know. I distrust his excuses. He said he would certainly return today, and there, he hasn't after all.

FINOLA. But today is not yet over. Oh, you needn't fear. He will return before tomorrow.

THE O'HEYNES. Ah, this is the way you are perpetually making excuses for him, Finola.

FINOLA [*a little confused*]. Father, why do you say so?

THE O'HEYNES. I understand it all. Another girl would not be so forgiving as you are, Finola.

FINOLA. I have nothing to forgive.

THE O'HEYNES. That is well, child. But, believe me, I had far rather he had married you than Maeve.

FINOLA. Oh, no. He always liked Maeve from the first, and no one else. I never at any time doubted that, father.

THE O'HEYNES. Well, this is certainly a queer way of showing his affection for her.

FINOLA. I suppose it would be, if there were no reason for it.

THE O'HEYNES [*indignantly*]. To think he should have put off coming until his very wedding morning. He deserves to lose her after leaving her all this time. Oh, the persistent ill-luck that has pursued me all through life.

FINOLA. I'm sure I can't think how you consider it ill-luck to be on the eve of having all your wishes fulfilled.

THE O'HEYNES. Ah, that is just it, child. I have so often been on the eve of having my wishes fulfilled: and then somehow the unforeseen has come about: and all my hopes have gone from me. I am surely the most unfortunate of men.

FINOLA. Father dear, you must not despond in this way.

THE O'HEYNES. To think of all the anxiety your sister has caused me, Finola, and the trouble she put me to before she would accept this rich young Englishman. She must have been mad. As if the coming into this place of such a suitor was an everyday event to her.

FINOLA [*pensively*]. He never for a moment interested her somehow. It was very strange, his coming—wasn't it?

THE O'HEYNES. Was there ever such good fortune? I advertise the fishing of my river in the papers. He arrives here last summer, and takes it at once. To be sure it is splendid salmon fishing—but that it should have brought such a tenant as Hugh Fitz Walter—and that he should have fallen in love with Maeve—well—

FINOLA [*with a sigh*]. Well, father, you ought to be content with such good fortune.

THE O'HEYNES [*despondingly*]. Ah, I am afraid it is too good to come to anything. But just think that after all he should be the one to wreck this good fortune— Oh, I am distracted. [*He begins to work his hands and tear his hair.*]

FINOLA [*alarmed*]. Father, don't fret in this way. It is bad for your health. And you know there is no reason for it.

THE O'HEYNES [*feebly*]. Oh, child, if you could only realize how I have waited and waited for this—for the time when fortune would enable our family to resume its fitting position in the country! Hugh has at last promised me this fortune. Is it surprising that I should be anxious, when I see the danger of his failing me?

FINOLA [*inadvertently*]. He is not the one who will fail you, father.

THE O'HEYNES [*with a quick suspicion*]. You think Maeve is more likely to—eh? Where is she?

FINOLA. Oh, don't trouble about her. She is safe.

THE O'HEYNES. I noticed she was taking to her old habits lately. I had again to forbid her to wander through the country at night.

FINOLA [*as if laughing the matter off*]. You must not mind these wanderings of hers. They are very harmless, father.

THE O'HEYNES [*anxiously*]. Does she still talk of this strange one she is in love with?

FINOLA. Oh, that is nothing. Don't trouble about it.

THE O'HEYNES. I am not so sure of what you say, Finola.

I'll take my oath she is thinking about some good-for-nothing fellow after all.

FINOLA. No—no, nothing of the kind. You don't understand her.

THE O'HEYNES. Indeed I don't, child.

FINOLA. It is not often easy to do so. She seems to live by the brain as we live by the heart.

THE O'HEYNES. She seems to me quite regardless of realities.

FINOLA. Those feelings and impulses which are in our hearts and which govern our affections, with her are all in the head. This sounds strange: but it is the only way I can account for her nature.

THE O'HEYNES [*surprised*]. In the head?

FINOLA. Yes—that is why she appears so cold, and, as you say, regardless of realities. I even think if this one she loves were to become a reality, he would cease to fascinate her.

THE O'HEYNES [*curiously*]. Have you ever found out who he is?

FINOLA. No—not altogether.

THE O'HEYNES. I wonder what put such an extravagant idea in her head.

FINOLA. I think I know.

THE O'HEYNES. Well, what is it?

FINOLA. Would you believe it, father, I think it is those books that belonged to Uncle Bryan.

THE O'HEYNES. You mean those books up in the top room. They are mostly about ancient Greece, aren't they?

FINOLA. Yes. She is always poring over them and looking at their pictures—white statues and beautiful wall ornaments which she told me were in Greece. And then she showed me other books too, with pictures of pillars and arches—all ornamented likes those in the abbey here. Then I have seen her take the writings of Uncle Bryan and study them with all these pictures before her.

THE O'HEYNES. Poor Bryan's writings, do you say? I didn't think there were any here. I thought the Society he belonged to, took them all. [*With plaintive regret.*] My poor brother Bryan; he was a great scholar. They used to talk of him in Dublin. They said if he had lived to complete his book, it would have made him famous.

FINOLA. What was he writing about when he died, father?

THE O'HEYNES. Let me see—I think his work was to be called *The Influence of Greek Art on Celtic Ornament* or something of the sort.

FINOLA. That must have been it; for Maeve is always talking of that, and of the brotherhood of the Greek and Celtic races, and of a curious unreal beauty besides, which she says the Greeks invented. She thinks she has discovered something similar in the Celt.

THE O'HEYNES. Is that what you say she is in love with?

FINOLA [*with earnest conviction*]. I verily believe so, father. [*Then after a moment's consideration.*] Still it often seems to me she must have some individual in her mind besides.

THE O'HEYNES. I thought that was the case.

FINOLA. Oh—not what you think.

THE O'HEYNES. What then, child?

FINOLA. I don't know—she speaks of his beauty as if it had some sort of likeness to the Celtic ornament she is so much in love with.

THE O'HEYNES. Ah, she must have discovered this in the writings of Bryan. He had all sorts of odd theories about everything, poor fellow.

FINOLA. Yes, and she is as full of theories. She says that because Celtic ornament is as rare and delicate as the Greek, so her pattern of Celtic youth must, in the same way, equal the perfection of Greek youth.

THE O'HEYNES [*astonished*]. My goodness, is the whole of life like this to her?

FINOLA. Ah, now you understand what I meant when I told you that everything with her seemed to be only in the head.

THE O'HEYNES [*seriously*]. Yes, Finola, and nothing in the heart. She has no warm feelings of the heart. She was always cold and distant from her earliest childhood.

FINOLA. No, I would not say so much. I think it is only her imagination that has absorbed all the warmth of her nature.

THE O'HEYNES. What you say is the same thing, my dear. Whatever may be the cause, depend upon it, she has no feeling.

FINOLA. Oh, don't say that, father.

THE O'HEYNES. Oh, no, she hasn't, Finola; and I don't wonder that this young man's affection should at last weary of her apathy.

FINOLA. It is not any want of affection that has delayed him, father.

THE O'HEYNES. I cannot believe any more in his affection. [*Querulously.*] Why is he not here? Why is he not here?

FINOLA. You will surely see him very soon. For goodness' sake, do not fret so. Go in, and try to rest.

THE O'HEYNES. Rest—I cannot rest. How can I rest with this anxiety gnawing at me?

FINOLA. Oh, this miserable pride and position. They are ruining your health and peace.

THE O'HEYNES [*with a sudden reviving of energy*]. Not they, my girl, indeed—why do you say so? Why should what are good for every other man be bad for old Colman O'Heynes?

FINOLA. Yes, yes, father dear, I know. But somehow we have been so happy and united in our seclusion here. We are going to be divided.

THE O'HEYNES. How divided?

FINOLA. Maeve will soon leave us.

THE O'HEYNES. Ah—yes, of course.

FINOLA. Let that be sufficient. Let us at least not try to go out into the world.

THE O'HEYNES. Why not, Finola?

FINOLA. The world is such a great lonely place.

THE O'HEYNES. But my lost position—the lost dignity of our family. I have that to reassert. When my rich son-in-law comes there will be an end of our poverty.

FINOLA. You are the Prince of Burren. Is not the royalty of our race acknowledged? What place can we find in a grotesque world of plutocrats and shopkeeper peers? This change in our life seems unnatural to me. And then that wicked old Peg Inerny is always talking.

THE O'HEYNES [*sharply*]. Eh—what does she say?

FINOLA. Oh, nothing definite—nothing but insinuations and mystery, till I feel quite terrified.

THE O'HEYNES. She has been the curse of our house; and now the infernal witch has bewitched your sister.

FINOLA. I don't think that—I hope not. Maeve is only fascinated by her strange tales—the past, always the past.

THE O'HEYNES. Ay, it was the same way with your poor mother and this Peg Inerny who was a servant here long ago, and put it into her head to call your sister by the name of Maeve. Peg Inerny, I know, had some sinister object for this.

FINOLA. Oh, no, no.

THE O'HEYNES. Ah—wait a while.

FINOLA [*with a scared look*]. Father, don't forebode evil. Try and be contented—try and check this restlessness that is urging you to change your life. Let us go in. [*As they move to the left.*] Look at our old castle. How spectral those giant ash-trees rise up around it from the pale March grass. How peaceful they all look in the sunset. Would it not be misery to leave that peace for a world where there is at least no peace.

[HUGH FITZ WALTER—*a good-looking young Englishman of about five and twenty, dressed in a tweed suit—enters at the right.*]

HUGH [*eagerly*]. So I have arrived, you see, at last.

THE O'HEYNES [*turning*]. Who is that?—what, Hugh?

HUGH. It is I.

THE O'HEYNES. And so it is.—Heaven be praised. I thought you were never coming, Hugh. [*He shakes him by the hand.*]

FINOLA [*also shaking him by the hand*]. I am so glad you have come—at last.

HUGH. But I wrote to you my reason for not getting here sooner.

THE O'HEYNES. Yes, I know, of course. But why should you have put off coming like this till the very last?

HUGH. Haven't I explained to you again and again how my affairs delayed me?

THE O'HEYNES [*peevishly*]. Yes—yes—explanations. You have caused me, Hugh, the greatest anxiety for all that.

HUGH. I assure you, O'Heynes, this delay was sorely against my will: and I am sorry you have had any anxiety on my account. Why you have, indeed, I cannot understand.

THE O'HEYNES. My mind has been a prey to all sorts of doubts and forebodings.

HUGH [*alarmed*]. Good gracious. What is this for? Isn't Maeve well? How is she?

THE O'HEYNES [*impatiently*]. Oh, she is well—well enough.

HUGH. You are hiding something from me, O'Heynes.

THE O'HEYNES. No—not at all.

HUGH. I, too, was anxious. That is why I hurried here at once after my arrival in the village.

THE O'HEYNES [*suspiciously*]. Eh—why were you anxious?

HUGH. I had not heard about her from Finola for some days.

THE O'HEYNES. There is nothing the matter with her except what has come by your protracted absence.

HUGH [*frightened*]. What has come to her? You alarm me.

THE O'HEYNES. Only a return of her strange ways that used to trouble me before her engagement to you. That is all.

HUGH [*with visible relief*]. Oh—that is all.

THE O'HEYNES [*involuntarily*]. She frightens me sometimes.

HUGH. In what way?

[THE O'HEYNES *hesitates and looks confused.*]

FINOLA. Oh, don't worry her about such things. Hush, here she comes.

[MAEVE O'HEYNES *enters from the back.*]

HUGH. Oh, Maeve, what is it—?

[MAEVE *starts when she perceives him.*]

HUGH [*goes eagerly to her, but is checked by the chillness of her manner, then taking her hand which she gives apathetically*]. I hope you are not angry, Maeve. I came as soon as it was possible for me.

MAEVE [*with some recovered composure*]. Oh—for that— I am not angry in the least—I am not angry at all.

HUGH. You looked as if something disturbed you.

FINOLA. Hugh, it is only her surprise at suddenly seeing you.

THE O'HEYNES. Yes, indeed, when you have disappointed her so often. But, thank heaven, you have arrived safe at last. Come, Finola, come, now I can rest. I feel I want rest after this suspense. Come, let us go indoors.

[*Exeunt* THE O'HEYNES *and* FINOLA O'HEYNES *at left.*]

HUGH [*to* MAEVE]. Well, I am back at last; and you— you are so silent and forgetful there among those old stones.

MAEVE [*as if recalled to herself*]. No. I am in reality thinking of this very thing.

HUGH. Of my coming?

MAEVE. Yes.

HUGH. It has no interest for you one way or the other?

MAEVE. Oh, yes. But I cannot understand father's reason for being so troubled about it.

HUGH. Of course not. As if I wouldn't return on the first opportunity to you. Why do you seem annoyed that I should tell you this?

MAEVE [*restlessly*]. Somehow there seem such cross-purposes in this world of ours.

HUGH. Cross-purposes— How so?

MAEVE. Oh, I don't know—persons seem to give others what those others don't want from them, but want from some one else.

HUGH. That is indeed a world of cross-purposes.

MAEVE [*sadly*]. Don't you see that it is just so with us here?

HUGH [*dejectedly*]. You mean that I give what is not wanted.

MAEVE. Yes, and that another would give you what you want from some one else.

HUGH. Who is that other?

MAEVE. The one whom you once appeared to like best.

HUGH. You are the one I always liked best in the world.

MAEVE. The world did not think so.

HUGH. Indeed?—You puzzle me. Explain what you are saying.

MAEVE [*with a certain embarrassment*]. I thought you liked my sister better than me.

HUGH. Than you? Oh, no—impossible. I know you don't believe what you are saying.

MAEVE. But you appeared to be so much more intimate with her than you have been with me.

HUGH. Ah, that is just it. I have the greatest affection for Finola. I admire her goodness and unselfishness. She has indeed the disposition of an angel.

MAEVE. And yet you could leave her for one so less worthy, as I am.

HUGH. You shall not say you are less worthy; I can see no fault in you.

MAEVE. Oh, why did you ever leave Finola?

HUGH. You forget we were never more than friends. She is one of my very dearest friends.

MAEVE. And you were never engaged to her?

HUGH. Never. It was only when I despaired of your consent that I thought for a while of Finola. But it was no use. Your image always rose up between us. I soon understood that for me you were the only one in the world. [*Pause.*]

MAEVE [*absently*]. The only one in the world. What happiness it must be to find the one who is so much as that.

HUGH. It may also be misery—that is, in a certain sense.

MAEVE [*a little surprise*]. Really? How can it be misery?

HUGH. When we know that nothing of what we feel is returned.

MAEVE [*abstractedly*]. I should not have thought that much mattered.

HUGH. Do you say this because I persist in loving you through all your contempt of my love?

MAEVE. Oh, no—I was not thinking of you at all.

HUGH. What was your reason then for saying it?

MAEVE [*with a pensive deliberation*]. I should have imagined that if one really loved, one would shrink from a return of love.

HUGH [*surprised*]. You wouldn't like your love returned?

MAEVE. Ah, no, for I think if it were, the beauty of love could come to an end in the lover.

HUGH. How very strange. But why should I think so? Yours is the reasoning of one who has never known love.

MAEVE. So you think I have never known love?

HUGH. Certainly. [*Pause.*] Have you?

MAEVE. Well, I can tell you truly that I have.

HUGH [*in a serious tone*]. Is that really so?

MAEVE. Yes.

HUGH [*with a sudden suspicion*]. Do you love some one now?

MAEVE [*quietly*]. Yes.

HUGH [*growing excited*]. Who is he?

MAEVE [*wearily*]. Oh, what is the use of telling you?

HUGH. Who is he, I say? For pity's sake speak.

MAEVE. You would never understand.

HUGH [*bitterly*]. I should understand only too well.

MAEVE. Look around you, then.

HUGH [*puzzled, looking around him*]. Well? I see no one.

MAEVE [*scornfully*]. I knew you would not understand.

HUGH [*wondering*]. I see nothing but these ruins—that mysterious round tower—the stony mountains—and your gray castle through the leafless boughs of great ash-trees.

MAEVE [*with a visionary look in her eyes*]. And you see nothing but these?

HUGH. Oh, what is this mystery? Will you tell me?

MAEVE [*smiling ecstatically*]. Among all these that you see—listen to what Gráinne says in the old poem—

"There lives a one
   On whom I would love to gaze long,
   For whom I would give the whole world,
   All, all, though it is a delusion."

HUGH [*downcast*]. You are mocking me.

MAEVE [*gently*]. Oh, no.—How can you think so? Are not all things beautiful that remind us of our love?

HUGH [*after looking at her calmly for some time*]. Yes, you are right. How strange you are. I do not understand you. Among us simple men you seem like one of your golden fairies. What is the name you call them?

MAEVE. Tuatha de Danann, those tall beautiful children of the Dagda Mor. It is said they were the old people of Erin and were afterwards worshiped as gods.

HUGH. But you do not believe they are really gods?

MAEVE. Oh, no—only a race whose great beauty still haunts our land. [*Sadly.*] They were too beautiful to compare with me.

HUGH. They could not be more beautiful than you are.

You don't know how beautiful you are to me. No—if you knew, you would not be so indifferent. Ah, I realize but too well how little you care for me. You would never have consented to be my wife but for your father: you are doing it all for your father—not for me.

MAEVE. Oh, why do you go back to all that? Have I not consented? And is not that the main thing?

HUGH [*resignedly*]. Yes—I suppose I must be satisfied. I must only trust to time for winning you completely.

MAEVE [*with mysterious significance*]. Let us all trust to time.

HUGH [*brightening*]. May I put my trust in time?

MAEVE. You must ask that question of Time himself.

HUGH. Oh, I am confident of his answer.

MAEVE. And I, too, am confident in Time.

[*Exeunt leisurely at the left.*]

[*As they are going,* PEG INERNY—*a little old woman in a ragged red frieze petticoat, a black frieze cloak raised up to partially cover her head, and with dark woolen stockings worn away at the bare soles of her feet—enters stealthily from among the ruins at back. Muttering indistinctly she follows the two for a while, then squats down on a stone and gazes fixedly at the cairn.*]

[*After a pause* MAEVE *and* FINOLA O'HEYNES *enter at the left.*]

FINOLA. Oh, Maeve, why do you come out here again?

MAEVE [*joyfully*]. He is gone. Until tomorrow, at least, I shall be free.

FINOLA. Poor Hugh.

MAEVE. He is gone; and I will make the most of my little liberty. I have to say good-by to beauty. How this moonlit night—this Irish night comes like a fawn!

[FINOLA *perceives* PEG INERNY *and stands as if transfixed.*]

MAEVE. What's the matter, Finola? [*Turns and looks.*] Oh, it is only Peg Inerny.

FINOLA. Come away, Maeve, for heaven's sake come. I have left father sleeping in the hall; and if he awakes he is sure to call me, and ask where you are.

MAEVE [*not heeding* FINOLA]. Peg, Peg, I have not seen you for many days. What has brought you here tonight?

PEG [*rousing herself slowly and looking steadily at*

MAEVE]. I come to take a last farewell of my Princess on the night before her wedding day.

MAEVE [*with a rigid melancholy*]. Yes, I shall never return here, Peg.

PEG. Do you think you will ever leave, Princess?

FINOLA. Oh, what is that she says? I am terrified.

MAEVE [*carelessly*]. You are always alarmed at one thing or another, Finola.

FINOLA [*uneasily*]. No—no—but didn't you hear her?

PEG [*to* FINOLA]. Princess, do not fear a poor old woman.

FINOLA. Why will you always call us princesses?

PEG. Isn't your father a prince? The Prince of Burren?

MAEVE [*impatiently*]. A prince indeed. It is a mockery now to call him that.

PEG. The O'Heynes is none the less a prince whatever he may have done to put shame on his race.

MAEVE [*helplessly*]. Oh, what a misfortune it was.

FINOLA [*expostulating*]. Maeve—darling.

PEG [*slyly*]. They told me my Princess Maeve was content to marry her young Englishman.

MAEVE [*with suppressed scorn*]. Ha—no one ever troubled before to consider whether she was or not.

PEG. He is so rich—so rich with his grand English house and possessions.

MAEVE. Yes, indeed—and that is how the whole tragedy has come about.

PEG. I was sure you cared not, Princess, for this world's riches.

MAEVE [*sadly*]. Heaven knows I never had any greed of them.

FINOLA. Oh, Maeve, I thought you had done with these complaints once and for all.

MAEVE [*pained and irresolute*]. So I, too, thought—once perhaps. But today in the abbey—it was so beautiful. Something seemed to come back to me.

PEG. It was haunting you, Princess? The day-ghost, eh?

MAEVE [*with a wan look*]. The day-ghost. Oh, the wistful pleading of a day-ghost!

FINOLA [*frightened*]. Why do you say that, Maeve?

MAEVE. Ah—if you saw him—but you never have, Finola.

FINOLA. Saw him—good heavens, where?

MAEVE [*pointing to the round tower*]. In the masterwork of Goban—in the mountains too.

PEG. Your love is dreaming among the rocks of these mountains, Princess.

MAEVE [*with a sort of ecstasy*]. Oh, how I have grown to love these stony mountains.

PEG. They are the pleasure haunts of many a beautiful ghost.

MAEVE. The many beautiful buried in that cairn.

PEG. Oh, what a world there is underneath that cairn.

MAEVE [*pensively*]. Yes, the great beautiful Queen Maeve who reigned over Connacht hundreds of years ago—she is buried in that cairn, you say?

PEG. Haven't I often told you so, Princess?

FINOLA. But I have always understood that Queen Maeve was buried at Rathcroghan in County Roscommon.

PEG. No, Princess, she is here.

FINOLA [*inquiringly*]. Can you know that?

PEG. Can I know? I can know many things. [*With a low laugh.*] Indeed I ought to know where Queen Maeve is.

MAEVE. Why you especially, Peg?

PEG. Haven't I dwelt in her palace, child?

FINOLA [*timidly approaching* MAEVE]. That is a strange thing to say.

PEG [*continuing with a sort of inward satisfaction*]. Yes, I have dwelt in her palace. Ha—ha—does anyone think that I could bear my miserable outcast life in the world if I could not live the other life also? Oh, my sweet ladies, you don't know the grandeur of that other life.

MAEVE [*eagerly*]. Tell me, do tell me of that other life.

FINOLA. Maeve—take care—don't ask such a thing.

MAEVE [*impatiently*]. Oh, Finola, you mustn't prevent me in this way. [*To* PEG INERNY.] Tell me.

PEG. A life among the people with beautiful looks.

MAEVE [*suddenly delighted*]. With beautiful looks!

PEG. Yes, Princess— Oh, just so graceful and clean as you are yourself. I often think you must be one of them.

MAEVE. Tell me more about those people.

PEG. They are now ruled over by the great Queen Maeve.

MAEVE [*puzzled*]. But—she is dead, isn't she? Didn't you say she was buried in the cairn?

PEG [*with an enigmatical grimace*]. Yes, yes, Princess—
but not dead— Oh, I never said that she was dead.

MAEVE. What new and wonderful tale are you now telling
me?

PEG. Haven't I told you before that Queen Maeve has ever
been watchful of you?

MAEVE [*surprised*]. No—you have not. What does this
mean?

PEG. Just fancy, Princess, it was she who had you called
after herself.

FINOLA [*excitedly*]. Maeve, don't believe her. How is this
possible?

PEG. Ah, Princess Finola, didn't you ever know that I was
once a servant in the Castle?

FINOLA [*restraining herself*]. Yes, I believe you were. It
was a very long time ago, was it not?

PEG. When your beautiful sister here was born.

FINOLA. Well then, supposing you were, what has that
to do with Queen Maeve naming my sister?

PEG [*slyly*]. Oh—only 'twas I made them think of calling
her Maeve.

FINOLA. But you said Queen Maeve did so?

PEG [*with veiled significance*]. Haven't I told you of the
other life I lead, sweet Princess Finola?

FINOLA [*starts, then looking awed and mystified at* PEG
INERNY, *says in a trembling voice*]. Maeve, she is a wicked
woman. It is not right to hold any intercourse with her.

MAEVE [*who has been listening with a troubled expression*]. Ah me, I am the most miserable one in the world.

FINOLA [*terrified*]. Dearest, for pity's sake don't—don't
give way to such a feeling.

MAEVE [*despairingly*]. My father—oh, my father.

PEG. I know it was for his sake alone that you promised to
marry this Hugh Fitz Walter.

MAEVE. Yes, father will become rich and great—but my
heart will break.

FINOLA [*anxiously*]. No— No, Maeve, you must remember
how good and kind Hugh is. He will surely never cause you
unhappiness.

MAEVE. How could he be anything but unhappiness to me,
when I can only think of my beloved?

PEG [*insidiously*]. That one who haunts the mountains and the beautiful old buildings, Princess—

MAEVE. My beloved whom I am leaving forever!

FINOLA [*throwing her arms around her sister*]. Hush—you must not think of him any more, Maeve.

PEG. Ah—you cling to her like ivy, my Lady Finola. You were the one made for clinging. You were the wife that would have been best for the Englishman.

MAEVE. Oh, if he could but understand that this is so.

PEG. They never can, Princess. Dwellers in the valley are always looking at the heights above them.

MAEVE [*sadly*]. I am no longer on those heights. I have fallen from them miserably, and have become [*looking at* FINOLA] like the ivy in the valley.

PEG. Not yet—you are still on the heights. No, you are still like the tall smooth larch on the top of the mountain.

MAEVE [*dejectedly*]. Ah, no, not any longer.

PEG. Come then, to the mountains, Princess—there you will believe it.

FINOLA [*restraining her*]. Maeve, Maeve, do not go. It will kill father if he hears you have wandered away tonight.

PEG. See how bright it is. The night is lit for your visit. [MAEVE *appears to hesitate.*] Beware of the ivy clinging around the larch, Princess Maeve. It will kill the fairy growth of the larch.

MAEVE [*restlessly*]. Let me go, Finola, let me go.

FINOLA. I will not, Maeve.

MAEVE. Let me go to the mountains for this last time; I promise to return soon.

FINOLA. Oh, sister, do not go there tonight.

MAEVE. How white the moon rays dance upon the mountains.

PEG. It is the mountains, Princess, that are white with the dancing feet of the fairies.

MAEVE [*desperately*]. I must go there tonight.

FINOLA. You shall not, Maeve.

MAEVE [*gazing fondly on the mountains*]. Oh, beauty of my day-dreams come forth from the mountains.

PEG. Princess, what is it that you see?

MAEVE [*with transport*]. My love, like an exhalation from the earth to the stars!

PEG [*moving towards the back*]. Come, Princess, come.

MAEVE. I am coming.

FINOLA [*with a sudden determination*]. Then I shall go too. I could not bear the suspense of your absence. [*Distant voice of* THE O'HEYNES *is heard several times calling* "Finola."] Good heavens, there is father calling. [*Runs to the left and listens in great agitation while the calling is repeated.*] Yes, father, yes, father.

[*Exeunt* MAEVE O'HEYNES *and* PEG INERNY *quickly at the back.*]

FINOLA. If he finds she has gone he will be so distressed. I must not tell him. Oh, Maeve, why, why have you gone? Yes, father—coming—coming. [*Exit at left.*]

ACT II

SCENE: *The exterior of O'Heynes Castle. At the left a large square tower with its two roof gables facing right and left, and Irish battlements which carry two high chimneys, one at front and one at back of roof. On ground level at front is the pointed Gothic entrance-door, over which a square-headed window lights a room above, while on the side facing the right above a hall window, is another square-headed window belonging to the same upper room. Around, great leafless ash-trees grow upon the pale green grass. Some way off at the right is the cairn with the abbey ruins beyond; and stony mountain ranges, as in the first act, form a background to the whole scene.*

It is a frosty night with a very bright moon.

FINOLA O'HEYNES, *closely muffled, comes out through the door of the castle.*

FINOLA. Maeve. Are you there, Maeve? [*Pause.*] Maeve. [*Goes to the right and peers about.*] I don't see any sign of her. Oh dear, oh dear, I wonder does she intend to come back. [*With an anxious and undecided look.*] I don't know which way to search for her. Stop—I will try this path leading to the mountains. [*Exit at back behind the Castle.*]

[MAEVE O'HEYNES, *looking very pale and listless, enters from the right.*]

MAEVE [*gazing forlorn around the scene*]. Oh, moon and mountain and ruin, give a voice to my infinite sadness!

[*Pause.*]

[FINOLA O'HEYNES *reënters from behind the Castle.*]

FINOLA. O sister, you are here!

MAEVE [*slowly*]. Yes.

FINOLA. Thank heaven, you have returned. [*She advances toward her.*]

MAEVE. I said I would return, Finola.

FINOLA. Oh, I was so frightened. Aren't you perished without a cloak on, this bitter night?

MAEVE [*wearily*]. Is it so cold?

FINOLA [*surprised*]. Cold? You must feel this biting frosty air?

MAEVE. No—not particularly.

FINOLA [*feeling the hands and face of* MAEVE]. Why, Maeve, you are like ice.

MAEVE [*as if remembering*]. Like ice. How beautiful to be like the ice!

FINOLA. Oh, come in, come in from the cold.

MAEVE. No—let me wait here, in the moonlight.

FINOLA. Darling, you will get dreadfully ill—and on your wedding morning too.

MAEVE [*with a shudder*]. What—it is not yet the day?

FINOLA. Midnight has just passed—yes, this is your wedding day.

MAEVE [*mournfully*]. Oh, so soon—so soon.

FINOLA. Far better had it been sooner, my poor sister.

MAEVE. Oh, don't say that, Finola.

FINOLA. Yes, yes, this long delay since your engagement has brought the old trouble upon you again.

MAEVE [*with a scornful smile*]. Do you think I was ever really reconciled to my fate?

FINOLA. And yet—and yet—you seemed happy for a while.

MAEVE. No—never really. I was only talked into a false sort of happiness, Finola.

FINOLA [*expostulating*]. Oh, how can you say that?

MAEVE. Yes, I deceived myself there among you. You all seemed so happy and were so kind and indulgent to me, that I wished to believe this marriage was for the best.

FINOLA. And you never really believed it?

MAEVE. Never—I was soon certain that I never did.

FINOLA. When was that?

MAEVE. When he went to England to arrange with his lawyers, and this family happiness that encircled me gradually disappeared—

FINOLA. Do you think so? I am sure father and I have never changed.

MAEVE. Perhaps not, but you understand, I was left more to myself and had time to think over what I had done. [*Despairingly.*] Ah, then I saw that I never could be reconciled to my fate.

FINOLA. Darling, you should not have encouraged such a thought. It will leave you, when you are married and away from here.

MAEVE. Oh, the sacrifice—I make it for father's sake.

FINOLA. Be sure your sacrifice for father's sake will have its reward.

MAEVE. It is a cruel sacrifice. And yet it must be—

FINOLA. Poor Hugh. At all events he is unchanged.

MAEVE. I too am unchanged, Finola. Don't you see it after what I have told you?

FINOLA. I suppose so. But have you always disliked him? You do not hate him?

MAEVE. Oh, but if you were to see him Finola, in the light he appears to me—

FINOLA. How does he appear to you, dear?

MAEVE [*with sudden vehemence*]. A bandit—a plunderer!

FINOLA. Maeve, what are you saying?

MAEVE. Yes, I say a bandit, like his English predecessors who ruined every beautiful thing we ever had.

FINOLA [*frightened*]. Sister, how can you accuse him of that?

MAEVE [*bitterly*]. Yes, he has come finally to ruin every beautiful thing.

FINOLA. He, who is so generous? Why, instead of destroying, is he not restoring the dignity of our ancient Celtic house?

MAEVE [*scornfully*]. Yes, I know what such restoration means. It is bought at too great a price, I can tell you. It is like that great restoration of a family's pride by Strongbow, who first brought our humiliation upon us.

FINOLA. No—I cannot see the likeness, Maeve.

MAEVE. Don't you remember the conditions of the English noble whom the Irish king Diarmid called to his aid?

FINOLA. Was it not, if Strongbow regained for Diarmid his kingdom he was to marry the king's daughter Eva?

MAEVE. Yes, and then become heir to Diarmid. He succeeded in regaining the kingdom and the conditions were fulfilled, weren't they?

FINOLA. They were.

MAEVE. And thus with the power that was given him he subdued and ruined the ancient splendor of Erin. The old, old story! Poor Eva, you were sacrificed—a sweet symbol of your country in her subjection.

FINOLA. That may be, but still I can't understand in what way Hugh is to injure our country.

MAEVE. By killing the last flame of her life.

FINOLA. The last flame of our country's life? How is that?

MAEVE. Yes, the last light of her life.

FINOLA. What is this last light?

MAEVE [*with a child's smile and as if forgetful of all sorrows*]. The fairy lamp of Celtic Beauty!

FINOLA [*after a moment, in a very gentle voice*]. Dearest, it is impossible he ever could do this thing.

MAEVE. Is he not destroying my chosen way of life—that life which alone may keep the flame alight? Am I not the last?

FINOLA. The last? Why should you think that you are the last?

MAEVE. Listen and I will tell you, Finola. You have heard Peg Inerny speak of her other life, and of having dwelt in the palace of Queen Maeve.

FINOLA [*nervously*]. Yes, what of her?

MAEVE. This very night after I had left her upon the mountain I thought I saw her beckoning to me in the abbey. I followed her while she went past the round tower to the cairn which now was glowing against a sky that had turned crimson. With a gesture the old woman seemed to open the cairn, and then stood transformed in a curious region of fresh green suffused with saffron light, so that I saw her tall, and beautiful, and marvelously pale of face, and crowned with a golden diadem not so golden as her hair. And I heard her say these words in ancient Gaelic: "Last Princess of Erin, thou art a lonely dweller among strange peoples; but I the great Queen Maeve have watched thee from thy birth, for thou wert to be the vestal of our country's last beauty. Behold whom thy love hath called to life. Mark him well, for already his hour of dissolution hath come." And I looked and saw him who was beauty standing by the round tower. With a feeling of nothingness, I fell upon my knees and bent down to the earth. When I looked again he was not there. Then a company of ancient Celts bore a covered form upon their shoulders; while a choir of rose-crowned boys sang ·dirges with violet voices of frail, lace-like beauty. And then buried their dead one by the round tower, and over his grave they raised a great ogham stone. And again I heard the voice of the Queen: "They have buried thy dead beauty, Princess. Thou hast killed him by deserting thy chosen way of life; for there are no more who live for beauty." Then in my desolation I seemed to lose consciousness of all save these last words of the queen: "Yet, Princess, I will come and comfort thee again tonight." And with a start I discovered that I was sitting alone in the moonlight by the round tower. And I looked, and I could not find the great ogham stone that they had raised over my beloved.

FINOLA. And so you were only dreaming after all.

MAEVE. Yes, it must have only been a dream—for my beloved is not dead.

FINOLA. Nor will Queen Maeve come to you again tonight.

MAEVE. Do not be so sure of that, Finola.

FINOLA [*in a frightened voice*]. Oh, heavens! there she is.

MAEVE [*starting*]. Who?

FINOLA. Peg Inerny.

[PEG INERNY *enters from the right.*]

PEG. My noble ladies.

FINOLA [*angrily*]. What do you want?

PEG. Oh, I never thought you could be so sharp, Lady Finola.

FINOLA [*with the desperation of terror*]. Go—you are here for no good purpose.

MAEVE [*deprecatingly*]. Finola.

PEG [*to* FINOLA]. Won't you give me the liberty of a wild beast to walk about at night, my dear?

FINOLA [*shrieking*]. Go, I say, or I will let loose the dogs of the Castle upon you.

MAEVE. Finola, for goodness' sake, what are you saying? What wrong has she ever done to any of us?

FINOLA. Oh, yes, don't I know her evil intentions towards you?

MAEVE. I feel sure she has never done me harm.

PEG [*to* MAEVE]. Sweet Princess, you'll rejoice for the gentleness you have shown me.

FINOLA [*to* PEG INERNY]. I will call my father up if you don't leave at once. Come, sister, come into the castle.

PEG. Good night, Sweet Maeve—sleep—sleep—and dream. [*Exit at right.*]

MAEVE [*yearningly*]. And dream—oh, that I could dream again tonight, that dream!

FINOLA. Don't think of it any more, dearest. Come in to rest.

MAEVE. No—let me stay awhile longer here.

FINOLA. But you will be frozen, Maeve. I wonder you ever awoke again after falling asleep in the abbey.

MAEVE. Let me stay, Finola, I do not feel the cold.

FINOLA. It is because you are already so cold.

MAEVE. My love is so divinely cold.

FINOLA. Ah, that is a strange sort of love.

MAEVE [*wistfully*]. He is the only one I have ever loved. Let me stay. I hear him coming.

FINOLA [*frightened*]. You hear him—?

MAEVE [*pointing towards the abbey*]. Yes, there—far away—coming on the wings of the March wind. Don't you hear?

FINOLA. I hear the bitter wind, Maeve, through our old ash-trees.

MAEVE [*smiling in reverie*]. The fairy March wind which races at twilight over our fields, turning them to that strange pale beauty, like the beauty of a fairy's face.—Oh, it is fit that my beloved should ride on such a steed.

FINOLA. Dearest, you must go to rest. He will never come. He is dead.

MAEVE. He is not dead. He will come. I know he will. But the way is long. A long—long way.

FINOLA. A long way, indeed, without beginning and without end.

MAEVE. It began from the land of everlasting youth.

FINOLA. You have often told me of that land, Tir-nan-ogue, is it not?

MAEVE. The Celtic dream-land of ideal beauty. There he lives in never-fading freshness of youth. [*With a steadfast visionary look.*] I am haunted by a boyish face close hooded with short gold hair—and every movement of his slender faultless body goes straight to my heart like a fairy melody. Oh, he has a long way to journey:—for that land of beauty was never so far away as it is tonight.

FINOLA [*sadly*]. It never was nearer, my poor sister. Come, I will see you to your rest.

MAEVE. I must rest alone, Finola. You must not follow me to my room.

FINOLA. Why not, dear?

MAEVE. Oh, do not. Leave me to myself.

FINOLA [*with a sigh*]. Very well, if you wish it.

MAEVE [*going*]. Good night.

FINOLA. Good night, dear.

MAEVE [*quickly turning and throwing her arms around* FINOLA]. Good night—good-by— Oh, my darling, good-by.

FINOLA [*consolingly*]. My poor Maeve, it is not yet the time for parting.

MAEVE. Who knows where I must go, when my beloved shall come. [*Exit hurriedly by door leading into the Castle.*]

FINOLA [*wonderingly*]. What does she mean by those words? [*With a reassured air.*] Oh, she is tired, poor sister. That is what it is. And I suppose her mind is confused with her imaginary difficulties. But all will come well in good time. [*Exit by door leading into the Castle. Pause.*]

[MAEVE O'HEYNES *appears at the window of the Castle, above the hall window facing the right, and slowly opens the casement.*]

MAEVE [*leaning out*]. Oh, the beautiful frosty night! I cannot keep it from me. The greatest beauty like the old Greek sculpture is always cold! My Prince of the hoar dew! My golden love, let me see you once more in that aureole of crimson sky! [*With an infinite longing.*] Oh, that the beauty I saw in my dream could return to me now. [*With sudden terror.*] But tomorrow, how shall I face the misery of tomorrow? Oh, pity me, pity me— [*Calmer.*] And yet I have always known that my beloved would deliver me from bondage. [*With a gradually weaker voice as she sinks upon a chair.*] But I am weary of waiting—weary—weary—it is hard to resist the longing for sleep. [*She sighs as she reclines back out of sight in an angle of the window.*]

[*Pause.*]

[*There is a soft music of harps, while the aurora borealis arises and glows in the sky. Soon a ghostly procession is seen to emerge like vapor from the neighborhood of the cairn. Presently as it advances it grows more distinct and then is discovered to consist of* QUEEN MAEVE, *tall, pale faced and fair-haired, in a golden crown and gold embroidered robes; of* BOY PAGES *in garlanded tunics and wearing wreaths of roses upon their heads; of ancient Irish harpers with their harps; of chieftains and warriors in conical caps; of people, etc. As they approach near to the Castle,* MAEVE O'HEYNES *enters from the door at its front, and stands looking on in wonder. They halt; and the harpers cease playing on their harps.*]

CHORUS OF BOY PAGES [*singing in broad solemn unison*].
       Every hill which is at this Oenach
       Hath under it heroes and Queens,
       And poets and distributors,
       And fair fierce women.

[*The harpers recommence their music.*]

MAEVE [*with a thrill of happiness*]. Ah, that song of Dorban I know so well. And this is Queen Maeve again.

[*The harpers cease their music.*]

CHORUS OF BOY PAGES.
       Hast seen our warriors? In their hands are silver shields
       Ornamented with white silver signs—
       They wield blue flaming swords
       And carry red horns with metal mountings.

MAEVE [*listening*]. Now they are chanting the lay of Fiachna son of Reta.

A BOY PAGE [*singing alone*].
       Obedient to the settled order of the battle,
       Preceding their prince of gracious mien

They march across blue lances,
Those troops of white warriors with knotted hair.
CHORUS OF BOY PAGES.
Then march across blue lances,
Those troops of white warriors with knotted hair.
[*The harpers recommence their music.*]
QUEEN MAEVE. Princess, I come, as I have promised.
MAEVE [*approaching and falling on her knees*]. My
Queen— Oh, save me, my Queen.
QUEEN MAEVE. O last of my daughters in the land, what
help can I give you?
MAEVE. My beloved—where is he?
QUEEN MAEVE. He is coming over the mountains. He is
coming to you over the mountains.
MAEVE [*rising*]. Yes, I knew he was coming on the fairy
March wind.
QUEEN MAEVE. Your love is so great that you divine his
coming? and yet you can suffer bondage?
MAEVE. How shall I escape the stranger's bondage?
QUEEN MAEVE. I will take you to the land of joy.
MAEVE. To Tir-nan-ogue?—O Queen, do you rule in Tir-
nan-ogue?
QUEEN MAEVE. The empire of the Gael is in Tir-nan-ogue.
There during life he is at peace in the building of beauty
from the past.
MAEVE. And so the land you reign in is the home of living
men.
QUEEN MAEVE. Each man who comes to his ideal has come
to Tir-nan-ogue.
MAEVE. And thus we see you so young and so beautiful
after all those two thousand years!
QUEEN MAEVE. Your fame also shall remain beautiful and
young.
MAEVE. Of what kind is the happiness that makes Tir-nan-
ogue happy?
QUEEN MAEVE. Happiness in the present as sweet as the
remembrance of happiness.
MAEVE. There shall my happiness be great indeed.
QUEEN MAEVE. You remember much happiness?
MAEVE. I remember beauty.
QUEEN MAEVE. Those who love beauty shall see beauty.

MAEVE. The immortal beauty of form!

QUEEN MAEVE. Form that will awaken genius!

MAEVE. Form is my beauty and my love!

[*The harpers cease their music.*]

CHORUS OF BOY PAGES.

Their strength, great as it is, cannot be less,
They are sons of queens and kings,
On the heads of all a comely
Growth of hair yellow like gold.

A BOY PAGE.

Their bodies are graceful and majestic,
Their eyes with a look of power have the eyeball blue.
Their teeth are brilliant like glass,
Their lips are red and thin.

CHORUS OF BOY PAGES.

Their bodies are graceful and majestic,
These sons of queens and kings.

[*The harpers recommence their music.*]

MAEVE. So Fiachna is made to sing when the poet tells how the hero came from the land of the gods. I love that poem!

QUEEN MAEVE. I have all the poems—the greatest those that are lost. Come into my land; and they that made them shall sing them, and their music shall turn all things to beauty.

MAEVE. Queen, I have seen that land afar.

QUEEN MAEVE. You also have seen Tir-nan-ogue?

MAEVE. In my dreams, in my day-dreams.

QUEEN MAEVE. Daughter, it is passing sweet when our day-dreams come true.

MAEVE. Oh, let me see the beloved of my day-dreams.

QUEEN MAEVE. Your Prince of the hoar dew, when he comes, will give you rest.

MAEVE. Rest without pain or fear of bondage?

QUEEN MAEVE. Rest in beauty—a beauty which is transcendently cold.

MAEVE. Oh, let me see that beauty. I have sought it in vain on earth.

QUEEN MAEVE. He is coming, he is coming over the mountains. You shall speak to him when he is come.

MAEVE [*with a sudden disconsolate look*]. I will never speak to him.

QUEEN MAEVE. Why, wayward child?

MAEVE. Queen, I cannot. The sight of such beauty will make me speechless.

QUEEN MAEVE. Then shall you find peace in his beauty.

MAEVE. But, oh, my Queen, let me see him.

QUEEN MAEVE. You shall see him in the Northern lights of Tir-nan-ogue.

MAEVE. And his beauty shall be my joy in an ideal land.

QUEEN MAEVE. I am waiting for you, poor weary child.

MAEVE. The land where my day-dreams will come true!

QUEEN MAEVE. See, the Northern lights are passing before the dawn. We must not tarry.

MAEVE. I am ready, my beautiful Queen.

QUEEN MAEVE. Then come with the Northern lights, beautiful ice maiden!

MAEVE. I shall see my beauty—my love—! [*Half swooning she falls on the neck of* QUEEN MAEVE.]

[*The harpers cease their music.*]

CHORUS OF BOY PAGES.

Noble and melodious music thou dost hear;
Thou goest from kingdom to kingdom
Drinking from goblets of massy gold,
Thou wilt discourse with thy beloved.

A BOY PAGE.

We have carried from the plain Mag Mell
Thirty caldrons, thirty horns for drinking,
We have carried from it the lamentation sung by Mear,
Daughter of Eochaid the Dumb.

[*The harpers recommence their music.*]

CHORUS OF BOY PAGES.

What a marvel in Tir-nan-ogue
That mead should fall with each shower,
Drinking from goblets of massy gold,
Thou wilt discourse with thy beloved.

[*During this song all, including* MAEVE O'HEYNES, *have gradually moved off towards the cairn and faded away with the aurora borealis, so that, when the music ceases, no trace of them remains. A faint gray light of dawn now prevails; and then the whole scene, at the approach of sunrise, is discovered to be completely white with a thick coating of hoar frost. After awhile* HUGH FITZ WALTER, *muffled and carrying a large bunch of flowers, enters from the left.*]

HUGH. I can wait no longer. I must come to her Castle with the first light. How fine it looks decked out with the hoar frost! Oh, I hope she is safe and well; let these be my morning offering before she awakes. [*He lays the flowers by the doorway of the Castle.*]

[THE O'HEYNES, *also muffled, enters from the left.*]

THE O'HEYNES [*looking in the direction of* HUGH]. Ah! you, too, are out early this morning.

HUGH. Yes. Somehow I felt I had to come.

THE O'HEYNES. What a blessing you are here at last, Hugh. [*He grasps him by the hand.*]

HUGH. I wish I could have returned sooner.

THE O'HEYNES. I wish you could have. Well, let that be.

HUGH. But why are you also about at this hour of the morning? I did not expect to see anyone stirring.

THE O'HEYNES [*peevishly*]. I could not sleep these hours past with thinking and thinking. Then something made me get up, and see what would happen.

HUGH [*anxiously*]. What would happen? Heavens! what do you expect to happen?

THE O'HEYNES. Oh, nothing, nothing, I suppose. Only my mind will not let me rest.

HUGH. Do you know I, too, was very uneasy about things last night.

THE O'HEYNES [*suspiciously*]. You, why? What reason could you have had?

HUGH [*with rather a forced laugh*]. Oh, none, of course. How could I?

THE O'HEYNES. Of course not—of course not. But come in to the fire, Hugh, and warm yourself. There has been a great frost last night.

HUGH. Yes, the whole country is white, as if it were covered with snow.

THE O'HEYNES. A March frost soon melts before the sun. See, it is already rising. The day is going to be a glorious one.

HUGH. There is an old saying— "Happy is the bride the sun shines on."

[*As they go towards the door of the Castle,* FINOLA O'HEYNES *enters from it.*]

FINOLA. Oh, what lovely flowers!

HUGH. I brought them for Maeve. She is not yet awake?

FINOLA. No. I gave orders she was not to be disturbed. It was very late last night when she went to rest; and she seemed so tired.

HUGH. Then I would not have her disturbed for worlds. Will you bring her these flowers, Finola, when she awakes?

[PEG INERNY *enters from the right*.]

PEG. When she awakes—? Ah—my Princess Maeve—do you think she will care for such flowers now?

HUGH [*in a subdued voice*]. Why not? Why do you say she would not?

PEG. Oh, it's a cold morning, a cruel cold morning.

FINOLA. Go away from this place.—Let me never see you again.

PEG. I have never before been refused the shelter of O'Heynes Castle.

HUGH. O'Heynes Castle is never the better for your presence. I understand you are always importuning Miss O'Heynes.

THE O'HEYNES. Come, we must not be hard to the old woman on such a day as this. Go round to the kitchen, Peg, and get something to eat.

PEG. Yes, some food. I want some food and warmth, Prince—I have been out all night, and I am famished.

THE O'HEYNES. Well, then, get all you wish. The Castle hall is open to everyone in honor of my daughter's wedding today.

HUGH. Yes, we must try to make everyone happy today— even this wicked old woman.

PEG [*with a sinister look*]. I suppose you also, my brave Englishman, think you ought to be happy.

HUGH. Why—of course. Don't you know I am to be married today?

PEG [*almost contemptuously*]. You married to the Princess Maeve?

HUGH [*bridling up*]. Yes.

PEG [*mockingly*]. Well, well, how queer that you should think so!

FINOLA [*with a scared expression*]. There is misfortune in those words.

THE O'HEYNES. Peg Inerny, you are awakening my forebodings again.

PEG [*humbly*]. Oh, Prince, I can't say otherwise.

HUGH [*indignantly*]. What old woman's talk is this?

PEG [*with a quiet prophetic triumph*]. You think I am only an old woman; but I tell you that Erin can never be subdued.

HUGH. I should like to know what that has to do with the matter?

PEG [*smiling insidiously*]. Perhaps the Englishman may think that he already holds her? Ah, she will slip like a fairy from his grasp. [*She laughs low and sardonically.*]

FINOLA [*excitedly to* PEG INERNY]. Leave the place at once, you wicked woman. Oh, drive her away, Hugh, before she says any more.

HUGH [*advances to* PEG INERNY, *who draws herself up defiantly. He then steps back, saying, with a forced laugh*]. What do I care for her? I shall soon be married and far away.

PEG. Take care, my fine Englishman, if your Irish Princess hasn't already slipped from you like a fairy.

THE O'HEYNES [*nervously*]. What do you mean, Peg Inerny?

PEG. Oh, my Prince, just before dawn upon the mountains—I saw her.

HUGH [*with a look of terror*]. You saw her?

PEG [*with a smile of ecstasy*]. Yes, I saw my Princess Maeve!

HUGH [*turning perplexed to* THE O'HEYNES *and to* FINOLA]. But—but didn't you say she was there in the Castle?

THE O'HEYNES [*with a helpless look*]. I thought so. I am sure I thought so. Didn't you say she was here, Finola?

FINOLA [*in a hollow voice*]. Yes, father. [*As if petrified she now slowly retreats towards the Castle door, keeping her eyes always fixed on* PEG INERNY.]

HUGH. Oh, that Maeve should be wandering over the mountains on such a night as this.

THE O'HEYNES [*confusedly*]. I knew some misfortune was coming. What has happened?

PEG [*with increasing ecstasy*]. If you had only seen her,

as I saw her upon the mountain—she was so beautiful—so happy. You would have died at the sight of such beauty, my Englishman.

HUGH [*with a look of bitterness and despair*]. As if I required to be persuaded of her beauty!

PEG [*quietly*]. And you will never see it again.

[*Exit* FINOLA O'HEYNES *by door leading into the Castle.*]

HUGH [*suddenly subdued*]. Never again—why never again?

PEG. It has gone to where he is.

HUGH [*wildly*]. He—he—who is he? Speak at once. Don't you see you torture me?

PEG. The beauty that she loves.

HUGH [*growing quieter*]. Ah, I understand—only that.

PEG [*calmly triumphant and ecstatic*]. Like the glory of the Northern lights was his face upon the mountains. And when she saw him, her own face shone like a star.

HUGH [*as if transfixed*]. Oh, what does all this mean? [*Recovering himself.*] Ha—ha—it is nothing. Of course you are only raving. That's what it is. Anyone can see that.

THE O'HEYNES [*with an agonized look*]. She has given utterance to my worst forebodings. Tell what you saw next, Peg Inerny.

PEG. The dawn came then; and Princess Maeve went out from my sight with the stars!

[*Short pause.*]

[*Cries of* "Help!" *are heard within the Castle. Then* FINOLA O'HEYNES, *with a scared face, appears at the window over the entrance-door, and throws the casement open violently.*]

FINOLA [*wailing*]. Oh, heavens, oh, my heavens—oh—[*Looks across the room towards the window facing the abbey at right, and after a moment's awful silence says in a voice of terror.*]—Maeve—she is sitting there at the open window—dead.

GROUP V

PLAYS OF THE MODERN MOVEMENT

FIFTY years in the life of a race-literature, consciously in-
sulated from the beginning, seems too little time for such a
literature to crack its elementary mold and flutter out from
the risky category of the literary curiosity. Irish dramatists,
realizing the necessity of this action, are gradually casting off
what has come to be a universal preoccupation with provin-
cialisms of thought and speech. And thus they are merging
into the larger field of world-literature. Since Ibsen, the
drama of small countries has taken this direction successfully.
The drama of today, having shifted its interest and emphasis
from the body to the mind of man, is become thereby common property to all nations. It is substituting nationalistic
plays, which lend themselves comfortably to universal consideration and a universally intelligible treatment, in the place of
more picturesque, perhaps, but less profound, emotional plays
dealing with local types and characters, and depending too
heavily for their success on the exploitation of some esoteric
atmosphere. The remarkable increase in the number of foreign plays produced each year in New York and London
gives ample evidence of this new dramatic internationalism.
Luigi Pirandello's *Six Characters in Search of an Author*,
Kaiser's *From Morn to Midnight*, Benavente's *The Bonds of
Interest*, Andreyev's *He Who Gets Slapped*, Molnar's *Liliom*,
Capek's *R. U. R.*, and Heijermann's *The Good Hope* are a few
of the foreign plays produced successfully in New York in the
last few years. They were successful because they treated abstract questions or imaginative subjects of general interest
quite apart from the parochialisms imposed upon them by geo-
graphical limitations. Seeing these plays we do not say, "How
Italian this one is." or "How true that one is of life in Ger-
many." Rather, we remark on the intellectual interest they
contain for us, and on the vitality and freshness of the methods
used in presenting the ideas to us.

The stability of Irish society at the present time under the new independent government practically eliminates any need for plays of a vituperative or locally circumscribed nature. Certainly the new dramatists, profiting by the pioneering of their predecessors, should embrace new methods and find a world market for their dramatic goods. With more than six hundred amateur acting groups and a large number of professional theaters extant at this writing, there should be no lack of encouragement to playwrights who want to experiment in the wider field. Ireland is drama-mad. Spontaneous dramatization of any casual situation occurs everywhere. The drama, or rather the acting of it, is not confined to the theater alone. In the market-place, in pubs, or at public meetings one may detect a certain theatrical instinct of the people finding an outlet. This mimetic gift may again be explained psychologically: the make-believe taking precedence before the actual. Certainly, then, the playwrights cannot complain of any lack of interest in the drama. However, the dilemma they find themselves in is this: how they may preserve the tenets of their original purpose to build a drama in the native tradition (which means writing of the peasantry in the Anglo-Irish idiom or in Gaelic) and, at the same time, contribute to the demands of an international dramatic field. The latter course is not impossible, in fact it is being done, haltingly to be sure, but done nevertheless in a few of the smaller amateur groups in and around Dublin. We need have no doubt of the Irishman's ability to enter the international field. We have learned to discredit, I hope, the peevish assertions George Moore makes in *Hail and Farewell* to the effect that an Irishman is incapable of any profundity of thought or emotion.

It does not necessarily follow that the Irish drama should be forced to change its complexion completely to conform to the changing taste either of its critics or its audiences, and become ponderously intellectual at the expense of its special poetic and æsthetic qualities. Neither should it necessarily forego the Irish idiom. But it must break away from the restrictions of the outworn peasant play toward a new expansion and development, toward a new humanism, before it can be considered along with the best of our modern dramatic literatures in the future. To take this path the Irish must first bring themselves to the common opinion that the national tradition has been established, the national identity manifested, and the national patriotic conscience eased. They must believe that, as a dramatic medium expressing and reflecting the modern times, the peasant play, as such, is exhausted, and that clinging to it will bring about the drama's slow strangulation as the result of its own confinement. The Irish Drama League and the Dublin Gate Theatre Studio, both semi-amateur organizations, substantiate the argument that Ireland is becoming more and more receptive to this idea of dramatic internationalism as it becomes more and more impatient with the peasant play tradition. The Gate, for example, has successfully completed its second season. They have produced sixteen plays of repute by a wide group of Irish and foreign authors and not one of the plays has been of the peasant type. *Juggernaut* by David Sears and *The Old Lady Says "No!"* by E. W. Tocher are two thoroughly Irish plays in their repertoire which are not circumscribed by conventions tending to limit their appeal in other countries. *The Old Lady Says "No!"* is the first Irish expressionistic play. Unfortunately it relies too much on topical allusions concerning present day Dublin to hold our interest throughout. It will be well to watch the activities of these groups of producers and authors in the future.

That the old-fashioned peasant play is gradually reaching its nadir and is being superseded by a type of play deriving directly from it yet indicative of the changing temper of the times is apparent in *Juno and the Paycock* by Sean O'Casey. The subject of this and the remaining plays by this author is still, in a sense, the peasant character, but it is the peasant character in process of disintegration as the result of its being transplanted from the country hut to the city tenement. Sean O'Casey, former laborer and hod-carrier, himself a product of the backwash of Dublin's tenement district, has become the most arresting figure in the modern Irish theater, as well as its *enfant terrible*. He has risen from total obscurity with four plays: *Juno and the Paycock* and *The Shadow of a Gunman*, 1925; *The Plow and the Stars*, 1926; and his latest work, *The Silver Tassie*, 1928.[1] It is this so-called shifting of dramatic interest from the country to the city which sets

[1] New York: The Macmillan Company.

O'Casey's plays off as new departures from the old tradition, and causes them to be placed in this final category of modern plays. O'Casey is interested in the realistic presentation of the effect of environment on his characters. All his plays take place at some period of stress. The action in *Juno and the Paycock* goes on amid the civil warfare in 1922; *The Shadow of a Gunman* in the uprising of 1920; *The Plow and the Stars* during the 1916 rebellion; and *The Silver Tassie* during the Great War. As a result, the presence of impending disaster hangs over these Dublin slums like a pall, and the people of the plays are caught and held at a point of great intensity brought about by the feverish uncertainty of the war atmosphere. O'Casey underwent experiences later included in his writings, and his biography should be studied to see how the temper of his plays was affected by his personal life during these convulsive times. He had many opportunities to watch the reactions of his fellows in the slums during this abnormal period at first-hand, and his observations are recorded with an uncanny sense of the demands of the theater. If his plays are harsh and brutal criticisms of the period and of the people, it is because his life among the tenement-dwellers was hard and bitter, although, now and then, he can light up the slum's sordid ugliness with the revelation of some simple unspoiled beauty. It is possible for him to do this because he is as swift with sympathy where he thinks it is deserved as he is with vilification and ironic abuse. There is no Yeatsian somnambulism in O'Casey's creative genius. He is all crude strength and fire. The violent discrepancy between these two author's artistic creeds, interesting because it marks the old and the new tradition in Irish drama, is clearly shown in the publication of personal correspondence between O'Casey and the Abbey directorate in general, and Yeats in particular, which grew out of the latter's refusal to produce *The Silver Tassie*. Although the publication of the letters was regrettable and in extremely bad taste, it is a good indication of the factional strife still burning in some parts of the otherwise peaceful Irish dramatic world. The correspondence appears in the June 9, 1928, issue of *The Irish Statesman*.

O'Casey is considered by many the only Irish playwright who can thus far compare with John M. Synge, although it is difficult to discover an adequate basis on which to judge them together. Generally considered, O'Casey displays a narrower breadth of sympathy for his characters than did Synge, and less of that author's culture and poetic detachment, but he compensates for this lack by the speed and vigor of his scenes, the sureness of his grasp on his material as he describes character in prolific detail, and what is the possession of every true genius, an absolute artistic independence. His rapid rise from the sewer to the stage has been phenomenal, bearing witness to the theatrical genius which seems almost instinctive to the Irish people.

Like many of his predecessors, this new standard-bearer exposes a vulnerable spot in his armor by the manner in which he manipulates and elaborates plots. In *Juno and the Paycock* the plot itself is negligible. The misinterpretation of the will, on which the tragedy depends, seems accidental rather than inevitable. But this may after all be a minor consideration when there is so much else of worth to be found. O'Casey reproduces in detail the brawling, kaleidoscopic life in convincing terms, but it is not merely a photographic reproduction. Out of this wealth of incident and multitude of characters we can grasp a thread of significance running through the plays, a theme in undertone: the desire to live for ideals and principles frustrated and made incompatible by the wretched, poverty-stricken circumstances of the city. He contrasts in quick succession those few who regard principles above life with the many (they are usually older men) who love the word for the dramatic effect they hope to gain by its use. In *The Plough and the Stars* we feel the irony behind the sacrifice Jack Clitheroe and Lieutenant Langon make for the sake of those others who make a mockery of patriotism by their contemptible conduct.

If O'Casey sees any hope for the future of these people in their degrading environment, that hope transpires in the conduct of his women characters. This is especially true of Juno Boyle and, in lesser degree, of her daughter, Mary in *Juno and the Paycock*. Like Maurya, in the one criterion for all Irish tragedy, *Riders to the Sea*, Juno is a pitiful rather than a truly tragic figure. A chain of unfortunate events bears her spirit heavily down and she cries aloud her grief. That is all. The greatest fault she has, and the one which finally proves her undoing, is her long indulgence of the wretched "Captain." She behaves in too negative a fashion to be described as a tragic heroine, whose true function, if we follow Aristotle, lies in positively breasting the waves of disaster, but, then, she is like all Irish tragic heroines —of the Christian, not the Greek Pagan, type, and we seek and find in her some last vestige of nobility and genuineness remaining in this drunken, chaotic world. Calm, forgiving, and strong in sorrow, she goes through the play like a breath of clean air. Mary, too, has some desire for self-improvement which she clings to, rather selfishly, in spite of her environment, but fails to rise above it through the treachery of an educated cad whose hide O'Casey's pen does not fail to scratch in passing. The son Johnny's hysterical and sinister presence intensifies the cruelty of the surroundings and brings the horror of the civil strife close to hand. The scene in which he is carried off to be killed is packed with conflicting emotions.

O'Casey makes us laugh at the antics of Captain Boyle as he doubles and redoubles throughout the play like a hare before the dogs, but we take away at last a bitter remembrance of him and of his disloyal companion, Joxer Daly. He needs our pity rather than our laughter. This applies most strongly to his actions in the final scene. Here is the most relentless and devastating criticism of Irish character we have had from a playwright since the beginning of the literary movement, and here is revealed the Ireland of which we must be ashamed, with all its sodden inertia, its brutality, and its future hopelessness.

O'Casey's star may be ascending still. Let us hope that it is; but in *The Silver Tassie* he gives evidence of relinquishing a medium and a method in which he was most effective for the sake of a different subject matter and a different technique incongruous with his former style. *The Silver Tassie* opens in the familiar Dublin tenement but the last acts move away from realism into the realm of philosophic expressionism, and the result is an awkward and indecisive play. It may be that O'Casey is in grave danger of making the mistake Eugene O'Neill is guilty of in his last play, the mistake of thinking himself a better philosopher than he is a dramatist and story-teller (the two terms are, of course, synonymous). We have no quarrel with his obviously sincere attempt to discover new methods and new departures, but we do regret his throwing overboard the type of play he was beginning to master at a time when its usefulness does not seem to be exhausted.

Some conclusions may be drawn from *The Big House* which can be applied in general to all the other plays of the modern Irish movement. It is an intensely realistic approach to another class in Irish society as typical as the slum class of the O'Casey plays, though perhaps less exploited in the theater—the aristocracy. *The Big House* is devoid of all sentimentality and romanticism, but abounds in satire. The strain of mysticism is again apparent here, Ulick's ghostly voice adding that striking Irish quality to the play. It is written with the sure and delicate touch of a master of dialogue with incisive insight and sensitive understanding of both sides of a difficult question. For all the delicacy in its writing, *The Big House* contains an imposing thesis. It proves that the truly noble character cannot be intimidated by an unthinking show of force even in a world which, since it is organized on the principles of democracy, relegates class-consciousness to the department of the clinical psychologist. The author is showing how the gentry reacted to their being arbitrarily squashed during the "troubles" between two opposing forces, each acting on sudden and unreasonable impulse. The successful reception of this play in Ireland, a country so frequently shackled in its expression in the past by political and religious prejudices, augurs well for the future. Many good political plays have been omitted from this book because they were better politics than they were dramatic literature. They may have been omitted with entire justification if they had had no provocative human beings like Kate Alcock and St. Leger in them. *The Big House* has many social and political implications, but what interests me more is the dramatic flowering of Kate Alcock's character. We are far away from the tumult of those hectic days, and so will they be before she has ceased to live as an extraordinary theater-personality.

Lennox Robinson, above all other Irish dramatists of the present day, has given evidence of a sure and steady artistic progression consonant with the gradual enrichening of his dramatic experience as producer, actor, and member of the

Board of Directors of the Abbey Theater. The success of his own plays there, often presenting a totally different point of view than that held by the audience, continues to prove that Ireland is no longer too barbaric to receive another's candid opinion into its theater without attempting to wreck the same. He shows by this play that he has reached a high point of excellence in writing for an adult theater, and the play reveals, by its successful reception, an Ireland standing upon its own feet and weighing all questions, political, religious, or artistic, with an open mind.

JUNO AND THE PAYCOCK

A TRAGEDY IN THREE ACTS

By Sean O'Casey

THE CHARACTERS IN THE PLAY

"CAPTAIN" JACK BOYLE
JUNO BOYLE, *his wife*
JOHNNY BOYLE } *their children*
MARY BOYLE
"JOXER" DALY
MRS. MAISIE MADIGAN
"NEEDLE" NUGENT, *a tailor*
MRS. TANCRED

Residents in the Tenement.

JERRY DEVINE
CHARLIE BENTHAM, *a school teacher*
AN IRREGULAR MOBILIZER
TWO IRREGULARS
A COAL-BLOCK VENDOR
A SEWING MACHINE MAN
TWO FURNITURE REMOVAL MEN
TWO NEIGHBORS

SCENE

ACT I.—The living apartment of a two-roomed tenancy of the Boyle family, in a tenement house in Dublin.

ACT II.—The same.

ACT III.—The same.

A few days elapse between Acts I and II, and two months between Acts II and III.

During Act III the curtain is lowered for a few minutes to denote the lapse of one hour.

Period of the play, 1922.

ACT I

SCENE: *The living room of a two-room tenancy occupied by the* BOYLE *family in a tenement house in Dublin. Left, a door leading to another part of the house; left of door a window looking into the street; at back a dresser; farther to right at back, a window looking into the back of the house. Between the window and the dresser is a picture of the Virgin; below the picture, on a bracket, is a crimson bowl in which a floating votive light is burning. Farther to the right is a small bed partly concealed by cretonne hangings strung on a twine. To the right is the fireplace; near the fireplace is a door leading to the other room. Beside the fireplace is a box containing coal. On the mantelshelf is an alarm clock lying on its face. In a corner near the window looking into the back is a galvanized bath. A table and some chairs. On the table are breakfast things for one. A teapot is on the hob and a frying-pan stands inside the fender. There are a few books on the dresser and one on the table. Leaning against the dresser is a long-handled shovel—the kind invariably used by laborers when turning concrete or mixing mortar.* JOHNNY BOYLE *is sitting crouched beside the fire.* MARY *with her jumper off —it is lying on the back of a chair—is arranging her hair before a tiny mirror perched on the table. Beside the mirror is stretched out the morning paper, which she looks at when she isn't gazing into the mirror. She is a well-made and good-looking girl of twenty-two. Two forces are working in her mind—one, through the circumstances of her life, pulling her back; the other, through the influence of books she has read, pushing her forward. The opposing forces are apparent in her speech and her manners, both of which are degraded by her environment, and improved by her acquaintance—slight though it be—with literature. The time is early forenoon.*

MARY [*looking at the paper*]. On a little byroad, out beyant Finglas, he was found.

[MRS. BOYLE *enters by door on right; she has been shopping and carries a small parcel in her hand. She is forty-*

*five years of age, and twenty years ago she must have been
a pretty woman; but her face has now assumed that look
which ultimately settles down upon the faces of the women
of the working-class: a look of listless monotony and harassed
anxiety, blending with an expression of mechanical resistance.
Were circumstances favorable, she would probably be a handsome, active and clever woman.*]

Mrs. Boyle. Isn't he come in yet?

Mary. No, mother.

Mrs. Boyle. Oh, he'll come in when he likes; struttin'
about the town like a paycock with Joxer, I suppose. I hear
all about Mrs. Tancred's son is in this mornin's paper.

Mary. The full details are in it this mornin'; seven wounds
he had—one entherin' the neck, with an exit wound beneath the left shoulder blade; another in the left breast pene-
thratin' the heart, an' . . .

Johnny [*springing up from the fire*]. Oh, quit that
readin', for God's sake! Are yous losin' all your feelin's?
It'll soon be that none of yous'll read anythin' that's not
about butcherin'! [*He goes quickly into the room on left.*]

Mary. He's gettin' very sensitive, all of a sudden!

Mrs. Boyle. I'll read it myself, Mary, by an' by, when
I come home. Everybody's sayin' that he was a die-hard—
thanks be to God that Johnny had nothin' to do with him
this long time. . . . [*Opening the parcel and taking out
some sausages, which she places on a plate.*] Ah, then, if that
father o' yours doesn't come in soon for his breakfast, he
may go without any; I'll not wait much longer for him.

Mary. Can't you let him get it himself when he comes in?

Mrs. Boyle. Yes, an' let him bring in Joxer Daly along
with him? Ay, that's what he'd like, an' that's what he's
waitin' for—till he thinks I'm gone to work, an' then sail
in with the boul' Joxer, to burn all the coal an' dhrink all
the tea in the place, to show them what a good Samaritan
he is! But I'll stop here till he comes in, if I have to wait
till tomorrow mornin'.

Voice of Johnny inside. Mother!

Mrs. Boyle. Yis?

Voice of Johnny. Bring us in a dhrink o' wather.

Mrs. Boyle. Bring in that fella a dhrink o' wather, for
God's sake, Mary.

MARY. Isn't he big an' able enough to come out an' get it himself?

MRS. BOYLE. If you weren't well yourself you'd like somebody to bring you in a dhrink o' wather. [*She brings in drink and returns.*]

MRS. BOYLE. Isn't it terrible to have to be waitin' this way! You'd think he was bringin' twenty poun's a week into the house the way he's going on. He wore out the Health Insurance long ago, he's afther wearin' out the un-employment dole, an', now, he's thryin' to wear out me! An' constantly singin', no less, when he ought always to be on his knees offerin' up a Novena for a job!

MARY [*tying a ribbon, fillet-wise around her head*]. I don't like this ribbon, ma; I think I'll wear the green— it looks betther than the blue.

MRS. BOYLE. Ah, wear whatever ribbon you like, girl, only don't be botherin' me. I don't know what a girl on strike wants to be wearin' a ribbon round her head for or silk stockin's on her legs either; it's wearin' them things that make the employers think they're givin' yous too much money.

MARY. The hour is past now when we'll ask the employ-ers' permission to wear what we like.

MRS. BOYLE. I don't know why you wanted to walk out for Jennie Claffey; up to this you never had a good word for her.

MARY. What's the use of belongin' to a Trades Union if you won't stand up for your principles? Why did they sack her? It was a clear case of victimization. We couldn't let her walk the streets, could we?

MRS. BOYLE. No, of course yous couldn't—yous wanted to keep her company. Wan victim wasn't enough. When the employers sacrifice wan victim, the Trades Unions go wan betther be sacrificin' a hundred.

MARY. It doesn't matther what you say, ma—a princi-ple's a principle.

MRS. BOYLE. Yis; an' when I go into oul' Murphy's to-morrow, an' he gets to know that, instead o' payin' all, I'm goin' to borry more, what'll he say when I tell him a principle's a principle? What'll we do if he refuses to give us any more on tick?

MARY. He daren't refuse—if he does, can't you tell him he's paid?

MRS. BOYLE. It's lookin' as if he was paid, whether he refuses or no.

[JOHNNY *appears at the door on left. He can be plainly seen now; he is a thin delicate fellow, something younger than* MARY. *He has evidently gone through a rough time. His face is pale and drawn; there is a tremulous look of indefinite fear in his eyes. The left sleeve of his coat is empty, and he walks with a slight halt.*]

JOHNNY. I was lyin' down; I thought yous were gone. Oul' Simon Mackay is thrampin' about like a horse over me head, an' I can't sleep with him—they're like thunder-claps in me brain! The curse o'—God forgive me for goin' to curse!

MRS. BOYLE. There, now; go back an' lie down again, an' I'll bring you in a nice cup o' tay.

JOHNNY. Tay, tay, tay! You're always thinkin' o' tay. If a man was dyin', you'd thry to make him swally a cup o' tay! [*He goes back.*]

MRS. BOYLE. I don't know what's goin' to be done with him. The bullet he got in the hip in Easter Week was bad enough, but the bomb that shatthered his arm in the fight in O'Connell Street put the finishin' touch on him. I knew he was makin' a fool of himself. God knows I went down on me bended knees to him not to go agen the Free State.

MARY. He stuck to his principles, an', no matther how you may argue, ma, a principle's a principle.

VOICE OF JOHNNY. Is Mary goin' to stay here?

MARY. No, I'm not goin' to stay here; you can't expect me to be always at your beck an' call, can you?

VOICE OF JOHNNY. I won't stop here be meself!

MRS. BOYLE. Amn't I nicely handicapped with the whole o' yous! I don't know what any o' yous ud do without your ma. [*To* JOHNNY.] Your father'll be here in a minute, an' if you want anythin', he'll get it for you.

JOHNNY. I hate assin' him for anythin'. . . . He hates to be assed to stir. . . . Is the light lightin' before the picture o' the Virgin?

MRS. BOYLE. Yis, yis! The wan inside to St. Anthony isn't enough, but he must have another wan to the Virgin here!

[JERRY DEVINE *enters hastily. He is about twenty-five, well-set, active and earnest. He is a type, becoming very common now in the Labor Movement, of a mind knowing enough to make the mass of his associates, who know less, a power, and too little to broaden that power for the benefit of all.* MARY *seizes her jumper and runs hastily into room left.*]

JERRY [*breathless*]. Where's the Captain, Mrs. Boyle; where's the Captain?

MRS. BOYLE. You may well ass a body that: he's wherever Joxer Daly is—dhrinkin' in some snug or another.

JERRY. Father Farrell is just afther stoppin' to tell me to run up an' get him to go to the new job that's goin' on in Rathmines; his cousin is foreman o' the job, an' Father Farrell was speakin' to him about poor Johnny an' his father bein' idle so long, an' the foreman told Father Farrell to send the Captain up an' he'd give him a start—I wondher where I'd find him?

MRS. BOYLE. You'll find he's ayther in Ryan's or Foley's.

JERRY. I'll run round to Ryan's—I know it's a great house o' Joxer's. [*He rushes out.*]

MRS. BOYLE [*piteously*]. There now, he'll miss that job, or I know for what! If he gets win' o' the word, he'll not come back till evenin', so that it'll be too late. There'll never be any good got out o' him so long as he goes with that shouldher-shruggin' Joxer. I killin' meself workin', an' he sthruttin' about from mornin' till night like a paycock!

[*The steps of two persons are heard coming up a flight of stairs. They are the footsteps of* CAPTAIN BOYLE *and* JOXER. CAPTAIN BOYLE *is singing in a deep, sonorous, self-honoring voice.*]

THE CAPTAIN. Sweet Spirit, hear me prayer! Hear . . . oh . . . hear . . . me prayer . . . hear, oh, hear . . . Oh, he . . . ar . . . oh,   he . . . ar . . . me . . . pray . . . er!

JOXER [*outside*]. Ah, that's a darlin' song, a daaarlin' song!

MRS. BOYLE [*viciously*]. Sweet spirit hear his prayer! Ah, then, I'll take me solemn affeydavey, it's not for a job he's prayin'! [*She sits down on the bed so that the cretonne hangings hide her from the view of those entering.*]

[THE CAPTAIN *comes slowly in. He is a man of about sixty; stout, gray-haired and stocky. His neck is short, and his head looks like a stone ball that one sometimes sees on top of a gate-post. His cheeks, reddish-purple, are puffed out, as if he were always repressing an almost irrepressible ejaculation. On his upper lip is a crisp, tightly cropped mustache; he carries himself with the upper part of his body slightly thrown back, and his stomach slightly thrust forward. His walk is a slow, consequential strut. His clothes are dingy, and he wears a faded seaman's cap with a glazed peak.*]

BOYLE [*to* JOXER, *who is still outside*]. Come on, come on in, Joxer; she's gone out long ago, man. If there's nothing else to be got, we'll furrage out a cup o' tay, anyway. It's the only bit I get in comfort when she's away. 'Tisn't Juno should be her pet name at all, but Deirdre of the Sorras, for she's always grousin'.

[JOXER *steps cautiously into the room. He may be younger than* THE CAPTAIN *but he looks a lot older. His face is like a bundle of crinkled paper; his eyes have a cunning twinkle; he is spare and loosely built; he has a habit of constantly shrugging his shoulders with a peculiar twitching movement, meant to be ingratiating. His face is invariably ornamented with a grin.*]

JOXER. It's a terrible thing to be tied to a woman that's always grousin'. I don't know how you stick it—it ud put years on me. It's a good job she has to be so often away, for [*with a shrug*] when the cat's away, the mice can play!

BOYLE [*with a commanding and complacent gesture*]. Pull over to the fire, Joxer, an' we'll have a cup o' tay in a minute.

JOXER. Ah, a cup o' tay's a darlin' thing, a daaarlin' thing —the cup that cheers but doesn't . . .

[JOXER'S *rhapsody is cut short by the sight of* JUNO' *coming forward and confronting the two cronies. Both are stupefied.*]

MRS. BOYLE [*with sweet irony—poking the fire, and turning her head to glare at* JOXER]. Pull over to the fire, Joxer Daly, an' we'll have a cup o' tay in a minute! Are you sure, now, you wouldn't like an egg?

JOXER. I can't stop, Mrs. Boyle; I'm in a desperate hurry, a desperate hurry.

Mrs. Boyle. Pull over to the fire, Joxer Daly; people is always far more comfortabler here than they are in their own place.

[Joxer *makes hastily for the door.* Boyle *stirs to follow him; thinks of something to relieve the situation—stops, and says suddenly*]: Joxer!

Joxer [*at door ready to bolt*]. Yis?

Boyle. You know the foreman o' that job that's goin' on down in Killesther, don't you, Joxer?

Joxer [*puzzled*]. Foreman—Killesther?

Boyle [*with a meaning look*]. He's a butty o' yours, isn't he?

Joxer [*the truth dawning on him*]. The foreman at Killesther—oh yis, yis. He's an oul' butty o' mine—oh, he's a darlin' man, a daarlin' man.

Boyle. Oh, then, it's a sure thing. It's a pity we didn't go down at breakfast first thing this mornin'—we might ha' been working now; but you didn't know it then.

Joxer [*with a shrug*]. It's betther late than never.

Boyle. It's nearly time we got a start, anyhow; I'm fed up knockin' round, doin' nothin'. He promised you—gave you the straight tip?

Joxer. Yis. "Come down on the blow o' dinner," says he, "an' I'll start you, an' any friend you like to brin' with you." Ah, says I, you're a darlin' man, a daaarlin' man.

Boyle. Well, it couldn't come at a betther time—we're a long time waitin' for it.

Joxer. Indeed we were; but it's a long lane that has no turnin'.

Boyle. The blow up for dinner is at one—wait till I see what time it 'tis. [*He goes over to the mantelpiece, and gingerly lifts the clock.*]

Mrs. Boyle. Min' now, how you go on fiddlin' with that clock—you know the least little thing sets it asthray.

Boyle. The job couldn't come at a betther time; I'm feelin' in great fettle, Joxer. I'd hardly believe I ever had a pain in me legs, an' last week I was nearly crippled with them.

Joxer. That's betther an' betther; ah, God never shut wan door but he opened another!

Boyle. It's only eleven o'clock; we've lashins o' time.

I'll slip on me oul' moleskins afther breakfast, an' we can saunther down at our ayse. [*Putting his hand on the shovel.*] I think, Joxer, we'd betther bring our shovels?

JOXER. Yis, Captain, yis; it's betther to go fully prepared an' ready for all eventualities. You bring your long-tailed shovel, an' I'll bring me navvy. We mighten' want them, an', then agen, we might: for want of a nail the shoe was lost, for want of a shoe the horse was lost, an' for want of a horse the man was lost—aw, that's a darlin' proverb, a daarlin' . . .

[*As* JOXER *is finishing his sentence,* MRS. BOYLE *approaches the door and* JOXER *retreats hurriedly. She shuts the door with a bang.*]

BOYLE [*suggestively*]. We won't be long pullin' ourselves together agen when I'm working for a few weeks.

[MRS. BOYLE *takes no notice.*]

BOYLE. The foreman on the job is an oul' butty o' Joxer's; I have an idea that I know him meself. [*Silence.*] . . . There's a button off the back o' me moleskin trousers. . . . If you leave out a needle an' thread I'll sew it on meself. . . . Thanks be to God, the pains in me legs is gone, anyhow!

MRS. BOYLE [*with a burst*]. Look here, Mr. Jacky Boyle, them yarns won't go down with Juno. I know you an' Joxer Daly of an oul' date, an', if you think you're able to come it over me with them fairy tales, you're in the wrong shop.

BOYLE [*coughing subduedly to relieve the tenseness of the situation*]. U-u-u-ugh.

MRS. BOYLE. Butty o' Joxer's! Oh, you'll do a lot o' good as long as you continue to be a butty o' Joxer's!

BOYLE. U-u-u-ugh.

MRS. BOYLE. Shovel! Ah, then, me boyo, you'd do far more work with a knife an' fork than ever you'll do with a shovel! If there was e'er a genuine job goin' you'd be dh'other way about—not able to lift your arms with the pains in your legs! Your poor wife slavin' to keep the bit in your mouth, an' you gallivantin' about all the day like a paycock!

BOYLE. It ud be betther for a man to be dead, betther for a man to be dead.

MRS. BOYLE [*ignoring the interruption*]. Everybody

callin' you "Captain," an' you only wanst on the wather, in an oul' collier from here to Liverpool, when anybody, to listen or look at you, ud take you for a second Christo For Columbus!

BOYLE. Are you never goin' to give us a rest?

MRS. BOYLE. Oh, you're never tired o' lookin' for a rest.

BOYLE. D'ye want to dhrive me out o' the house?

MRS. BOYLE. It ud be easier to dhrive you out o' the house than to dhrive you into a job. Here, sit down an' take your breakfast—it may be the last you'll get, for I don't know where the next is goin' to come from.

BOYLE. If I get this job we'll be all right.

MRS. BOYLE. Did ye see Jerry Devine?

BOYLE [*testily*]. No, I didn't see him.

MRS. BOYLE. No, but you seen Joxer. Well, he was here lookin' for you.

BOYLE. Well, let him look!

MRS. BOYLE. Oh, indeed, he may well look, for it ud be hard for him to see you, an' you stuck in Ryan's snug.

BOYLE. I wasn't in Ryan's snug—I don't go into Ryan's.

MRS. BOYLE. Oh, is there a mad dog there? Well, if you weren't in Ryan's you were in Foley's.

BOYLE. I'm telling you for the last three weeks I haven't tasted a dhrop of intoxicatin' liquor. I wasn't in ayther wan snug or dh'other—I could swear that on a prayer-book—I'm as innocent as the child unborn!

MRS. BOYLE. Well, if you'd been in for your breakfast you'd ha' seen him.

BOYLE [*suspiciously*]. What does he want me for?

MRS. BOYLE. He'll be back any minute an' then you'll soon know.

BOYLE. I'll dhrop out an' see if I can meet him.

MRS. BOYLE. You'll sit down an' take your breakfast, an' let me go to me work, for I'm an hour late already waitin' for you.

BOYLE. You needn't ha' waited, for I'll take no breakfast —I've a little spirit left in me still!

MRS. BOYLE. Are you goin' to have your breakfast—yes or no?

BOYLE [*too proud to yield*]. I'll have no breakfast—yous

can keep your breakfast. [*Plaintively.*] I'll knock out a bit somewhere, never fear.

MRS. BOYLE. Nobody's goin' to coax you—don't think that. [*She vigorously replaces the pan and the sausages in the press.*]

BOYLE. I've a little spirit left in me still.

[JERRY DEVINE *enters hastily.*]

JERRY. Oh, here you are at last! I've been searchin' for you everywhere. The foreman in Foley's told me you hadn't left the snug with Joxer ten minutes before I went in.

MRS. BOYLE. An' he swearin' on the holy prayer-book that he wasn't in no snug!

BOYLE [*to* JERRY]. What business is it o' yours whether I was in a snug or no? What do you want to be gallopin' about afther me for? Is a man not to be allowed to leave his house for a minute without havin' a pack o' spies, pimps an' informers cantherin' at his heels?

JERRY. Oh, you're takin' a wrong view of it, Mr. Boyle; I simply was anxious to do you a good turn. I have a message for you from Father Farrell: he says that if you go to the job that's on in Rathmines, an' ask for Foreman Mangan, you'll get a start.

BOYLE. That's all right, but I don't want the motions of me body to be watched the way an asthronomer ud watch a star. If you're folleyin' Mary aself, you've no pereeogative to be folleyin' me. [*Suddenly catching his thigh.*] U-ugh, I'm afther gettin' a terrible twinge in me right leg!

Mrs. Boyle. Oh, it won't be very long now till it travels into your left wan. It's miraculous that whenever he scents a job in front of him, his legs begin to fail him! Then, me bucko, if you lose this chance, you may go an' furrage for yourself!

JERRY. This job'll last for some time too, Captain, an' as soon as the foundations are in, it'll be cushy enough.

BOYLE. Won't it be a climbin' job? How d'ye expect me to be able to go up a ladder with these legs? An', if I get up aself, how am I goin' to get down agen?

MRS. BOYLE [*viciously*]. Get wan o' the laborers to carry you down in a hod! You can't climb a laddher, but you can skip like a goat into a snug!

JERRY. I wouldn't let meself be let down that easy, Mr. Boyle; a little exercise, now, might do you all the good in the world.

BOYLE. It's a docthor you should have been, Devine— maybe you know more about the pains in me legs than meself that has them?

JERRY [*irritated*]. Oh, I know nothin' about the pains in your legs; I've brought the message that Father Farrell gave me, an' that's all I can do.

MRS. BOYLE. Here, sit down an' take your breakfast, an' go an' get ready; an' don't be actin' as if you couldn't pull a wing out of a dead bee.

BOYLE. I want no breakfast, I tell you; it ud choke me afther all that's been said. I've a little spirit left in me still.

MRS. BOYLE. Well, let's see your spirit, then, an' go in at wanst an' put on your moleskin trousers!

BOYLE [*moving towards the door on left*]. It ud be betther for a man to be dead! U-ugh! There's another twinge in me other leg! Nobody but meself knows the sufferin' I'm goin' through with the pains in these legs o' mine! [*He goes into the room on left as* MARY *comes out with her hat in her hand.*]

MRS. BOYLE. I'll have to push off now, for I'm terrible late already, but I was determined to stay an' hunt that Joxer this time. [*She goes off.*]

JERRY. Are you going out, Mary?

MARY. It looks like it when I'm putting on my hat, doesn't it?

JERRY. The bitther word agen, Mary.

MARY. You won't allow me to be friendly with you; if I thry, you deliberately misundherstand it.

JERRY. I didn't always misundherstand it; you were often delighted to have the arms of Jerry around you.

·MARY. If you go on talkin' like this, Jerry Devine, you'll make me hate you!

JERRY. Well, let it be either a weddin' or a wake! Listen, Mary, I'm standin' for the Secretaryship of our Union. There's only one opposin' me; I'm popular with all the men, an' a good speaker—all are sayin' that I'll get elected.

MARY. Well?

JERRY. The job's worth three hundred an' fifty pounds

a year, Mary. You an' I could live nice an' cosily on that; it would lift you out o' this place an' . . .

MARY. I haven't time to listen to you now—I have to go. [*She is going out when* JERRY *bars the way.*]

JERRY [*appealingly*]. Mary, what's come over you with me for the last few weeks? You hardly speak to me, an' then only a word with a face o' bitterness on it. Have you forgotten, Mary, all the happy evenin's that were as sweet as the scented hawthorn that sheltered the sides o' the road as we saunthered through the country?

MARY. That's all over now. When you get your new job, Jerry, you won't be long findin' a girl far betther than I am for your sweetheart.

JERRY. Never, never, Mary! No matther what happens you'll always be the same to me.

MARY. I must be off; please let me go, Jerry.

JERRY. I'll go a bit o' the way with you.

MARY. You needn't, thanks; I want to be by meself.

JERRY [*catching her arm*]. You're goin' to meet another fella; you've clicked with someone else, me lady!

MARY. That's no concern o' yours, Jerry Devine; let me go!

JERRY. I saw yous comin' out o' the Cornflower Dance Class, an' you hangin' on his arm—a thin, lanky strip of a Micky Dazzler, with a walkin'-stick an' gloves!

VOICE OF JOHNNY [*loudly*]. What are you doin' there —pullin' about everything!

VOICE OF BOYLE [*loudly and viciously*]. I'm puttin' on me moleskin trousers!

MARY. You're hurtin' me arm! Let me go, or I'll scream, an' then you'll have the oul' fella out on top of us!

JERRY. Don't be so hard on a fella, Mary, don't be so hard.

BOYLE [*appearing at the door*]. What's the meanin' of all this hillabaloo?

MARY. Let me go, let me go!

BOYLE. D'ye hear me—what's all this hillabaloo about?

JERRY [*plaintively*]. Will you not give us one kind word, one kind word, Mary?

BOYLE. D'ye hear me talkin' to yous? What's all this hillabaloo for?

JERRY. Let me kiss your hand, your little, tiny, white hand!

BOYLE. Your little, tiny, white hand—are you takin' leave o' your senses, man?

[MARY *breaks away and rushes out.*]

BOYLE. This is nice goin's on in front of her father!

JERRY. Ah, dhry up, for God's sake! [*He follows* MARY.]

BOYLE. Chiselurs don't care a damn now about their parents, they're bringin' their fathers' gray hairs down with sorra to the grave, an' laughin' at it, laughin' at it. Ah, I suppose it's just the same everywhere—the whole worl's in a state o' chassis! [*He sits by the fire.*] Breakfast! Well, they can keep their breakfast for me. Not if they went down on their bended knees would I take it—I'll show them I've a little spirit left in me still! [*He goes over to the press, takes out a plate and looks at it.*] Sassige! Well, let her keep her sassige. [*He returns to the fire, takes up the teapot and gives it a gentle shake.*] The tea's wet right enough. [*A pause; he rises, goes to the press, takes out the sausage, puts it on the pan, and puts both on the fire. He attends the sausage with a fork.*]

BOYLE [*singing*].

When the robins nest agen,
And the flowers are in bloom,
When the Springtime's sunny smile seems to banish all
    sorrow an' gloom;
Then me bonny blue-ey'd lad, if me heart be true till
    then—
He's promised he'll come back to me,
When the robins nest agen!

[*He lifts his head at the high note, and then drops his eyes to the pan.*]

BOYLE [*singing*]:

When the . . .

[*Steps are heard approaching; he whips the pan off the fire and puts it under the bed, then sits down at the fire. The door opens and a bearded man looking in says*]:

You don't happen to want a sewin' machine?

BOYLE [*furiously*]. No, I don't want e'er a sewin' machine! [*He returns the pan to the fire, and commences to sing again.*]

BOYLE [*singing*].

> When the robins nest agen,
> And the flowers they are in bloom,
> He's . . .

[*A thundering knock is heard at the street door.*]

BOYLE. There's a terrible tatheraraa—that's a stranger—that's nobody belongin' to the house. [*Another loud knock.*]

JOXER [*sticking his head in at the door*]. Did ye hear them tatherarahs?

BOYLE. Well, Joxer, I'm not deaf.

JOHNNY [*appearing in his shirt and trousers at the door on left; his face is anxious and his voice is tremulous*]. Who's that at the door; who's that at the door? Who gave that knock—d'ye yous hear me—are yous deaf or dhrunk or what?

BOYLE [*to* JOHNNY]. How the hell do I know who 'tis? Joxer, stick your head out o' the window an' see.

JOXER. An' mebbe get a bullet in the kisser? Ah, none o' them thricks for Joxer! It's betther to be a coward than a corpse!

BOYLE [*looking cautiously out of the window*]. It's a fella in a thrench coat.

JOHNNY. Holy Mary, Mother o' God, I . . .

BOYLE. He's goin' away—he must ha' got tired knockin'.

[JOHNNY *returns to the room on left.*]

BOYLE. Sit down an' have a cup o' tay, Joxer.

JOXER. I'm afraid the missus ud pop in on us agen before we'd know where we are. Somethin's tellin' me to go at wanst.

BOYLE. Don't be superstitious, man; we're Dublin men, an' not boyos that's only afther comin' up from the bog o' Allen—though if she did come in, right enough, we'd be caught like rats in a thrap.

JOXER. An' you know the sort she is—she wouldn't listen to reason—an' wanse bitten twice shy.

BOYLE [*going over to the window at back*]. If the worst came to the worst, you could dart out here, Joxer; it's only a dhrop of a few feet to the roof of the return room, an' the first minute she goes into dh'other room, I'll give you the bend, an' you can slip in an' away.

JOXER [*yielding to the temptation*]. Ah, I won't stop very long anyhow. [*Picking up a book from the table.*] Whose is the buk?

BOYLE. Aw, one o' Mary's; she's always readin' lately— nothin' but thrash, too. There's one I was lookin' at dh'other day: three stories, *The Doll's House, Ghosts,* an' *The Wild Duck*—Buks only fit for chiselurs!

JOXER. Didja ever rade *Elizabeth, or Th' Exile o' Sibayria . . .* ah, it's a darlin' story, a daarlin' story!

·BOYLE. You eat your sassige, an' never min' *Th' Exile o' Sibayria.*

[*Both sit down;* BOYLE *fills out tea, pours gravy on* JOXER'S *plate, and keeps the sausage for himself.*]

JOXER. What are you wearin' your moleskin trousers for?

BOYLE. I have to go to a job, Joxer. Just afther you'd gone, Devine kem runnin' in to tell us that Father Farrell said if I went down to the job that's goin' on in Rathmines I'd get a start.

JOXER. Be the holy, that's good news!

BOYLE. How is it good news? I wondher if you were in my condition, would you call it good news?

JOXER. I thought . . .

BOYLE. You thought! You think too. sudden sometimes, Joxer. D'ye know, I'm hardly able to crawl with the pains in me legs!

JOXER. Yis, yis; I forgot the pains in your legs. I know you can do nothin' while they're at you.

BOYLE. You forgot; I don't think any of yous realize the state I'm in with the pains in me legs. What ud happen if I had to carry a bag o' cement?

JOXER. Ah, any man havin' the like of them pains id be down an' out, down an' out.

BOYLE. I wouldn't mind if he had said it to meself; but, no, oh no, he rushes in an' shouts it out in front o' Juno, an' you know what Juno is, Joxer. We all know Devine knows a little more than the rest of us, but he doesn't act as if he did; he's a good boy, sober, able to talk an' all that, but still . . .

JOXER. Oh ay; able to argufy, but still . . .

BOYLE. If he's runnin' afther Mary, aself, he's not goin' to be runnin' afther me. Captain Boyle's able to take care of himself. Afther all, I'm not gettin' brought up on Virol. I never heard him usin' a curse; I don't believe he was ever dhrunk in his life—sure he's not like a Christian at all!

JOXER. You're afther takin' the word out o' me mouth —afther all, a Christian's natural, but he's unnatural.

BOYLE. His oul' fella was just the same—a Wicklow man.

JOXER. A Wicklow man! That explains the whole thing. I've met many a Wicklow man in me time, but I never met wan that was any good.

BOYLE. "Father Farrell," says he, "sent me down to tell you." Father Farrell! . . . D'ye know, Joxer, I never like to be beholden to any o' the clergy.

JOXER. It's dangerous, right enough.

BOYLE. If they do anything for you, they'd want you to be livin' in the Chapel. . . . I'm goin' to tell you somethin', Joxer, that I wouldn't tell to anybody else—the clergy always had too much power over the people in this unfortunate country.

JOXER. You could sing that if you had an air to it!

BOYLE [*becoming enthusiastic*]. Didn't they prevent the people in forty-seven from seizin' the corn, an' they starvin'; didn't they down Parnell; didn't they say that hell wasn't hot enough nor eternity long enough to punish the Fenians? We don't forget, we don't forget them things, Joxer. If they've taken everything else from us, Joxer, they've left us our memory.

JOXER [*emotionally*]. For mem'ry's the only friend that grief can call its own, that grief . . . can . . . call . . . its own!

BOYLE. Father Farrell's beginnin' to take a great intherest in Captain Boyle; because of what Johnny did for his country, says he to me wan day. It's a curious way to reward Johnny be makin' his poor oul' father work. But, that's what the clergy want, Joxer—work, work, work for me an' you; havin' us mulin' from mornin' till night, so that they may be in bether fettle when they come hoppin' round for their dues! Job! Well, let him give his job to wan of his hymn-singin', prayer-spoutin', craw-thumpin' Confraternity men!

[*The voice of a coal-block vendor is heard chanting in the street.*]

VOICE OF COAL VENDOR. Blocks . . . coal-blocks! Blocks . . . coal-blocks!

JOXER. God be with the young days when you were steppin' the deck of a manly ship, with the win' blowin' a hurricane through the masts, an' the only sound you'd hear was, "Port your helm!" an' the only answer, "Port it is, sir!"

BOYLE. Them was days, Joxer, them was days. Nothin' was too hot or too heavy for me then. Sailin' from the Gulf o' Mexico to the Antanartic Ocean. I seen things, I seen things, Joxer, that no mortal man should speak about that knows his Catechism. Ofen, an' ofen, when I was fixed to the wheel with a marlinspike, an' the win's blowin' fierce an' the waves lashin' an' lashin', till you'd think every minute was goin' to be your last, an' it blowed, an' blowed —blew is the right word, Joxer, but blowed is what the sailors use. . . .

JOXER. Aw, it's a darlin' word, a daarlin' word.

BOYLE. An', as it blowed an' blowed, I ofen looked up at the sky an' assed meself the question—what is the stars, what is the stars?

VOICE OF COAL VENDOR. Any blocks, coal-blocks; blocks, coal-blocks!

JOXER. Ah, that's the question, that's the question—what is the stars?

BOYLE. An' then, I'd have another look, an' I'd ass meself —what is the moon?

JOXER. Ah, that's the question—what is the moon, what is the moon?

[*Rapid steps are heard coming towards the door.* BOYLE *makes desperate efforts to hide everything;* JOXER *rushes to the window in a frantic effort to get out;* BOYLE *begins to innocently lilt—"Oh, me darlin' Jennie, I will be thrue to thee," when the door is opened, and the black face of the* COAL VENDOR *appears.*]

THE COAL VENDOR. D'yes want any blocks?

BOYLE [*with a roar*]. No, we don't want any blocks!

JOXER [*coming back with a sigh of relief*]. That's after puttin' the heart across me—I could ha' sworn it was Juno.

I'd betther be goin', Captain; you couldn't tell the minute Juno'd hop in on us.

BOYLE. Let her hop in; we may as well have it out first as at last. I've made up me mind—I'm not goin' to do only what she damn well likes.

JOXER. Them sentiments does you credit, Captain; I don't like to say anything as between man an' wife, but I say as a butty, as a butty, Captain, that you've stuck it too long, an' that it's about time you showed a little spunk.

> How can a man die betther than facin' fearful odds,
> For th' ashes of his fathers an' the temples of his gods.

BOYLE. She has her rights—there's no one denyin' it, but haven't I me rights too?

JOXER. Of course you have—the sacred rights o' man!

BOYLE. Today, Joxer, there's goin' to be issued a proclamation be me, establishin' an independent Republic, an' Juno'll have to take an oath of allegiance.

JOXER. Be firm, be firm, Captain; the first few minutes'll be the worst:—if you gently touch a nettle it'll sting you for your pains; grasp it like a lad of mettle, an' as soft as silk remains!

VOICE OF JUNO OUTSIDE. Can't stop, Mrs. Madigan—I haven't a minute!

JOXER [*flying out of the window*]. Holy God, here she is!

BOYLE [*packing the things away with a rush in the press*]. I knew that fella ud stop till she was in on top of us! [*He sits down by the fire.*]

[JUNO *enters hastily; she is flurried and excited.*]

JUNO. Oh, you're in—you must have been only afther comin' in?

BOYLE. No, I never went out.

JUNO. It's curious, then, you never heard the knockin'. [*She puts her coat and hat on bed.*]

BOYLE. Knockin'? Of course I heard the knockin'.

JUNO. An' why didn't you open the door, then? I suppose you were so busy with Joxer that you hadn't time.

BOYLE. I haven't seen Joxer since I seen him before. Joxer! What ud bring Joxer here?

JUNO. D'ye mean to tell me that the pair of yous wasn't collogin' together here when me back was turned?

BOYLE. What ud we be collogin' together about? I have somethin' else to think of besides collogin' with Joxer. I can swear on all the holy prayer-books . . .

MRS. BOYLE. That you weren't in no snug! Go on in at wanst now, an' take aff that moleskin trousers o' yours, an' put on a collar an' tie to smarten yourself up a bit. There's a visitor comin' with Mary in a minute, an' he has great news for you.

BOYLE. A job, I suppose; let us get wan first before we start lookin' for another.

MRS. BOYLE. That's the thing that's able to put the win' up you. Well, it's no job, but news that'll give you the chance o' your life.

BOYLE. What's all the mysthery about?

MRS. BOYLE. G'win an' take off the moleskin trousers when you're told!

[BOYLE *goes into room on left.*]

[MRS. BOYLE *tidies up the room, puts the shovel under the bed, and goes to the press.*]

MRS. BOYLE. Oh, God bless us, looka the way everythin's thrun about! Oh, Joxer was here, Joxer was here!

[MARY *enters with* CHARLIE BENTHAM; *he is a young man of twenty-five, tall, good-looking, with a very high opinion of himself generally. He is dressed in a brown coat, brown knee-breeches, gray stockings, a brown sweater, with a deep blue tie; he carries gloves and a walking-stick.*]

MRS. BOYLE [*fussing round*]. Come in, Mr. Bentham; sit down, Mr. Bentham, in this chair; it's more comfortabler than that, Mr. Bentham. Himself'll be here in a minute; he's just takin' off his trousers.

MARY. Mother!

BENTHAM. Please don't put yourself to any trouble, Mrs. Boyle—I'm quite all right there, thank you.

MRS. BOYLE. An' to think of you knowin' Mary, an' she knowin' the news you had for us, an' wouldn't let on; but it's all the more welcomer now, for we were on our last lap!

VOICE OF JOHNNY INSIDE. What are you kickin' up all the racket for?

BOYLE [*roughly*]. I'm takin' off me moleskin trousers!

JOHNNY. Can't you do it, then, without lettin' th' whole house know you're takin' off your trousers? What d'ye want puttin' them on an' takin' them off again?

BOYLE. Will you let me alone, will you let me alone? Am I never goin' to be done thryin' to please th' whole o' yous?

MRS. BOYLE [*to* BENTHAM]. You must excuse th' state o' th' place, Mr. Bentham; th' minute I turn me back that man o' mine always makes a litther o' th' place, a litther o' th' place.

BENTHAM. Don't worry, Mrs. Boyle; it's all right, I assure . . .

BOYLE [*inside*]. Where's me braces; where in th' name o' God did I leave me braces. . . . Ay, did you see where I put me braces?

JOHNNY [*inside, calling out*]. Ma, will you come in here an' take da away ou' o' this or he'll dhrive me mad.

MRS. BOYLE [*going towards door*]. Dear, dear, dear, that man'll be lookin' for somethin' on th' day o' Judgment. [*Looking into room and calling to* BOYLE.] Look at your braces, man, hangin' round your neck!

BOYLE [*inside*]. Aw, Holy God!

MRS. BOYLE [*calling*]. Johnny, Johnny, come out here for a minute.

JOHNNY. Oh, leave Johnny alone, an' don't be annoyin' him!

MRS. BOYLE. Come on, Johnny, till I inthroduce you to Mr. Bentham. [*To* BENTHAM.] Me son, Mr. Bentham; he's afther goin' through the mill. He was only a chiselur of a Boy Scout in Easter Week, when he got hit in the hip; and his arm was blew off in the fight in O'Connell Street. [JOHNNY *comes in.*] Here he is, Mr. Bentham; Mr. Bentham, Johnny. None can deny he done his bit for Irelan', if that's going to do him any good.

JOHNNY [*boastfully*]. I'd do it agen, ma, I'd do it agen; for a principle's a principle.

MRS. BOYLE. Ah, you lost your best principle, me boy, when you lost your arm; them's the only sort o' principles that's any good to a workin' man.

JOHNNY. Ireland only half free'll never be at peace while she has a son left to pull a trigger.

MRS. BOYLE. To be sure, to be sure—no bread's a lot betther than half a loaf. [*Calling loudly in to* BOYLE.] Will you hurry up there?

[BOYLE *enters in his best trousers, which aren't too good, and looks very uncomfortable in his collar and tie.*]

MRS. BOYLE. This is me husband; Mr. Boyle, Mr. Bentham.

BENTHAM. Ah, very glad to know you, Mr. Boyle. How are you?

BOYLE. Ah, I'm not too well at all; I suffer terrible with pains in me legs. Juno can tell you there what . . .

MRS. BOYLE. You won't have many pains in your legs when you hear what Mr. Bentham has to tell you.

BENTHAM. Juno! What an interesting name! It reminds one of Homer's glorious story of ancient gods and heroes.

BOYLE. Yis, doesn't it? You see, Juno was born an' christened in June; I met her in June; we were married in June, an' Johnny was born in June, so wan day I says to her, "You should ha' been called Juno," an' the name stuck to her ever since.

MRS. BOYLE. Here, we can talk o' them things agen; let Mr. Bentham say what he has to say now.

BENTHAM. Well, Mr. Boyle, I suppose you'll remember a Mr. Ellison of Santry—he's a relative of yours, I think.

BOYLE [*viciously*]. Is it that prognosticator an' procrastinator! Of course I remember him.

BENTHAM. Well, he's dead, Mr. Boyle . . .

BOYLE. Sorra many'll go into mournin' for him.

MRS. BOYLE. Wait till you hear what Mr. Bentham has to say, an' then, maybe, you'll change your opinion.

BENTHAM. A week before he died he sent for me to write his will for him. He told me that there were two only that he wished to leave his property to: his second cousin Michael Finnegan of Santry, and John Boyle, his first cousin of Dublin.

BOYLE [*excitedly*]. Me, is it me, me?

BENTHAM. You, Mr. Boyle; I'll read a copy of the will that I have here with me, which has been duly filed in the Court of Probate. [*He takes a paper from his pocket and reads*]:

"*6th February* 1922.

"This is the last Will and Testament of William Ellison, of Santry, in the County of Dublin. I hereby order and wish my property to be sold and divided as follows:—

"Twenty pounds to the St. Vincent De Paul Society.

"Sixty pounds for Masses for the repose of my soul (five shillings for Each Mass).

"The rest of my property to be divided between my first and second cousins.

"I hereby appoint Timothy Buckly, of Santry, and Hugh Brierly, of Coolock, to be my Executors.

(Signed)   WILLIAM ELLISON.
             HUGH BRIERLY.
             TIMOTHY BUCKLY.
             CHARLES BENTHAM, N.T."

BOYLE [*eagerly*]. An' how much'll be comin' out of it, Mr. Bentham?

BENTHAM. The Executors told me that half of the property would be anything between fifteen hundred and two thousand pounds.

MARY. A fortune, father, a fortune!

JOHNNY. We'll be able to get out o' this place now, an' go somewhere we're not known.

MRS. BOYLE. You won't have to trouble about a job for a while, Jack.

BOYLE [*fervently*]. I'll never doubt the goodness o' God agen.

BENTHAM. I congratulate you, Mr. Boyle. [*They shake hands.*]

BOYLE. An' now, Mr. Bentham, you'll have to have a wet.

BENTHAM. A wet?

BOYLE. A wet—a jar—a boul!

MRS. BOYLE. Jack, you're speakin' to Mr. Bentham, an' not to Joxer.

BOYLE [*solemnly*]. Juno . . . Mary . . . Johnny . . . we'll have to go into mournin' at wanst. . . . I never expected that poor Bill ud die so sudden. . . . Well, we all have to die some day . . . you, Juno, today . . . an' me, maybe, tomorrow. . . . It's sad, but it can't be helped. . . . Requiescat in pace . . . or, usin' our oul' tongue like St. Patrick or St. Briget, Guh sayeree jeea ayera!

MARY. Oh, father, that's not Rest in Peace; that's God save Ireland.

BOYLE. U-u-ugh, it's all the same—isn't it a prayer? . . . Juno, I'm done with Joxer; he's nothin' but a prognosticator an' a . . .

JOXER [*climbing angrily through the window and bounding into the room*]. You're done with Joxer, are you? Maybe you thought I'd stop on the roof all the night for you! Joxer out on the roof with the win' blowin' through him was nothin' to you an' your friend with the collar an' tie!

MRS. BOYLE. What in the name o' God brought you out on the roof; what were you doin' there?

JOXER [*ironically*]. I was dhreamin' I was standin' on the bridge of a ship, an' she sailin' the Antartic Ocean, an' it blowed, an' blowed, an' I lookin' up at the sky an' sayin', what is the stars, what is the stars?

MRS. BOYLE [*opening the door and standing at it*]. Here, get ou' o' this, Joxer Daly; I was always thinkin' you had a slate off.

JOXER [*moving to the door*]. I have to laugh every time I look at the deep sea sailor; an' a row on a river ud make him seasick!

BOYLE. Get ou' o' this before I take the law into me own hands!

JOXER [*going out*]. Say aw rewaeawr, but not good-by. Lookin' for work, an' prayin' to God he won't get it! [*He goes.*]

MRS. BOYLE. I'm tired tellin' you what Joxer was; maybe now you see yourself the kind he is.

·BOYLE. He'll never blow the froth off a pint o' mine agen, that's a sure thing. Johnny . . . Mary . . . you're to keep yourselves to yourselves for the future. Juno, I'm done with Joxer. . . . I'm a new man from this out. . . . [*Clasping* JUNO's *hand, and singing emotionally*.]:

Oh, me darlin' Juno, I will be thrue to thee;
Me own, me darlin' Juno, you're all the world to me.

ACT II

SCENE: *The same, but the furniture is more plentiful, and of a vulgar nature. A glaringly upholstered armchair and lounge; cheap pictures and photos everywhere. Every available spot is ornamented with huge vases filled with artificial flowers. Crossed festoons of colored paper chains stretch from end to end of ceiling. On the table is an old attaché case. It is about six in the evening, and two days after the First Act.* BOYLE, *in his shirt-sleeves, is voluptuously stretched on the sofa; he is smoking a clay pipe. He is half asleep. A lamp is lighting on the table. After a few moments' pause the voice of* JOXER *is heard singing softly outside at the door*—"Me pipe I'll smoke, as I dhrive me moke—are you there, Mor . . . ee . . . ar . . . i . . . teee!"

BOYLE [*leaping up, takes a pen in his hand and busies himself with papers*]. Come along, Joxer, me son, come along.

JOXER [*putting his head in*]. Are you be yourself?

BOYLE. Come on, come on; that doesn't matther; I'm masther now, an' I'm goin' to remain masther.

[JOXER *comes in.*]

JOXER. How d'ye feel now, as a man o' money?

BOYLE [*solemnly*]. It's a responsibility, Joxer, a great responsibility.

JOXER. I suppose 'tis now, though you wouldn't think it.

BOYLE. Joxer, han' me over that attackey case on the table there. [JOXER *hands the case.*] Ever since the Will has passed I've run hundhreds o' dockyments through me han's —I tell you, you have to keep your wits about you. [*He busies himself with papers.*]

JOXER. Well, I won't disturb you; I'll dhrop in when . . .

BOYLE [*hastily*]. It's all right, Joxer, this is the last one to be signed today. [*He signs a paper, puts it into the case, which he shuts with a snap, and sits back pompously in the chair.*] Now, Joxer, you want to see me; I'm at your service —what can I do for you, me man?

JOXER. I've just dhropped in with the three pounds five

shillings that Mrs. Madigan riz on the blankets an' table for you, an' she says you're to be in no hurry payin' it back.

BOYLE. She won't be long without it; I expect the first check for a couple o' hundhred any day. There's the five bob for yourself—go on, take it, man; it'll not be the last you'll get from the Captain. Now an' agen we have our differ, but we're there together all the time.

JOXER. Me for you, an' you for me, like the two Musketeers.

BOYLE. Father Farrell stopped me today an' tole me how glad he was I fell in for the money.

JOXER. He'll be stoppin' you often enough now; I suppose it was "Mr." Boyle with him?

BOYLE. He shuk me be the han'. . . .

JOXER [*ironically*]. I met with Napper Tandy, an' he shuk me be the han'!

BOYLE. You're seldom asthray, Joxer, but you're wrong shipped this time. What you're sayin' of Father Farrel is very near to blasfeemey. I don't like anyone to talk disrespectful of Father Farrell.

JOXER. You're takin' me up wrong, Captain; I wouldn't let a word be said agen Father Farrell—the heart o' the rowl, that's what he is; I always said he was a darlin' man, a daarlin' man.

BOYLE. Comin' up the stairs who did I meet but that bummer, Nugent. "I seen you talkin' to Father Farrell," says he, with a grin on him. "He'll be folleyin' you," says he, "like a Guardian Angel from this out"—all the time the oul' grin on him, Joxer.

JOXER. I never seen him yet but he had that oul' grin on him!

BOYLE. "Mr. Nugent," says I, "Father Farrell is a man o' the people, an', as far as I know the History o' me country, the priests was always in the van of the fight for Irelan's freedom."

JOXER [*fervently*]:

Who was it led the van, Soggart Aroon?
Since the fight first began, Soggart Aroon?

BOYLE. "Who are you tellin'?" says he. "Didn't they let down the Fenians, an' didn't they do in Parnell? An' now . . ." "You ought to be ashamed o' yourself," says I,

interruptin' him, "not to know the History o' your country." An' I left him gawkin' where he was.

JOXER. Where ignorance 's bliss 'tis folly to be wise; I
wondher did he ever read the Story o' Irelan'.

BOYLE. Be J. L. Sullivan? Don't you know he didn't.

JOXER. Ah, it's a darlin' buk, a daarlin' buk!

BOYLE. You'd betther be goin', now, Joxer, his Majesty,
Bentham, 'll be here any minute, now.

JOXER. Be the way things is lookin', it'll be a match between him an' Mary. She's thrun over Jerry altogether. Well,
I hope it will, for he's a darlin' man.

BOYLE. I'm glad you think so—I don't. [*Irritably.*] What's
darlin' about him?

JOXER [*nonplussed*]. I only seen him twiced; if you want to
know me, come an' live with me.

BOYLE. He's too ignified for me—to hear him talk you'd
think he knew as much as a Boney's Oraculum. He's given up
his job as teacher, an' is goin' to become a solicitor in Dublin
—he's been studyin' law. I suppose he thinks I'll set him up,
but he's wrong shipped. An' th' other fella—Jerry's as bad.
The two o' them ud give you a pain in your face, listenin' to
them; Jerry believin' in nothin', an' Bentham believin' in
everythin'. One that says all is God an' no man; an' th' other
that says all is man an' no God!

JOXER. Well, I'll be off now.

BOYLE. Don't forget to dhrop down afther awhile; we'll
have a quiet jar, an' a song or two.

JOXER. Never fear.

BOYLE. An' tell Mrs. Madigan that I hope we'll have the
pleasure of her organization at our little enthertainment.

JOXER. Righto; we'll come down together. [*He goes out.*]

[JOHNNY *comes from room on left, and sits down moodily
at the fire.* BOYLE *looks at him for a few moments, and shakes
his head. He fills his pipe.*]

VOICE OF JUNO AT THE DOOR. Open the door, Jack; this
thing has me nearly kilt with the weight.

[BOYLE *opens the door.* JUNO *enters carrying the box of a
gramophone, followed by* MARY *carrying the horn, and some
parcels.* JUNO *leaves the box on the table and flops into a
chair.*]

JUNO. Carryin' that from Henry Street was no joke.

BOYLE. U-u-ugh, that's a grand-lookin' insthrument—how much was it?

JUNO. Pound down, an' five to be paid at two shillin's a week.

BOYLE. That's reasonable enough.

JUNO. I'm afraid we're runnin' into too much debt; first the furniture, an' now this.

BOYLE. The whole lot won't be much out of two thousand pounds.

MARY. I don't know what you wanted a gramophone for— I know Charlie hates them; he says they're destructive of real music.

BOYLE. Desthructive of music—that fella ud give you a pain in your face. All a gramophone wants is to be properly played; it's thrue wondher is only felt when everythin's quiet —what a gramophone wants is dead silence!

MARY. But, father, Jerry says the same; afther all, you can only appreciate music when your ear is properly trained.

BOYLE. That's another fella ud give you a pain in your face. Properly thrained! I suppose you couldn't appreciate football unless your fut was properly thrained.

MRS. BOYLE [*to* MARY]. Go on in ower that an' dress, or Charlie 'll be in on you, an' tea nor nothin 'll be ready.

[MARY *goes into room left.*]

MRS. BOYLE [*arranging table for tea*]. You didn't look at our new gramophone, Johnny?

JOHNNY. 'Tisn't gramophones I'm thinking of.

MRS. BOYLE. An' what is it you're thinkin' of, allanna?

JOHNNY. Nothin', nothin', nothin'.

MRS. BOYLE. Sure, you must be thinkin' of somethin'; it's yourself that has yourself the way y'are; sleepin' wan night in me sisther's, an' the nex' in your father's brother's—you'll get no rest goin' on that way.

JOHNNY. I can rest nowhere, nowhere, nowhere.

MRS. BOYLE. Sure, you're not thryin' to rest anywhere.

JOHNNY. Let me alone, let me alone, let me alone, for God's sake.

[*A knock at street door.*]

MRS. BOYLE [*in a flutter*]. Here he is; here's Mr. Bentham!

BOYLE. Well, there's room for him; it's a pity there's not a brass band to play him in.

Mrs. Boyle. We'll han' the tea round, an' not be clus-thered round the table, as if we never seen nothin'.

[*Steps are heard approaching, and* Juno, *opening the door, allows* Bentham *to enter.*]

Juno. Give your hat an' stick to Jack, there . . . sit down, Mr. Bentham . . . no, not there . . . in th' easy chair be the fire . . . there, that's better. Mary'll be out to you in a minute.

Boyle [*solemnly*]. I seen be the paper this mornin' that Consols was down half per cent. That's serious, min' you, an' shows the whole counthry's in a state o' chassis.

Mrs. Boyle. What's Consols, Jack?

Boyle. Consols? Oh, Consols is—oh, there's no use tellin' women what Consols is—th' wouldn't undherstand.

Bentham. It's just as you were saying, Mr. Boyle . . .

[Mary *enters charmingly dressed.*]

Bentham. Oh, good evening, Mary; how pretty you're looking!

Mary [*archly*]. Am I?

Boyle. We were just talkin' when you kem in, Mary, I was tellin' Mr. Bentham that the whole counthry's in a state o' chassis.

Mary [*to* Bentham]. Would you prefer the green or the blue ribbon round me hair, Charlie?

Mrs. Boyle. Mary, your father's speakin'.

Boyle [*rapidly*]. I was jus' tellin' Mr. Bentham that the whole counthry's in a state o' chassis.

Mary. I'm sure you're frettin', da, whether it is or no.

Mrs. Boyle. With all our churches an' religions, the worl's not a bit the betther.

Boyle [*with a commanding gesture*]. Tay!

[Mary *and* Mrs. Boyle *dispense the tea.*]

Mrs. Boyle. An' Irelan's takin' a leaf out o' the worl's buk; when we got the makin' of our own laws I thought we'd never stop to look behind us, but instead of that we never stopped to look before us! If the people ud folley up their religion betther there'd be a betther chance for us—what do you think, Mr. Bentham?

Bentham. I'm afraid I can't venture to express an opin-ion on that point, Mrs. Boyle; dogma has no attraction for me.

MRS. BOYLE. I forgot you didn't hold with us: what's this you said you were?

BENTHAM. A Theosophist, Mrs. Boyle.

MRS. BOYLE. An' what in the name o' God 's a Theosophist?

BOYLE. A Theosophist, Juno, 's a—tell her, Mr. Bentham, tell her.

BENTHAM. It's hard to explain in a few words: Theosophy's founded on The Vedas, the religious books of the East. Its central theme is the existence of an all-pervading Spirit—the Life-Breath. Nothing really exists but this one Universal Life-Breath. And whatever even seems to exist separately from this Life-Breath, doesn't really exist at all. It is all vital force in man, in all animals, and in all vegetation. This Life-Breath is called the Prawna.

MRS. BOYLE. The Prawna! What a comical name!

BOYLE. Prawna; yis, the Prawna. [*Blowing gently through his lips.*] That's the Prawna!

MRS. BOYLE. Whist, whist, Jack.

BENTHAM. The happiness of man depends upon his sympathy with this Spirit. Men who have reached a high state of excellence are called Yogi. Some men become Yogi in a short time, it may take others millions of years.

BOYLE. Yogi! I seen hundhreds of them in the streets o' San Francisco.

BENTHAM. It is said by these Yogi that if we practice certain mental exercises that we would have powers denied to others—for instance, the faculty of seeing things that happen miles and miles away.

MRS. BOYLE. I wouldn't care to meddle with that sort o' belief; it's a very curious religion, altogether.

BOYLE. What's curious about it? Isn't all religions curious? If they weren't, you wouldn't get anyone to believe them. But religions is passin' away—they've had their day like everything else. Take the real Dublin people, f'rinstance: they know more about Charlie Chaplin an' Tommy Mix than they do about SS. Peter an' Paul!

MRS. BOYLE. You don't believe in ghosts, Mr. Bentham?

MARY. Don't you know he doesn't, mother?

BENTHAM. I don't know, that, Mary. Scientists are beginning to think that what we call ghosts are sometimes seen by persons of a certain nature. They say that sensational actions, such as the killing of a person, demand great energy, and that that energy lingers in the place where the action occurred. People may live in the place and see nothing, when someone may come along whose personality has some peculiar connection with the energy of the place, and, in a flash, the person sees the whole affair.

JOHNNY [*rising swiftly, pale and affected*]. What sort o' talk is this to be goin' on with? Is there nothin' betther to be talkin' about but the killin' o' people? My God, isn't it bad enough for these things to happen without talkin' about them! [*He hurriedly goes into the room on left.*]

BENTHAM. Oh, I'm very sorry, Mrs. Boyle! I never thought . . .

MRS. BOYLE [*apologetically*]. Never mind, Mr. Bentham, he's very touchy. [*A frightened scream is heard from* JOHNNY *inside.*]

MRS. BOYLE. Mother of God, what's that?

[*He rushes out again, his face pale, his lips twitching, his limbs trembling.*]

JOHNNY. Shut the door, shut the door, quick, for God's sake! Great God, have mercy on me! Blessed Mother o' God, shelther me, shelther your son!

MRS. BOYLE [*catching him in her arms*]. What's wrong with you? What ails you? Sit down, sit down, here, on the bed . . . there now . . . there now.

MARY. Johnny, Johnny, what ails you?

JOHNNY. I seen him, I seen him . . . kneelin' in front o' the statue . . . merciful Jesus, have pity on me!

MRS. BOYLE [*to* BOYLE]. Get him a glass o' whiskey . . . quick, man, an' don't stand gawkin'.

[BOYLE *gets the whiskey.*]

JOHNNY. Sit here, sit here, mother . . . between me an' the door.

MRS. BOYLE. I'll sit beside you as long as you like, only tell me what was it came across you at all?

JOHNNY [*after taking some drink*]. I seen him. . . . I seen Robbie Tancred kneelin' down before the statue . . . an' the red light shinin' on him . . . an' when I went in . . . he turned an' looked at me . . . an' I seen the woun's bleedin' in his breast. . . . Oh, why did he look at me like that . . . it wasn't my fault that he was done in. . . . Mother o' God, keep him away from me!

MRS. BOYLE. There, there, child, you've imagined it all. There was nothin' there at all—it was the red light you seen, an' the talk we had put all the rest into your head. Here, dhrink more o' this—it'll do you good. . . . An', now, stretch yourself down on the bed for a little. [*To* BOYLE.] Go in, Jack, an' show him it was only in his own head it was.

BOYLE [*making no move*]. E-e-e-e-eh; it's all nonsense; it was only a shadda he saw.

MARY. Mother o' God, he made me heart lep!

BENTHAM. It was simply due to an overwrought imagination—we all get that way at times.

MRS. BOYLE. There, dear, lie down in the bed, an' I'll put the quilt across you . . . e-e-e-eh, that's it . . . you'll be as right as the mail in a few minutes.

JOHNNY. Mother, go into the room an' see if the light's lightin' before the statue.

MRS. BOYLE [*to* BOYLE]. Jack, run in, an' see if the light's lightin' before the statue.

BOYLE [*to* MARY]. Mary, slip in an' see if the light's lightin' before the statue.

[MARY *hesitates to go in*.]

BENTHAM. It's all right; Mary, I'll go. [*He goes into the room; remains for a few moments, and returns.*]

BENTHAM. Everything's just as it was—the light burning bravely before the statue.

BOYLE. Of course; I knew it was all nonsense.

[*A knock at the door.*]

BOYLE [*going to open the door*]. E-e-e-e-eh.

[*He opens it, and* JOXER, *followed by* MRS. MADIGAN, *enters.* MRS. MADIGAN *is a strong, dapper little woman of about forty-five; her face is almost always a widespread smile of complacency. She is a woman who, in manner at least, can mourn with them that mourn, and rejoice with them that do rejoice. When she is feeling comfortable, she is inclined to be reminiscent; when others say anything, or following a statement made by herself, she has a habit of putting her head a little to one side, and nodding it rapidly several times in suc-*

cession, like a bird pecking at a hard berry. Indeed, she has a good deal of the bird in her, but the bird instinct is by no means a melodious one. She is ignorant, vulgar and forward, but her heart is generous withal. For instance, she would help a neighbor's sick child; she would probably kill the child, but her intentions would be to cure it; she would be more at home helping a drayman to lift a fallen horse. She is dressed in a rather soiled gray dress and a vivid purple blouse; in her hair is a huge comb, ornamented with huge colored beads. She enters with a gliding step, beaming smile and nodding head. BOYLE *receives them effusively.*]

BOYLE. Come on in, Mrs. Madigan; come on in; I was afraid you weren't comin'. . . . [*Slyly.*] There's some peo-ple able to dhress, ay, Joxer?

JOXER. Fair as the blossoms that bloom in the May, an' sweet as the scent of the new mown hay. . . . Ah, well she may wear them.

MRS. MADIGAN [*looking at* MARY]. I know some as are as sweet as the blossoms that bloom in the May—oh, no names, no pack dhrill!

BOYLE. An', now, I'll inthroduce the pair o' yous to Mary's intended: Mr. Bentham, this is Mrs. Madigan, an oul' back-parlor neighbor, that, if she could help it at all, ud never see a body shuk!

BENTHAM [*rising, and tentatively shaking the hand of* MRS. MADIGAN]. I'm sure, it's a great pleasure to know you, Mrs. Madigan.

MRS. MADIGAN. An' I'm goin' to tell you, Mr. Bentham, you're goin' to get as nice a bit o' skirt in Mary, there, as ever you seen in your puff. Not like some of the dhressed up dolls that's knockin' about lookin' for men when it's a skelpin' they want. I remember as well as I remember yes-therday, the day she was born—of a Tuesday, the twenty-fifth o' June, in the year nineteen-one, at thirty-three min-utes past wan in the day be Foley's clock, the pub at the corner o' the street. A cowld day it was too, for the season o' the year, an' I remember sayin' to Joxer, there, who I met comin' up th' stairs, that the new arrival in Boyle's ud grow up a hardy chiselur if it lived, an that she'd be somethin' one o' these days that nobody suspected, an' so signs on it, here she is today, goin' to be married to a young man lookin' as if he'd be fit to commensurate in any position in life it ud please God to call him!

BOYLE [*effusively*]. Sit down, Mrs. Madigan, sit down, me oul' sport. [*To* BENTHAM.] This is Joxer Daly, Past Chief Ranger of the Dear Little Shamrock Branch of the Irish National Foresters, an oul' front-top neighbor, that never despaired, even in the darkest days of Ireland's sorra.

JOXER. Nil desperandum, Captain, nil desperandum.

BOYLE. Sit down, Joxer, sit down. The two of us was often in a tight corner.

MRS. BOYLE. Ay, in Foley's snug!

JOXER. An' we kem out of it flyin', we kem out of it flyin', Captain.

BOYLE. An', now, for a dhrink—I know yous won't refuse an oul' friend.

MRS. MADIGAN [*to* JUNO]. Is Johnny not well, Mrs. . . .

MRS. BOYLE [*warningly*]. S-s-s-sh.

MRS. MADIGAN. Oh, the poor darlin'.

BOYLE. Well, Mrs. Madigan, is it tea or what?

MRS. MADIGAN. Well, speakin' for meself, I jus' had me tea a minute ago, an' I'm afraid to dhrink any more—I'm never the same when I dhrink too much tay. Thanks, all the same, Mr. Boyle.

BOYLE. Well, what about a bottle o' stout or a dhrop o' whiskey?

MRS. MADIGAN. A bottle o' stout ud be a little too heavy for me stummock afther me tay. . . . A-a-ah, I'll thry the ball o' malt.

[BOYLE *prepares the whiskey.*]

MRS. MADIGAN. There's nothin' like a ball o' malt occasional like—too much of it isn't good. [*To* BOYLE, *who is adding water.*] Ah, God, Johnny, don't put too much wather on it! [*She drinks.*] I suppose yous'll be lavin' this place.

BOYLE. I'm looking for a place near the sea; I'd like the place that you might say was me cradle, to be me grave as well. The sea is always callin' me.

JOXER. She is callin', callin', callin', in the win' an' on the sea.

BOYLE. Another dhrop o' whiskey, Mrs. Madigan?

MRS. MADIGAN. Well, now, it ud be hard to refuse seein' the suspicious times that's in it.

BOYLE [*with a commanding gesture*]. Song! . . . Juno . . . Mary . . . "Home to Our Mount'ins"!

MRS. MADIGAN [*enthusiastically*]. Hear, hear!

JOXER. Oh, tha's a darlin' song, a daarlin' song!

MARY [*bashfully*]. Ah, no, da; I'm not in a singin' humor.

MRS. MADIGAN. Gawn with you, child, an' you only goin' to be marrid; I remember as well as I remember yestherday, —it was on a lovely August evenin', exactly, accordin' to date, fifteen years ago, come the Tuesday folleyin' the nex' that's comin' on, when me own man [*the Lord be good to him*] an' me was sittin' shy together in a doty little nook on a counthry road, adjacent to The Stiles. "That'll scratch your lovely, little white neck," says he, ketchin' hould of a danglin' bramble branch, holdin' clusters of the loveliest flowers you ever seen, an' breakin' it off, so that his arm fell, accidental like, roun' me waist, an' as I felt it tightenin', an' tightenin', an' tightenin', I thought me buzzum was every minute goin' to burst out into a roystherin' song about

> The little green leaves that were shakin' on the threes,
> The gallivantin' büttherflies, an' buzzin' o' the bees!

BOYLE. Ordher for the song!

JUNO. Come on, Mary—we'll do our best.

[JUNO *and* MARY *stand up, and choosing a suitable position, sing simply "Home to Our Mountains." They bow to company, and return to their places.*]

BOYLE [*emotionally, at the end of song*]. Lull . . . me . . . to . . . rest!

JOXER [*clapping his hands*]. Bravo, bravo! Darlin' girulls, darlin' girulls!

MRS. MADIGAN. Juno, I never seen you in betther form.

BENTHAM. Very nicely rendered indeed.

MRS. MADIGAN. A noble call, a noble call!

MRS. BOYLE. What about yourself, Mrs. Madigan?

[*After some coaxing,* MRS. MADIGAN *rises, and in a quavering voice sings the following verse*]:

> If I were a blackbird I'd whistle and sing;
> I'd follow the ship that my thrue love was in;
> An' on the top riggin', I'd there build me nest,
> An' at night I would sleep on me Willie's white breast!

[*Becoming husky, amid applause, she sits down.*]

MRS. MADIGAN. Ah, me voice is too husky now, Juno; though I remember the time when Maisie Madigan could sing like a nightingale at matin' time. I remember as well as I remember yesterday, at a party given to celebrate the comin' of the first chiselur to Annie an' Benny Jimeson—who was the barber, yous may remember, in Henrietta Street, that, afther Easter Week, hung out a green, white an' orange pole, an', then, when the Tans started their Jazz dancin', whipped it in agen, an' stuck out a red, white an' blue wan instead, given as an excuse that a barber's pole was strictly non-political—singin' "An' You'll Remember Me," with the top notes quiverin' in a dead hush of pethrified attention, folleyed by a clappin' o' han's that shuk the tumblers on the table, an' capped be Jimeson, the barber, sayin' that it was the best rendherin' of "You'll Remember Me" he ever heard in his natural!

BOYLE [*peremptorily*]. Ordher for Joxer's song!

JOXER. Ah, no, I couldn't; don't ass me, Captain.

BOYLE. Joxer's song, Joxer's song—give us wan of your shut-eyed wans. [JOXER *settles himself in his chair; takes a drink; clears his throat; solemnly closes his eyes, and begins to sing in a very querulous voice*]:

> She is far from the lan' where her young hero sleeps,
> An' lovers around her are sighing [*He hesitates.*]
> An' lovers around her are sighin' . . . sighin' . . . sighin' . . .

[*A pause.*]
BOYLE [*imitating* JOXER]:

> And lovers around her are sighing!

What's the use of you thryin' to sing the song if you don't know it?

MARY. Thry another one, Mr. Daly—maybe you'd be more fortunate.

MRS. MADIGAN. Gawn, Joxer, thry another wan.

JOXER [*starting again*]:

I have heard the mavis singin' his love song to the morn;
I have seen the dew-dhrop clingin' to the rose jus' newly
born; but . . . but . . . [*frantically*] to the rose
jus' newly born . . . newly born . . . born.

JOHNNY. Mother, put on the gramophone, for God's sake, an' stop Joxer's bawlin'.

BOYLE [*commandingly*]. Gramophone! . . . I hate to see fellas thryin' to do what they're not able to do.

[BOYLE *arranges the gramophone, and is about to start it, when voices are heard of persons descending the stairs.*]

MRS. BOYLE [*warningly*]. Whisht, Jack, don't put it on, don't put it on yet; this must be poor Mrs. Tancred comin' down to go to the hospital—I forgot all about them bringin' the body to the church tonight. Open the door, Mary, an' give them a bit o' light.

[MARY *opens the door, and* MRS. TANCRED—*a very old woman, obviously shaken by the death of her son—appears, accompanied by several neighbors. The first few phrases are spoken before they appear.*]

FIRST NEIGHBOR. It's a sad journey we're goin' on, but God's good, an' the Republicans won't be always down.

MRS. TANCRED. Ah, what good is that to me now? Whether they're up or down—it won't bring me darlin' boy from the grave.

MRS. BOYLE. Come in an' have a hot cup o' tay, Mrs. Tancred, before you go.

MRS. TANCRED. Ah, I can take nothin' now, Mrs. Boyle—I won't be long afther him.

FIRST NEIGHBOR. Still an' all, he died a noble death, an' we'll bury him like a king.

MRS. TANCRED. An' I'll go on livin' like a pauper. Ah, what's the pains I suffered bringin' him into the world to carry him to his cradle, to the pains I'm sufferin' now, carryin' him out o' the world to bring him to his grave!

MARY. It would be better for you not to go at all, Mrs. Tancred, but to stay at home beside the fire with some o' the neighbors.

MRS. TANCRED. I seen the first of him, an' I'll see the last of him.

MRS. BOYLE. You'd want a shawl, Mrs. Tancred; it's a cowld night, an' the win's blowin' sharp.

MRS. MADIGAN [*rushing out*]. I've a shawl above.

MRS. TANCRED. Me home is gone, now; he was me only child, an' to think that he was lyin' for a whole night stretched out on the side of a lonely counthry lane, with his head, his darlin' head, that I ofen kissed an' fondled, half hidden in the wather of a runnin' brook. An' I'm told he was the leadher of the ambush where me nex' door neighbor, Mrs. Mannin', lost her Free State soldier son. An' now here's the two of us oul' women, standin' one on each side of a scales o' sorra, balanced be the bodies of our two dead darlin' sons. [MRS. MADIGAN *returns, and wraps a shawl around her.*] God bless you, Mrs. Madigan. . . . [*She moves slowly towards the door.*] Mother o' God, Mother o' God, have pity on the pair of us! . . . O Blessed Virgin, where were you when me darlin' son was riddled with bullets, when me darlin' son was riddled with bullets! . . . Sacred Heart of the Crucified Jesus, take away our hearts o' stone . . . an' give us hearts o' flesh! . . . Take away this murdherin' hate . . . an' give us Thine own eternal love! [*They pass out of the room.*]

MRS. BOYLE [*explanatorily to* BENTHAM]. That was Mrs. Tancred of the two-pair back; her son was found, e'er yestherday, lyin' out beyant Finglas riddled with bullets. A diehard he was, be all accounts. He was a nice quiet boy, but lattherly he went to hell, with his Republic first, an' Republic last an' Republic over all. He ofen took tea with us here, in the oul' days, an' Johnny, there, an' him used to be always together.

JOHNNY. Am I always to be havin' to tell you that he was no friend o' mine? I never cared for him, an' he could never stick me. It's not because he was Commandant of the Battalion that I was Quarthermasther of, that we were friends.

MRS. BOYLE. He's gone, now—the Lord be good to him! God help his poor oul' creature of a mother, for no matther whose friend or enemy he was, he was her poor son.

BENTHAM. The whole thing is terrible, Mrs. Boyle; but the only way to deal with a mad dog is to destroy him.

MRS. BOYLE. An' to think of me forgettin' about him bein'

brought to the church tonight, an' we singin' an' all, but it was well we hadn't the gramophone goin', anyhow.

BOYLE. Even if we had aself. We've nothin' to do with these things, one way or t'other. That's the Government's business, an' let them do what we're payin' them for doin'.

MRS. BOYLE. I'd like to know how a body's not to mind these things; look at the way they're afther leavin' the people in this very house. Hasn't the whole house, nearly, been massacreed? There's young Mrs. Dougherty's husband with his leg off; Mrs. Travers that had her son blew up be a mine in Inchegeela, in Co. Cork; Mrs. Mannin' that lost wan of her sons in an ambush a few weeks ago, an' now, poor Mrs. Tancred's only child gone West with his body made a collandher of. Sure, if it's not our business, I don't know whose business it is.

BOYLE. Here, there, that's enough about them things; they don't affect us, an' we needn't give a damn. If they want a wake, well, let them have a wake. When I was a sailor, I was always resigned to meet with a wathery grave; an', if they want to be soldiers, well, there's no use o' them squealin' when they meet a soldier's fate.

JOXER. Let me like a soldier fall—me breast expandin' to th' ball!

MRS. BOYLE. In wan way, she deserves all she got; for lately, she let th' die-hards make an open house of th' place; an' for th' last couple of months, either when th' sun was risin', or when th' sun was settin', you had C.I.D. men burstin' into your room, assin' you where were you born, where were you christened, where were you married, an' where would you be buried!

JOHNNY. For God's sake, let us have no more o' this talk.

MRS. MADIGAN. What about Mr. Boyle's song before we start th' gramophone?

MARY [*getting her hat, and putting it on*]. Mother, Charlie and I are goin' out for a little sthroll.

MRS. BOYLE. All right, darlin'.

BENTHAM [*going out with* MARY]. We won't be long away, Mrs. Boyle.

MRS. MADIGAN. Gwan, Captain, gwan.

BOYLE. E-e-e-e-eh, I'd want to have a few more jars in me, before I'd be in fettle for singin'.

JOXER. Give us that poem you writ t'other day. [*To the rest.*] Aw, it's a darlin' poem, a daarlin' poem.

MRS. BOYLE. God bless us, is he startin' to write poetry!

BOYLE [*rising to his feet*]. E-e-e-e-eh. [*He recites in an emotional, consequential manner the following verses*]:

> Shawn an' I were friends, sir, to me he was all in all.
> His work was very heavy and his wages were very small.
> None betther on th' beach as Docker, I'll go bail,
> 'Tis now I'm feelin' lonely, for today he lies in jail.
> He was not what some call pious—seldom at church or
>   prayer;
> For the greatest scoundrels I know, sir, goes every Sunday
>   there.
> Fond of his pint—well, rather, but hated the Boss by
>   creed
> But never refused a copper to comfort a pal in need.

E-e-e-e-eh. [*He sits down.*]

MRS. MADIGAN. Grand, grand; you should folley that up, you should folley that up.

JOXER. It's a daarlin' poem!

BOYLE [*delightedly*]. E-e-e-e-eh.

JOHNNY. Are yous goin' to put on th' gramophone to-night, or are yous not?

MRS. BOYLE. Gwan, Jack, put on a record.

MRS. MADIGAN. Gwan, Captain, gwan.

BOYLE. Well, yous'll want to keep a dead silence.

[*He sets a record, starts the machine, and it begins to play* "If you're Irish, come into the Parlor." *As the tune is in full blare, the door is suddenly opened by a brisk, little bald-headed man, dressed circumspectly in a black suit; he glares fiercely at all in the room; he is* "NEEDLE" NUGENT, *a tailor. He carries his hat in his hand.*]

NUGENT [*loudly, above the noise of the gramophone*]. Are yous goin' to have that thing bawlin' an' the funeral of Mrs. Tancred's son passin' the house? Have none of yous any respect for the Irish people's National regard for the dead?

[BOYLE *stops the gramophone.*]

MRS. BOYLE. Maybe, Needle Nugent, it's nearly time we

had a little less respect for the dead, an' a little more regard for the livin'.

MRS. MADIGAN. We don't want you, Mr. Nugent, to teach us what we learned at our mother's knee. You don't look yourself as if you were dyin' of grief; if y'ass Maisie Madigan anything, I'd call you a real thrue die-hard an' live-soft Republican, attendin' Republican funerals in the day, an' stoppin' up half the night makin' suits for the Civic Guards!

[*Persons are heard running down to the street, some saying,* "Here it is, here it is." NUGENT *withdraws, and the rest, except* JOHNNY, *go to the window looking into the street, and look out. Sounds of a crowd coming nearer are heard; portion are singing*]:

> To Jesus' Heart all burning
> With fervent love for men,
> My heart with fondest yearning
> Shall raise its joyful strain.
> While ages course along,
> Blest be with loudest song,
> The Sacred Heart of Jesus
> By every heart and tongue.

MRS. BOYLE. Here's the hearse, here's the hearse!

BOYLE. There's t'oul' mother walkin' behin' the coffin.

MRS. MADIGAN. You can hardly see the coffin with the wreaths.

JOXER. Oh, it's a darlin' funeral, a daarlin' funeral!

MRS. MADIGAN. We'd have a betther view from the street.

BOYLE. Yes—this place ud give you a crick in your neck. [*They leave the room, and go down.* JOHNNY *sits moodily by the fire.*]

[*A young man enters; he looks at* JOHNNY *for a moment.*]

THE YOUNG MAN. Quarthermasther Boyle.

JOHNNY [*with a start*]. The Mobilizer!

THE YOUNG MAN. You're not at the funeral?

JOHNNY. I'm not well.

THE YOUNG MAN. I'm glad I've found you; you were stoppin' at your aunt's; I called there but you'd gone. I've to give you an ordher to attend a Battalion Staff meetin' the night afther tomorrow.

JOHNNY. Where?

THE YOUNG MAN. I don't know; you're to meet me at the Pillar at eight o'clock; then we're to go to a place I'll be told of tonight; there we'll meet a mothor that'll bring us to the meeting. They think you might be able to know somethin' about them that gave the bend where Commandant Tancred was shelterin'.

JOHNNY. I'm not goin', then. I know nothing about Tancred.

THE YOUNG MAN [*at the door*]. You'd betther come for your own sake—remember your oath.

JOHNNY [*passionately*]. I won't go! Haven't I done enough for Ireland! I've lost me arm, an' me hip's desthroyed so that I'll never be able to walk right agen! Good God, haven't I done enough for Ireland?

THE YOUNG MAN. Boyle, no man can do enough for Ireland! [*He goes.*]

[*Faintly in the distance the crowd is heard saying:*]

Hail, Mary, full of grace, the Lord is with Thee;
Blessed art Thou amongst women, and blessed, etc.

ACT III

SCENE: *The same as Act II. It is about half-past six on a November evening; a bright fire is burning in the grate; MARY, dressed to go out, is sitting on a chair by the fire, leaning forward, her hands under her chin, her elbows on her knees. A look of dejection, mingled with uncertain anxiety, is on her face. A lamp, turned low, is lighting on the table. The votive light under the picture of the Virgin, gleams more redly than ever. MRS. BOYLE is putting on her hat and coat. It is two months later.*

MRS. BOYLE. An' has Bentham never even written to you since—not one line for the past month?

MARY [*tonelessly*]. Not even a line, mother.

MRS. BOYLE. That's very curious. . . . What came between the two of yous at all? To leave you so sudden, an' yous so great together. . . . To go away t' England, an' not to even leave you his address. . . . The way he was always bringin' you to dances, I thought he was mad afther you. Are you sure you said nothin' to him?

MARY. No, mother—at least nothing that could possibly explain his givin' me up.

MRS. BOYLE. You know you're a bit hasty at times, Mary, an' say things you shouldn't say.

MARY. I never said to him what I shouldn't say, I'm sure of that.

MRS. BOYLE. How are you sure of it?

MARY. Because I love him with all my heart and soul, mother. Why, I don't know; I often thought to myself that he wasn't the man poor Jerry was, but I couldn't help loving him, all the same.

MRS. BOYLE. But you shouldn't be frettin' the way you are; when a woman loses a man, she never knows what she's afther losin', to be sure, but, then, she never knows what she's afther gainin', either. You're not the one girl of a month ago—you look like one pinin' away. It's long ago I had a right to bring you to the doctor, instead of waitin' till to-night.

MARY. There's no necessity, really, mother, to go to the doctor; nothing serious is wrong with me—I'm run down and disappointed, that's all.

MRS. BOYLE. I'll not wait another minute; I don't like the look of you at all. . . . I'm afraid we made a mistake in throwin' over poor Jerry. . . . He'd have been betther for you than that Bentham.

MARY. Mother, the best man for a woman is the one for whom she has the most love, and Charlie had it all.

MRS. BOYLE. Well, there's one thing to be said for him—he couldn't have been thinkin' of the money, or he wouldn't ha' left you . . . it must ha' been somethin' else.

MARY [*wearily*]. I don't know . . . I don't know, mother . . . only I think . . .

MRS. BOYLE. What d'ye think?

MARY. I imagine . . . he thought . . . we weren't . . . good enough for him.

MRS. BOYLE. An' what was he himself, only a school teacher? Though I don't blame him for fightin' shy of people like that Joxer fella an' that oul' Madigan wan—nice sort o' people for your father to inthroduce to a man like Mr. Bentham. You might have told me all about this before now, Mary; I don't know why you like to hide everything from your mother; you knew Bentham, an' I'd ha' known nothin' about it if it hadn't bin for the Will; an' it was only today, afther long coaxin', that you let out that he'd left you.

MARY. It would have been useless to tell you—you wouldn't understand.

MRS. BOYLE [*hurt*]. Maybe not. . . . Maybe I wouldn't understand. . . . Well, we'll be off now. [*She goes over to door left, and speaks to* BOYLE *inside.*]

MRS. BOYLE. We're goin' now to the doctor's. Are you goin' to get up this evenin'?

BOYLE [*from inside*]. The pains in me legs is terrible! It's me should be poppin' off to the doctor instead o' Mary, the way I feel.

MRS. BOYLE. Sorra mend you! A nice way you were in last night—carried in in a frog's march, dead to the world. If that's the way you'll go on when you get the money it'll be the grave for you, an asylum for me and the Poorhouse for Johnny.

BOYLE. I thought you were goin'?

MRS. BOYLE. That's what has you as you are—you can't bear to be spoken to. Knowin' the way we are, up to our ears in debt, it's a wondher you wouldn't ha' got up to go to th' solicitor's an' see if we could ha' gettin' a little o' the money even.

BOYLE [*shouting*]. I can't be goin' up there night, noon an' mornin', can I? He can't give the money till he gets it, can he? I can't get blood out of a turnip, can I?

MRS. BOYLE. It's nearly two months since we heard of the Will, an' the money seems as far off as ever. . . . I suppose you know we owe twenty poun's to oul' Murphy?

BOYLE. I've a faint recollection of you tellin' me that before.

MRS. BOYLE. Well, you'll go over to the shop yourself for the things in future—I'll face him no more.

BOYLE. I thought you said you were goin'?

MRS. BOYLE. I'm goin' now; come on, Mary.

BOYLE. Ey, Juno, ey!

MRS. BOYLE. Well, what d'ye want now?

BOYLE. Is there e'er a bottle o' stout left?

MRS. BOYLE. There's two o' them here still.

BOYLE. Show us in one o' them an' leave t'other there till I get up. An' throw us in the paper that's on the table, an' the bottle o' Sloan's Liniment that's in th' drawer.

MRS. BOYLE [*getting the liniment and the stout*]. What paper is it you want—the *Catholic News?*

BOYLE. The *Catholic News! The News o' the World!*

[MRS. BOYLE *brings in the things asked for and comes out again.*]

MRS. BOYLE [*at door*]. Mind the candle, now, an' don't burn the house over our heads. I left t'other bottle o' stout on the table. [*She puts bottle of stout on table. She goes out with* MARY. *A cork is heard popping inside.*]

[*A pause; then outside the door is heard the voice of* JOXER *lilting softly:* "Me pipe I'll smoke, as I dhrive me moke . . . are you . . . there . . . More . . . aar . . . i . . . tee!" *A gentle knock is heard and, after a pause, the door opens, and* JOXER, *followed by* NUGENT, *enters.*]

JOXER. Be God, they must be all out; I was thinkin' there was somethin' up when he didn't answer the signal. We seen Juno an' Mary goin', but I didn't see him, an' it's very seldom he escapes me.

NUGENT. He's not goin' to escape me—he's not goin' to be let go to the fair altogether.

JOXER. Sure, the house couldn't hould them lately; an' he goin' about like a mastherpiece of the Free State counthry; forgettin' their friends; forgettin' God—wouldn't even lift his hat passin' a chapel! Sure they were bound to get a dhrop! An' you really think there's no money comin' to him afther all?

NUGENT. Not as much as a red rex, man; I've been a bit anxious this long time over me money, an' I went up to the solicitor's to find out all I could—ah, man, they were goin' to throw me down the stairs. They toul' me that the oul' cock himself had the stairs worn away comin' up afther it, an' they black in the face tellin' him he'd get nothin'. Some way or another that the Will is writ he won't be entitled to get as much as a make!

JOXER. Ah, I thought there was somethin' curious about the whole thing; I've bin havin' sthrange dhreams for the last couple o' weeks. An' I notice that that Bentham fella doesn't be comin' here now—there must be somethin' on the mat there too. Anyhow, who, in the name o' God, ud leave anythin' to that oul' bummer? Sure it ud be unnatural. An' the way Juno an' him's been throwin' their weight about for the last few months! Ah, him that goes a borrowin' goes a sorrowin'!

NUGENT. Well, he's not goin' to throw his weight about in the suit I made for him much longer. I'm tellin' you seven poun's aren't to be found growin' on the bushes these days.

JOXER. An' there isn't hardly a neighbor in the whole street that hasn't lent him money on the strength of what he was goin' to get, but they're after backing the wrong horse. Wasn't it a mercy o' God that I'd nothin' to give him! The softy I am, you know, I'd ha' lent him me last juice! I must have had somebody's good prayers. Ah, afther all, an honest man's the noblest work o' God!

[BOYLE *coughs inside.*]

JOXER. Whisht, damn it, he must be inside in bed.

NUGENT. Inside o' bed or outside of it he's goin' to pay me for that suit, or give it back—he'll not climb up my back as easily as he thinks.

JOXER. Gwan in at wanst, man, an' get it off him, an' don't be a fool.

NUGENT [*going to door left, opening it and looking in*]. Ah, don't disturb yourself, Mr. Boyle; I hope you're not sick?

BOYLE. Th' oul' legs, Mr. Nugent; the oul' legs.

NUGENT. I just called over to see if you could let me have anything off the suit?

BOYLE. E-e-e-e-eh, how much is this it is?

NUGENT. It's the same as it was at the start—seven poun's.

BOYLE. I'm glad you kem, Mr. Nugent; I want a good heavy top-coat—Irish frieze, if you have it. How much would a top-coat like that be now?

NUGENT. About six poun's.

BOYLE. Six poun's—six an' seven, six an' seven is thirteen —that'll be thirteen poun's I'll owe you.

[JOXER *slips the bottle of stout that is on the table into his pocket.* NUGENT *rushes into the room, and returns with suit on his arm; he pauses at the door.*]

NUGENT. You'll owe me no thirteen poun's. Maybe you think you're betther able to owe it than pay it!

BOYLE [*frantically*]. Here, come back to hell ower that—where're you goin' with them clothes o' mine?

NUGENT. Where am I goin' with them clothes o' yours? Well, I like your damn cheek!

BOYLE. Here, what am I goin' to dhress meself in when I'm goin' out?

NUGENT. What do I care what you dhress yourself in? You can put yourself in a bolsther cover, if you like. [*He goes towards the other door, followed by* JOXER.]

JOXER. What'll he dhress himself in! Gentleman Jack an' his frieze coat!

[*They go out.*]

BOYLE [*inside*]. Ey, Nugent, ey, Mr. Nugent, Mr. Nugent!

[*After a pause* BOYLE *enters hastily, buttoning the braces of his moleskin trousers; his coat and vest are on his arm; he throws these on a chair and hurries to the door on right.*]

BOYLE. Ey, Mr. Nugent, Mr. Nugent!

JOXER [*meeting him at the door*]. What's up, what's wrong, Captain?

BOYLE. Nugent's been here an' took away me suit—the only things I had to go out in!

JOXER. Tuk your suit—for God's sake! An' what were you doin' while he was takin' them?

BOYLE. I was in bed when he stole in like a thief in the night, an' before I knew even what he was thinkin' of, he whipped them from the chair, an' was off like a redshank!

JOXER. An' what, in the name o' God, did he do that for?

BOYLE. What did he do it for? How the hell do I know what he done it for? Jealousy an' spite, I suppose.

JOXER. Did he not say what he done it for?

BOYLE. Amn't I afther tellin' you that he had them whipped up an' was gone before I could open me mouth?

JOXER. That was a very sudden thing to do; there mus' be somethin' behin' it. Did he hear anythin', I wondher?

BOYLE. Did he hear anythin'?—you talk very queer, Joxer—what could he hear?

JOXER. About you not gettin' the money, in some way or t'other?

BOYLE. An' what ud prevent me from gettin' th' money?

JOXER. That's jus' what I was thinkin'—what ud prevent you from gettin' the money—nothin', as far as I can see.

BOYLE [*looking round for bottle of stout with an exclamation*]. Aw, holy God!

JOXER. What's up, Jack?

BOYLE. He must have afther lifted the bottle o' stout that Juno left on the table!

JOXER [*horrified*]. Ah, no, ah, no! He wouldn't be afther doin' that, now.

BOYLE. An' who done it then? Juno left a bottle o' stout here, an' it's gone—it didn't walk, did it?

JOXER. Oh, that's shockin'; ah, man's inhumanity to man makes countless thousands mourn!

MRS. MADIGAN [*appearing at the door*]. I hope I'm not disturbin' you in any discussion on your forthcomin' legacy —if I may use the word—an' that you'll let me have a barny for a minute or two with you, Mr. Boyle.

BOYLE [*uneasily*]. To be sure, Mrs. Madigan—an oul' friend's always welcome.

JOXER. Come in the evenin', come in th' mornin'; come when you're assed, or come without warnin', Mrs. Madigan.

BOYLE. Sit down, Mrs. Madigan.

MRS. MADIGAN [*ominously*]. Th' few words I have to say can be said standin'. Puttin' aside all formularies, I suppose you remember me lendin' you some time ago three poun's that I raised on blankets an' furniture in me uncle's?

BOYLE. I remember it well. I have it recorded in me book —three poun's five shillin's from Maisie Madigan, raised on articles pawned; an', item: fourpence, given to make up the price of a pint, on th' principle that no bird ever flew on wan wing; all to be repaid at par, when the ship comes home.

MRS. MADIGAN. Well, ever since I shoved in the blankets I've been perishing with th' cowld, an' I've decided, if I'll be too hot in th' nex' world aself, I'm not goin' to be too cowld in this wan; an' consequently, I want me three poun's, if you please.

BOYLE. This is a very sudden demand, Mrs. Madigan, an' can't be met; but I'm willing to give you a receipt in full, in full.

Mrs. Madigan. Come on, out with th' money, an' don't be jack-actin'.

Boyle. You can't get blood out of a turnip, can you?

Mrs. Madigan [*rushing over and shaking him*]. Gimme me money, y'oul' reprobate, or I'll shake the worth of it out of you!

Boyle. Ey, houl' on, there; houl' on, there! You'll wait for your money now, me lassie!

Mrs. Madigan [*looking around the room and seeing the gramophone*]. I'll wait for it, will I? Well, I'll not wait long; if I can't get th' cash, I'll get th' worth of it. [*She catches up the gramophone.*]

Boyle. Ey, ey, there, wher'r you goin' with that?

Mrs. Madigan. I'm goin' to th' pawn to get me three quid five shillin's; I'll brin' you th' ticket, an' then you can do what you like, me bucko.

Boyle. You can't touch that, you can't touch that! It's not my property, an' it's not ped for yet!

Mrs. Madigan. So much th' better. It'll be an ayse to me conscience, for I'm takin' what doesn't belong to you. You're not goin' to be swankin' it like a paycock with Maisie Madigan's money—I'll pull some o' th' gorgeous feathers out o' your tail! [*She goes off with the gramophone.*]

Boyle. What's th' world comin' to at all? I ass you, Joxer Daly, is there any morality left anywhere?

Joxer. I wouldn't ha' believed it, only I seen it with me own two eyes. I didn't think Maisie Madigan was that sort of a woman; she has either a sup taken, or she's heard somethin'.

Boyle. Heard somethin'—about what, if it's not any harm to ass you?

Joxer. She must ha' heard some rumor or other that you weren't goin' to get th' money.

Boyle. Who says I'm not goin' to get th' money?

Joxer. Sure, I know—I was only sayin'.

Boyle. Only sayin' what?

Joxer. Nothin'.

Boyle. You were goin' to say somethin', don't be a twisther.

Joxer [*angrily*]. Who's a twisther?

BOYLE. Why don't you speak your mind, then?

JOXER. You never twisted yourself—no, you wouldn't know how!

BOYLE. Did you ever know me to twist; did you ever know me to twist?

JOXER [*fiercely*]. Did you ever do anythin' else! Sure, you can't believe a word that comes out o' your mouth.

BOYLE. Here, get out, ower o' this; I always knew you were a prognosticator an' a procrastinator!

JOXER [*going out as* JOHNNY *comes in*]. The anchor's weighed, farewell, re . . . mem . . . ber . . . me. Jacky Boyle, Esquire, infernal rogue an' damned liar!

JOHNNY. Joxer an' you at it agen?—when are you goin' to have a little respect for yourself, an' not be always makin' a show of us all?

BOYLE. Are you goin' to lecture me now?

JOHNNY. Is mother back from the doctor yet, with Mary?

[MRS. BOYLE *enters; it is apparent from the serious look on her face that something has happened. She takes off her hat and coat without a word and puts them by. She then sits down near the fire, and there is a few moments' pause.*]

BOYLE. Well, what did the doctor say about Mary?

MRS. BOYLE [*in an earnest manner and with suppressed agitation*]. Sit down here, Jack; I've something to say to you . . . about Mary.

BOYLE [*awed by her manner*]. About . . . Mary?

MRS. BOYLE. Close that door there and sit down here.

BOYLE [*closing the door*]. More trouble in our native land, is it? [*He sits down.*] Well, what is it?

MRS. BOYLE. It's about Mary.

BOYLE. Well, what about Mary—there's nothin' wrong with her, is there ?

MRS. BOYLE. I'm sorry to say there's a gradle wrong with her.

BOYLE. A gradle wrong with her! [*Peevishly.*] First Johnny an' now Mary; is the whole house goin' to become an hospital! It's not consumption, is it?

MRS. BOYLE. No . . . it's not consumption . . . it's worse.

JOHNNY. Worse! Well, we'll have to get her into some place ower this, there's no one here to mind her.

MRS. BOYLE. We'll all have to mind her now. You might as well know now, Johnny, as another time. [*To* BOYLE.] D'ye know what the doctor said to me about her, Jack?

BOYLE. How ud I know—I wasn't there, was I?

MRS. BOYLE. He told me to get her married at wanst.

BOYLE. Married at wanst! An' why did he say the like o' that?

MRS. BOYLE. Because Mary's goin' to have a baby in a short time.

BOYLE. Goin' to have a baby!—my God, what'll Bentham say when he hears that?

MRS. BOYLE. Are you blind, man, that you can't see that it was Bentham that has done this wrong to her?

BOYLE [*passionately*]. Then he'll marry her, he'll have to marry her!

MRS. BOYLE. You know he's gone to England, an' God knows where he is now.

BOYLE. I'll folley him, I'll folley him, an' bring him back, an' make him do her justice. The scoundrel, I might ha' known what he was, with his yogees an' his prawna!

MRS. BOYLE. We'll have to keep it quiet till we see what we can do.

BOYLE. Oh, isn't this a nice thing to come on top o' me, an' the state I'm in! A pretty show I'll be to Joxer an' to that oul' wan, Madigan! Amn't I afther goin' through enough without havin' to go through this!

MRS. BOYLE. What you an' I'll have to go through'll be nothin' to what poor Mary'll have to go through; for you an' me is middlin' old, an' most of our years is spent; but Mary'll have maybe forty years to face an' handle, an' every wan of them'll be tainted with a bitther memory.

BOYLE. Where is she? Where is she till I tell her off? I'm tellin' you when I'm done with her she'll be a sorry girl!

MRS. BOYLE. I left her in me sisther's till I came to speak to you. You'll say nothin' to her, Jack; ever since she left school she's earned her livin', an' your fatherly care never throubled the poor girl.

BOYLE. Gwan, take her part agen her father! But I'll let you see whether I'll say nothin' to her or no! Her an' her readin'! That's more o' th' blasted nonsense that has the house fallin' down on top of us! What did th' likes of her, born in a tenement house, want with readin'? Her readin's afther bringin' her to a nice pass—oh, it's madnin', madnin', madnin'!

MRS. BOYLE. When she comes back say nothin' to her, Jack, or she'll leave this place.

BOYLE. Leave this place! Ay, she'll leave this place, an' quick too!

MRS. BOYLE. If Mary goes, I'll go with her.

BOYLE. Well, go with her! Well, go, th' pair o' yous! I lived before I seen yous, an' I can live when yous are gone. Isn't this a nice thing to come rollin' in on top o' me afther all your prayin' to St. Anthony an' The Little Flower. An' she's a child o' Mary, too—I wonder what'll the nuns think of her now? An' it'll be bellows'd all over th' disthrict before you could say Jack Robinson; an' whenever I'm seen they'll whisper, "That's th' father of Mary Boyle that had th' kid be th' swank she used to go with; d'ye know, d'ye know?" To be sure they'll know—more about it than I will meself!

JOHNNY. She should be dhriven out o' th' house she's brought disgrace on!

MRS. BOYLE. Hush, you, Johnny. We needn't let it be bellows'd all over the place; all we've got to do is to leave this place quietly an' go somewhere where we're not known, an' nobody'll be th' wiser.

BOYLE. You're talkin' like a two-year-oul', woman. Where'll we get a place ou' o' this?—places aren't that easily got.

MRS. BOYLE. But, Jack, when we get the money . . .

BOYLE. Money—what money?

MRS. BOYLE. Why, oul' Ellison's money, of course.

BOYLE. There's no money comin' from oul' Ellison, or anyone else. Since you're heard of wan throuble, you might as well hear of another. There's no money comin' to us at all—the Will's a wash-out!

MRS. BOYLE. What are you sayin', man—no money?

JOHNNY. How could it be a wash-out?

BOYLE. The boyo that's afther doin' it to Mary done it to me as well. The thick made out the Will wrong; he said in th' Will, only first cousin an' second cousin, instead of men-tionin' our names, an' now anyone that thinks he's a first cousin or second cousin t'oul' Ellison can claim the money as

well as me, an' they're springin' up in hundreds, an' comin'
from America an' Australia, thinkin' to get their whack out
of it, while all the time the lawyers is gobblin' it up, till
there's not as much as ud buy a stockin' for your lovely
daughter's baby!

MRS. BOYLE. I don't believe it, I don't believe it, I don't
believe it!

JOHNNY. Why did you say nothin' about this before?

MRS. BOYLE. You're not serious, Jack; you're not serious!

BOYLE. I'm tellin' you the scholar, Bentham, made a
banjax o' th' Will; instead o' saying', "th' rest o' me property
to be divided between me first cousin, Jack Boyle, an' me
second cousin, Mick Finnegan, o' Santhry," he writ down
only, "me first an' second cousins," an 'the world an' his
wife are afther th' property now.

MRS. BOYLE. Now I know why Bentham left poor Mary
in th' lurch; I can see it all now—oh, is there not even a middlin' honest man left in th' world?

JOHNNY [*to* BOYLE]. An' you let us run into debt, an'
you borreyed money from everybody to fill yourself with
beer. An' now, you tell us the whole thing's a wash-out! Oh,
if it's thrue, I'm done with you, for you're worse than me
sisther Mary!

BOYLE. You hole your tongue, d'ye hear? I'll not take any
lip from you. Go an' get Bentham if you want satisfaction
for all that's afther happenin' us.

JOHNNY. I won't hole me tongue, I won't hole me tongue!
I'll tell you what I think of you, father an' all as you are
. . . you . . .

MRS. BOYLE. Johnny, Johnny, Johnny, for God's sake, be
quiet!

JOHNNY. I'll not be quiet, I'll not be quiet; he's a nice
father, isn't he? Is it any wondher Mary went asthray,
when . . .

MRS. BOYLE. Johnny, Johnny, for my sake be quiet—for
your mother's sake!

BOYLE. I'm goin' out now to have a few dhrinks with th'
last few makes I have, an 'tell that lassie o' yours not to be
here when I come back; for if I lay me eyes on her, I'll lay
me han's on her, an' if I lay me han's on her, I won't be ac-
countable for me actions!

JOHNNY. Take care somebody doesn't lay his han's on you —y'oul' . . .

MRS. BOYLE. Johnny, Johnny!

BOYLE [*at door, about to go out*]. Oh, a nice son, an' a nicer daughter, I have. [*Calling loudly upstairs.*] Joxer, Joxer, are you there?

JOXER [*from a distance*]. I'm here, More . . . ee . . . aar . . . i . . . tee!

BOYLE. I'm goin' down to Foley's—are you comin'?

JOXER. Come with you? With that sweet call me heart is stirred; I'm only waiting for the word, an' I'll be with you, like a bird!

[BOYLE *and* JOXER *pass the door going out.*]

JOHNNY [*throwing himself on the bed*]. I've a nice sisther, an' a nice father, there's no bettin' on it. I wish to God a bullet or a bomb had whipped me ou' o' this long ago! Not one o' yous, not one o' yous, have any thought for me!

MRS. BOYLE [*with passionate remonstrance*]. If you don't whisht, Johnny, you'll drive me mad. Who has kep' th' home together for the past few years—only me. An' who'll have to bear th' biggest part o' this throuble but me—but whinin' an' whingin' isn't goin' to do any good.

JOHNNY. You're to blame yourself for a gradle of it—givin' him his own way in everything, an' never assin' to check him, no matther what he done. Why didn't you look afther th' money? why . . .

[*There is a knock at the door;* MRS. BOYLE *opens it;* JOHNNY *rises on his elbow to look and listen; two men enter.*]

FIRST MAN. We've been sent up be th' Manager of the Hibernian Furnishing Co., Mrs. Boyle, to take back the furniture that was got a while ago.

MRS. BOYLE. Yous'll touch nothin' here—how do I know who yous are?

FIRST MAN [*showing a paper*]. There's the ordher, ma'am. [*Reading.*] A chest o' drawers, a table, wan easy an' two ordinary chairs; wan mirror; wan chestherfield divan, an' a wardrobe an' two vases. [*To his comrade.*] Come on, Bill, it's afther knockin' off time already.

JOHNNY. For God's sake, mother, run down to Foley's an' bring father back, or we'll be left without a stick.

[*The men carry out the table.*]

MRS. BOYLE. What good would it be? You heard what he said before he went out.

JOHNNY. Can't you thry? He ought to be here, an' the like of this goin' on.

[MRS. BOYLE *puts a shawl around her, as* MARY *enters.*]

MARY. What's up, mother? I met men carryin' away the table, an' everybody's talking about us not gettin' the money after all.

MRS. BOYLE. Everythin's gone wrong, Mary, everythin'. We're not gettin' a penny out o' the will, not a penny— I'll tell you all when I come back; I'm goin' for your father. [*She runs out.*]

JOHNNY [*to* MARY, *who has sat down by the fire*]. It's a wondher you're not ashamed to show your face here, afther what has happened.

[JERRY *enters slowly; there is a look of earnest hope on his face. He looks at* MARY *for a few moments.*]

JERRY [*softly*]. Mary!

[MARY *does not answer.*]

JERRY. Mary, I want to speak to you for a few moments, may I?

[MARY *remains silent;* JOHNNY *goes slowly into room on left.*

JERRY. Your mother has told me everything, Mary, and I have come to you. . . . I have come to tell you, Mary, that my love for you is greater and deeper than ever. . . .

MARY [*with a sob*]. Oh, Jerry, Jerry, say no more; all that is over now; anything like that is impossible now!

JERRY. Impossible? Why do you talk like that, Mary?

MARY. After all that has happened.

JERRY. What does it matter what has happened? We are young enough to be able to forget all those things. [*He catches her hand.*] Mary, Mary, I am pleading for your love. With Labor, Mary, humanity is above everything; we are the Leaders in the fight for a new life. I want to forget Bentham, I want to forget that you left me—even for awhile.

MARY. Oh, Jerry, Jerry, you haven't the bitter word of scorn for me after all.

JERRY [*passionately*]. Scorn! I love you, love you, Mary!

MARY [*rising, and looking him in the eyes*]. Even though . . .

JERRY. Even though you threw me over for another man; even though you gave me many a bitter word!

MARY. Yes, yes, I know; but you love me, even though . . . even though . . . I'm . . . goin' . . . goin' . . . [*He looks at her questioningly, and fear gathers in his eyes.*] Ah, I was thinkin' so. . . . You don't know everything!

JERRY [*poignantly*]. Surely to God, Mary, you don't mean that . . . that . . . that . . .

MARY. Now you know all, Jerry; now you know all!

JERRY. My God, Mary, have you fallen as low as that?

MARY. Yes, Jerry, as you say, I have fallen as low as that.

JERRY. I didn't mean it that way, Mary . . . it came on me so sudden, that I didn't mind what I was sayin'. . . . I never expected this—your mother never told me. . . . I'm sorry . . . God knows, I'm sorry for you, Mary.

MARY. Let us say no more, Jerry; I don't blame you for thinkin' it's terrible. . . . I suppose it is. . . . Everybody'll think the same. . . . It's only as I expected—your humanity is just as narrow as the humanity of the others.

JERRY. I'm sorry, all the same. . . . I shouldn't have troubled you. . . . I wouldn't if I'd known . . . if I can do anything for you . . . Mary . . . I will. [*He turns to go, and halts at the door.*]

MARY. Do you remember, Jerry, the verses you read when you gave the lecture in the Socialist Rooms some time ago, on Humanity's Strife with Nature?

JERRY. The verses—no; I don't remember them.

MARY. I do. They're runnin' in me head now—

> An' we felt the power that fashion'd
> All the lovely things we saw,
> That created all the murmur
> Of an everlasting law,
> Was a hand of force an' beauty,
> With an eagle's tearin' claw.
>
> Then we saw our globe of beauty
> Was an ugly thing as well,
> A hymn divine whose chorus

Was an agonizin' yell;
Like the story of a demon,
That an angel had to tell.

Like a glowin' picture by a
Hand unsteady, brought to ruin;
Like her craters, if their deadness
Could give life unto the moon;
Like the agonizing horror
Of a violin out of tune.

[*There is a pause, and* DEVINE *goes slowly out.*]
JOHNNY [*returning*]. Is he gone?
MARY. Yes.
[*The two men reënter.*]
FIRST MAN. We can't wait any longer for t'oul' fella—
sorry, miss, but we have to live as well as th' nex' man.
[*They carry out some things.*]
JOHNNY. Oh, isn't this terrible! . . . I suppose you told
him everything . . . couldn't you have waited for a few
days . . . he'd have stopped th' takin' of the things, if you'd
kep' your mouth shut. Are you burnin' to tell every one
of the shame you've brought on us?
MARY [*snatching up her hat and coat*]. Oh, this is un-
bearable! [*She rushes out.*]
FIRST MAN [*reëntering*]. We'll take the chest o' drawers
next—it's the heaviest.
[*The votive light flickers for a moment, and goes out.*]
JOHNNY [*in a cry of fear*]. Mother o' God, the light's
after goin' out!
FIRST MAN. You put the win' up me the way you bawled
that time. The oil's all gone, that's all.
JOHNNY [*with an agonizing cry*]. Mother o' God, there's
a shot I'm after gettin'!
FIRST MAN. What's wrong with you, man? Is it a fit
you're takin'?
JOHNNY. I'm after feelin' a pain in me breast, like the
tearin' by of a bullet!
FIRST MAN. He's goin' mad—it's a wondher they'd leave
a chap like that here be himself.
[Two IRREGULARS *enter swiftly; they carry revolvers;*

one goes over to JOHNNY; *the other covers the two furniture men.*]

FIRST IRREGULAR [*to the men, quietly and incisively*].
Who are you—what are yous doin' here—quick!

FIRST MAN. Removin' furniture that's not paid for.

IRREGULAR. Get over to the other end of the room an'
turn your faces to the wall—quick.

[*The two men turn their faces to the wall, with their
hands up.*]

SECOND IRREGULAR [*to* JOHNNY]. Come on, Sean Boyle,
you're wanted; some of us have a word to say to
you.

JOHNNY. I'm sick, I can't—what do you want with me?

SECOND IRREGULAR. Come on, come on; we've a distance
to go, an' haven't much time—come on.

JOHNNY. I'm an oul' comrade—yous wouldn't shoot an
oul' comrade.

SECOND IRREGULAR. Poor Tancred was an oul' comrade
o' yours, but you didn't think o' that when you gave him
away to the gang that sent him to his grave. But we've
no time to waste; come on—here, Dermot, ketch his arm.
[*To* JOHNNY.] Have you your beads?

JOHNNY. Me beads! Why do you ass me that, why do you
ass me that?

SECOND IRREGULAR. Go on, go on, march!

JOHNNY. Are yous goin' to do in a comrade—look at
me arm, I lost it for Ireland.

SECOND IRREGULAR. Commandant Tancred lost his life
for Ireland.

JOHNNY. Sacred Heart of Jesus, have mercy on me!
Mother o' God, pray for me—be with me now in the agonies
o' death! . . . Hail, Mary, full o' grace . . . the Lord is
. . . with Thee.

[*They drag out* JOHNNY BOYLE, *and the curtain falls.
When it rises again the most of the furniture is gone.* MARY
and MRS. BOYLE, *one on each side, are sitting in a darkened
room, by the fire; it is an hour later.*]

MRS. BOYLE. I'll not wait much longer . . .what did they
bring him away in the mothor for? Nugent says he thinks
they had guns . . . is me throubles never goin' to be over?
. . . If anything ud happen to poor Johnny, I think I'd lose

me mind. . . . I'll go to the Police Station, surely they ought to be able to do somethin'.

[*Below is heard the sound of voices.*]

MRS. BOYLE. Whisht, is that something? Maybe, it's your rather, though when I left him in Foley's he was hardly able to lift his head. Whisht!

[*A knock at the door, and the voice of* MRS. MADIGAN, *speaking very softly*]:

Mrs. Boyle, Mrs. Boyle.

[MRS. BOYLE *opens the door.*]

MRS. MADIGAN. Oh, Mrs. Boyle, God an' His Blessed Mother be with you this night!

MRS. BOYLE [*calmly*]. What is it, Mrs. Madigan? It's Johnny—something about Johnny.

MRS. MADIGAN. God send it's not, God send it's not Johnny!

MRS. BOYLE. Don't keep me waitin', Mrs. Madigan; I've gone through so much lately that I feel able for anything.

MRS. MADIGAN. Two polismen below wantin' you.

MRS. BOYLE. Wantin' me; an' why do they want me?

MRS. MADIGAN. Some poor fella's been found, an' they think it's, it's . . .

MRS. BOYLE. Johnny, Johnny!

MARY [*with her arms round her mother*]. Oh, mother, mother, me poor, darlin' mother.

MRS. BOYLE. Hush, hush, darlin'; you'll shortly have your own throuble to bear. [*To* MRS. MADIGAN.] An' why do the polis think it's Johnny, Mrs. Madigan?

MRS. MADIGAN. Because one o' the doctors knew him when he was attendin' with his poor arm.

MRS. BOYLE. Oh, it's thrue, then; it's Johnny, it's me son, me own son!

MARY. Oh, it's thrue, it's thrue what Jerry Devine says —there isn't a God, there isn't a God; if there was He wouldn't let these things happen!

MRS. BOYLE. Mary, Mary, you mustn't say them things. We'll want all the help we can get from God an' His Blessed Mother now! These things have nothin' to do with the Will o' God. Ah, what can God do agen the stupidity o' men!

MRS. MADIGAN. The polis want you to go with them to the hospital to see the poor body—they're waitin' below.

Mrs. Boyle. We'll go. Come, Mary, an' we'll never come back here agen. Let your father furrage for himself now; I've done all I could an' it was all no use—he'll be hopeless till the end of his days. I've got a little room in me sisther's where we'll stop till your throuble is over, an' then we'll work together for the sake of the baby.

Mary. My poor little child that'll have no father!

Mrs. Boyle. It'll have what's far betther—it'll have two mothers.

[*A rough voice shouting from below*]:
Are yous goin' to keep us waitin' for yous all night?

Mrs. Madigan [*going to the door, and shouting down*]. Take your hour, there, take your hour! If yous are in such a hurry, skip off, then, for nobody wants you here—if they did yous wouldn't be found. For you're the same as yous were undher the British Government—never where yous are wanted! As far as I can see, the polis as polis, in this city, is Null an' Void!

Mrs. Boyle. We'll go, Mary, we'll go; you to see your poor dead brother, an' me to see me poor dead son!

Mary. I dhread it, mother, I dhread it!

Mrs. Boyle. I forgot, Mary, I forgot; your poor oul' selfish mother was only thinkin' of herself. No, no, you mustn't come—it wouldn't be good for you. You go on to me sisther's an' I'll face th' ordeal meself. Maybe I didn't feel sorry enough for Mrs. Tancred when her poor son was found as Johnny's been found now—because he was a Diehard! Ah, why didn't I remember that then he wasn't a Die-hard or a Stater, but only a poor dead son! It's well I remember all that she said—an' it's my turn to say it now: What was the pain I suffered, Johnny, bringin' you into the world to carry you to your cradle to the pains I'll suffer carryin' you out o' the world to bring you to your grave! Mother o' God, Mother o' God, have pity on us all! Blessed Virgin, where were you when me darlin' son was riddled with bullets, when me darlin' son was riddled with bullets? Sacred Heart o' Jesus, take away our hearts o' stone, and give us hearts o' flesh! Take away this murdherin' hate, an' give us Thine own eternal love! [*They all go slowly out.*]

[*There is a pause; then a sound of shuffling steps on the*

stairs outside. The door opens and BOYLE *and* JOXER, *both of them very drunk, enter.*]

BOYLE. I'm able to go no farther. . . . Two polis, ey . . . what were they doin' here, I wondher? . . . Up to no good, anyhow . . . an' Juno an' that lovely daughter o' mine with them. [*Taking a sixpence from his pocket and looking at it.*] Wan single, solithary tanner left out of all I borreyed. . . . [*He lets it fall.*] The last o' the Mohicans. . . . The blinds is down, Joxer, the blinds is down!

JOXER [*walking unsteadily across the room, and anchoring at the bed*]. Put all . . . your throubles . . . in your oul' kit bag . . . an' smile . . . smile . . . smile!

BOYLE. The counthry'll have to steady itself . . . it's goin' . . . to hell. . . . Where'r all . . . the chairs . . . gone to . . . steady itself, Joxer. . . . Chairs'll . . . have to . . . steady themselves. . . . No matther . . . what any- one may . . . say. . . . Irelan' sober . . . is Irelan' . . . free.

JOXER [*stretching himself on the bed*]. Chains . . . an' . . . slaveree . . . that's a darlin' motto . . . a daaarlin' . . . motto!

BOYLE. If th' worst comes . . . to th' worse . . . I can join a . . . flyin' . . . column. . . . I done . . . me bit . . . in Easther Week . . . had no business . . . to . . . be . . . there . . . but Captain Boyle's Captain Boyle!

JOXER. Breathes there a man with soul . . . so . . . de . . . ad . . . this . . . me . . . o . . . wn, me nat . . . ive l . . . an'!

BOYLE [*subsiding into a sitting posture on the floor*]. Com- mandant Kelly died . . . in them . . . arms . . . Joxer. . . . Tell me Volunteer Butties . . . says he . . . that . . . I died for . . . Irelan'!

JOXER. D'jever rade Willie . . . Reilly . . . an' his . . . own . . . Colleen . . . Bawn? It's a darlin' story, a daarl- in' story!

BOYLE. I'm telling you . . . Joxer . . . th' whole worl's . . . in a terr . . . ible state o' . . . chassis!

THE BIG HOUSE

FOUR SCENES IN ITS LIFE

By Lennox Robinson

CHARACTERS

In the order of their appearance.

ATKINS
REV. HENRY BROWN
CAPTAIN MONTGOMERY DESPARD
KATE ALCOCK
ST. LEGER ALCOCK
VANDALEUR O'NEILL
MRS. ALCOCK
ANNIE DALY
THREE YOUNG MEN

SCENE I. The drawing room at Ballydonal House.
A November morning, 1918.
SCENE II. The dining room at Ballydonal House.
A June evening, 1921.
SCENE III. The same. A February night, 1923.
SCENE IV. A corner of the garden early the next morning.

SCENE I: *The large drawing room at Ballydonal House. The*
room must give the impression of size, on a small stage one
of its sides must not be seen but should be "masked" by
a large Chinese screen. At the back are two large windows,
they can be either Georgian type or mock-Gothic, there
are heavy curtains on them. On the side of the room which
is seen is a door up stage and, lower down, a fireplace. A
profusion of furniture, some good, some bad, profusion of
small unimportant pictures, photographs, china on the
walls; the effect of all being a comfortable room contain-

*ing the vestigia of generations, the mid-Victorian vestigia
prevailing. There is a bright fire and bright sunshine outside the windows. It is about ten-thirty on a November
morning, 1918. The room is empty. A door on the unseen
side of the room opens and the voice of* ATKINS, *the butler,
is heard.*

ATKINS. Mr. Brown to see you, sir.

[MR. BROWN *appears round the screen, a middle-aged,
bearded clergyman.*]

BROWN [*looking round the room*]. Atkins! Atkins!

ATKINS [*coming back but still unseen*]. Did you call,
sir?

BROWN. Mr. Alcock isn't here.

ATKINS [*coming into sight round the screen and looking
round the room. He is a small stout man of sixty-five, his
gait is a little rolling, his voice a little thick, he is obviously
a little drunk.*] I beg your pardon, your reverence, he was
here a minute ago. [*He crosses to the door above the fireplace, opens it and looks into the next room. He shuts it
again.*] There's no one in the small drawing room but Captain
Despard. I'll send looking for him.

BROWN. Thank you.

ATKINS. He'll likely have walked out to the yard to see
do they understand about the bell.

BROWN. What bell?

ATKINS. The big bell, Father—your reverence, I mean—
the yard bell. It's to be rung at eleven o'clock and it's not
been rung these twenty years.

BROWN. I see. Part of the celebrations?

ATKINS. But indeed he needn't be bothering. I have Paddy
O'Reilly tutored in the bell. He's to be there since ten o'clock,
the rope in his hand, the cook's alarm clock hanging on the
wall in front of his face and on the stroke of eleven he's to
start bell-ringing, ring for a quarter of an hour and then
walk into the kitchen for the bottle of stout the master's
after ordering for him.

BROWN. I see. Well, it's a great day.

ATKINS. It is, Father.

BROWN. You'll be expecting your grandson home now.
Is he still in Salonika?

ATKINS. He is. When he couldn't get through them Dardanelles he gev up and he's sitting in Salonika ever since.

BROWN. He's been luckier than some. . . . Will you try and find Mr. Alcock? I can't wait long, I have a lot to do this morning.

ATKINS. I will, your reverence. There's the papers—this morning's *Constitution* and Saturday's *Irish Times*. We don't get it till the morning now since the second post was cut off, bad luck to it. But I suppose it's the same way at the rectory.

BROWN. It is indeed.

ATKINS. Ah well, please God now the Germans are bet we'll have posts and sugar and everything back the way it used to be long ago. Will I bring you a glass of sherry while you're waiting?

BROWN. No, thank you.

ATKINS. You'll excuse me for asking, Father—your reverence, I mean—I forgot you were so mad for the temperance. I'll have the master for you now as fast as I can get him. [*He ambles out.* MR. BROWN *opens the* Irish Times *and glances at it. From the door above the fire enters* CAPTAIN DESPARD, *twenty-five years old, in uniform, he limps a little. He stops on seeing* BROWN.]

BROWN [*going to him, holding out his hand*]. How d'ye do? You are Captain Despard, I'm sure.

DESPARD. Oh—ah—yes.

BROWN. My name is Brown, I'm the parson here. St. Leger —Mr. Alcock—told me you were coming here.

DESPARD. Oh—yes.

BROWN. You've been having a nasty time with your foot, haven't you? Is it better?

DESPARD. Nearly all right. I hope I'll be able to go back in another week or ten days.

BROWN. But fortunately there'll be nothing to go back to.

DESPARD. Nothing?

BROWN. No war. Only half an hour more of it, thank goodness.

DESPARD. I doubt if it's as over as people think it is.

BROWN. But President Wilson's terms—

DESPARD. Those damned Yankees—beg pardon—but this

Armistice business is a bad mistake, we should have marched through to Berlin.

BROWN. Hm! But if we get all we want without losing another man or killing another man—

DESPARD. Oh, losing! Killing! It's not a picnic.

BROWN. No, indeed, it isn't. . . . You were very good to poor Reginald. It made a great difference to Mrs. Alcock to know there was a friend with him when he died.

DESPARD. There wasn't much I could do.

BROWN. Still, it made a difference. Have you ever come across her other boy, Ulick?

DESPARD. Only once. A rather quiet dull sort of chap, isn't he? Not like poor old Reg.

BROWN. No, he's very different from Reginald. . . . I suppose you have no idea where Mr. Alcock is?

DESPARD. I haven't seen him since breakfast.

BROWN. Atkins is supposed to be looking for him, but Atkins is a little—well, he started to celebrate early.

DESPARD. Atkins? Oh, that's the butler. Why, he started to celebrate last night. You should have seen him handing round the soup. It was a marvel, but not a drop spilled.

BROWN. Poor Atkins. It's his one failing.

DESPARD. Typically Irish old fellow, isn't he?

BROWN. I hope not.

DESPARD. Oh, but he's a delightful old chap. And the rest of it doesn't seem to be so awfully Irish.

BROWN. The rest of it?

DESPARD. Well, the house itself, the way it's run, and—and everything.

BROWN. Do they read *Castle Rackrent* in the trenches?

DESPARD [*staring*]. I don't think so, never heard of it. What do you mean?

BROWN. Nothing. I withdraw my insinuation. I started by thinking how blunderingly English your conclusions were, I beg your pardon. Second thoughts make me give you credit for exceedingly sharp penetration.

DESPARD. Oh, thank you.

BROWN. I'm sure you're thinking that we haven't known each other long enough for me to say that sort of thing to you. But here in the country fresh acquaintances are so rare that I've got into the impolite habit of taking short cuts. You must forgive me.

DESPARD. Oh, rot. There's nothing to forgive. I suppose I was a bit taken aback by your talking of my penetration. What the dickens have I penetrated?

BROWN. Mr. Alcock told me you have never been in Ireland before. You've been in this house for a day and two nights and in that short time you've put your finger on the great fact that it is not typical. It isn't. It's a protest against the type.

DESPARD. The type being?

BROWN. Not quite what you think it is. Not always slovenly and ramshackle. The difference doesn't lie in the obvious things you've seen, it's not that this room is clean and decent and comfortable. Irish country houses frequently are that, it's not that your dinner was eatable and your bath hot—

DESPARD. Oh well, Irish hospitality—it's traditional, you know.

BROWN. But is St. Leger traditional, is Kate—Miss Alcock?

DESPARD. She's a jolly fine girl.

BROWN. You won't realize how fine until you see the others!

DESPARD. What others? She's the only daughter.

BROWN. I mean the types. Without an idea. With no culture. Ignorant. Don't know whether the portraits that hang in their dining rooms are eighteenth-century masterpieces or photogravures, don't know if the silver they use every day is old Irish or modern Brummagem. Don't know the history of their own family, don't know Irish history. Have nothing but a few religious prejudices and very good health. Can't even grow decent flowers.

DESPARD. Well, they're great sportswomen, Irish sportswomen are traditional, you know.

BROWN. That's the least Irish thing about them, your real Irishwoman despises sport, she thinks its only use is keeping the men out of mischief. And the Irish gentleman! Ignorant. Asleep. Look at their libraries. A splendid collection of eighteenth-century classics, twenty volumes of sermons of the early nineteenth century—after that nothing. They're divorced from all reality.

DESPARD. Oh, I say!

BROWN. Absurd of me to blaze out like this, isn't it? But I know what I'm talking about. My name's as common as dirt, but I'm from County Wexford and County Wexford Browns fancy themselves. They came over with your people once upon a time. I'm attacking my own class. And I'm extraordinarily interested in watching this house and the fight it's making.

DESPARD. Fight? What the dickens is it fighting for?

BROWN. Its life.

[KATE ALCOCK *comes in, her arms are full of Michaelmas daisies.*]

BROWN. Ah, Kate! Good morning.

KATE. Mr. Brown! I haven't a finger. Aren't they lovely? They're lasting so long this year. What a morning. Such sunshine. You've made each other's acquaintance?

BROWN. Yes.

KATE. You've heard the great news of course? Aunt Kat wired to father from London first thing this morning, we knew it at breakfast time.

BROWN. Miss Doyle at the Post Office made no bones of sharing the news, the whole village knew it before you did and she sent a messenger to the rectory on a bicycle.

KATE. Well, I don't blame her. Can you believe that the horrible thing will be killed dead at eleven o'clock, in less than half an hour?

BROWN. Captain Despard doesn't believe it will be killed.

KATE. Oh, soldiers are such optimists. Where's the boss?

BROWN. He's being looked for.

KATE. You're coming to dinner tonight, I hope. With this news it's going to be a celebration.

BROWN. That's what I called in to say. Alice's cold is almost gone, and she'll be delighted to come, for, as you say, it will be an occasion.

KATE. It's only ourselves, you know, not a dinner-party.

BROWN. Gracious, we didn't expect a dinner-party. When were you at a dinner-party last, Kate? Here, in County Cork, I mean?

KATE. Mother and I were counting up the other day. Not since the first winter of the war when those people took Knock for the shooting. They were awful bounders, but they did manage to gather fifteen people for a dinner-party. . . . My goodness, Monty, you're going to have a dull time of it here. . . . I told the boss it was cruel to invite you.

DESPARD. You forget. I invited myself.

KATE. Well, on your own head be it. We tried having Colonials here for their leave, men, you know, who had no relations or friends to go to. The South Africans didn't mind much, but the Australians always, after one day, sent themselves telegrams recalling themselves to the front. . . . I must get some more vases. Here's the boss.

[MR. ALCOCK *comes in,* KATE *goes out.*]

ALCOCK. Henry!

BROWN. Good morning, St. Leger. I couldn't let you know yesterday whether Alice would be well enough to come over tonight. I've come now to tell you that she can.

ALCOCK. Good. You've heard the news?

BROWN. Yes.

ALCOCK. In our quiet way we're going to let things rip tonight, I depend on Captain Despard to make things lively.

DESPARD. Don't expect too much from me.

ALCOCK. Oh, I've another string to my bow. [*To* BROWN.] I've just been down to that place you don't approve of— the wine-cellar.

BROWN. Atkins has been looking for you.

ALCOCK. I didn't see him, and I should have thought his feet would have turned instinctively in that direction. If anyone knows the way to the cellar he does. I haven't been there for six months or more but, thanks to Atkins, it's like Mother Hubbard's cupboard. You know all we take—a little claret at dinner, my small whiskey before I go to bed— but Atkins! My dear Despard, that old chap has an unerring palate. I bought a couple of dozen of cheap Burgundy, not bad at all, but cheap, I thought I'd buy him off with them. He tried one bottle but then concentrated on my best Pommard, and there's only one bottle of brandy left. He seems to have a conscience about champagne, it is sacred in his sight and you shall have plenty of it tonight.

BROWN. You can leave my name out of it.

ALCOCK. Hang it all, the night of the Armistice you must make an exception. Mrs. Brown is T.T., but I'm sure she'll drink her glass tonight like a good 'un.

BROWN. I wouldn't put it past her. Women seem to be able to square their consciences in a way we can't.

ALCOCK. By the way, I'm glad I've seen you beforehand. Tonight *is* an occasion and we'll drink a toast—the King and Victory. But not a word. No speeches or anything like that. Mary's feeling it a bit, of course. I know Reg is very much in her mind and if we once started to say things anything might happen.

BROWN. You needn't be afraid, I won't want to say anything, I couldn't trust myself. I'll be thinking of Dick.

ALCOCK. Of course. [*To* DESPARD.] He lost his only boy at Gallipoli. Such a splendid chap.

DESPARD. Rotten luck.

BROWN. When did you hear from Ulick?

ALCOCK. Yesterday. Fit as a fiddle. Only a few lines, things had been pretty strenuous of course.

BROWN. I wonder how soon you can expect him back.

ALCOCK. His mother has set her heart on having him for Christmas.

ATKINS [*unseen*]. Mr. O'Neill.

[*A gawky common-looking young man comes in.*]

ALCOCK. Hallo, Vandaleur.

VANDALEUR [*in a very marked brogue*]. Good morning, Alcock. Good morning, Mr. Brown.

ALCOCK. Mr. O'Neill, Captain Despard. [*They shake hands.*]

DESPARD. How d'ye do?

VANDALEUR. I hope ye're well. [*To* ALCOCK.] I was riding in this direction and me mother asked me to leave in a note, she and the gerr'ls want Mrs. Alcock and Kate to go over to tea next week. Here it is. 'Tis a bit crushed I'm afraid.

ALCOCK [*ringing the bell*]. I'll get it sent to Mary. Will you wait for the answer? Sit down.

VANDALEUR [*sitting*]. Thank ye. . . . Me fawther's sick.

ALCOCK. I'm sorry to hear that. Is he seriously ill?

VANDALEUR. I don't know. . . . I sold the black mare.

ALCOCK. Oh, did you get a good price?

VANDALEUR. Rotten.

BROWN. I'll go over and see your father this afternoon.

VANDALEUR. Ye needn't then.

BROWN. I can quite easily go, and if he's ill—

VANDALEUR. Sure he went to Cork by the morning train.

BROWN. Oh! Will he be back tonight?

VANDALEUR. Well, he was going to the doctor, and it would depind on what he said whether he'd end up the day in the hospital or in the County Club, but I think meself he'll be for the club.

BROWN. Oh! [*Enter* ATKINS.]

ALCOCK. Take this to the mistress please, and tell her that Mr. O'Neill is waiting for the answer.

ATKINS. Yes, sir [*he takes the note and goes*].

ALCOCK. Well, this is a great day, Vandaleur.

VANDALEUR. Indeed, 'tis wonderful weather for this time of year.

ALCOCK. I wasn't thinking of the weather.

VANDALEUR. There was a great turn-out for Dicky Smith's funeral a-Choosday, why weren't you there?

ALCOCK. I meant the war—the Armistice.

VANDALEUR. Oh, to be sure. Is it to be today or tomorrow?

ALCOCK. Within an hour.

VANDALEUR. Fancy that now. I suppose they'll fire off a big gun like or ring a bell.

DESPARD. Were you fighting?

VANDALEUR. I was not. [*To* ALCOCK.] I met Michael Dempsey on the avenue and he was telling me that you have some sheep sick and that one's after dying on you.

ALCOCK. Yes, Kate's in a great stew about it. But I've written to the "vet" and I heard from him this morning. He's going to wire this morning and let me know if he can come today or tomorrow.

VANDALEUR. Is it the fella from Knock you mean?

ALCOCK. Yes.

VANDALEUR. He's a bloody bad "vet." He lost me a mare and a foal last year. I'd rather have the district nurse than that fella. When they told me at home 'tother day that a cow was sick "Send for Mrs. Maguire," says I. "Send for

Mrs. Maguire." That's all I'd say. Wasn't I right, Captain?

[DESPARD *merely looks contemptuous*.]

BROWN. Well, I hope the cow survived.

VANDALEUR. Of course she did, she's lepping round giving gallons of milk. 'Tis all a cod, inspectors and departments and tillage. What the divil do the lads that make the regulations know about tillage? They wouldn't know the difference between wheat and oats.

ALCOCK. Well, we don't want to starve.

VANDALEUR. There's plenty to ate in this part of the country.

ALCOCK. But in the towns, in England—

VANDALEUR. Ah, let them go to the divil.

[MRS. ALCOCK *and* KATE *come in*.]

MRS. ALCOCK. Good morning, Van. Will you wait a minute while I write a note to your mother? I won't be long.

VANDALEUR. Sure there's no hurry. Good morning, Kate.

KATE. Good morning, Van. Sit down, don't mind me, I'm only doing these flowers.

VANDALEUR [*sitting*]. Flossie and Maggie and Helana and Gertie sent you their love.

KATE. Please give them my love.

VANDALEUR [*after a pause*]. Sissy sent you her love too.

KATE. Give my love to Sissy.

ALCOCK [*to* DESPARD]. Do you feel up to a stroll?

DESPARD. I'm afraid not. I've got to rest my foot as much as possible.

VANDALEUR. Are you after hurting your foot?

DESPARD. Yes.

ALCOCK. He got a nasty knock in France.

VANDALEUR. France?

DESPARD. There happens to be a war on there.

VANDALEUR. Sure I know. . . . Jerry Mangan's not the better of the fall he got, yet.

KATE. Oh, did he get a fall? I hadn't heard.

VANDALEUR. Lepping a small bit of a fence on that old red mare of his. Sure he's the rottenest rider in the country.

ALCOCK. I wish I had a horse to offer you, Despard, the only beast in the stables is the old carriage mare.

KATE. I'm sure the Goods or the O'Sullivans would lend him a horse.

VANDALEUR. Sure me fawther would lend him one. What about Prince Chawming?

DESPARD [*shortly*]. No, thank you.

VANDALEUR. He's quiet but a good goer and a very handy lepper. . . . You know him, Kate?

KATE. Yes. . . . Have you any flowers left, Van?

VANDALEUR. I don't know. 'Tis the gerr'ls looks after the flowers.

MRS. ALCOCK [*getting up*]. There, Van. Now don't forget it in your pocket.

VANDALEUR. I won't, Mrs. Alcock. Me mother sent you her love.

MRS. ALCOCK. Thank you.

VANDALEUR. And so did the gerr'ls. At least I didn't see Helana when I was leaving, but I'm sure she would have if I had seen her.

MRS. ALCOCK. Give them all my love and say I'm looking forward to seeing them next week. How's your father?

VANDALEUR. Sick.

BROWN. Are you in a great hurry, Van, or will you walk down the avenue with me?

VANDALEUR. Sure I'm in no hurry.

BROWN. Well, unfortunately, I am, so if you don't mind we'll be off now. I want to talk to you about the graveyard at Kilbeg. Good-by, Mrs. Alcock, till this evening.

MRS. ALCOCK. Seven-thirty. I'm so glad Alice is better, make her wrap up well.

ALCOCK. I'm sending the brougham for you at seven o'clock. Now don't start to protest, it's all been arranged.

BROWN. It's very kind of you. The little walk really wouldn't have done her any harm. . . . *Au revoir.*

[BROWN *goes to the door, while* VANDALEUR *awkwardly and formally shakes hands with everyone. He finishes with* DESPARD.]

VANDALEUR. You're sure you won't have Prince Chawming?

DESPARD. Certain. . . . Thanks.

BROWN. Come on, Vandaleur. [*They go out.*]

KATE. Go on, Monty, say it. Don't spare our feelings. "What a lout!" Or was it something worse, something unprintable?

DESPARD. In present company "lout" will have to do. Who is he? A farmer's son?

KATE [*laughing*]. Farmer's son! Vandaleur O'Neill!

ALCOCK. If family counts for anything he' gets full marks. A quarter of him is Irish—the best old Irish, the other three-quarters are successive English invasions. Compared to him we're second-rate interlopers. His father is first cousin and heir to Lord Rathconnell, but the father is drinking himself to death, he won't last a twelvemonth longer. Van doesn't drink, Van will be the next lord.

DESPARD. That clodhopper?

MRS. ALCOCK. Poor boy, it's not his fault, and he's really a good boy.

ALCOCK. No, it's not his fault, it's his wicked old father and his foolish mother. He was sent to a preparatory school in England; at the end of the first term he refused to go back, and his father and mother gave in. That's all the education he ever had. He can just sign his name, I suppose he can read. He's lived at home ever since with his father and mother and his five sisters.

KATE. Flossie and Sissy and Maggie and Gertie and "Helana"! And we've got to have tea with them all next week. Why did you say we'd go, mother?

MRS. ALCOCK. My dear, what could I do? Mrs. O'Neill asked me for *any* day next week. I couldn't say I was engaged for the whole week, that's simply unbelievable in Ballydonal.

KATE. I don't mind Van, I like poor Van. It's the "gerr'ls," as he calls them. What day did you say you'd go?

MRS. ALCOCK. Wednesday.

KATE. Thank God.

MRS. ALCOCK. Why?

KATE. I've two committees that afternoon.

MRS. ALCOCK. I don't believe it.

KATE. It's quite true. Poultry Society and Library.

MRS. ALCOCK. You and your committees!

KATE. They're better than tea with the O'Neills.

[ATKINS *appears*.]

ATKINS. There's a lad of the O'Flynns wishful to speak to your ladyship.

MRS. ALCOCK. Who?

ATKINS. One of the O'Flynns from the cross.

MRS. ALCOCK. Are you sure he doesn't want the master?

ATKINS. He asked specially for your ladyship.

MRS. ALCOCK. All right, I'll come. [ATKINS *goes.*] Atkins is drunk, St. Leger. He always ladyships me when he's drunk.

ALCOCK. Yes, my dear.

MRS. ALCOCK. Can't you do something? Can't you speak to him?

ALCOCK. Not much use while he's drunk. And I suppose there is some excuse this morning.

MRS. ALCOCK. If there wasn't you'd invent one. You're too easy-going.

ALCOCK. He's been here for more than forty years.

MRS. ALCOCK. Will you do what I've been asking you to do for the last twenty years? Will you get him to give you his key of the cellar?

ALCOCK. My dear, that would hurt his feelings.

MRS. ALCOCK. What about *my* feelings? Captain Despard will go back to England talking about us being so Irish. And I'm not Irish, Captain Despard, thank God. I'm a Hampshire woman, a respectable Hampshire woman, in exile, with a drunken Irish butler, and now I've got to go and talk to a "lad of the O'Flynns." Even after living here for twenty years I won't understand half of what he says. I suppose he wants a bottle of medicine for his old grandmother, or he wants to sell me a rabbit he's poached a hundred yards from our own front-door. [*Half vexed, half amused, she goes out.*]

DESPARD. Mrs. Alcock's quite wrong, I'm enjoying myself immensely.

ALCOCK. Ah, but that's just what you mustn't do. You mustn't "enjoy" us as if we were a comic story or a play. My wife would like you to take us as seriously as you'd take any country-house in England. She tries—she's tried for twenty-five years—to keep us serious, but always at our most proper moments Atkins or a lad of the O'Flynns keeps breaking in. You remember Dr. Johnson's friend?

DESPARD [*not remembering*]. Yes, oh yes.

ALCOCK. There's a great deal to be said for marrying out of your race. I like every now and then seeing Ballydonal through her foreign, hostile eyes. A touch of Hampshire does us no harm, keeps us from becoming like the O'Neills.

KATE. They married the foreigner, as you said yourself, but it didn't save them.

ALCOCK. True, it doesn't always work.

DESPARD. It's all part of what the padre was saying—that you're not the type.

ALCOCK. Oh, Brown talks a lot of nonsense. I keep telling him that we *are* the type, people like the O'Neills are the dreadful variants.

DESPARD. Is the padre himself up to type?

ALCOCK. He's a gentleman by birth and education—no, I'm afraid he's no longer the typical Irish parson. I believe you can be ordained now without having been to college—to what you and I would call a college. And the priests are as bad. Old Canon Maguire, who was here for forty years, was a traveled, cultivated gentleman, it was a pleasure and an honor to have him to dinner, but he's dead and gone and the new parish priest—impossible—a barbarian.

KATE. I'm sure priests are like soldiers. Didn't Bernard Shaw say that there are only two kinds of soldiers—young soldiers and old soldiers? There are only three kinds of priests, young, old and middle-aged. The old are, as father says, charmers, the middle-aged are rather dreadful generally, but I adore the curates, especially the Republican ones, they're such splendid workers.

DESPARD. Kate!

ALCOCK. Yes, she's hand-in-glove with them. The other day I came round a corner of the road, between here and the village, and I found a curate sitting on a pile of stones giving my daughter a lesson in Irish while she mended a puncture in his bicycle.

KATE. Well, he had cut his hand; I didn't want him to get the cut full of dirt. And he was a very old friend, a great pet, he got into trouble with the bishop in 1916.

DESPARD. About what?

ALCOCK [*dryly*]. Not theology!

KATE [*airily*]. Drilling and guns and a plan to blow up a military barracks.

DESPARD. Oh, no! Good God!

KATE. A fact.

DESPARD. Are the Protestant curates as bad as that?

KATE. Worse. They play tennis.

[MRS. ALCOCK *comes in.*]

MRS. ALCOCK. You must come, St. Leger, the boy is trying to get at you through me. Something about a brother of his who's been arrested. One of those Sinn Feiners, I think. He wants you to write "a bit of a note" to somewhere or someone, he's not sure to whom.

ALCOCK. Oh, these notes! Do you want a character, Despard, for some brother or cousin of yours whom I have never seen? I shall be delighted to give you one, I am a past master in the art of describing and praising the unknown. I'll come, Mary.

KATE [*to him as he goes out*]. Any wire from the "vet"?

ALCOCK. No, nothing so far.

[MR. *and* MRS. ALCOCK *go out.*]

KATE. Poor father!

DESPARD. Why poor?

KATE. Oh, I don't know. . . . Yes, I do. It's not his *metier*, all this.

DESPARD. This?

KATE. Notes to magistrates, sick sheep and general rural uplift. His place is in the music room, at his piano.

DESPARD. Does he play the piano?

KATE. Does he play—? Why, it's what he does do, much too well to be quite respectable in an Irish country gentleman. He was never intended for Ballydonal, he was in the Foreign Office, but his elder brother broke his neck hunting, and so he had to come back here.

DESPARD. Yes, it's no sort of a life for him or for you.

KATE. Oh, I'm not like father, I love it. . . . There's something I want you to tell me—how soon do you think we may expect Ulick home, not on leave, for good and all I mean? Supposing this armistice means peace, how soon is he likely to be able to get clear of the army?

DESPARD. Awfully hard to say. Three or four months perhaps, if he pushes hard.

KATE. Oh, he'll push like the dickens . . . December, January, February . . . he might be home in March.

DESPARD. Of course he might get some leave before then. Your mother told me he's due leave.

KATE. Yes, he hates fighting so much that he has a sort of conscience about pressing for leave and allows himself to be passed over. But if the war is over he'll have no conscience, he'll move heaven and earth to get out of the army.

DESPARD. To come and live here?

KATE. Yes. . . . And you go back to the law, I suppose?

DESPARD. Not if I can help it. I'll move heaven and earth to stay in the army.

KATE. You like it so much, Monty?

DESPARD. It's taught me what living is.

KATE. It seems to me like four years stolen out of life.

DESPARD. Yes, I know, it's been hard on girls, not much fun and all the men away. . . . Do you remember, Kate, what I said to you that night in London, the night before I went back to France?

KATE. I'm sure we all said a lot of silly things.

DESPARD. I said a lot of things to you, but I didn't say one thing. . . . I don't believe it's right for a chap to get engaged—married perhaps—when there's a war on. It's not fair to the girl. That's why I didn't ask you to marry me.

KATE. Oh, there were lots of other reasons. Feminine ones. That pretty Scotch girl, for instance.

DESPARD. Lulu Mackenzie? Nonsense. I liked you better than all the others rolled together.

KATE. That's only because I was Reggie's sister, your best friend's sister.

DESPARD. No, really. Do you remember Billie Dale? Vulgar little chap, but he had a knack of hitting the nail on the head. Well, *he* said to me that night, "Monty, the little Irish girl has all the others beaten to a frazzle."

KATE. That dreadful Mr. Dale!

DESPARD. As dreadful as you like, but it's God's truth.

KATE. To begin with, I'm not particularly little, I haven't gray eyes and long dark lashes, I don't speak with a fascinating brogue—

DESPARD. Your voice—

KATE. Stop! I remember you telling me that your favorite play was *Peg o' my Heart*. Well, I'm none of your Pegs. I don't go about with an Irish terrier under my arm, I don't much like dogs, I've no April moods, I don't go from tears to laughter in a moment, I don't believe I've cried once in ten years.

DESPARD. You're charming!

KATE. Much you know what I'm like! You've only known me in London spending a giddy fortnight there, on a holiday and consequently exactly the opposite of what I really am. I'm quite different here. Before you were out of your bath this morning I had fed my hens, when I've finished these flowers I'm going to garden till lunch—not a lady-like snipping off of dead flowers, really hard digging with a spade, forking dung probably. After lunch I go to the creamery for a committee meeting. I ride to the committee. I don't ride there on an unbroken pony, bare-backed, with my hair flying, I ride on a bicycle, a rather old and dirty bicycle, and I wear a rather old and dirty tweed coat and skirt. After the meeting I go to a poultry lecture, after the lecture to an Irish class. I'll have to leave the class early because you're here, and dinner tonight is an affair. If you weren't here I wouldn't be home in time for dinner, and I'd have tea and bread and jam when I came back. That's the real me, the me I like to be.

DESPARD. Yes, because you've never had the chance to be anything else.

KATE. I think I could have been other things.

DESPARD. You can be other things now.

KATE. Monty, are you asking me to marry you?

DESPARD. Of course.

KATE. I wish you wouldn't.

DESPARD. I can't help myself.

KATE. Oh, yes, you can. It's all sentimentalism, pegofmyheartiness.

DESPARD. You liked me in London. Don't you like me here?

KATE. It's different here, you're not part of my life here, you're part of the London holiday—a very nice part, Monty.

DESPARD. Make London your life, have Ballydonal for holiday.

KATE. Ah, there's Ulick.

DESPARD. What the devil—beg pardon—what has your brother got to do with it?

KATE. Everything.

DESPARD. Everything?

KATE. He's like me; we think Ballydonal *is* life, **our** life.

Of course, as long as Reggie was alive he was the eldest and he'd inherit, but he hated the country, he went straight from school into the army; he'd never want to live here. We planned that Ulick should rent the pláce from him or live here as sort of manager-agent. Ulick's all father isn't, a born farmer, a born public man, but he didn't depend merely on his instincts; he spent five years learning the newest and best ways of farming, and I've learnt lots of things you'd think silly and dull about poultry and milk and vegetables and bees, we were just ready to start here together—Ballydonal Limited—and then this horrible war came and upset everything, and I've been carrying on as best I could and Ulick's been drilling and marching and breaking his heart to be back, but now the war's over and Reggie's dead and—

DESPARD. Well?

KATE. I don't see why I shouldn't say it, even to his best friend. I'm glad Reggie's dead, glad he died like that, honorably, with letters after his name and mentioned in despatches and all that sort of thing. You knew him well, better than I did probably, and you knew he was handsome and popular, and that he gambled too much and drank too much and got himself mixed up in at least one very shady affair—

DESPARD. Reg was a bit reckless, but there was no harm in him. Just Irish high spirits.

KATE. Just Irish dissipation. Just what has tumbled the big houses into ruins or into the hands of the big graziers or into the hands of the Roman Catholic Church. Vandaleur O'Neills! Not poor Van himself, but the generations of your Irish high spirits that have gone to the making of Van. Reggie wouldn't have cared if he had dragged Ballydonal down. But Ulick and I do care—tremendously. We're going to hold our heads above water, hold Ballydonal above water, proudly and decently.

DESPARD. Milk and hens and turnips! It seems a poor ambition.

KATE. Oh, it's not milk for milk's sake exactly. Everything's mixed up in it, the country, the people, the whole thing.

DESPARD. Good Lord, you're not a Nationalist, are you?

KATE. I thought fervent Nationalism was part of the

make-up of your little gray-eyed Irish girl. . . . But no, I don't think I'm a Nationalist, I don't bother about politics, they crop up sometimes at committee meetings and are a great nuisance, and that's all I know about them.

DESPARD. But you learn Irish.

KATE. Yes. You learnt Latin.

DESPARD. I had to. It was part of the make-up of my career.

KATE. Irish is part of my make-up. I don't like it much; I don't suppose you liked Latin much. Ulick's better at it than I am; he really likes it, he even has managed to keep it up in spite of the war; he'll fit perfectly into the Bally-donal picture.

DESPARD. Hasn't it occurred to you that Ulick may marry? Where would you come in then?

KATE. I wouldn't come in, I'd go out.

DESPARD. So you'd much better marry me. I believe we'd make a good thing of marriage. I'd understand you. After all, my grandmother was Irish—from Ulster.

KATE. Ulster!

DESPARD. That's where I get my sense of humor from.

KATE. I see. . . . These Irish grandmothers!

DESPARD. Think it over, give me a chance. I'm here for a week anyway.

KATE. If I answered you now, Monty, I'd say "no." If you want me to think it over you must wait until I've seen Ulick.

DESPARD. I don't see the necessity of talking it over with him.

KATE. Oh, maybe I won't talk it over with him, but I just want to see him, see him here, and—and—oh, I do like you very much, Monty, but to live and work here with Ulick—!

DESPARD. Ten to one after France and the army this place will seem so desperately slow that he'll chuck it after a year.

KATE. If you only knew him! . . . Why, he comes here sometimes—I don't mean on leave—that's the only really Irish bit of me, I see him sometimes when he's not here at all.

DESPARD. What? Do you mean a ghost? Is this place haunted?

KATE. Sometimes. By Ulick. The night he enlisted he came, he stood on the gravel outside the hall-door, he looked so sad, so very sad. And twice I've seen him in the library standing at the bookcase where all the farming books are. And then only three nights ago.

DESPARD. Where?

KATE. I was coming back from the village, it was dusk, I had pushed my bicycle through the gate between the park and the grass-garden. I was closing the gate when I saw him coming up the drive towards me. He was walking very fast and he was looking very happy. He passed me, and I said "Ulick", I couldn't help it, he seemed so real. By that time he was on the hall-door steps, he turned round, gave me a smile and was gone.

DESPARD. By Jove!

KATE. That was just when the Armistice had begun to seem inevitable. He was dreaming it all over, you see, he was dreaming he was home. And you think he'd chuck it! How he's managed all this time to keep himself from deserting—!

DESPARD. He must be a rum chap. Well, everyone to their taste. But if you're right and he does stick here he'll be certain to marry. It will be part of his program; he'll marry one of O'Neill's sisters.

KATE. Monty, your Irish grandmother has given you a revolting imagination.

[MR. ALCOCK *comes back, the others separate a little self-consciously.*]

DESPARD. It's such a ripping morning, I think, foot or no foot, I must go out for a bit. I'll go and put on a pair of stronger shoes. May I come and watch you gardening, Kate?

KATE. Certainly. [*He goes.*]

KATE. Well, what did young O'Flynn want?

ALCOCK. Oh, just a note to the R.M. at Carrig. His brother has got himself into a bad mess, I'm afraid. He was suspected of being mixed up in that raid for arms at Carrigmore, and now three shotguns were found in the mattress of his bed.

KATE. What an uncomfortable place to put them. Did you give his brother the note?

ALCOCK. Of course. . . . I like Despard,

KATE. Do you?

ALCOCK. Don't you?

KATE. Oh, yes, quite.

ALCOCK. You saw a good deal of him in London last spring, didn't you?

KATE. Yes, he was staying with Aunt Kat for his leave, and then he got measles, and that kept him there longer so we saw a lot of each other.

ALCOCK. I know he was a great friend of Reggie's but Reggie never told us much about him. Who are his people?

KATE. Oh, the usual respectable English people with public-school temperaments. They think they're very poor, we'd call them quite rich.

ALCOCK. He's been a barrister, hasn't he? He'll go back to it after the war, I suppose?

KATE. Darling, don't try and be diplomatic. Have him into the library and ask him his income and his intentions. They are both entirely honorable. As you most obviously suspect—he wants to marry me.

ALCOCK. And you?

KATE. Am not at all sure that I want to marry him, and am not going to be rushed.

ALCOCK. I'd like you to marry, Kitty.

KATE. Thanks.

ALCOCK. That's the worst of living here. You meet no one you could, decently, marry.

KATE. I don't think I want to get married at all. I'm quite happy here, especially now Ulick's coming home.

ALCOCK. Ulick must marry, of course. You wouldn't be so happy then.

KATE. That's what Captain Despard threatened me with.

ALCOCK. I think if you really like Despard you'd be wise to take the chance of getting out of all this. Ballydonal's no life for an unmarried woman.

KATE. It's my life. I don't like marrying out of my life, out of my class—I don't mean that in a snobbish way, I'm sure the Despards are as good as we are—but they're different, they're English.

ALCOCK. You're half English yourself.

KATE. The English half of me seems swamped.

ALCOCK. How can you, if you stay here, marry into your class? Who is there to choose? Vandaleur?

KATE. No, not poor Van.

ALCOCK. There's not another house left within visiting distance except Carrigmore, and there are only two old women there. Get out of it, get away. You've done your duty by Ballydonal splendidly in Ulick's absence; now that he's coming back, quit.

KATE. Are you going to quit?

ALCOCK. Your mother would like to, but I think I'm too old to change. But, gracious, I'm going to quit in all kinds of other ways. My mind is full of letters of resignation.

KATE. From what?

ALCOCK. Everything. Every blessed committee and board I'm on. The Old Age Pensions, the Creamery, the Library, the District Council, the Hospital, the Select Vestry, the Diocesan Synod, the Agricultural Show, and all the other fifty committees. Ulick must take my place on them all. The moment he comes back I retire. I'm going then to play scales, nothing but scales, for a month.

KATE. Disgusting self-indulgence.

[ATKINS *comes in.*]

ATKINS [*presenting a telegram*]. The boy is waiting in case there's an answer.

ALCOCK [*taking it*]. Thank you. This will be from the "vet" [*A loud bell is heard.*] By Jove, we were forgetting! [*He looks at his watch.*] Eleven o'clock! Thank God.

KATE [*raising her arms with a gesture of relief*]. Oh, at last, at last.

ATKINS. He's ringing it too slow, the young divil. Wait till I talk to him. [*He hurries out.*]

KATE. We can begin to live again.

ALCOCK. Poor Reginald!

KATE. Yes, poor old Reg. [*They are silent for a little.*]

ALCOCK. Imagine London and Paris, how the flags must be flying and the bells ringing.

KATE. And imagine poor Berlin.

ALCOCK. I don't want to think about that. I spent such happy years there long ago—and Vienna too. Oh, well, they must be glad it's over. But they won't be junketing.

KATE. I'm glad we're here and that it's quiet. I'm so slow, I'll only take it in by degrees. I couldn't throw down my work now and start ragging. It wouldn't mean anything to me. I'll take a week to realize.

ALCOCK. The sunshine and your gay flowers will help us to take it in.

KATE. Yes. Michael Dempsey says—oh, the "vet", when is he coming, I promised to let Michael know the moment we heard.

ALCOCK. I forgot. [*He opens and reads the telegram,* KATE *has turned away.*]

KATE. I searched all through the sheep-book again last night, and I know a lot of things it's *not,* but I'm blessed if I know what it *is.* Michael persists in calling it a "blasht". Well, is he coming today? [*She turns and looks at her father, he looks at her strangely.*] What is it? . . . My darling, has anything happened?

ALCOCK [*with difficulty*]. Ulick.

KATE. Ulick? [*She snatches the telegram.*] "His Majesty deeply regrets . . . of wounds." Ulick? But the war is over.

ALCOCK. The eighth . . . three days ago.

KATE. Dead? . . . Ulick? . . . [*She begins to laugh hysterically.*] Listen to the bell, listen to the bell!

ALCOCK. My dear!

KATE. Victory! Victory!

ALCOCK. It *is.* For King, for Empire. That's what matters.

KATE. Damn King and Empire. They don't matter, not to us.

ALCOCK [*his arm round her*]. Hush, my dear, hush.

KATE [*breaking from him*]. I won't hush. Why should I? Ulick's life was here, here. All he loved, all he worked for.

ALCOCK. We must try and be proud—

KATE [*passionately*]. Never. Never in this world. I'll never be proud of it, I'll never pretend that it was anything but stupid and hateful. You and your King and your Empire! Much good they ever did Ulick, or me, or you.

ALCOCK. Stop, Kate, stop—

KATE. Stop your damned bell then.

[MRS. ALCOCK *hurries in, she goes straight to her husband and throws her arms round his neck.*]

MRS. ALCOCK. Do you hear it? Peace! Victory!

ALCOCK. Yes, yes, dear. [*Over her shoulder to* KATE.] Kate, please.

[KATE *goes out.*]

MRS. ALCOCK. Isn't it wonderful? But—so silly of me— I feel I want to cry. . . . It's Reggie, my poor dead Reggie.

ALCOCK. Of course, dear, of course.

MRS. ALCOCK. But I won't cry, I won't cry. I'll be proud of my dead, I'll think of my living. I'll think of Ulick.

ALCOCK. Yes . . . Ulick. . . .

MRS. ALCOCK. Won't Ulick laugh at us when he hears that we rang the poor old bell?

ALCOCK [*leading her to the sofa*]. My dear . . . I have something to tell you.

MRS. ALCOCK. Yes, but listen to the bell, it's ringing faster now, Paddy is ringing it *con amore;* he must be thinking of his beloved "Masther Ulick."

ALCOCK. I want to tell you . . . [*he stops*].

MRS. ALCOCK. Yes?

ALCOCK. I have had a telegram from the War Office.

MRS. ALCOCK. About Ulick?

ALCOCK. Yes, about Ulick.

MRS. ALCOCK. He's coming back? When?

ALCOCK. No. He's never coming back.

MRS. ALCOCK. Never? What do you mean? . . . What do you mean, St. Leger?

ALCOCK. My poor darling.

[*She stares at him, tries to say something, can't. His arm is round her and as he draws her to him the curtain falls. The bell is ringing quite merrily by this time.*]

SCENE II: *The dining room at Ballydonal. An evening in the latter part of June, 1921. Dinner is over, everything has disappeared from the table except dessert—a dish of strawberries.* MR. *and* MRS. ALCOCK *are sitting at the table, he wears a dinner jacket.*

MRS. ALCOCK. A few more strawberries, St. Leger?

ALCOCK. No, thank you.

MRS. ALCOCK. Just two or three—this big one. There are plenty left for Kate. [*She helps him to a few.*]

ALCOCK. Thanks. Take some yourself.

MRS. ALCOCK. I never remember having them so early as this, and so sweet.

ALCOCK. Of course the weather is exceptional.

MRS. ALCOCK. Yes. Brady says if we haven't rain soon these will be the last as well as the first. I wonder why weather is so difficult. It seems as if no weather was just the right weather. The roses are hardly worth the picking, they fade in a few hours.

ALCOCK. I love it. I love the heat. Do you remember that June in Rome—ninety-four or ninety-five, was it?—the heat and the roses?

MRS. ALCOCK. I remember. But even then the weather was wrong for the children, and I had to take them up to that horrible place in the hills.

ALCOCK. . . . How long ago it seems. . . . Like a different existence. . . .

MRS. ALCOCK. Yes. . . . It's nine years since we were abroad. Couldn't we manage to go this summer, even for a few weeks? There are such cheap trips again. I don't care how I go. I'll be a Polytechnic—whatever that means—or a Free Churcher, I'll stay at the scrubbiest *pensions,* I'll submit to being shown the Eiffel Tower from a char-à-banc—anything to get away.

ALCOCK. Isn't your sister going next month? Go with her.

MRS. ALCOCK. Not without you.

ALCOCK. I can't.

MRS. ALCOCK. What good does your staying here do?

ALCOCK. I'd be miserable away.

MRS. ALCOCK. You're miserable enough here in the middle of it, we're both miserable. Imagine the relief of being in a country whose politics mattered nothing to us.

ALCOCK. I don't believe I'd find it any relief. I'd always think I might have been able to do something if I'd stayed.

MRS. ALCOCK. You know you can't do anything. You can only wring your hands. It's much better to wash your hands of the whole thing.

ALCOCK. You're almost making an epigram.

MRS. ALCOCK. Am I? I know I'm talking common sense. I know that we're living in a community of criminal lunatics and that the sooner we get out of it the better.

ALCOCK. I'll wait till I'm put out.

MRS. ALCOCK. Burned out?

ALCOCK. Yes . . . Or starved out—that seems more likely.

MRS. ALCOCK [*with a sigh*]. Sometimes I envy the O'Neills. Kate had a letter today from Sissy O'Neill. They are with some relations in London and having a wonderfully gay time. Everyone makes no end of them because they've been burned out of the ancestral home. If London only knew what the ancestral home was like!

ALCOCK. Such an ugly house.

MRS. ALCOCK. Such a filthy house. Mrs. O'Neill once told me that the drawing room carpet had never been up in *her* time—and I believe her.

ALCOCK. I suppose the Irish refugees will soon become as *distingué* as the Russians. I understand that all the Russians are counts and princesses, all the Irish will be the descendants of kings. I can see the O'Neills having quite a success. I can see chivalrous young Englishmen laying their hearts at the large feet of Flossie and Helana.

MRS. ALCOCK. I can't quite see that. Englishmen at least know a pretty girl when they see one; no one could call those red-faced O'Neills pretty.

ALCOCK. Being burned out will have paled their cheeks. Kate, unburned, wouldn't have a look-in beside them, so, not to spoil her chances of matrimony, I'll stay.

MRS. ALCOCK. Don't talk rubbish. What good can you do? Your being here didn't save poor Maggie Leahy this afternoon.

ALCOCK [*sighing*]. No.

MRS. ALCOCK. All this murder has got to be put down ruthlessly. *You* can't be ruthless, so you'd better not be here while it's being put down.

ALCOCK. Ah, you admit it was murder.

MRS. ALCOCK. I admit nothing of the kind. Maggie's death was an accident—a most distressing one—but the ambush last night was murder pure and simple.

ALCOCK. I envy you, you have a wonderful power of discrimination.

MRS. ALCOCK. Right is right and wrong is wrong.

ALCOCK. Agreed.

MRS. ALCOCK. There are the eternal verities.

ALCOCK. No doubt there are, but what are they?

MRS. ALCOCK. You refuse to recognize them when you meet them, when they're as plain as the nose on your face.

ALCOCK. Oh, of course, England is right and Ireland is wrong, the Republicans commit murder, the Black and Tans commit—accidents.

MRS. ALCOCK. That's stupid—and unkind. I'm not as crude as that.

ALCOCK. Forgive me, my dear. I'm all on edge. Maggie Leahy's death seems the last straw. Let's talk of something else, something quite off the point—avalanches or irregular French verbs.

MRS. ALCOCK. I suppose I'm on edge too, that's why I say we both want a holiday. . . . Shall we have coffee here on the chance of Kate coming in?

ALCOCK. Yes.

[MRS. ALCOCK *rings.*]

ALCOCK. Even if I'd go away, Kate wouldn't.

MRS. ALCOCK. Kate, more than either of us, should go away. I'll try again to persuade her to go. The horrible affair this afternoon may have shaken her nerve.

ALCOCK. After all—though one would never have wanted them to come, all these horrors I mean, though one would have done everything in one's power to stop them—now that they're here it's all, in a sense, enriching. I mean Kate's life has been a richer, graver life than if she'd just played games and danced herself into matrimony. I don't believe she'd change places with her London cousins.

MRS. ALCOCK. More fool she then. They're all married, at least they will be next month when May marries, and Kate won't even go over to be bridesmaid! I've no patience with her.

[*Enter a parlor-maid*—ANNIE.]

MRS. ALCOCK. We'll have coffee here, please, Annie.

ANNIE. Yes, ma'am.

MRS. ALCOCK. I suppose Miss Kate hasn't come in yet?

ANNIE. I haven't seen her, ma'am.

MRS. ALCOCK. I wish she was safely home.

ALCOCK. There's been nothing fresh about poor Mrs. Leahy?

ANNIE. I'm told the husband is nearly demented.

ALCOCK. Poor fellow, no wonder! But it's not true, is it, that the baby was shot too?

ANNIE. I don't think so, sir. But of course I'd put nothing past them Tans.

MRS. ALCOCK. Bring us the coffee, please. Is cook keeping something hot for Miss Kate?

ANNIE. Yes, ma'am. . . . Father Doyle says they're a disgrace to civilization. [*She goes out.*]

MRS. ALCOCK. I don't trust that girl. Sly, like all Irish servants.

ALCOCK. Oh, I don't think so. But I must say I miss poor old Atkins. I often wish I hadn't pensioned him off. I met him in the village yesterday, he looked so extraordinarily well, I was strongly tempted to bring him back here with me.

MRS. ALCOCK. He's well because he hasn't the run of the cellar. A week here and he'd be as bad as ever.

ALCOCK. For all he'd find in the cellar now! I wonder if my grandfather is turning in his grave.

MRS. ALCOCK. Why should he?

ALCOCK. Oh, we must seem shockingly degenerate. No hunters in the stables, no swilling of claret, no card-playing. In this part of the country the eighteenth century lasted right down to the seventies, society even in my father's time was like one of Balzac's provincial novels. . . . Well, if grandfather upbraids me in the next world I'll retaliate by upbraiding him for stripping this room of its pictures. There was a Romney there, just opposite to me, my father remembered it as a child, and my great-granduncle hung over the fire—a dashing portrait of him in his admiral's dress with a sea-fight in the background, and they and all the others were sold to a little Jew in Limerick for a few beggarly pounds—they didn't even pay grandfather's racing debts.

MRS. ALCOCK. It was shameful of him to strip the house the way he did.

ALCOCK. I'm afraid I can't take a very high line about it, I grumble because he left me so little that *I* can sell. I really must get money somewhere.

MRS. ALCOCK. It made me simply furious this morning when I was walking back from the village and the Goods flashed past me in their motor choking me with dust. To think of all the rent they owe us! And their car isn't a Ford either, oh dear me no, some very expensive make Mrs. Brown told me. Is there no way of making them and all the others pay?

ALCOCK. None.

MRS. ALCOCK. I call them common thieves.

ALCOCK. Well, we can console ourselves with the thought that either the Republicans or the Black and Tans will commandeer their car one of these days.

[ANNIE *comes in with the coffee, which she puts before* MRS. ALCOCK *and goes out.*]

ALCOCK [*taking his coffee from* MRS. ALCOCK.] Thank you. . . . Aren't you having any?

MRS. ALCOCK. I don't think so.

ALCOCK. Why not?

MRS. ALCOCK. It would keep me awake.

ALCOCK. It never used to. Aren't you sleeping well?

MRS. ALCOCK. Not very—lately.

ALCOCK. Ah! lying awake imagining you hear the tread of strange feet on the gravel, a hammering on the door, a rattle of petrol tins, there's a click of a revolver, a scratch of a match, a—

MRS. ALCOCK. Don't, don't, St. Leger, *please!*

ALCOCK. My dear, are you really frightened?

MRS. ALCOCK. Terrified.

ALCOCK. I had no idea. . . . You really lie awake—?

MRS. ALCOCK. Listening. Till the light comes. Thank God the nights are short.

ALCOCK. How long has this been going on?

MRS. ALCOCK. Since the spring. No, always.

ALCOCK. Always?

MRS. ALCOCK. Never as bad as now, of course, but I've always felt strange, felt afraid.

ALCOCK. Good God! You've never got used to Ballydonal?

MRS. ALCOCK. Never quite used.

ALCOCK. It's always seemed a little foreign, a little queer? My dear Mary, why didn't you tell me?

MRS. ALCOCK. Oh, it's nothing to fuss about. I can stand it, I've stood it for more than twenty years. But I feel—

just for the sake of sleeping again—I'd like to spend a month or two in some very dull London suburb; Ealing, I think, for choice.

[KATE *comes in very pale and tired.*]

MRS. ALCOCK. My dear, how late you are, I was getting anxious. Do they know you're in? Mrs. Moloney is keeping something hot for you.

KATE. I came in the back way. Mrs. Moloney knows. She's sending me up some tea.

MRS. ALCOCK. Oh nonsense, you must have some dinner.

KATE. I couldn't, mother, really. I couldn't eat anything. [*She sits at the table.*]

MRS. ALCOCK. Just a little soup?

KATE. No really, thanks.

[ALCOCK *goes to the sideboard and pours something into a glass.*]

ALCOCK. Here, drink this.

KATE. What is it?

ALCOCK. Whiskey.

KATE. Oh, no, I couldn't, I don't want it—

ALCOCK. Now, no nonsense. Drink it down.

[*She does so. Suddenly she's afraid she's going to cry and gets up and goes to the window and stands looking out with her back to the room. Her mother is about to go to her.*]

ALCOCK [*in a low voice*]. Let her alone, she'll pull herself together.

MRS. ALCOCK [*low*]. She shouldn't have gone, we shouldn't have let her.

KATE [*turning round*]. I'm sorry. I'm all right now. [*She comes and sits down at the table.*]

ALCOCK. Do you want to talk, my dear, or would you rather be all alone?

KATE. I don't mind. . . . It was very dreadful but I don't think she can have suffered, Dr. Hennessy is sure it was instantaneous. She was sitting on the bank by the road with the baby in her arms, Pat was working in the field behind her. He never heard the lorry till it came round the corner from the cross. They only fired two shots he says. One of them hit her in the breast, I don't know how the poor baby escaped.

ALCOCK. But—but—the whole thing seems incredible.
. . . Were they blind drunk?

KATE. Nobody knows. I suppose they're in an awful state
of nerves and fury after the ambush last night. Father Doyle
is afraid they'll burn the village tonight.

ALCOCK. He was there—at the Leahys' cottage, I mean?

KATE. Yes, and Mrs. Brown came. Mr. Brown is away
until tomorrow. Mrs. Brown was splendid with all the children—six of them, imagine, and all so young. Pat was useless, simply blubbered like a child. Mrs. Murphy's taken the
baby, its arm got bruised when poor Maggie fell off the
bank.

MRS. ALCOCK. Can we send down anything? Food?

KATE. I think they've everything. I'll bring down a lot
of flowers tomorrow, Maggie liked flowers.

[*Enter* ANNIE *with the tea.*]

KATE. Thank you, Annie. [ANNIE *goes.*]

MRS. ALCOCK. Take a few strawberries, Kate. The first
this year.

KATE. Thanks. [*But she doesn't take any.*]

MRS. ALCOCK [*pouring her out some tea*]. That will do
you good.

KATE. Don't bother about me, I'll be all right. Go to the
drawing room, mother, please, I'd rather you would.

MRS. ALCOCK. I'd like to stay and see you eat a good
tea.

KATE. I'll do that all right. Please don't wait, do go.

MRS. ALCOCK. Will you promise me to eat something?

KATE. Yes, I promise.

MRS. ALCOCK. And if you feel you'd like something more
substantial, you've only got to ring the bell and Mrs. Moloney will send you up something nice.

KATE. Yes, I know.

MRS. ALCOCK. And you'll come to the drawing room
when you've finished?

KATE. Yes, I'll come. I won't be long.

MRS. ALCOCK. Come, St. Leger. [*She goes.* ALCOCK *follows her as far as the door and turns back.*]

ALCOCK. I don't like leaving you, Kitty.

KATE. I'm all right now. I was silly for a minute.

ALCOCK. Well, no wonder.

KATE. "And no one but the baby cried for poor Lorraine, Lorree." That's been running in my head all the evening. So silly, for we all cried. . . . I suppose I'll see some meaning in it some time. Of course we read of much worse horrors in the war, but to see it—and she was my nurse—a friend really—I gave her her wedding dress, do you remember? and the first baby was called after me.

ALCOCK. Yes, and Pat's father was gardener here for thirty years. They're really part of the family, one of ourselves.

KATE [*somberly*]. No, that's just what they're not.

ALCOCK. Not?

KATE. Not us, we're not them. That was the awful thing I realized this evening. There I was in that cottage with the neighbors and Father Doyle and Dr. Hennessy and I knew Maggie better than any of them, and I—I was an outsider.

ALCOCK. What do you mean?

KATE. Just what I say. An outsider. Something outside, different, away from them.

ALCOCK. When death is in question one feels, of course, that religion makes such a difference.

KATE. Yes, there was religion to make me feel outside but lots of other things too; education, I suppose, and tradition and—and everything that makes me me and them them. Between us and them, like the people in the Bible, there was a "great gulf fixed."

ALCOCK. I know no one who has made less of the gulf than you, Kitty. Your democracy shocks your mother.

KATE [*impatiently*]. Oh, yes, I threw a bridge across the gulf and ran across it and called Pat, Mick, and Larry by their Christian names, and hobnobbed with priests and creamery managers and Gaelic teachers—but it was only a bridge, the gulf remained and when the moment came they instinctively forced me to stand on the farther side. Oh, it wasn't only tonight I've felt it. I've been conscious of it ever since I've been conscious of anything, but I thought it could be broken down.

ALCOCK. Your politics aren't extreme enough.

KATE. It's not that. They could forgive me for not being an out-and-out Republican. There's something deeper, something that none of us can put into words, something instinctive, this "them" and "us" feeling.

ALCOCK. History.

KATE. I think I'd like it better if they hated us. That at least would make me feel that we had power, that we counted for something; it's very hard to forgive toleration.

ALCOCK. And it's hard for us not to seem to patronize.

KATE. I don't patronize, I never have. I sit on committees like every ordinary member. I sit with schoolchildren at the Gaelic classes because I'm such a dunce at Gaelic. We're as poor as mice, we don't keep up any style. We're as Irish as most of them, we're honest and hard working.

ALCOCK. I suppose they feel—

KATE. "They, they, they!" Why should · there be any "they"? I was made to feel in that cottage this evening that *I* had shot Mary, and yet they know perfectly well that I've no sympathy with the Auxiliaries.

ALCOCK. You're overwrought, my dear. You're exaggerating very much.

KATE. No, I'm not. What I'm saying is true, and you know it is. Van O'Neill is an ignorant clod, Father Doyle compared with him is a paragon of culture, but you're uncomfortable when Father Doyle comes here, you're not speaking your full mind to him, he's not speaking his full mind to you, but you're quite happy and easy with poor ignorant Van.

ALCOCK. I've known Van all his life.

KATE. I've known the people in the village all my life. I've worked with them, quarreled with them, loved them, but at the end of it all I find myself—just different.

ALCOCK. Maybe it's right we should be different.

KATE. How can it be right? I want to be the same.

ALCOCK. You'll never be that.

KATE. Why not?

ALCOCK. It will be always "them" and "us."

KATE. I feel sick and discouraged.

ALCOCK. And your mother feels frightened.

KATE. Frightened? Of what?

ALCOCK. Everything. She says she's never felt quite at home here.

KATE. Yes, it must be worse for her—no, it's worse for

me with the Irish side of me tormenting me. Let's give up,
chuck up the sponge.

ALCOCK. Kate!

KATE. We're "going, going, going—" like a battered
old piece of furniture at an auction. Let's smash the hammer down ourselves and cry "gone."

ALCOCK. Yes, go, Kate, go. You and your mother.

KATE. And you?

ALCOCK. No, no, I can't go yet.

KATE. Yet? What worse are you waiting for?

ALCOCK. I don't know.

KATE. I know. It's your devilish pride.

ALCOCK. I don't think so.

KATE. It's your devilish pride.

ALCOCK. No, no. It's—somehow I'd feel it physically impossible to go just now.

KATE. Yes. You're devilishly proud.

ALCOCK. Nonsense. . . . Your mother will be wondering
where I am. I'd better join her. Come to the drawing room
as soon as you can.

KATE. All right.

[ALCOCK *goes out.*]

[*Left to herself* KATE *drinks a little tea disheartedly. A
minute later* ANNIE *comes in.*]

ANNIE [*planting an egg on the table*]. Mrs. Moloney sent
this up, miss.

KATE. Oh, thanks, thank Mrs. Moloney.

ANNIE. Aren't you cold with the window open, miss?

KATE. I don't think so.

ANNIE. There's a terrible breeze blowing in. [*She half
closes the casement window.*]

KATE. It's getting very dark, isn't it, or is it very late?

ANNIE. 'Tis like as if there was going to be a storm, or
thunder maybe. [*She is going out.*]

KATE [*suddenly and decisively*]. Annie!

ANNIE. Yes, miss.

KATE. Shut the door. Come here. I want you to tell me
something.

ANNIE [*wonderingly*]. Yes, miss?

KATE. If the Black and Tans burn the village tonight will
we be burned out the next night?

ANNIE. Oh, miss!

KATE. Will we?

ANNIE. Such a thing to say!

KATE. Will we, will we?

ANNIE. Sure how could I say?

KATE. I know you can't say definitely "yes" or "no." But you can tell me whether you think it's likely. Your brother—well, I know what he is as well as you do—is he likely to look on us as a suitable reprisal?

ANNIE [*vaguely*]. Miss!

KATE. He burned the O'Neills.

ANNIE [*with contempt*]. Ah, sure, the O'Neills!

KATE. Exactly. That's what I want to know. Will there be any difference made between them and us? Will all the master has done for the district count for anything?

ANNIE. Everyone has a great respect for the master and for yourself too, miss.

KATE. I know. But how much respect? Enough to save us? I'm only asking as a matter of curiosity; if you tell me they will burn us I shan't do anything about it—as a matter of fact there's nothing to be done—but I just want to know.

ANNIE. I don't know why you ask me, miss.

KATE. I don't know why I shouldn't ask you. We've known each other ever since we were children; you know as much about what's going on in the village as any girl in it. I suspect that you know more than any girl. I want a straight answer to a straight question.

ANNIE. Ah, don't bother your head about such things, miss.

KATE. I see. . . . You won't answer me. . . . You're probably right not to. Thank you, you needn't wait. Thank Mrs. Moloney for sending me the egg.

ANNIE. Yes, miss. [*She goes out.*]

KATE [*to herself*]. A great gulf fixed. [*She remains brooding, she makes no attempt to eat anything but drinks a little tea. The door opens, DESPARD appears in the uniform of the Auxiliary Police. KATE doesn't stir, they look at each other silently for half a minute.*]

KATE. Why have you come? I told you not to.

DESPARD [*thickly, rather drunkenly*]. Professionally.

KATE. What?

DESPARD. Professionally. In the discharge of my duties.

KATE. Do you mean you're stationed here—in Ballydonal? I thought you were in Gormanstown?

DESPARD. Left. Why don't you read my letters?

KATE. I told you why.

DESPARD. Forgot. Shockin' memory.

KATE. I don't correspond with Auxiliaries.

DESPARD. No?

KATE. And I don't want them in this house.

DESPARD. No?

KATE. So will you please go?

DESPARD. This wonderful Irish hospitality! And I've come such a long way today, all the way from County Limerick.

KATE. Limerick?

DESPARD. Yes. The hell of a distance, but, as you were about to remark, lovely day for a drive.

KATE. Why? Why do you come?

DESPARD. Pleasure—and a duty. Pleasure to see you, duty to drop across and tell Ballydonal what we think of it.

KATE. To tell—? You—? I understand. How many of you are there?

DESPARD. Cars an' cars an' cars.

KATE. You're going to burn the village, I suppose?

DESPARD. Don't know. Depends.

KATE. Depends on whether you're drunk enough. You're drunk now but not very drunk.

DESPARD. You are going it, Kate.

KATE. What do you want here, in this house?

DESPARD. Stayed here once. Finding myself passing your gate felt it was only commonly polite to call on you.

KATE. Passing the gate . . . were you on the road between this and the village about four o'clock this afternoon?

DESPARD. No. Only just arrived.

KATE. Ah!

DESPARD. Why d'you ask?

KATE. Nothing.

DESPARD. My chaps searching your yard.

KATE. Searching the yard? In the name of goodness, for what?

DESPARD. Anything in trousers that might be hiding in loft or coach-house. Said I'd wait for them here. Damned rude, Kate, you might ask me to sit down or have a drink —*and* have a drink I mean.

KATE [*getting up*]. Take your men away, Captain Despard, take them away. You'll scare mother out of her wits. I give you my word of honor we're hiding no one in the house or in the yard.

DESPARD. Your word! My dear Kate! I said to the driver as we passed your gate "Taylor" (that's his name), "Taylor, that's Ballydonal House and there's a girl there who's as damned a little Sinn Feiner as any I know. Stop the car, turn round—"

KATE. Captain Despard—

DESPARD. Monty, Kate, Monty. This standoffishness, so uncalled for, unexpected—

KATE. Will you please, for the sake of the good friends we were once, go quietly away?

DESPARD. Remarked before—wonderful Irish hospitality, traditional. Well, I've learned not to wait to be asked. [*He sits down and pours himself out some whiskey.*]

KATE [*reaching for the decanter*]. Please, please, Monty—

DESPARD. Hands off! The dust of these roads. You wouldn't grudge an old friend a drink. [*He drinks.*] As you remarked, we were good friends. [KATE *moves towards the door*, DESPARD *gets between her and it.*] Where are you going?

KATE. To mother.

DESPARD. No. No warnings. Not allowed. You stay here, see? My business keep you here. House must be searched.

KATE. How ridiculous.

DESPARD [*suddenly blazing out*]. Yes, damned funny, like the ambush last night. Frightfully funny joke for the fellows who went west.

KATE. You know perfectly well we had nothing to do with the ambush.

DESPARD. Not guts enough. 'Scuse my language. But true. Whiners, that's what you are. "Why doesn't the Government. . . . Must establish law and order. . . . But Black and Tans are rather naughty." Compromise, conference, save your bacon. Wow, wow.

[KATE *turns away from the door and walks to the other side of the room.* DESPARD *goes back to the table and drinks again.*]

DESPARD. Your father used to brag of his cellar, I remember. How's the old boy?

KATE [*turning round*]. You realize that if you burn the village as a reprisal we'll probably be burned as another reprisal?

DESPARD. Unfortunate. Got to think of the murder of those chaps. Must punish. Must make Ballydonal squeal.

KATE. It was strangers did it, no one from this village.

DESPARD. Yes, always the naughty boys in the next parish. Heard that tale too often. Cuts no ice.

KATE. Monty, if I could bring those poor men back from the dead I'd do so, believe me I would. But they've been avenged. This afternoon a poor woman sitting by the road nursing a baby was shot dead by some Auxiliaries who were passing in a lorry. Won't you take that as your vengeance, and let the village alone?

DESPARD. Spying. I know these women.

KATE. She wasn't spying, she was only a poor laborer's wife sitting in the sunshine with her baby. I've known her all my life, she was my nurse when *I* was a baby.

DESPARD. Your nurse?

KATE. Yes. How would you feel if it had been your nurse.

DESPARD. Damnable.

KATE. Yes, damnable. It's all damnable, Monty, you and us and everything, but it won't be so damnable if because poor Maggie is dead you turn round your cars and go quietly home.

DESPARD. Home? What the hell d'you mean?

KATE. Home to Limerick.

DESPARD. Limerick? Home? Up Garryowen! More Irish than the Irish, you see.

KATE. Go home altogether, back to England, and we can be friends again.

DESPARD. Friends? Only friends?

KATE. Good friends.

DESPARD. I'd do a lot for you, Kitty.

KATE. I know you would. Do this.

DESPARD. Damn me, we will be friends again, Kitty, damn

me, we will. Give me a kiss and say you forgive and forget.

KATE. Oh, Monty, nonsense.

DESPARD. It's not nonsense. It's God's truth. Say you forget and forgive, kiss me and say you'll marry me and I'll spare the damned village.

KATE. Rubbish.

DESPARD. How rubbish?

KATE. This is County Cork, not third-rate melodrama.

DESPARD. What d'you mean?

KATE. You're behaving like the hero—or the villain—in a cheap novel.

DESPARD. You're damned superior.

KATE. You're not.

DESPARD. Won't quarrel with you, improves you to lose your temper. I'll kiss and be friends.

KATE. I won't.

DESPARD. Oh, yes, you will. . . . Come here.

KATE. Don't be silly.

DESPARD [*going to her*]. I mean it. Kiss me.

KATE. No.

DESPARD. Kiss me, you— [*He struggles with her, over-powers her, kisses her violently, repeatedly, suddenly he softens, grows tearfully tender.*] Kitty, Kitty, Kitty.

KATE. Monty, poor Monty.

DESPARD [*crying*]. Kitty, Kitty.

KATE [*soothing him*]. Hush, hush.

DESPARD. It's hell, Kitty, it's hell.

KATE. I know, I know.

DESPARD. You can't know how hellish.

KATE. My poor Monty.

DESPARD. The hot nights—that awful little barracks, the rotten chaps that are there, and never knowing when—who—

KATE. Yes, yes, I know.

DESPARD. It wasn't like this in France. I wish I were back there, I'd give my soul to be back there.

KATE. Get out of it. Give it up. Go back to England.

DESPARD [*shaking himself free of her*]. I'll see it through. The lice! We'll give 'em as hard as they give us and just a little bit harder.

[MR. ALCOCK *comes in.*]

ALCOCK. Your mother is wondering— Good gracious!

KATE. It's Captain Despard, father.

DESPARD. Evening, Mr. Alcock, how are you? Unexpected pleasure.

KATE. Captain Despard's men are just having a look round the yard. I explained, of course, that there was nobody—nothing—there for them to find and they will be gone in a few minutes. Perhaps you had better go to mother in case she hears anything and is frightened.

DESPARD. Not an unfriendly visit, Alcock, don't take it unfriendly.

ALCOCK. I'll take it as I please.

KATE. Will you go, father? I'll look after Captain Despard.

DESPARD. Yes, Kitty's turning duty into pleasure.

ALCOCK. Come on, Kitty.

DESPARD [*holding her arm*]. No, no, cruel—

ALCOCK [*suddenly exploding*]. Let my daughter alone.

KATE [*getting to* ALCOCK]. Father!

ALCOCK. Do your duty, damn you, as quickly as you can, and clear out of my house.

DESPARD. Mind what you're saying, Alcock.

ALCOCK. Mind your own business.

DESPARD. You're all my business. You and your lovely village and Kitty—

ALCOCK. Leave my daughter . . . [KATE *is trying to quiet him.*] Let me alone, Kitty.

KATE. Come to mother, father.

DESPARD. Yes, clear out of this, do you hear? Clear out, the two of you. [*He whips out his revolver.*]

ALCOCK. By God, if you threaten me—

KATE. Father, hush . . .

DESPARD. Upstairs with you. Hide. Under the bed.

ALCOCK. I see. You are drunk. Very pretty. Kate! [*He opens the door for her.*]

KATE. Not without you.

ALCOCK. I'm coming. [*To* DESPARD.] If you want us you will find us in the drawing room, my wife, my daughter and myself. You know the way, you have been a welcome guest here—when your uniform was a different one.

[ALCOCK *and* KATE *go out.*]

DESPARD. Old fool! [*The light has been fading, the room
is full of shadows. He gropes for his glass and knocks it over,
it breaks.*] Damn! [*He drinks straight from the decanter,
spilling the whiskey down his face. There is a sudden gust of
wind, the casement behind him blows open, the curtain blows
out into the room. He starts violently and swings round to
the window, his revolver in his hand.*] Hands up! Who are
you? Who are you, I say?

A WHISPER OUT OF THE DARKNESS. Ulick!

DESPARD. Ulick? Who are you? I warn you, don't come
in through that window, don't, I say. Hands up or I fire.
[*He fires rapidly in the direction of the window two or
three shots. The glass splinters and falls. He blows a whistle.*]
Taylor! Taylor! [*He fires again.*]

SCENE III: *An evening in February, 1923. The same scene
as the previous one, but the room is somewhat changed,
it is less emphatically a dining room and more of a sitting
room. A comfortable armchair is above the fire, and in it
Mrs. ALCOCK is sitting knitting and reading, the room
is lit by an oil lamp on the dining room table, and there
is a pair of candles on a little table beside Mrs. ALCOCK.
Half a minute after the curtain rises ANNIE comes into
the room, she has a large bundle of letters, newspapers,
and postal packages in her hand.*

ANNIE [*bringing them to Mrs. ALCOCK.*] The post,
ma'am.

MRS. ALCOCK. Letters! Oh, what a surprise!

ANNIE. And the postman said Miss Doyle told him to
tell you there'd be likely be a post going out tomorrow
about twelve o'clock.

MRS. ALCOCK. Tomorrow? I see. I'll have a lot of letters
to go. Will you tell the master that letters have come? He's
in the library.

ANNIE. Yes, ma'am. [*She goes out.*]

[*Mrs. ALCOCK sorts the mail and starts to open her own
letters. ALCOCK comes in, he is dressed in a dark lounge suit,
he has a sheet of paper—an unfinished letter in his hand.*]

MRS. ALCOCK. Letters, St. Leger. But only two from Kate!

ALCOCK. How is she?

MRS. ALCOCK. I haven't had time to read them yet. Those
are yours, they don't look very exciting, and there are all
these *Times* and the *Lit. Sup.* and *Punch* and *The Saturday
Review*—plenty of reading anyhow.

ALCOCK [*a little petulantly throwing the newspapers on
the table*]. I'll give up the *Times*. Newspapers are bad
enough taken in small daily doses, but when they arrive *en
masse* they are completely indigestible, they're only waste
of money.

MRS. ALCOCK. Only a few lines from Kate . . . had a
bit of a cold and very busy at the office . . . oh, she's changing her rooms, going to a boarding-house just off Blooms-
bury Square . . . Oh, imagine, St. Leger! Van O'Neill is
going to be married! Isn't that amazing?

ALCOCK. Well, why shouldn't he? Who's he marrying?

MRS. ALCOCK. Kate doesn't know, Sissy just sent her a
card asking her to go round to dinner and she'd tell her
about Van who was engaged to be married. . . . That *is*
exciting. . . . The next letter will tell me. [*She searches
for it and opens it.*]

ALCOCK [*opening and tearing up letters*]. No, I do *not*
want to lay down a hard tennis-court . . . *nor* install central heating . . . nor do I want to restock my cellar . . .
stupid advertisers are, have they no imagination, do they
never read the papers? . . . ah, a money-lender, he's more
in the picture . . . [*but he tears it up*] . . . your subscription . . . due . . . Yes, I expect it is, don't they wish they
may get it. . . . Your subscription . . . What a post, I can't
face it tonight.

MRS. ALCOCK [*having glanced through* KATE'S *other letter*]. This one is written earlier than the other, so we'll have
to wait to hear about Van. It would be just like him to
go and make a grand match. Look at Flossie marrying that
Bradford millionaire. [*She attacks other letters,* ALCOCK *bun-
dles his torn papers into the fire.*] . . . Oh, Margaret's gone
to Bournemouth, she likes the rooms and it's very mild she
says. She'll stay there till Easter, then she's due at the Cod-
dingtons, I must write to her tonight. . . . Did Annie tell
you that there's a post out tomorrow, at twelve?

ALCOCK. No.

MRS. ALCOCK. So if you have anything it must be ready by eleven. Have you finished your letter to Cosgrave?

ALCOCK [*troubled, getting the sheet of paper he has carried in with him*]. No. It doesn't satisfy me, I feel it's so inadequate. I'm sure he won't pay any attention to it—a letter from someone he's never seen, probably never heard of —in his place and with as much to do as he has, *I'd* pay no attention.

MRS. ALCOCK. Well, by writing you've done all you can do.

ALCOCK. You talk as if I was writing just to satisfy myself, not really with the object of saving Nicholas. You know it's come back on us like a boomerang—all these letters I've written for years and years recommending idle wastrels as being sober, industrious and entirely trustworthy. Now when I write something that's true, and when it's a matter of life and death no attention will be paid to it. I really think I should go to Dublin and try to see the President myself.

MRS. ALCOCK. What nonsense. In this weather. It's a terrible journey.

ALCOCK. I hate to leave you alone—if only Kitty wasn't in London. You wouldn't come with me?

MRS. ALCOCK. It's so unnecessary.

ALCOCK. It's a matter of life and death, and Nicholas is such a sterling fine fellow.

MRS. ALCOCK. Oh, they won't execute him. Condemning him to death is only to scare people. He'll be kept in prison for a couple of months and then he'll be made a cabinet minister. They're all the same gang.

ALCOCK. My dear, it's not all bluff; they *have* executed people. There's no shutting our eyes to the fact that Nicholas is in very grave danger.

MRS. ALCOCK. Well, he's got no one but himself to thank for the scrape he's in. You're not pretending you approve of what he's done?

ALCOCK. Of course not. But if I could make the President realize that he's not just disorderly, not the common kind of gun-man, that he's a man of very high principles and fine motives—

MRS. ALCOCK. Oh, every murder no doubt committed from the highest motives!

ALCOCK [*sighs, gives it up*]. I'll think it over tonight, if I could be even sure of the post getting quickly through to Dublin, but the mail might be raided, the letters might never get through at all.

MRS. ALCOCK. The letters are going all right now. Don't worry about it tonight anyway. Give me *Punch* and play me something.

ALCOCK [*handing her* Punch]. Here you are. [*He goes to a cottage piano.*] What shall I play?

MRS. ALCOCK. Anything you like. [*He sits at the piano, worrying, he doesn't play.*]

MRS. ALCOCK [*discovering something in* Punch]. Listen to this, St. Leger, this is rather good. "According to an evening paper Mr. G. F. Preston, London Telephone Controller, who is retiring at the end of this month, has held the post for eleven years. We congratulate him in spite of our suspicions that this is the wrong number." Really, *Punch* is very witty.

ALCOCK [*not listening*]. Yes.

MRS. ALCOCK. And listen to this: "A garden-party on a gigantic scale is to be held at Los Angeles. We understand that tickets will be issued to admit "bearer and one wife." Isn't that amusing? [*She notices that he is paying no attention.*] Do play something, dear, take your mind off things.

ALCOCK. Yes. [*He plays for a moment or two.*] This beastly piano, it's out of tune too. [*He gets up.*] I can't play it. There must be a fire in the music room tomorrow, the Steinway is getting damp.

MRS. ALCOCK. Very well.

ALCOCK. This room is cold too.

MRS. ALCOCK. You got perished sitting all the evening in that icy library. Sit near the fire and poke it up.

ALCOCK. Would you think it horrible of me to go to bed? I feel cold and cross. I'll only snap if I stay here.

MRS. ALCOCK. Yes, do go to bed, you look wretched. I'll bring you a hot drink in bed.

ALCOCK. Ah, you needn't bother.

MRS. ALCOCK. I'll bring it in a quarter of an hour. Take something to read, the *Saturday Review*—or take *Punch,* I can read it tomorrow.

ALCOCK. No, thanks, too contemporary. I have *Tristram*

Shandy upstairs. Sterne is pleasantly remote. Are you coming to bed soon?

MRS. ALCOCK. Yes, I won't be very long after you. [KATE *has entered very quietly, she is in hat and coat.*]

ALCOCK. Really I feel inclined never to get up, just lie in bed till the summer and read the classics, and never, never look at a newspaper or hear any horrible "news."

KATE. No, you're not going to bed as early as you think.

ALCOCK.   } Good gracious!
MRS. ALCOCK. } Kate!

[KATE *flings herself round her father, and then on her mother.*]

ALCOCK. Kitty, is it possible?

KATE. Looks like it.

MRS. ALCOCK. My dear! How? Why?

KATE. Sorry to take you by surprise like this—

ALCOCK. Oh, don't apologize.

KATE. But everything's so uncertain, I didn't know if I'd ever arrive.

MRS. ALCOCK. How did you get here? You're starving, I'm sure. Ring for Annie.

KATE. They know, they're bringing tea. I came on Lordan's lorry from Cork; my, such a jolting, three bridges down, and we had to take to the fields and pay toll to every farmer. I walked up from the village lugging my suitcase. [*To her mother.*] You're looking blooming. [*Looking at her father.*] The boss is a little—a little wizened—I think that's the word.

ALCOCK. I'll get my bloom back now that you've come.

KATE [*taking off her hat and coat and flinging herself into a chair*]. My, it's good to be back. As the man said when he saw Rome—"You can 'ave Rome." Well, you can 'ave London. Never again, my dears, never again, except for a fortnight's holiday once a year.

MRS. ALCOCK. Do you mean you've left for good—not just for a little holiday? But Mr. Scholes—?

KATE. I'm afraid you have me for good and all. Yesterday—or the day before—all this slow traveling has muddled my dates, I just felt I could bear it no longer. Columns in the papers about country-houses going up in flames, Senators being kidnapped and all kinds of thrilling goings-on, and there I was secretarying for Scholes, dear siring and dear madaming and referring to theirs of the ult. and the inst. No, it was not to be borne. So I just up and told him I was going and swept out.

MRS. ALCOCK. But surely you had to give him a month's notice?

KATE. Of course. That was what made him so cross. He didn't much mind my going—I'm a rotten secretary I expect—but he did mind my not giving him a month's notice. It hurt his sense of decency. Your countrymen are very queer, mother, the things that shock them—and the things that don't.

MRS. ALCOCK. Well, a bargain is a bargain.

KATE. Of course it is, darling.

ALCOCK. Oh, damn Scholes. You're here, that's the great thing.

MRS. ALCOCK. It's so disorderly, so—so Irish to run away like that.

KATE. I know it is, but I just felt "Oh, damn Scholes," and said it.

MRS. ALCOCK. You didn't, Kate.

KATE. Practically; getting back here was all that mattered. I suppose he can have the law on me if he likes but he won't, he's too decent, he's got a nice tame English secretary by this time and is blessing his stars to be rid of me. But you're quite right, mother, in saying it was so Irish of me to cut and run, that's why I ran, because I felt myself going to pieces.

MRS. ALCOCK. How, Kate?

KATE. Morally, mamma dear. You've no idea what it's like in London now, how an Irish girl feels, the things people say, the things the papers say, the "we-told-you-so-ness" of them all. Well you can take it in either of two ways, either you're a martyred émigré like Margaret de Burgh and are shown off and have people asked to meet you, and carry pictures of your castle *before* the fire and *after* the fire (so like an advertisement for a hair restorer or a baby food— why doesn't Shell or Pratts take it up "Before using our No. 1 spirit the castle was like this—after—!"), and you dress very plainly and get asked out to very good luncheons and talk of being betrayed by England, thrown to the wolves, call yourself an outpost of the Empire and how you made a gallant last stand and, altogether, are more "I-told-you-so" than anyone else. [*She pauses for breath.*]

ALCOCK. Jealous! *You* had no photographs, we're still intact.

KATE. Exactly. I had no photographs. So I had to take it the other way, which means that I simply went livid green. I just damned people, I insulted the émigrés, I loathed their long, gloomy, Protestant faces, their whines and their appetite for luncheons; I insulted the English, I told them it was none of their business what we did with our own country, and anyway as we'd beaten them it would be more becoming if they kept their mouths shut. I made myself thoroughly objectionable to everyone and then I suddenly realized that I was behaving like any Irish girl in a tenth-rate novelette written by some horrible Colonial, that I was being "so Irish" as mother calls me. That shocked me profoundly, and I knew that for my soul's salvation the sooner I left the better, and I realized I'd better leave quick or may be there'd be nothing to come back to. And here I am.

ALCOCK. We're not likely to be burned, I'm not a Senator.

MRS. ALCOCK. Thank God.

KATE. Well, anyway I'm here, and now I'll be able to be myself again. I'll criticize and dislike Irish people—some of them—and be either a Free Stater or a Republican, I suppose I've got to be one or the other. In London, you know, I was just blatantly Irish, I wouldn't stand a word against De Valera *or* Cosgrave. . . . Oh, mother darling, I know I'm a disappointment to you coming back like this after all the trouble you took and the strings you pulled to get Scholes to take me and I know you wanted me to marry some nice quiet Englishman—but I've stood it for nearly a year and I couldn't bear it any longer and no nice Englishman wanted to marry me—not even a nasty one—I've had no followers, not one. I'm a failure, I'm back on your hands —for keeps.

MRS. ALCOCK. It's lovely to have you.

ALCOCK. By Jove, it is. It's not been fun—this winter.

KATE. I suppose it hasn't. I suppose we've all been telling lies to each other for the last six months, you telling me everything was splendid and not to mind what the papers said, and I telling you that there was no place like London. . . . Well, we needn't pretend any more to each other. God, it's grand to be back to real things even if they're hideous things. In London—apart from the struggle to make a living—everything seems just sentimental play-acting. It's —it's fuzzy.

MRS. ALCOCK [*bitterly*]. Sentimental? If you want sentiment in its essence you have it here.

KATE. Yes, I know. But you'll die for it. It's not fuzzy to die.

ALCOCK. Oh, Kate—no, I won't bother you with it tonight.

KATE. What is it? No, do tell me. I'm back for everything bad and good.

ALCOCK. It's Nicholas O'Connor—you remember Nicholas, Jer. O'Connor's son?

KATE. Of course. Ulick thought so much of him, he got you to send him to the Model Farm. I thought you had put him in charge of the farms at Ballymacduff.

ALCOCK. He left early in the summer. He went very Republican you know. I lost sight of him, apparently he was in the West fighting all the autumn. He's been captured and condemned to death.

KATE. Nicholas! Oh, father!

ALCOCK. Yes. I only heard today. A three days' old paper I saw.

KATE. But can't something be done? Nicholas was one in a thousand.

ALCOCK. I know. I've written a letter to Cosgrave—half-written it, but it seems inadequate, I don't believe he'll pay much attention to it, he doesn't know me. I thought I ought to go to Dublin and see him but I didn't like leaving your mother.

KATE. Oh, go, I'm here now. Mother—imagine Nicholas —oh, it's too horrible.

ALCOCK. You've not come home to a picnic.

KATE. No. Forgive me for saying all those silly things, that was the end of the novelette, I'll try and be decent now. Yet I do like real things, if there has to be a battle I don't want it to be a sham fight. . . . How fond Ulick was of Nicholas. They used to fish together as boys, do you remember?

ALCOCK. Yes.

KATE. And they worked at Gaelic together in Ulick's holidays—but Ulick was better at Gaelic than Nick.

ALCOCK. I must save him, he was a decent fine fellow. Of course I don't approve of what he's done but— [*To* MRS. ALCOCK.] My dear, you won't mind my going now?

MRS. ALCOCK. No. It was wicked of me to try to stop your going before. God knows I don't wish his death . . . there's been enough killing. . . . His mother . . . [*she pulls herself together, she won't be "sentimental"*]. Why don't they bring your tea, Kate?

KATE. No hurry. I'm not hungry, too excited. Oh, Sissy O'Neill saw me off. You'll not be surprised to hear that she "sent her love." The amount of love the O'Neills are always sending, I wonder they have any left.

MRS. ALCOCK. And what's this about Van? I only got your letter tonight—five minutes before you came.

KATE. Oh, my dear, Van is making a splendid match.

MRS. ALCOCK. There, St. Leger! Who is she?

KATE. American, the usual millions but not the usual American, lives in England altogether and likes to be thought English, has an English accent which Sissy speaks of as "magnificent." She's crazy about horses, Van was at Rathconnell's hunting—he *can* ride, poor Van—they met in the hunting field, he courted her from the back of a horse, he proposed to her from the back of a horse—the only place he'd have any courage—and they're to be married next month.

MRS. ALCOCK. Well, if she admires the English accent what does she think of Van's?

KATE. She's obviously very much in love. But Van's has improved. You really wouldn't know any of the O'Neills, burning them out has done wonders for them. There's Flossie with her Bradford woolen man—countless thousands; Sissy in an office, her boss told me the other day she was "invaluable"; Gertie in Bond Street doing people's faces— Gertie who never washed her own! Maggie in a very comfortable little flat looking after her mother, and Helana in musical comedy. Can you beat it?

MRS. ALCOCK. It's wonderful, it's unbelievable.

KATE. Compared to them I feel I'm a thorough failure, a returned empty. [*She looks round the room.*] But—I knew there was something odd and queer—why, are you sitting here? What's that armchair doing and the table out of the small drawing room, why the school-room piano?

MRS. ALCOCK. Well, we haven't been using the drawing room this winter.

KATE. Why not?

MRS. ALCOCK. Oh, it doesn't seem worth while. Your father is out or in the library all day, we go to bed very early, no one ever calls—there's no one *to* call except the Browns, and they don't mind sitting in here—

ALCOCK. Don't mind her, Kitty; she's making decent, needless excuses. The truth is we're pretty nearly broke, and she's trying to run the house with only two servants, Annie and the cook. Every room less means a fire less.

KATE. I see. . . . You're eating next to nothing, of course; you always had the appetite of wrens, no wonder the boss looks pinched; it's about time I came home.

ALCOCK. Nonsense, we've plenty to eat.

MRS. ALCOCK. But he would give up wine—even his glass of thin grog before going to bed.

KATE. I've saved ten pounds; I wish it was more, but it's awfully hard to save in London. We'll go on a burst, *pâté de foie gras* for you and champagne for the boss.

MRS. ALCOCK. Darling!

KATE. I suppose no rents are coming in?

ALCOCK. Not a penny for three years.

KATE. Hm . . . We are shrinking, aren't we? Do you remember the first winter of the war we shut up the north wing and did without two servants, the next winter we cut off the central heating, that meant never sitting in the hall, now the drawing room's gone and the music room, too, I suppose. Soon we'll be reduced to a single bed-sitting room. . . . Do you think it all minds it—feels it—the house itself, I mean—Ballydonal?

ALCOCK. In all the generations it's seen, it must have learnt patience.

KATE. Yes, I suppose an immense toleration for the animals who run about through its passages and rooms, and who pull down a bit here and build it up again fifty years later, and cover its walls with paper and then wash the paper all off, who tear out its vitals to put in hot water pipes and then let the pipes go cold. And feather beds are banished to lofts and wax candles give place to lamps, and they should have gone before this to make place for acetylene or electric light, and none of us live any longer or are any the happier, but we scratch and alter, scratch and alter, generation after generation.

ALCOCK. You're becoming quite lyric, Kitty.

KATE. Sorry. But you see when I was away from it I could see it in a way I never could before. When I lived here I couldn't see the house for the rooms.

MRS. ALCOCK. They're awful, all those empty rooms on every side of us—above us all those garrets, below us cellars and empty cellars.

ALCOCK. Never mind, one of these days I'll sell it to the priests or the nuns.

MRS. ALCOCK. I wish you would.

KATE. Is it true that Castle Bewley is to be a training college for South African missionaries?

ALCOCK. Quite true. And Carrigmore, of course, has dedicated itself to the task of converting China. . . . One of these days Ireland will wake up and realize that all its best houses and much of its best land have passed into the hands of landlords who are entirely self-contained, who give no employment, who hold themselves aloof from the life of the community. A curious situation.

KATE. Well, the big houses have had their fling, drank claret deeply in their youth, gambled and horse-raced in their middle-age, so it's right they should be converted and turn pious in their old age. But I should think Castle Bewley would need not conversion but exorcism.

MRS. ALCOCK. I hear Annie coming. Here's your supper at last.

[*The door opens, three young men in trench coats and soft hats appear. The leader of them has a revolver.*]

LEADER. Mr. Alcock, you have five minutes to leave the house.

[*The* ALCOCKS *have risen, speechless.*]

ALCOCK. What do you want?

LEADER. You have five minutes to get out.

ALCOCK. You—you're going to—

LEADER. Blow it up and burn it. You have five minutes. Will you please leave as quickly as you can, you can take with you anything you like.

ALCOCK [*bewildered*]. Mary—

MRS. ALCOCK [*blazing with indignation, to the leader*]. You dare? You dare? I don't expect you to have sense, that would be asking too much, but have you no decency? Do you know what house you're in, do you know who you're speaking to? Have you ever heard of Ballydonal House? Have you ever heard of Mr. St. Leger Alcock?

LEADER. You have five minutes to leave.

MRS. ALCOCK. Don't stand there prating of your five minutes. I'm English, thank God, if I'd my way I'd have been out of this house five years ago, five and twenty years ago.

ALCOCK [*restraining her*]. Mary, my dear—

MRS. ALCOCK [*shaking him off*.] No, St. Leger . . . [*To the* LEADER.] I don't know your face, are you a stranger here? If you are, before you destroy Ballydonal House go down to the village and ask the first person you meet what this house means, ask if anyone was ever turned away hungry from its door, ask them about Mr. Alcock, what he's done for them, the years of his life he's spent on them, the money, the—the—oh, it's monstrous. What was he doing this very evening? Writing a letter to Cosgrave to try and save one of you—one of you who come now to—

ALCOCK. Stop, Mary. We're not begging off.

LEADER. I have my orders. Ye're to go and the sooner the better; I've other work to do tonight.

MRS. ALCOCK. Nicholas O'Connor. He was writing to save his life, and now you—

LEADER. He's after the fair. Nick was executed yesterday.

MRS. ALCOCK. Oh.

ALCOCK. Yesterday? Poor Nicholas!

MRS. ALCOCK. Is that why we're to be burnt? It won't bring him back to life!

LEADER. I'm not here to argue. . . . [*To* ALCOCK.] Will you get the women out? They'd better get some coats or something, the night is dry but it's cold.

[ANNIE *appears at the door in coat and hat.*]

ANNIE [*to* LEADER]. Me box and the cook's is in me room corded and all. Will you send the lads to fetch them down.

LEADER [*shortly*]. All right.

ANNIE [*insolently taking out a cigarette*]. Give me a light.

LEADER. A light?

ANNIE [*with a grin*]. You needn't tell me you've no matches. [*He gives her a box, she lights her cigarette.*] I suppose you'll give us a lift to the village.

LEADER. I will not. We're going the other way; I'll leave the boxes at the lodge.

ANNIE. You're not very civil. . . . [*To* MRS. ALCOCK.] You owe me a fortnight's wages. You can send it to me, care of Miss Doyle. [*She goes.*]

MRS. ALCOCK. She was packed and ready, she knew!

ALCOCK. Come, my dear. Come, Kate.

KATE [*blazing*]. No! they can blow me up here.

ALCOCK. Hush. No use talking like that. On with your coat. [*He helps her into her coat.*]

MRS. ALCOCK. St. Leger! The birds!

ALCOCK. Oh . . . [*To* LEADER.] It sounds quite ridiculous, but my wife has some canaries—two large cages—they're upstairs in the old nursery, if we could—?

LEADER [*to the men*]. Let ye bring them down and hurry. Where are they?

ALCOCK. Kate, will you show them where they are?

KATE. No.

ALCOCK. I'll show the way myself. . . . See that your mother wraps up well. Now come . . . [*He gets the women out, their heads are high; he turns at the door to the* LEADER.] It's up two flights, I'm afraid, and the cages are awkward things to carry—I'll just see that my wife has her warm coat. [*He disappears.*]

LEADER [*to men*]. When you have the birds and the servants' boxes out come back here. We'll put one mine here and another at the library door where Annie Daly showed us. I'll want two tins of petrol here and as many again in the hall, and . . . [*he is continuing his orders when the curtain falls*].

SCENE IV: *A corner of the garden. Two high stone walls form a right angle across which has been built a summer-house—a roof supported by a couple of pillars. Below the stone walls are flower borders, empty now except for some withered stems of plants, on the walls some withered creepers and perhaps some evergreen ones, rose-trees gone a little wild. In the summer-house and outside it on the path is a medley of furniture. It is just before sunrise, the morning after the previous scene, a cold light which grows brighter as the scene progresses. ATKINS, collarless, dressed very hastily, and MR. BROWN, also hastily dressed and very dirty, enter carrying between them a sofa.*

BROWN [*dropping his end*]. Just here, Atkins, we won't take it any further.

ATKINS. I'd like to get it into the summer-house.

BROWN. There's not room. We'll get a cart later on and get all these things over to the rectory.

ATKINS [*rather futilely dusting the sofa*]. The murdering rascals. Will we bring the rest of the things, your reverence?

BROWN. I think they're as well on the gravel as they are here—now the summer-house is full. For a wonder it doesn't look like rain. Michael will have an eye to them.

ATKINS. Oh, then, I know the sort of an eye Michael Dempsey will have to them, a covetous, thieving eye.

BROWN. Atkins!

ATKINS. Faith, Mary Dempsey will be living like a lady from this out, lolling back on her ladyship's cushions and drinking her tea out of her ladyship's cups.

BROWN. Nonsense. Michael is as honest as the day.

ATKINS. God help you, your reverence, 'tis little you know the class of people that's in this place. I was as innocent as yourself until I went to live beyond in the village. There's neither religion nor decency in the village, a low, thieving, murdering lot. Oh, my eyes were opened, I assure you. I learned things that surprised me, indeed and I did. Thanks be to God I come from the County Tipperary and never set foot in County Cork till I took service with the poor master's father.

BROWN [*sitting on the sofa and lighting a pipe*]. I thought I remembered hearing that Tipperary had a reputation for wildness.

ATKINS. To be sure it has, but it's decent kind of wildness; you wouldn't find a thing happening there like what happened here last night—burning Ballydonal House! God forgive me, I could curse like a tinker when I think of it. They're a low, mean, murdering crew, the people in this place, not a one of them would come up with me to lend a hand when the blaze of light on the window woke me this morning, but you'll see they'll be up in an hour's time, nosing around, picking up this thing and that, "saving them" moryah, "keeping them safe for Mr. Alcock against the time he'll be wanting them." Do you know what I'd like to see this minute better than anything else in the world?

BROWN. What?

ATKINS. A regiment of English soldiers and my grandson in the middle of them marching into the village, horse, foot and artillery, and making smithereens of the dirty little houses is there and the dirty little people is living in them, and maybe then they'd know what it is to feel the way the poor mistress feels this minute with her lovely house destroyed on her and she without a roof to shelter her.

BROWN. No, no, you wouldn't wish them that. They're not responsible for what's happened.

ATKINS. Bedad, then, I'd make them responsible, and mark you me, it will come to that yet, and maybe quicker than any of us expect.

BROWN. Come to what?

ATKINS. People high up and low down screeching to the English to come back and protect them from themselves.

BROWN. I don't think that day will ever come.

ATKINS. Indeed and it will. God knows we need protection. How can we live in peace in a little country where everyone knows everyone else and every third man you meet is your second cousin? Sure 'tis well known that relations never agree and every man in Ireland is his own relation.

[*Enter* KATE.]

KATE. Here you are. I've been looking everywhere for you. Wouldn't you like a cup of tea? Michael kindled a fire in the coach-house and we've all been having tea.

BROWN. No, thanks, I'm having a pipe instead.

KATE. We've all been washing under the pump. I'm rather proud of the result.

BROWN. I've sent a message to the Goods asking them to send over a car to bring you all across to the rectory.

KATE. Oh, we could walk.

BROWN. The Goods may as well do that much for you.

ATKINS. Them Goods!

BROWN. You might have a look and see whether the car is there, Atkins. They won't know where to find us.

ATKINS. Very well, your reverence. [*He goes out.*]

BROWN. Poor old Atkins is in a state of tearing indignation. He takes it all as a personal insult to the family.

KATE. Yes. . . . What an amount of stuff you've got here!

BROWN. I gave up when the summer-house was full, we'll get it all up to the rectory before night, there are plenty of empty houses in the yard.

KATE [*looking into the summer-house*]. What a mixture!

BROWN. It is, rather.

KATE. My God, look! [*She pulls out a picture—Leighton's "Wedded."*] I saved that, Mr. Brown, I saved it, a picture I've always hated and at any rate it's only a cheap reprint. I struggled through smoke and flame to save it and I never remembered till too late those fine Hones in the hall.

BROWN. How could you remember in all the excitement? I do wish I had known an hour earlier than I did.

KATE. Yes, if we'd had someone with a clear head—father was no use, once he found that there was no chance of saving the beloved Steinway, he just went numb. Mother, though you'd never have thought it, was the best of us, she kept her head and her sense, she made for the right things, made me get the miniatures and made father get at the safe and the papers.

BROWN. And Atkins?

KATE. Instinctively went for big pieces of furniture, things he'd known all his life, it meant that the nice Chippendale stuff was saved but also this hideous sofa. [*She sits on it.*] I suppose I'm a little hysterical but I can only feel everything—since the horror of the mine—as supremely ridiculous. If you could have seen us—but you can easily imagine it—literally risking our lives for the sake of certain bits of wood and china and glass. And we're supposed to be educated and intelligent and (as you'd remind me) we have immortal souls, but savages from darkest Africa couldn't have fought more desperately for some uncouth image of their god than we did for some piece of wood absurdly carved, for miniatures of our forebears, for Leighton's "Wedded." Pure fetish worship. Now that the excitement is over I realize what savages we were and what a nuisance this jetsam is going to be, so much better if everything had been burned. It's awful to think that we'll have to start again to live up to the Chippendale suite. Couldn't we—oh, don't you think we could—have a little private bonfire here of the contents of the summer-house?

BROWN. The complications with the insurance people would be awful.

KATE. I suppose so. And anyway mother has the Chippendales in the coach-house. Joking apart, I'd like to have saved some of the books, a few of Ulick's for old sake's sake.

BROWN. Could you get nothing from the library?

KATE. Nothing. The explosion blocked the door and it went on fire at once. Oh, well, a lot of them were very dusty, and most of them I had never read, and God with amazing foresight has created Mr. Andrew Carnegie.

BROWN. I'm glad that Ulick didn't live to see this, it would have broken his heart.

KATE. I wonder would it. We thought very much alike, Ulick and I, and do I look as if my heart was broken?

BROWN. I can't say you do. . . . I expect in your inmost soul you're glad to be quit of it all.

KATE. Glad? I feel—exalted! If only you knew what I feel and I'll tell you—but not now, here's father. Poor darling, he doesn't look exalted, we must get him to the rectory as soon as possible.

[*Enter* ALCOCK.]

ALCOCK. Your mother is wondering where you are.

KATE. I'll go to her. Is she still in the coach-house?

ALCOCK. Yes. I left her feeding the birds.

KATE. Right. I'll be back again. [*She goes.*]

BROWN. Sit down, St. Leger.

ALCOCK [*sitting on the sofa*]. I feel tired.

BROWN. Of course. Have a pipe.

ALCOCK. No, thanks. [*Feeling in his pocket.*] I don't believe I have a pipe.

BROWN. I have a second one—if you don't mind.

ALCOCK. I feel a pipe would make me sick—like a schoolboy. Silly, isn't it. But I'll try a cigarette.

BROWN. The Goods are sending a conveyance to bring you to the rectory and after breakfast I shall pack you all off to bed.

ALCOCK. Yes.

BROWN. Kate is fine.

ALCOCK. Yes. I'm not and I'm not going to try to be fine. I feel as if nothing matters any more, as if everything was over.

BROWN. Ay.

ALCOCK. And that I'm just damned glad it's all over and that there's no reason to make an effort any more, no need to pretend ever again.

BROWN. To pretend what?

ALCOCK. That all this—all life here mattered—to me personally I mean, that I really cared what happened.

BROWN. You cared a lot, my dear man, you've been breaking your heart for four years.

ALCOCK. Because I hate stupidity and cruelty and waste, but not for any other reason. I'd have felt just the same if this had been Abyssinia.

BROWN. I doubt it. . . . And what happens now?

ALCOCK. I haven't an idea. I don't intend to have an idea.

BROWN. Kate—?

ALCOCK. Exactly. Kate. I feel it's Kate's show. I leave it all to her and to my wife. My God, it's a relief to have it all over. I've felt for so many years like a bad actor cast for a part far too heroic for his talents, I haven't had technique enough for it, I haven't in any way been big enough for it, the audience has realized at last what I realized years ago, it's hissed me off the stage and sitting here in the wings wiping off my make-up I'm feeling devilishly relieved, almost happy, but at the same time I feel distinctly sick in the stomach.

BROWN. You want a nip of spirits—whiskey or brandy.

ALCOCK. Henry, I'm surprised at you!

BROWN. Oh, for your stomach's sake. There's some at the rectory. For years I've been preaching total abstinence and boasting that I'd never let a drop of the accursed stuff under my roof and I discovered the other day that all the time my wife was squirreling a bottle of brandy—on the top of the wardrobe in my dressing-room of all places—keeping it for emergencies, she said. It's been there for twenty years. Aren't women the dickens?

ALCOCK. Excellent Alice! It was probably twenty years old to start with. It will be worth drinking. Do you think she'll consider me an emergency?

BROWN. Surely.

[*Enter* MRS. ALCOCK *and* KATE.]

MRS. ALCOCK [*fussily*]. Now, St. Leger, there's a message from the Goods to say they're sending a car, it will be here in five minutes. Are you ready to come?

ALCOCK. Quite.

MRS. ALCOCK. We'll take the birds with us, they're all right, I fed them just now. Kate has arranged with Michael to have all the things brought over to the rectory and stored there for the present, of course we couldn't trust them here for an hour, and we'll order a motor to take us to Cork this afternoon.

BROWN. Oh, won't you stay at the rectory? We've plenty of room, you're all welcome as long as ever you like to stay.

MRS. ALCOCK. I know it sounds rude but I'd rather go. They've burned us out, we've our pride still, I hope—at least I have—I know when I'm not wanted, I take the hint and go and I hope to goodness I never come back.

[BROWN *sighs*.]

MRS. ALCOCK. Yes, I know it sounds horrible to you, dear Mr. Brown, our best friend here, our oldest friend, but it's because you're such an old friend I can't pretend. But we'll only be parted from you for a little while. You must follow us, we'll get you some lovely quiet English parish with an ancient beautiful church and you'll be able to put flowers and a crucifix on the altar without your congregation thinking that you are heading straight for Rome.

BROWN. Dear Mrs. Alcock!

Mrs. Alcock. I mean it. You can't pretend that you'd prefer the horrible bare barrack of a church you have here. St. Leger sits here as if he was dead, but I don't feel a bit dead, I'm an old woman, I suppose, but I feel as if life was just beginning for me. Even if we never get a penny of compensation for all this—and I suppose we'll get something —we can't be worse off than we've been here trying to support this white elephant of a house. We'll go to Bournemouth, my sister's there, we'll go to furnished lodgings. Oh, the peace of English furnished lodgings, the beautiful dull respectability of Bournemouth.

Alcock. Bournemouth after Ballydonal!

Mrs. Alcock. Don't get sentimental, St. Leger. Or do, if you like. Have a broken heart, it's quite a comfortable thing to have in a place like Bournemouth.

Alcock. What does Kate say?

Kate. It sounds a good plan.

Mrs. Alcock. Of course it's a good plan.

Brown. You can leave my English parish out of it. I've been fighting with my Select Vestry for twenty years, they'd think they'd won if I left.

Kate. Oh, I meant for mother and the boss.

Mrs. Alcock. It's easy to run up to London from Bournemouth, Kate. You can go up for long week-ends.

Kate. Don't bother about me. I'm not in that picture.

Mrs. Alcock. Where are you then?

Kate. Here. Right here.

Mrs. Alcock. Rubbish.

Kate. We'll get to Cork this evening, we sleep there and go on to England tomorrow or the next day. We go to Bournemouth, I find you really nice, stuffy, respectable lodgings, I hire a good piano, I stay with you till the Vicar calls on you—that launches you into society—and then I'm coming back.

Mrs. Alcock. My dear! Nonsense.

Kate [low, almost singing it]. I'm coming back, I'm coming back, I'm coming back.

Mrs. Alcock. Where to?

Kate. Atkins' pantry, I think. Did you notice how wonderfully Providence almost completely spared it? I want three pieces of corrugated iron to make a roof and a few little odds and ends—Mr. Brown must get them for me. [Brown *laughs.*]

Mrs. Alcock. Oh, I see it's a joke.

Kate. No, it isn't. The corrugated iron part is but the rest isn't. As we are planning our futures I may as well say what I have to say now as later. I am coming back to live here at Ballydonal.

Alcock. Is this bravado or mere obstinacy?

Mrs. Alcock. As I said before, I have my pride, I know when I'm not wanted.

Kate. I have my pride too. Until last night I thought we were not wanted, that's what sickened me, that's what drove me to work in London, I saw everything sweeping past us and leaving us behind, high and dry like some old wreck, useless and forgotten, I couldn't bear that—my beastly conceit, I suppose.

Mrs. Alcock. And after last night do you feel you're wanted?

Kate. I can't flatter myself that we're wanted, but we're not forgotten—ignored.

Mrs. Alcock. I could have put up with being forgotten, there are some ways of being remembered—

Kate. I know. "Say it with petrol!" But still, even to have it said that way, to have it said any way—

Brown. By Jove, I see. Last night showed you that you still mattered.

Kate. More than ever we mattered before. When those men came in I was furiously angry, I'd have shot them if I had a gun, but deep down in me there was something exulting, something saying, "This is real."

Alcock. Your passion for reality, Kitty!

Kate. I mean it was sincere. I've seen time after time father having interviews with people like those young men about one thing or another, but they were never quite real interviews, father wasn't real or they weren't real, but last night!— Did you notice they kept their hats on?

Mrs. Alcock. I've no doubt they did.

Kate. I don't think they meant to be rude, it was just typical of their attitude towards us, they sort of kept on their hats in their minds. We were equals—except that they had revolvers and we hadn't. It was—it was grand.

MRS. ALCOCK. Well, if it pleases you to know that you're hated, to know that there's no gratitude in the country for all your father has done, you have ample reason for rejoicing. I suppose Annie's falseness and insolence was a great pleasure to you too.

KATE. No, Annie was hateful. But they didn't like her falseness, you could feel they didn't . . . It's not quite that they hate us, it's fear. They're afraid of us.

ALCOCK. "They," "us"! Do you remember, Kate, the evening after Maggie Leahy was shot?

KATE. Yes. But now I don't want to give up the "they" and "us," I glory in it. I was wrong, we were all wrong, in trying to find a common platform, in pretending we weren't different from every Pat and Mick in the village. Do you remember that gray filly we had long ago that I christened "Pearl" and Michael always called it "Perr'l" and so we all called it "Perr'l" not to seem to criticize Michael's pronunciation? That's a trifling example, but it's the sort of democratic snobbishness we went in for. We were ashamed of everything, ashamed of our birth, ashamed of our good education, ashamed of our religion, ashamed that we dined in the evenings and that we dressed for dinner, and, after all, our shame didn't save us or we wouldn't be sitting here on the remnants of our furniture.

ALCOCK. And what can save you now, it's too late?

KATE. If it was too late they wouldn't have bothered to burn us; *they* don't think it's too late so why should we? They're afraid of us still.

MRS. ALCOCK [*with a bitter laugh*]. We do look formidable, don't we?

KATE. We are formidable if we care to make ourselves so, if we give up our poor attempt to pretend we're not different. We must glory in our difference, be as proud of it as they are of theirs.

BROWN. But why?

KATE. Why? What do you mean?

BROWN. Why "must" you glory?

KATE. Why, because we're what we are. Ireland is not more theirs than ours.

BROWN. Or ours than theirs.

KATE. Exactly. But do let's leave them to see their own

point of view. We've spent so much time sympathetically seeing theirs that we've lost sight of our own. Ah, Mr. Brown, you've been as bad as any.

BROWN. As bad?

KATE. How many converts have you made during the twenty years you've been rector of Ballydonal?

BROWN. Converts? I'm not ministering among the heathen.

KATE. Shouldn't you feel, as a Protestant parson, that Roman Catholics are next thing to heathens? If you don't feel like that why are you a parson?

BROWN [*smiling*]. Do you want me to turn to souperism?

KATE. Why not? You used to rail at the Irish country gentleman and say that he was putting up no fight. What sort of a fight have you put up? If you really believed in your Protestantism you wouldn't hesitate at a trifle like souperism.

BROWN. You'll never get me to stoop to that.

KATE. Oh, well, religion's not my business and I'm too fond of you to quarrel with you but you'll have to go, all you amiable Protestant parsons, and make room for parsons who believe in their religion enough to fight for souls with every weapon that God has put into their hands. If they don't come, Protestantism itself goes.

ALCOCK. It's going now.

KATE. Because the Mr. Browns are letting it slip through their fingers just as you'd let Ballydonal slip through yours.

ALCOCK. It seems to me it's been snatched.

KATE. Pooh! What's a house? Bricks and stones. Aren't there plenty of both in the world. We'll build it up again.

MRS. ALCOCK. Nonsense. Never. Not for me.

KATE. I'll build it for myself. I'll build it with my own hands if I'm put to it. I believe in Ballydonal, it's my life, it's my faith, it's my country.

ALCOCK. My dear, don't. Don't waste your life here. If you were a man, if you were Ulick, I wouldn't say a word to stop you, but a single woman!—

KATE. I must marry if I can. That's another thing Mr. Brown must look out for me; three pieces of corrugated iron and a husband, please, Mr. Brown.

BROWN. I wish I could get you the husband as easily as the other. What sort of husband do you want?

KATE. Well, I ought to marry someone like Van O'Neill but I'd like to marry wildly, out of all reason, I'd . . . like to marry a— [*She stops.*]

MRS. ALCOCK. Well Kate, who?

KATE. No, it's a dream, it's quite impossible. But I should like to marry a Republican Catholic curate.

MRS. ALCOCK. Kate!

KATE. I've always adored them.

[ATKINS *comes in.*]

ATKINS. The Goods' car is here now, sir.

MRS. ALCOCK. Thank goodness, it puts an end to this ridiculous conversation. St. Leger, wake up, come along.

ALCOCK [*getting up slowly*]. Yes, I suppose so.

MRS. ALCOCK. Take my arm.

ALCOCK. My dear, you should take mine.

MRS. ALCOCK. I don't need it. Come.

ALCOCK [*as he goes out*]. Bournemouth after Ballydonal!

MRS. ALCOCK. Ssh! [*They go out.*]

BROWN. I believe you mean it, Kate; I see it in your eye.

KATE. Every word of it. Go after them, I have a word to say to Atkins.

[MR. BROWN *goes out.*]

KATE. We're going to Cork this afternoon, Atkins, and then to England. The master will send you your money as usual. Here's something to go on with. [*She hands him a pound note.*]

ATKINS. You're going away, miss? Ah, sure, it had to be.

KATE. But in a few weeks, in a month or two, I'm coming back.

ATKINS. You're what, miss?

KATE. Coming back to live here for good.

ATKINS. Thank God for that.

KATE. You can tell it in the village. [*She goes out.*]

ATKINS [*looking after her*]. God bless Miss Kate. [*He looks at the furniture.*] The murdering ruffians! [*He is lifting a chair into the summer-house, he drops it and starts back in terror.*] Miss Kate, Miss Kate, Miss Kate!

KATE [*coming back quickly*]. What is it, Atkins? What's the matter?

ATKINS [*babbling*]. I seen him there—in the summer-house—as clear as the day—Master Ulick—

KATE. Ulick? Go away, Atkins, go away. [*She pushes him out. She turns to the summer-house and speaks softly.*] Ulick! Are you there? . . . [*Her face lights up.*] Oh, my dear, you've come to me again, after all these years. . . . And you're smiling, so I'm right, it's what you'd have done. . . . [*A pause, she seems to listen to someone talking.*] Yes. . . . Yes. . . . So—kiss me, my dear. . . . [*She raises her face as if she were being kissed, she closes her eyes.*]

BIOGRAPHIES AND PLAY LISTS

PADRAIC COLUM

PADRAIC COLUM was born in Longford on Dec. 8, 1881, and was educated in the Irish National Schools. He was actively associated with the early beginning of the dramatic movement. He was one of the founders and the editor of the *Irish Review* from 1911 to 1913. He came to the United States in 1914 and has made it his residence from that time. In 1923 he was invited to make a survey of the mythology and folklore of the Hawaiian Islands. Since coming to America he has written many children's books as well as books of travel in Ireland, including the very popular *Road Round Ireland*.

He is a regular contributor to magazines in the United States and Ireland.

He lives in New Canaan, Connecticut.

Plays: *The Saxon Shillin'*, produced 1902.
      The Kingdom of the Young, produced 1902.
      The Foleys, 1902.
      Eoghan's Wife, 1902.
      Broken Soil (revised as *The Fiddler's House*, 1907).
      The Land, 1905.
      Thomas Muskerry, 1910.
      The Desert, 1912.
      Three Plays, 1917 (containing: *The Fiddler's House; The Land;* and *Thomas Muskerry*).
      Balloon, 1929.

GEORGE FITZMAURICE

VERY little is known about this author. Born in Ireland, his greatest popular success came in 1907 when *The Country*

Dressmaker was produced in the Abbey. After that he was practically ignored as a playwright. His last play noted below is of far less value than his previous works.

Plays: *The Country Dressmaker,* 1907.
　　　The Pie-Dish, 1908.
　　　Five Plays, 1915 (containing: *The Country Dressmaker; The Moonlighter; The Magic Glasses; The Pie-Dish; The Dandy Dolls*).
　　　'Twixt the Giltenans and the Carmodys, 1923.

LADY GREGORY

LADY ISABELLA AUGUSTA GREGORY was born in Galway in 1859. She has served The National Theatre Society and the Abbey Theatre since the first days, with wisdom and patience. Mention has already been made of her books on Irish folklore. The Kiltartan dialect, in which many of her plays are written, although it is an artificial idiom, has all the charm and spirit of actual peasant speech. A "chapter in her autobiography," including a summary of the early vicissitudes of the national drama is charmingly told in *Our Irish Theatre.*

Plays: *Twenty Five,* produced 1903.
　　　Seven Short Plays, 1909 (containing: *Spreading the News; Hyacinth Halvey; The Traveling Man; The Rising of the Moon; The Jackdaw; The Workhouse Ward; The Gaol Gate*).
　　　The Image, 1910.
　　　The Kiltartan Molière, dialect versions of *Le Medecin Malgré Lui; Les Fourberies de Scapin; L'Avare.* 1910.
　　　Irish Folk-History Plays, two volumes, 1912.
　　　　Volume 1. The Tragedies—*Grania; Kincora; Devorgilla.*
　　　　Volume 2. The Comedies—*Canavans; White Cockade; Deliverer.*
　　　New Comedies, 1913 (containing: *The Bogie Men; The Full Moon; Coats; Damer's Gold; McDonough's Wife*).
　　　The Dragon, 1920.

The Image and Other Plays, 1922 (containing: *The Image; Hanrahan's Oath; Shanwalla; The Wrens*).

Three Wonder Plays, 1922 (containing: *The Dragon; Aristotle's Bell; The Jester*).

The Story Brought by Brigit, a Passion Play in Three Acts, 1924.

Three Last Plays, 1928 (containing: *Sancho's Master; Dave; The Would-be-Gentleman*).

Douglas Hyde

Dr. Douglas Hyde was born in Ireland. He was educated at Trinity College, Dublin, receiving his B.A. degree there in 1884, and LL.D. in 1887. From 1894 to 1895 he was President of the Irish National Literary Society, and served the Gaelic League in the same capacity from 1893 to 1915. In addition to the works mentioned elsewhere in this book, his English renditions of the Irish *Love Songs of Connacht* are examples of his admirable skill both as a poet and as a Gaelic scholar.

Plays: *The Bursting of the Bubble,* 1903.
  Drama Breite Criosta; Nativity Play in Irish, translated by Lady Gregory, 1903.
  The Tinker and the Fairy, 1905.
  The Poorhouse (with Lady Gregory), produced 1907.
  The Marriage, produced 1911.

Edward Martyn

Edward Martyn attended Belvedere School in Dublin; and Beaumont, Windsor, later completing his education at Christ Church, Oxford. He was one of the original founders of the Irish dramatic movement. He served as President of Sinn Fein for four years, 1904–1908. In 1914 he founded at Dublin The Irish Theatre, "for the production of native non-peasant plays, plays in the Irish language, and translations of Continental master dramas." He was a promoter of the Gaelic League and of other Irish educational projects. He was a Governor of the University College in Galway. He died on December 5, 1923.

Plays: *The Heather Field and Maeve,* 1899.
      The Tale of a Town, 1902.
      The Enchanted Sea, 1902.
      The Placehunters.
      Grangecolman, 1912.
      The Dream Physician, produced 1914.

T. C. MURRAY

T. C. MURRAY was born in County Cork in 1873 and received his early education at St. Patrick's Training College from which he graduated in 1891. In addition to his success in the fields of poetry and drama, he has filled with distinction the position of Headmaster of Inchicore Model Schools, Dublin, since 1915.

Plays: *The Wheel of Fortune,* 1909.
      Birthright, 1910, revised 1928.
      Maurice Harte, 1912.
      Sovereign Love, 1913.
      Spring, 1918.
      The Briery Gap, 1918.
      Aftermath, 1922.
      Autumn Fire, 1924.
      The Pipe in the Fields, 1928.
      The Blind Wolf, 1928.

SEAN O'CASEY

SEAN O'CASEY was born in Dublin. He has had no formal education. As a boy he sold newspapers on the streets of Dublin instead of going to school. He aided in the organization of and served as a soldier in the Irish Citizen Army, and took active part in the fighting during the 1916 rebellion. His first known publications are not plays. They are two pamphlets issued under the Gaelic form of O'Casey's name: Sean o Cathasaigh. One is a *History of the Irish Citizen Army* (1918), and the other is a pamphlet entitled *The Story of Thomas Ashe,* a patriot in the revolt. He received for *Juno and the Paycock* the Hawthornden Prize for the best play in English by an author under forty years of age, 1926. His most important plays have already been noted. He lives in London.

PADRAIC PEARSE

PATRICK HENRY PEARSE was the son of an English father and an Irish mother. He was born in Dublin in 1879, and was educated by the Christian Brothers. He received the B.A. degree from Royal University and later his B.L., although he never practiced law. He devoted himself entirely to political teaching. He founded St. Enda's School, Dublin; was an ardent member and prominent promoter of the Gaelic League. He was the editor of a Gaelic Magazine, *An Claidheamh Solus,* and founded a short-lived weekly paper, *An Barr Buadh.* He was executed for fulfilling the principles he had advocated in these journals.

He was elected President of the Irish Provisional Government in Easter Week, 1916, fell into the hands of the British at the Dublin Post Office, and was shortly afterwards court-martialed and shot, May 3, 1916. In addition to his plays, his Political Speeches and Writings are published (Maunsel and Co., 1916), as well as his prose stories and *Songs of the Irish Rebels and Specimens from an Irish Anthology* (1918).

Plays: published in *Collected Works,* Dublin 1917:
> *The Singer*
> *The King, a morality.*
> *The Master.*
> *Iosagan.*

LENNOX ROBINSON

LENNOX ROBINSON was born in County Cork in 1886 and was educated at the Bandon Grammar School. He is a mem-

ber of the Board of Directors of the Abbey Theatre. He fulfilled the office of manager for that organization from 1910
to 1914 and from 1919 to 1923, when he became its Producer. He holds this responsible position at the present time.

Plays: *The Clancy Name,* produced 1908.
      The Cross Roads, 1909.
      Harvest, 1910.
      Patriots, 1912.
      The Dreamers, 1915.
      The White Headed Boy, 1916.
      The Lost Leader, 1918.
      The Round Table, 1924.
      Crabbed Youth and Age, 1924.
      Never the Time and the Place, 1924.
      Plays, 1928 (containing: *The Round Table; Crabbed
         Youth and Age; Portrait; The White Blackbird;
         The Big House; Give a Dog—*).
      The Far-off Hills, 1929.
      Ever the Twain, 1929.

GEORGE WILLIAM RUSSELL (A.E.; O.L.S.; Y.O.)

DR. RUSSELL was born in Lurgan, County Armagh, April
10, 1867. He was educated at Rathmine's School. He has
distinguished himself and his country by his many writings
on philosophical subjects, by his fearless and wise editorship
of *The Irish Statesman,* formerly *The Irish Homestead,* and
by his kind and understanding criticism of the works of
many younger Irish writers. He has published many poems
and essays of a mystical nature, and is an accomplished
painter. He served for some years as Vice President of the
National Theatre Society.

· He is the recipient of honorary degrees from Yale University and from Trinity College, Dublin. His collected
poems were published in 1926.

JOHN M. SYNGE

JOHN M. SYNGE was born at Rathfarnum, Dublin, in 1871.
He received his B.A. from Trinity College, Dublin, in 1892,

and thereafter settled in Paris where he attempted to write criticisms of French literature. Acting on the advice of W. B. Yeats, he returned to Ireland and wrote accounts of the life he found in the Aran Islands. The germs of his plays may be found in these descriptions in *The Aran Islands* and *Wicklow and Kerry*. Students should consult M. Bourgeois' *Life and Works of John M. Synge* for a more detailed account of this author. He died of cancer in a Dublin hospital in 1909.

Plays: *The Tinker's Wedding*, written about 1902.
    In the Shadow of the Glen, produced 1903.
    Riders to the Sea, produced 1904.
    The Well of the Saints, produced 1905.
    The Playboy of the Western World, produced 1907.
    Deirdre of the Sorrows, produced 1910.

W. B. Yeats

WILLIAM BUTLER YEATS was born in Sandymount, Co. Dublin on June 13, 1865. He received his early education at Godolphin School, Hammersmith, and at Erasmus School, Dublin. Influenced by his father, who was a painter of distinction, at the age of eighteen he decided on a career in art. After studying in this field for three years he forsook it for literature. Since that time he has become one of the outstanding men of letters in Europe. He holds an honorary degree of Doctor of Letters from Trinity College, Dublin. He served as a member of the first Irish Free State Senate from 1922 to 1928 and is a member of the Board of Directors of the Abbey Theatre. In 1923 he was awarded the Nobel Prize for Literature. Much of his time in the last few years has been spent in Italy, where he makes his winter home. In the following list, the titles of his many poems and essays have been omitted.

Plays: *Countess Cathleen*, 1892.
    The Land of Heart's Desire, 1894.
    The Shadowy Waters, 1900.
    Diarmaid and Grania (with George Moore), unpublished.

Kathleen ni Houlihan, 1902.

Where There is Nothing (with Lady Gregory), 1903.

The Hour Glass and Other Plays, 1904 (containing:
    *The Hour Glass; Kathleen ni Houlihan; A Pot of
    Broth*).

The Unicorn from the Stars (with Lady Gregory),
    1904.

The King's Threshold, 1904.

On Baile's Strand, 1904.

Deirdre, 1907.

Plays for an Irish Theatre, 1911 (containing: *Deirdre;
    The Green Helmet; On Baile's Strand; The King's
    Threshold; The Shadowy Waters; The Hour
    Glass; Kathleen ni Houlihan*).

Four Plays for Dancers, 1921 (containing: *At the
    Hawk's Well; The Only Jealousy of Emer; The
    Dreaming of the Bones; Calvary*).

The Player Queen, 1922.

The Resurrection, 1927.

Œdipus the King, a version for the modern stage, 1928.

Œdipus at Colonnus, 1929.

GLOSSARY

Fighting the Waves, a ballet based on the *Only Jealousy of Emer,* was presented in the Abbey Theater in August, 1929.

THE TWISTING OF THE ROPE

PAGE 126 Oisin, or Ossian: pronounced Usheen' or Isheen'. Oisin was the son of Finn mac Coul. He is the supposed author of the "Ossianic Ballads," hence his designation as the "Gaelic Homer."

Fenians: an ancient Irish tribe led by Finn. Fenians is a contraction of Fianna Eirinn.

" 127 Donal no Greina: pronounced Dahnahl no gryna.

" 132 Ohone-y-o, go deo: pronounced achōnya gō jō.

" 134 lebidins: paltry fools.

go deo, ma neoir: pronounced go-jo, ma nyor, —forever, by my tears.

" 135 bán, acushla dilis: pronounced bawn, akooshla deelish—my white one, my darling girl.

THE DANDY DOLLS

PAGE 137 moryah: an ironical expression meaning "I don't think," or "bosh."

tasby: strength, resolution.

bosthoon: a boorish fellow.

" 138 Such a grah: such an unholy love.

clevvy: an open cupboard.

" 139 loppeens: rag or stocking on the foot in place of a boot. The meaning here is probably "claws."

" 140 dilisk: pronounced dilsk, a sea plant which grows on rocks.

" 141 screed: rag.

" 143 linnhe: pronounced linna, a barn attached to a cottage.

pratie: potato.

" 144 gom: fool.

" 152 smadher: break into pieces.

" 153 treenahayla: mixed up in great confusion.

" 154 bad scran: bad luck.

meila murdhre: thousand murders.

RIDERS TO THE SEA

PAGE 165 poteen: pronounced potcheen, an illicitly-distilled liquor.

PAGE 204 feis: pronounced fesh, an Irish language festival.

" 206 Tá go breagh!: pronounced thaw gu brah, Very
fine!

" 208 ráméish: pronounced raw-may-ish, fine, foolish
talk.

" 211 ciseán: pronounced kish-aun, a turf-basket.
bacal: pronounced bok-ol, a heap.

" 218 A Thighearna!: pronounced a heer-na, O Lord!

" 219 ban: pronounced baan, a pasture field.

" 227 Dia linn as muire Mháthaír!: pronounced dee-a
ling us mir-ra waw-hir, God and the Mother
of God to us!

" 228 A Muire Mháthaír!: pronounced mir-ra wawhir,
Mother Mary!

" 230 a chuíd!: pronounced a kwid, my share of the
world.

THE SINGER

PAGE 236 Maire ni Fhiannachta: pronounced Mawrya nĭ
feenachta.
Sighle: pronounced sheela.
Maoilsheachlainn: pronounced Mwee-hŏ'-klinn.
Diarmaid: pronounced dyermid.

" 239 fosaidheacht: pronounced fŏ'-say-ookt. A shelter.
mám: pronounced mawn, a mountain pass, a
hill.

" 240 Uachtar Ard: pronounced Ooktar ahrd, the
present village of Oughterard.
Cois-Fhairrge: pronounced Coosh-fareja.
boreen, a narrow path from the main road to
the house.

" 242 Cnoc an Teachta: pronounced nuck an teeakta.

" 243 The Gall, the foreigners or strangers.

" 246 camán, a stick used in playing hurley.

" 249 Deibhidhe: pronounced Day-vee-da, an old Irish
verse form.

" 251 shuiler: pronounced sheeler, a wandering singer.

" 256 Aileach: pronounced Ay lock.

MAEVE

PAGE 258 The O'Heynes: the custom survives here of designating the head of a clan or tribe as *the* chief member.

Maeve: pronounced Mayv.

" 259 Oenach: pronounced Ō'nah.

" 270 Tuatha de Danaan: pronounced Too-atha-de Dahnahn, an ancient Gaelic race descended from the Gods. When they were overthrown by the Milesians, they became a fairy tribe.

" 283 Fiachna, son of Reta, was a warrior from the land of the Gods who, with Loegaire Liban, the son of the King of Connacht, invaded and conquered the stronghold of Mag Mell in the Land of the Dead. His purpose was to rescue his wife who had been abducted thither. The two warriors remained to jointly rule the Country of the Dead.

" 286 Eochaid: pronounced Yo-hee.